THE SOCIAL
REALITY
OF CRIME

RICHARD QUINNEY
New York University

LITTLE, BROWN AND COMPANY   Boston

Published simultaneously in Canada
by Little, Brown & Company (Canada) Limited

PRINTED IN THE UNITED STATES OF AMERICA

Preface

My purpose in this book is to provide a reorientation to the study of crime. I have attempted to accomplish this task by developing a theoretical perspective by means of which research and writing in criminology can be reinterpreted.

The nominalistic position is my starting point: a thing exists only when it is given a name; any phenomenon is real to us only when we can imagine it. Without imagination there would be nothing to experience. So it is with crime. In our relationships with others we construct a *social reality of crime*. This reality is both conceptual and phenomenal, a world of meanings and events constructed in reference to crime.

This theoretical approach to crime consists of several related processes: (1) how criminal definitions are formulated; (2) how criminal definitions are applied; (3) how behavior patterns develop in relation to criminal definitions; and (4) how criminal conceptions are constructed. The social reality of crime is constantly being created.

I have felt it necessary to reinterpret criminology for more than academic reasons. Much of our criminology lacks a sense of the contemporary. I seek a sociology of crime that fits into our own times. I am, also, explicitly interested in the ideals of justice and individual freedom. When we find ourselves able to examine crime as a human construct, then we can raise questions about the justice of criminal law. It is my hope that the theory of the social reality of crime has the power of forcing us to consider libertarian ideals. I contend that a relevant criminology can be attained only when we allow our personal values to provide a vision for the study of crime.

Richard Quinney

Contents

3 APPLICATION OF CRIMINAL DEFINITIONS

THE SOCIAL
REALITY
OF CRIME

1

A Theory
of Crime

CHAPTER ONE

The Social
Reality of
Crime

The history of contemporary sociology is characterized by a progressive loss in faith — faith that anything exists beyond man's imagination. We are consequently being led to new assumptions about our craft and the substance of our labors. New ways of attacking old problems are making this a dynamic period for sociology.

Perhaps in no other sociological realm is intellectual revisionism more apparent than in the study of crime. In these pages I will indicate how current thoughts and trends in the sociological study of crime can culminate in a theory of crime. The theory that I will present — *the theory of the social reality of crime* — rests upon theoretical and methodological assumptions that reflect the happenings of our time; it is meant to provide an understanding of crime that is relevant to our contemporary experiences.[1]

ASSUMPTIONS: EXPLANATION
IN THE STUDY OF CRIME

Until fairly recent times studies and writings in criminology were shaped almost entirely by the criminologist's interest in "the crim-

---

[1] An earlier version of the theory of the social reality of crime was contained in a paper I presented at the 63rd annual meeting of the American Sociological Association, August 28, 1968. This chapter is a revision of my later paper, "The Social Reality of Crime," in Jack D. Douglas (ed.), *Crime and Justice in American Society* (Indianapolis: Bobbs-Merrill, 1970).

inal." In the last few years, however, those who study crime have
realized that crime is relative to different legal systems, that an absolute conception of crime — outside of legal definitions — had to be
replaced by a relativistic (that is, legalistic) conception. Many criminologists have therefore turned to studying how criminal definitions
are constructed and applied in a society.

Two schools of thought have developed. Some argue that crime
is properly studied by examining the offender and his behavior.
Others are convinced that the criminal law is the correct object:
how it is formulated, enforced, and administered. The two need not
become deadlocked in polemics. The long overdue interest in criminal definitions happily corrects the absurdities brought about by
studying the offender alone; the two approaches actually comple-
ment one another. A synthesis of the criminal behavior and criminal
definition approaches can provide a new theoretical framework for
the study of crime.

The theory I am proposing rests upon certain assumptions about
theoretical explanation: these assumptions are in regard to (1) ontology, (2) epistemology, (3) causation, and (4) theory construction.

Ontology. What is the world really like? I mean, what is it we
pretend to separate ourselves from when we go about our observations? I adopt a nominalistic position contrary to that of the posi-
tivists. Accordingly, I can accept no universal essences. The mind
is unable to frame a concept that corresponds to an objective reality.
We cannot be certain of an objective reality beyond man's conception of it. Thus, we have no reason to believe in the objective existence of anything. We must, instead, formulate theories that give
meaning to our experiences.[2]

Epistemology. Implied in the ontological assumption is the epis-
temological assumption that we as observers cannot "copy" anything
that may be regarded as an objective reality, since we are skeptical
of the existence of such a reality. Our observations, instead, are
based on our own mental *constructions,* not on essences beyond our

---

[2] I have developed this position in *The Problem of Crime* (New York:
Dodd, Mead, 1970), chap. 3.

experiences. Expressed in a more romantic way: "Beauty is in the eye of the beholder." Thus, our concern is not with any correspondence between "objective reality" and observation, but between observation and the utility of such observations in understanding our own subjective, multiple social worlds.

Causation. Much of criminological theory, based on positivistic assumptions, has sought to explain the "causes" of crime. That search continues, but the modern concept of causation employed in the philosophy of science is considerably different from that used by criminologists.[3] The strategy toward causation that I propose for a theory of crime is consistent with the above assumptions about the world and the way in which we understand it, as well as with current usage in the philosophy of science. This strategy has three parts.

First, causal explanation need not be the sole interest of criminologists.[4] The objective of any science is not to formulate and verify theories of causation, but to construct an order among observables. Explanations as generalized answers to the question "why?" may be presented in other than causal form. For example, explanations in terms of probability statements, functional relationships, and developmental stages can be formulated into propositions that do not depend upon causal explanation. A science of human social behavior is obviously possible without the notion of causation.

Second, a statement of causation does not necessarily state the

[3] For a discussion of the usage of causation in modern philosophy of science and in the physical sciences, see Percy W. Bridgman, "Determinism in Modern Science," in Sidney Hook (ed.), *Determinism and Freedom in the Age of Modern Science* (New York: Collier, 1961), pp. 57–75; Mario Bunge, *Causality: The Place of the Causal Principle in Modern Science* (New York: The World Publishing Co., 1963); Werner Heisenberg, *Physics and Philosophy: The Revolution in Modern Science* (New York: Harper & Row, 1958).

[4] Alternatives in causal explanation have been suggested in Hermanus Bianchi, *Position and Subject Matter of Criminology: Inquiry Concerning Theoretical Criminology* (Amsterdam: North Holland, 1956); Nathaniel Cantor, "The Search for Causes of Crime," *Journal of Criminal Law, Criminology and Police Science,* 22 (March–April, 1932), pp. 854–863; Peter Lejins, "Pragmatic Etiology of Delinquent Behavior," *Social Forces,* 29 (March, 1951), pp. 317–321; David Matza, *Delinquency and Drift* (New York: John Wiley, 1964); Walter C. Reckless, *Criminal Behavior* (New York: McGraw-Hill, 1940). Acceptance of causal analysis in contemporary criminology is found in Travis Hirshi and Hanan C. Selvin, *Delinquency Research: An Appraisal of Analytic Methods* (New York: The Free Press, 1967).

nature of reality, but is a *methodological construction* of the observer: "Causes certainly are connected by effects; but this is
because our theories connect them, not because the world is held
together by cosmic glue."[5] The scientist who defines a causal relationship has to see that it is a construct imposed by himself in
order to give meaning to a significant theoretical problem. Confused,
we often inadvertently turn the causational construct into a description of reality.[6] Initially a heuristic device, a methodological tool,
causation does not necessarily describe the substance of our observations.

Third, we must not use the causational construct as it has often
been applied in physical science. Causative explanations of crime
have tended in particular to be based on the mechanistic conception
of causation. What is required in the explanation of crime, *if* a
causative explanation is formulated, is a conception of causation
that is attuned to the nature of social phenomena.

The world of social phenomena studied by the social scientist has
meaning for the human beings living within it. The world of nature,
on the other hand, which the physical scientist studies, means nothing to the physical objects. Therefore, the social scientist's constructs
have to be founded upon the *social reality* created by man: "The
constructs of the social sciences are, so to speak, constructs of the
second degree, that is, constructs of the constructs made by the
actors on the social scene, whose behavior the social scientist has to
observe and to explain in accordance with the procedural rules of
his science."[7] As social scientists we may well conceive of a *substantive causal process*, as part of a social reality that is constructed by
man, and distinct from the causal constructs formulated as methodological devices by the physical scientist. Thus, causation could be
used substantively to explain crime in the special sense of *social
causation*. To the extent that man defines situations, that is, con-

[5] Norwood Russell Hanson, *Patterns of Discovery* (Cambridge: Cambridge
University Press, 1965), p. 64.

[6] On the confusion between nominal and real constructs in general, see
Robert Bierstedt, "Nominal and Real Definitions in Sociological Theory," in
Llewellyn Gross (ed.), *Symposium in Sociological Theory* (Evanston, Ill.: Row,
Peterson, 1959), pp. 121–144.

[7] Alfred Schutz, "Concept and Theory Formation in the Social Sciences," in
Maurice Nathanson (ed.), *Philosophy of the Social Sciences* (New York: Random House, 1963), p. 242.

structs his own world in relation to others, the student of social life may conceive of a social causation as part of a social reality.

Theory Construction. The appropriate structure of a theory is far from certain in sociology. Many have worked toward establishing a research methodology, but little has been done about developing theoretical methods. Since we lack criteria for building theories, Homans has suggested that a theory must consist of propositions that state relationships and form a deductive system.[8] But we cannot ignore explanations that may be formulated in forms other than the deductive. These may contain propositions which are not deductive, but which are probabilistic, functional, or genetic.[9] Such propositions need not necessarily be deductive, in the sense that another set of propositions must be deduced from them in order for the original set of propositions to be regarded as a theory.

More important, propositions must be consistent with one another and must be integrated into a system.[10] The conclusions drawn from one proposition must not contradict those derived from another, and any conclusions obtained from the theory must be derivable within the system. Other standards to be adhered to in constructing theories are: the propositions must be testable; their validity must be determined by subsequent research; and they must be useful, enabling us to understand the problem that inspired us to formulate the theory.

Within the theory that I am constructing are several propositions that are consistent and integrated into a theoretical system. One or more specific statements express in probability form the relationships within the proposition. Further, the propositions are arranged according to a *system of proposition units*. The propositions express relationships that are both coexistent and sequential. The theory

[8] George Casper Homans, "Contemporary Theory in Sociology," in Robert E. L. Faris (ed.), *Handbook of Modern Sociology* (Chicago: Rand McNally, 1964), pp. 951–977.

[9] See Robert Brown, *Explanation in Social Science* (Chicago: Aldine, 1963); Morris R. Cohen and Ernest Nagel, *An Introduction to Logic and Scientific Method* (New York: Harcourt, Brace, 1934), pp. 197–222; Abraham Kaplan, *The Conduct of Inquiry: Methodology for the Behavioral Sciences* (San Francisco: Chandler Publishing Co., 1964), pp. 327–369.

[10] David Miller, *Scientific Sociology: Theory and Method* (Englewood Cliffs, N.J.: Prentice-Hall, 1967), pp. 9–10.

thus assumes that patterns of phenomena develop over a period of time.[11] Each proposition unit within the theoretical model requires explanation, and each unit relates to the others. Ultimately, the theoretical system provides the basis for an integrated theory of crime.

ASSUMPTIONS: MAN AND SOCIETY IN A THEORY OF CRIME

In studying any social phenomenon we must hold to some general perspective. Two of those used by sociologists, and by most social analysts for that matter, are the *static* and the *dynamic* interpretations of society. Either is equally plausible, though most sociologists take the static viewpoint.[12] This emphasis has relegated forces and events, such as deviance and crime, which do not appear to be conducive to stability and consensus, to the pathologies of society.

My theory of crime, however, is based on the dynamic perspective. The theory is based on these assumptions about man and society: (1) process, (2) conflict, (3) power, and (4) social action.

Process. The dynamic aspect of social relations may be referred to as "social process." Though in analyzing society we use static descriptions, that is, we define the structure and function of social relations, we must be aware that social phenomena fluctuate continually.[13]

We apply this assumption to all social phenomena that have duration and undergo change, that is, all those which interest the sociologist. A social process is a continuous series of actions, taking place in time, and leading to a special kind of result: "a system of social

[11] For discussions of sequential theories, see Howard S. Becker, *Outsiders: Studies in the Sociology of Deviance* (New York: The Free Press of Glencoe, 1963), pp. 22–25; Clarence Schrag, "Elements of Theoretical Analysis in Sociology," in Llewellyn Gross (ed.), *Sociological Theory: Inquiries and Paradigms* (New York: Harper & Row, 1967), pp. 242–244.

[12] See Robert A. Nisbet, *The Sociological Tradition* (New York: Basic Books, 1966); Reinhard Bendix and Bennett Berger, "Images of Society and Problems of Concept Formation in Sociology," in Gross, *Symposium on Sociological Theory*, pp. 92–118.

[13] Howard Becker, *Systematic Sociology on the Basis of the Beziehungslehre and Gebildelehre of Leopold von Wiess* (New York: John Wiley & Sons, 1932).

change taking place within a defined situation and exhibiting a particular order of change through the operation of forces present from the first within the situation."[14] Any particular phenomenon, in turn, is viewed as contributing to the dynamics of the total process. As in the "modern systems approach," social phenomena are seen as generating out of an interrelated whole.[15] The methodological implication of the process assumption is that any social phenomenon may be viewed as part of a complex network of events, structures, and underlying processes.

Conflict. In any society conflicts between persons, social units, or cultural elements are inevitable, the normal consequences of social life. Conflict is especially prevalent in societies with diverse value systems and normative groups. Experience teaches that we cannot expect to find consensus on all or most values and norms in such societies.

Two models of society contrast sharply: one is regarded as "conflict" and the other, "consensus." With the consensus model we describe social structure as a functionally integrated system held together in equilibrium. In the conflict model, on the other hand, we find that societies and social organizations are shaped by diversity, coercion, and change. The differences between these contending but complementary conceptions of society have been best characterized by Dahrendorf.[16] According to his study, we assume in postulating the consensus (or integrative) model of society that: (1) society is a relatively persistent, stable structure, (2) it is well integrated, (3) every element has a function — it helps maintain the system, and (4) a functioning social structure is based on a consensus on values. For the conflict (or coercion) model of society, on the other hand, we assume that: (1) at every point society is subject to change, (2) it displays at every point dissensus and conflict, (3) every element contributes to change, and (4) it is based on the coercion of some of its members by others. In other words, so-

[14] Robert MacIver, *Social Causation* (New York: Ginn, 1942), p. 130.
[15] Walter Buckley, "A Methodological Note," in Thomas J. Scheff, *Being Mentally Ill* (Chicago: Aldine, 1966), pp. 201–205.
[16] Ralf Dahrendorf, *Class and Class Conflict in Industrial Society* (Stanford: Stanford University Press, 1959), pp. 161–162.

ciety is held together by force and constraint and is characterized by ubiquitous conflicts that result in continuous change: "values are ruling rather than common, enforced rather than accepted, at any given point of time."[17]

Although in society as a whole conflict may be general, according to the conflict model, it is still likely that we will find stability and consensus on values among subunits in the society. Groups with their own cultural elements are found in most societies, leading to social differentiation with conflict between the social units; nonetheless integration and stability may appear within specific social groups: "Although the total larger society may be diverse internally and may form only a loosely integrated system, within each subculture there may be high integration of institutions and close conformity of individuals to the patterns sanctioned by their own group."[18]

Conflict need not necessarily disrupt society. Some sociologists have been interested in the *functions* of social conflict, "that is to say, with those consequences of social conflict which make for an increase rather than a decrease in the adaptation or adjustment of particular social relationships or groups."[19] It seems that conflict can promote cooperation, establish group boundaries, and unite social factions. Furthermore, it may lead to new patterns that may in the long run be beneficial to the whole society or to parts of it.[20] Any doubts about its functional possibilities have been dispelled by Dahrendorf: "I would suggest . . . that all that is creativity, innovation, and development in the life of the individual, his group, and his society is due, to no small extent, to the operation of conflicts between group and group, individual and individual, emotion and emotion within one individual. This fundamental fact alone seems to me to justify the value judgment that conflict is essentially 'good' and 'desirable.' "[21] Conflict is not always the disruptive agent in a

[17] Ralf Dahrendorf, "Out of Utopia: Toward a Reorientation in Sociological Analysis," *American Journal of Sociology*, 67 (September, 1958), p. 127.

[18] Robin M. Williams, Jr., *American Society*, 2nd ed. (New York: Alfred A. Knopf, 1960), p. 375.

[19] Lewis A. Coser, *The Functions of Social Conflict* (New York: The Free Press, 1956), p. 8.

[20] Lewis A. Coser, "Social Conflict and the Theory of Social Change," *British Journal of Sociology*, 8 (September, 1957), pp. 197–207.

[21] Dahrendorf, *Class and Class Conflict in Industrial Society*, p. 208. The importance of conflict in society is also discussed in, among other works, George

society; at certain times it may be meaningful to see it as a cohesive force.

Power. The conflict conception of society leads us to assume that coherence is assured in any social unit by coercion and constraint. In other words, *power* is the basic characteristic of social organization. "This means that in every social organization some positions are entrusted with a right to exercise control over other positions in order to ensure effective coercion; it means, in other words, that there is a differential distribution of power and authority."[22] Thus, conflict and power are inextricably linked in the conception of society presented here. The differential distribution of power produces conflict between competing groups, and conflict, in turn, is rooted in the competition for power. Wherever men live together conflict and a struggle for power will be found.

Power, then, is the ability of persons and groups to determine the conduct of other persons and groups.[23] It is utilized not for its own sake, but is the vehicle for the enforcement of scarce values in society, whether the values are material, moral, or otherwise. The use of power affects the distribution of values and values affect the distribution of power. The "authoritative allocation of values" is essential to any society.[24] In any society, institutional means are used to officially establish and enforce sets of values for the entire population.

Simmel, *Conflict,* trans. Kurt H. Wolff (New York: The Free Press, 1955); Irving Louis Horowitz, "Consensus, Conflict and Cooperation: A Sociological Inventory," *Social Forces,* 41 (December, 1962), pp. 177–188; Raymond W. Mack, "The Components of Social Conflict," *Social Problems,* 12 (Spring, 1965), pp. 388–397.

[22] Dahrendorf, *Class and Class Conflict in Industrial Society,* p. 165.

[23] Max Weber, *From Max Weber: Essays in Sociology,* trans. H. H. Gerth and C. Wright Mills (New York: Oxford University Press, 1946); Hans Gerth and C. Wright Mills, *Character and Social Structure* (New York: Harcourt, Brace, 1953), especially pp. 192–273; C. Wright Mills, *The Power Elite* (New York: Oxford University Press, 1956); George Simmel, *The Sociology of George Simmel,* trans. Kurt H. Wolff (New York: The Free Press, 1950), pp. 181–186; Robert Bierstedt, "An Analysis of Social Power," *American Sociological Review,* 15 (December, 1950), pp. 730–738.

[24] David Easton, *The Political System* (New York: Alfred A. Knopf, 1953), p. 137. Similar ideas are found in Harold D. Lasswell, *Politics: Who Gets What, When, How* (New York: McGraw-Hill, 1936); Harold D. Lasswell and Abraham Kaplan, *Power and Society* (New Haven: Yale University Press, 1950).

Power and the allocation of values are basic in forming *public policy*. Groups with special *interests* become so well organized that they are able to influence the policies that are to affect all persons. These interest groups exert their influence at every level and branch of government in order to have their own values and interests represented in the policy decisions.[25] Any interest group's ability to influence public policy depends on the group's position in the political power structure. Furthermore, access to the formation of public policy is unequally distributed because of the structural arrangements of the political state. "Access is one of the advantages unequally distributed by such arrangements; that is, in consequence of the structural peculiarities of our government some groups have better and more varied opportunities to influence key points of decision than do others."[26] Groups that have the power to gain access to the decision-making process also inevitably control the lives of others.

A major assumption in my conception of society, therefore, is the importance of interest groups in shaping public policy. Public policy is formed so as to represent the interests and values of groups that are in positions of power. Rather than accept the pluralistic

[25] Among the vast amount of literature on interest groups, see Donald C. Blaisdell, *American Democracy Under Pressure* (New York: Ronald Press, 1957); V. O. Key, Jr., *Politics, Parties, and Pressure Groups* (New York: Thomas Y. Crowell, 1959); Earl Latham, *Group Basis of Politics* (Ithaca, N.Y.: Cornell University Press, 1952); David Truman, *The Governmental Process* (New York: Alfred A. Knopf, 1951); Henry W. Ehrmann (ed.), *Interest Groups on Four Continents* (Pittsburgh: University of Pittsburgh Press, 1958); Henry A. Turner, "How Pressure Groups Operate," *Annals of the American Academy of Political and Social Science*, 319 (September, 1958), pp. 63–72; Richard W. Gable, "Interest Groups as Policy Shapers," *Annals of the American Academy of Political and Social Science*, 319 (September, 1958), pp. 84–93; Murray S. Stedman, "Pressure Group and the American Tradition," *Annals of the American Academy of Political and Social Science*, 319 (September, 1958), pp. 123–219. For documentation on the influence of specific interest groups, see Robert Engler, *The Politics of Oil* (New York: Macmillan, 1961); Oliver Garceau, *The Political Life of the American Medical Association* (Cambridge: Harvard University Press, 1941); Charles M. Hardin, *The Politics of Agriculture: Soil Conservation and the Struggle for Power in Rural America* (New York: The Free Press of Glencoe, 1962); Grant McConnell, *Private Power and American Democracy* (New York: Alfred A. Knopf, 1966); Harry A. Millis and Royal E. Montgomery, *Organized Labor* (New York: McGraw-Hill, 1945); Warner Schilling, Paul Y. Hammond, and Glenn H. Snyder, *Strategy, Politics and Defense* (New York: Columbia University Press, 1962); William R. Willoughby, *The St. Lawrence Waterway: A Study in Politics and Diplomacy* (Madison: University of Wisconsin Press, 1961).

[26] Truman, *The Governmental Process*, p. 322.

conception of the political process, which assumes that all groups make themselves heard in policy decision-making, I am relying upon a conception that assumes an unequal distribution of power in formulating and administering public policy.[27]

Social Action. An assumption of man that is consistent with the conflict-power conception of society asserts that man's actions are purposive and meaningful, that man engages in voluntary behavior. This *humanistic* conception of man contrasts with the oversocialized conception of man. Man is, after all, capable of considering alternative actions, of breaking from the established social order.[28] Once he gains an awareness of self, by being a member of society, he is able to choose his actions. The extent to which he does conform depends in large measure upon his own self-control.[29] Nonconformity may also be part of the process of finding self-identity. It is thus *against* something that the self can emerge.[30]

By conceiving of man as able to reason and choose courses of action, we may see him as changing and becoming, rather than merely being.[31] The kind of culture that man develops shapes his

[27] Evaluations of the pluralistic and power approaches are found in Peter Bachrach and Morton S. Baratz, "Two Faces of Power," *American Political Science Review,* 61 (December, 1962), pp. 947–952; Thomas I. Cook, "The Political System: The Stubborn Search for a Science of Politics," *Journal of Philosophy,* 51 (February, 1954), pp. 128–137; Charles S. Hyneman, *The Study of Politics* (Urbana: University of Illinois Press, 1959); William C. Mitchell, "Politics as the Allocation of Values: A Critique," *Ethics,* 71 (January, 1961), pp. 79–89; Talcott Parsons, "The Distribution of Power in American Society," *World Politics,* 10 (October, 1957), pp. 123–143; Charles Perrow, "The Sociological Perspective and Political Pluralism," *Social Research,* 31 (Winter, 1964), pp. 411–422.

[28] For essentially this aspect of man see Peter Berger, *Invitation to Sociology: A Humanistic Perspective* (New York: Doubleday, 1963), chap. 6; Max Mark, "What Image of Man for Political Science?" *Western Political Quarterly,* 15 (December, 1962), pp. 593–604; Dennis Wrong, "The Oversocialized Conception of Man in Modern Sociology," *American Sociological Review,* 26 (April, 1961), pp. 183–193.

[29] Tamotsu Shibutani, *Society and Personality: An Interactionist Approach to Social Psychology* (Englewood Cliffs, N.J.: Prentice-Hall, 1961), especially pp. 60, 91–94, 276–278. Also see S. F. Nadel, "Social Control and Self-Regulation," *Social Forces,* 31 (March, 1953), pp. 265–273.

[30] Erving Goffman, *Asylums* (New York: Doubleday, 1961), pp. 318–320.

[31] Richard A. Schermerhorn, "Man the Unfinished," *Sociological Quarterly,* 4 (Winter, 1963), pp. 5–17; Gordon W. Allport, *Becoming: Basic Considerations for a Psychology of Personality* (New Haven: Yale University Press, 1955).

ability to be creative. Through his culture he may develop the capacity to have greater freedom of action.[32] Not only is he shaped by his physical, social, and cultural experiences, he is able to select what he is to experience and develop. The belief in realizing unutilized human potential is growing and should be incorporated in a contemporary conception of human behavior.[33]

The *social action* frame of reference that serves as the basis of the humanistic conception of man is drawn from the work of such writers as Weber, Znaniecki, MacIver, Nadel, Parsons, and Becker.[34] It was originally suggested by Max Weber: "Action is social in so far as, by virtue of the subjective meaning attached to it by the acting individual (or individuals), it takes account of the behavior of others and is thereby oriented in its own course."[35] Hence, human behavior is *intentional*, has *meaning* for the actors, is *goal-oriented*, and takes place with an *awareness* of the consequences of behavior.

Because man engages in social action, a *social reality* is created. That is, man in interaction with others constructs a meaningful world of everyday life.

> It is the world of cultural objects and social institutions into which we are all born, within which we have to find our bearings, and with which we have to come to terms. From the outset, we, the actors on the social scene, experience the world we live in as a world both of nature and of culture, not as a private but as an intersubjective one, that is, as a world common to all of us, either actually given or potentially accessible to everyone; and this involves intercommunication and language.[36]

Social reality consists of both the social meanings and the products of the subjective world of persons. Man, accordingly, con-

[32] Herbert J. Muller, *The Uses of the Past* (New York: Oxford University Press, 1952), especially pp. 40–42.

[33] Julian Huxley, *New Bottles for New Wines* (New York: Harper, 1957).

[34] Florian Znaniecki, *Social Actions* (New York: Farrar and Rinehart, 1936); MacIver, *Social Causation*; S. F. Nadel, *Foundations of Social Anthropology* (New York: The Free Press, 1951); Talcott Parsons, *The Structure of Social Action* (New York: The Free Press, 1949); Howard Becker, *Through Values to Social Interpretation* (Durham: Duke University Press, 1950).

[35] Max Weber, *The Theory of Social and Economic Organization*, trans. A. M. Henderson and Talcott Parsons (New York: The Free Press), p. 88.

[36] Alfred Schutz, *The Problem of Social Reality: Collected Papers I* (The Hague: Martinus Nijhoff, 1962), p. 53.

structs activities and patterns of actions as he attaches meaning to his everyday existence.[37] Social reality is thus both a *conceptual reality* and a *phenomenal reality*. Having constructed social reality, man finds a world of meanings and events that is real to him as a conscious social being.

THEORY: THE SOCIAL REALITY OF CRIME

The theory contains six propositions and a number of statements within the propositions. With the first proposition I define crime. The next four are the explanatory units. In the final proposition the other five are collected to form a composite describing the social reality of crime. The propositions and their integration into a theory of crime reflect the assumptions about explanation and about man and society outlined above.[38]

PROPOSITION 1 (DEFINITION OF CRIME): *Crime is a definition of human conduct that is created by authorized agents in a politically organized society.*

This is the essential starting point in the theory — a definition of crime — which itself is based on the concept of definition. Crime is a *definition* of behavior that is conferred on some persons by others. Agents of the law (legislators, police, prosecutors, and judges), representing segments of a politically organized society, are responsible for formulating and administering criminal law. Persons and behaviors, therefore, become criminal because of the *formulation* and *application* of criminal definitions. Thus, *crime is created.*

By viewing crime as a definition, we are able to avoid the commonly used "clinical perspective," which leads one to concentrate on the quality of the act and to assume that criminal behavior is an

[37] See Peter L. Berger and Thomas Luckmann, *The Social Construction of Reality* (Garden City, N.Y.: Doubleday, 1966).

[38] For earlier background material, see Richard Quinney, "A Conception of Man and Society for Criminology," *Sociological Quarterly,* 6 (Spring, 1965), pp. 119–127; ·Quinney, "Crime in Political Perspective," *American Behavioral Scientist,* 8 (December, 1964), pp. 19–22; Quinney, "Is Criminal Behavior Deviant Behavior?" *British Journal of Criminology,* 5 (April, 1965), pp. 132–142.

individual pathology.[39] Crime is not inherent in behavior, but is a judgment made by some about the actions and characteristics of others.[40] This proposition allows us to focus on the formulation and administration of the criminal law as it touches upon the behaviors that become defined as criminal. Crime is seen as a result of a process which culminates in the defining of persons and behaviors as criminal. It follows, then, that *the greater the number of criminal definitions formulated and applied, the greater the amount of crime.*

PROPOSITION 2 (FORMULATION OF CRIMINAL DEFINITIONS): *Criminal definitions describe behaviors that conflict with the interests of the segments of society that have the power to shape public policy.*

Criminal definitions are formulated according to the interests of those *segments* (types of social groupings) of society which have the *power* to translate their interests into *public policy*. The interests — based on desires, values, and norms — which are ultimately incorporated into the criminal law are those which are treasured by the dominant interest groups in the society.[41] In other words, those who

---

[39] See Jane R. Mercer, "Social System Perspective and Clinical Perspective: Frames of Reference for Understanding Career Patterns of Persons Labelled as Mentally Retarded," *Social Problems,* 13 (Summer, 1966), pp. 18–34.

[40] This perspective in the study of social deviance has been developed in Becker, *Outsiders;* Kai T. Erikson, "Notes on the Sociology of Deviance," *Social Problems,* 9 (Spring, 1962), pp. 307–314; John I. Kitsuse, "Societal Reactions to Deviant Behavior: Problems of Theory and Method," *Social Problems,* 9 (Winter, 1962), pp. 247–256. Also see Ronald L. Akers, "Problems in the Sociology of Deviance: Social Definitions and Behavior," *Social Forces,* 46 (June, 1968), pp. 455–465; David J. Bordua, "Recent Trends: Deviant Behavior and Social Control," *Annals of the American Academy of Political and Social Science,* 369 (January, 1967), pp. 149–163; Jack P. Gibbs, "Conceptions of Deviant Behavior: The Old and the New," *Pacific Sociological Review,* 9 (Spring, 1966), pp. 9–14; Clarence R. Jeffery, "The Structure of American Criminological Thinking," *Journal of Criminal Law, Criminology and Police Science,* 46 (January–February, 1956), pp. 658–672; Austin T. Turk, "Prospects for Theories of Criminal Behavior," *Journal of Criminal Law, Criminology and Police Science,* 55 (December, 1964), pp. 454–461.

[41] See Richard C. Fuller, "Morals and the Criminal Law," *Journal of Criminal Law, Criminology and Police Science,* 32 (March–April, 1942), pp. 624–630; Thorsten Sellin, *Culture Conflict and Crime* (New York: Social Science Research Council, 1938), pp. 21–25; Clarence R. Jeffery, "Crime, Law and Social Structure," *Journal of Criminal Law, Criminology and Police Science,* 47 (November-December, 1956), pp. 423–435; John J. Honigmann, "Value Conflict and Legislation," *Social Problems,* 7 (Summer, 1959), pp. 34–40; George Rusche and Otto Kirchheimer, *Punishment and Social Structure* (New York: Columbia

have the ability to have their interests represented in public policy regulate the formulation of criminal definitions.

That criminal definitions are formulated is one of the most obvious manifestations of *conflict* in society. By formulating criminal law (including legislative statutes, administrative rulings, and judicial decisions), some segments of society protect and perpetuate their own interests. Criminal definitions exist, therefore, because some segments of society are in conflict with others.[42] By formulating criminal definitions these segments are able to control the behavior of persons in other segments. It follows that *the greater the conflict in interests between the segments of a society, the greater the probability that the power segments will formulate criminal definitions.*

The interests of the power segments of society are reflected not only in the content of criminal definitions and the kinds of penal sanctions attached to them, but also in the *legal policies* stipulating how those who come to be defined as "criminal" are to be handled. Hence, procedural rules are created for enforcing and administering the criminal law. Policies are also established on programs for treating and punishing the criminally defined and for controlling and preventing crime. In the initial criminal definitions or the subsequent procedures, and in correctional and penal programs or policies of crime control and prevention, the segments of society that have power and interests to protect are instrumental in regulating the behavior of those who have conflicting interests and less power.[43]

University Press, 1939); Roscoe Pound, *An Introduction to the Philosophy of Law* (New Haven: Yale University Press, 1922).

[42] I am obviously indebted to the conflict formulation of George B. Vold, *Theoretical Criminology* (New York: Oxford University Press, 1958), especially pp. 203–242. A recent conflict approach to crime is found in Austin T. Turk, "Conflict and Criminality," *American Sociological Review*, 31 (June, 1966), pp. 338–352.

[43] Considerable support for this proposition is found in the following studies: William J. Chambliss, "A Sociological Analysis of the Law of Vagrancy," *Social Problems*, 12 (Summer, 1964), pp. 66–77; Kai T. Erikson, *Wayward Puritans* (New York: John Wiley, 1966); Jerome Hall, *Theft, Law and Society*, 2nd ed. (Indianapolis: Bobbs-Merrill, 1952); Clarence R. Jeffery, "The Development of Crime in Early England," *Journal of Criminal Law, Criminology and Police Science*, 47 (March–April, 1957), pp. 647–666; Alfred R. Lindesmith, *The Addict and the Law* (Bloomington: Indiana University Press, 1965); Rusche and Kirchheimer, *Punishment and Social Structure;* Andrew Sinclair, *Era of Excess: A Social History of the Prohibition Movement* (New York: Harper & Row, 1964); Edwin H. Sutherland, "The Sexual Psychopath

Finally, law changes with modifications in the interest structure. When the interests that underlie a criminal law are no longer relevant to groups in power, the law will be reinterpreted or altered to incorporate the dominant interests. Hence, *the probability that criminal definitions will be formulated is increased by such factors as (1) changing social conditions, (2) emerging interests, (3) increasing demands that political, economic, and religious interests be protected, and (4) changing conceptions of the public interest.* The social history of law reflects changes in the interest structure of society.

PROPOSITION 3 (APPLICATION OF CRIMINAL DEFINITIONS): *Criminal definitions are applied by the segments of society that have the power to shape the enforcement and administration of criminal law.*

The powerful interests intervene in all stages in which criminal definitions are created. Since interests cannot be effectively protected by merely formulating criminal law, enforcement and administration of the law are required. The interests of the powerful, therefore, operate in *applying* criminal definitions. Consequently, crime is "political behavior and the criminal becomes in fact a member of a 'minority group' without sufficient public support to dominate the control of the police power of the state."[44] Those whose interests conflict with the interests represented in the law must either change their behavior or possibly find it defined as "criminal."

The probability that criminal definitions will be applied varies according to the extent to which the behaviors of the powerless conflict with the interests of the power segments. Law enforcement efforts and judicial activity are likely to be increased when the interests of the powerful are threatened by the opposition's behavior. Fluctuations and variations in the application of criminal definitions reflect shifts in the relations of the various segments in the power structure of society.

Law," *Journal of Criminal Law, Criminology and Police Science,* 40 (January–February, 1950), pp. 543–554.

[44] Vold, *Theoretical Criminology,* p. 202. Also see Irving Louis Horowitz and Martin Liebowitz, "Social Deviance and Political Marginality: Toward a Redefinition of the Relation Between Sociology and Politics," *Social Problems,* 15 (Winter, 1968), pp. 280–296.

Obviously, the criminal law is not applied directly by the powerful segments. They delegate enforcement and administration of the law to authorized *legal agents,* who, nevertheless, represent their interests. In fact, the security in office of legal agents depends on their ability to represent the society's dominant interests.

Because the interest groups responsible for creating criminal definitions are physically separated from the groups to which the authority to enforce and administer law is delegated, local conditions affect the manner in which criminal definitions are applied.[45] In particular, communities vary in the law enforcement and administration of justice they expect. Application is also affected by the visibility of acts in a community and by its norms about reporting possible offenses. Especially important are the occupational organization and ideology of the legal agents.[46] Thus, *the probability that criminal definitions will be applied is influenced by such community and organizational factors as (1) community expectations of law enforcement and administration, (2) the visibility and public reporting of offenses, and (3) the occupational organization, ideology, and actions of the legal agents to whom the authority to enforce and*

[45] See Michael Banton, *The Policeman and the Community* (London: Tavistock, 1964); Egon Bittner, "The Police on Skid-Row: A Study of Peace Keeping," *American Sociological Review,* 32 (October, 1967), pp. 699–715; John P. Clark, "Isolation of the Police: A Comparison of the British and American Situations," *Journal of Criminal Law, Criminology and Police Science,* 56 (September, 1965), pp. 307–319; Nathan Goldman, *The Differential Selection of Juvenile Offenders for Court Appearance* (New York National Council on Crime and Delinquency, 1963); James Q. Wilson, *Varieties of Police Behavior* (Cambridge: Harvard University Press, 1968).

[46] Abraham S. Blumberg, *Criminal Justice* (Chicago: Quadrangle Books, 1967); David J. Bordua and Albert J. Reiss, Jr., "Command, Control and Charisma: Reflections on Police Bureaucracy," *American Journal of Sociology,* 72 (July, 1966), pp. 68–76; Aaron V. Cicourel, *The Social Organization of Juvenile Justice* (New York: John Wiley, 1968); Arthur Niederhoffer, *Behind the Shield: The Police in Urban Society* (Garden City, N.Y.: Doubleday, 1967); Jerome H. Skolnick, *Justice Without Trial: Law Enforcement in Democratic Society* (New York: John Wiley, 1966); Arthur L. Stinchcombe, "Institutions of Privacy in the Determination of Police Administrative Practice," *American Journal of Sociology,* 69 (September, 1963), pp. 150–160; David Sudnow, "Normal Crimes: Sociological Features of the Penal Code in a Public Defender Office," *Social Problems,* 12 (Winter, 1965), pp. 255–276; William A. Westley, "Violence and the Police," *American Journal of Sociology,* 59 (July, 1953), pp. 34–41; Arthur Lewis Wood, *Criminal Lawyer* (New Haven: College & University Press, 1967).

administer criminal law is delegated. Such factors determine how the dominant interests of society are implemented in the application of criminal definitions.

The probability that criminal definitions will be applied in *specific situations* depends on the actions of the legal agents. In the final analysis, a criminal definition is applied according to an *evaluation* by someone charged with the authority to enforce and administer the law. In the course of "criminalization," a criminal label may be affixed to a person because of real or fancied attributes: "Indeed, a person is evaluated, either favorably or unfavorably, not because he *does* something, or even because he *is* something, but because others react to their perceptions of him as offensive or inoffensive."[47] Evaluation by the definers is affected by the way in which the suspect handles the situation, but ultimately their evaluations and subsequent decisions determine the criminality of human acts. Hence, *the more legal agents evaluate behaviors and persons as worthy of criminal definition, the greater the probability that criminal definitions will be applied.*

PROPOSITION 4 (DEVELOPMENT OF BEHAVIOR PATTERNS IN RELATION TO CRIMINAL DEFINITIONS): *Behavior patterns are structured in segmentally organized society in relation to criminal definitions, and within this context persons engage in actions that have relative probabilities of being defined as criminal.*

Although behavior varies, all behaviors are similar in that they represent the *behavior patterns* of segments of society. Therefore, all persons — whether they create criminal definitions or are the objects of criminal definitions — act according to *normative systems* learned in relative social and cultural settings.[48] Since it is not the

---

[47] Turk, "Conflict and Criminality," p. 340. For research on the evaluation of suspects by policemen, see Irving Piliavin and Scott Briar, "Police Encounters with Juveniles," *American Journal of Sociology*, 70 (September, 1964), pp. 206–214.

[48] Assumed within the theory of the social reality of crime is Sutherland's theory of differential association. See Edwin H. Sutherland, *Principles of Criminology*, 4th ed. (Philadelphia: J. B. Lippincott, 1947). An analysis of the differential association theory is found in Melvin L. De Fleur and Richard Quinney, "A Reformulation of Sutherland's Differential Association Theory and a Strategy for Empirical Verification," *Journal of Research in Crime and Delinquency*, 3 (January, 1966), pp. 1–22.

quality of the behavior but the action taken against the behavior that makes it criminal, that which is defined as criminal in any society is relative to the behavior patterns of the segments of society that formulate and apply criminal definitions. Consequently, *persons in the segments of society whose behavior patterns are not represented in formulating and applying criminal definitions are more likely to act in ways that will be defined as criminal than those in the segments that formulate and apply criminal definitions.*

Once behavior patterns are established with some regularity within the respective segments of society, individuals are provided with a framework for developing *personal action patterns*. These patterns continually develop for each person as he moves from one experience to another. It is the development of these patterns that gives his behavior its own substance in relation to criminal definitions.

Man constructs his own patterns of action in participating with others. It follows, then, that *the probability that a person will develop action patterns that have a high potential of being defined as criminal depends on the relative substance of (1) structured opportunities, (2) learning experiences, (3) interpersonal associations and identifications, and (4) self-conceptions.* Throughout his experiences, each person creates a conception of himself as a social being. Thus prepared, he behaves according to the anticipated consequences of his actions.[49]

During experiences shared by the criminal definers and the criminally defined, personal action patterns develop among the criminally defined because they are so defined. After such persons have had continued experience in being criminally defined, they learn to manipulate the application of criminal definitions.[50]

Furthermore, those who have been defined as criminal begin to conceive of themselves as criminal; as they adjust to the definitions

---

[49] On the operant nature of criminally defined behavior, see Robert L. Burgess and Ronald L. Akers, "A Differential Association-Reinforcement Theory of Criminal Behavior," *Social Problems,* 14 (Fall, 1966), pp. 128–147; C. R. Jeffery, "Criminal Behavior and Learning Theory," *Journal of Criminal Law, Criminology and Police Science,* 56 (September, 1965), pp. 294–300.

[50] A discussion of the part the person plays in manipulating the deviant defining situation is found in Judith Lorber, "Deviance as Performance: The Case of Illness," *Social Problems,* 14 (Winter, 1967), pp. 302–310.

imposed upon them, they learn to play the role of the criminal.[51] Because of others' reactions, therefore, persons may develop personal action patterns that increase the likelihood of their being defined as criminal in the future. That is, *increased experience with criminal definitions increases the probability of developing actions that may be subsequently defined as criminal.*

Thus, both the criminal definers and the criminally defined are involved in reciprocal action patterns. The patterns of both the definers and the defined are shaped by their common, continued, and related experiences. The fate of each is bound to that of the other.

PROPOSITION 5 (CONSTRUCTION OF CRIMINAL CONCEPTIONS): *Conceptions of crime are constructed and diffused in the segments of society by various means of communication.*

The "real world" is a social construction: man with the help of others creates the world in which he lives. Social reality is thus the world a group of people create and believe in as their own. This reality is constructed according to the kind of "knowledge" they develop, the ideas they are exposed to, the manner in which they select information to fit the world they are shaping, and the manner in which they interpret these conceptions.[52] Man behaves in reference to the *social meanings* he attaches to his experiences.

Among the constructions that develop in a society are those which determine what man regards as crime. Wherever we find the concept of crime, there we will find conceptions about the relevance of crime, the offender's characteristics, and the relation of crime to the social order.[53] These conceptions are constructed by communication. In fact, *the construction of criminal conceptions depends on the por-*

[51] Edwin M. Lemert, *Human Deviance, Social Problems, and Social Control* (Englewood Cliffs, N.J.: Prentice-Hall, 1964), pp. 40–64; Edwin M. Lemert, *Social Pathology* (New York: McGraw-Hill, 1951), pp. 3–98. A related and earlier discussion is in Frank Tannenbaum, *Crime and the Community* (New York: Columbia University Press, 1938), pp. 3–81.

[52] See Berger and Luckmann, *The Social Construction of Reality.* Relevant research on the diffusion of information is discussed in Everett M. Rogers, *Diffusion of Innovations* (New York: The Free Press of Glencoe, 1962).

[53] Research on public conceptions of crime is only beginning. See Alexander L. Clark and Jack P. Gibbs, "Social Control: A Reformulation," *Social Problems,* 12 (Spring, 1965), pp. 398–415; Thomas E. Dow, Jr., "The Role of Identification in Conditioning Public Attitude Toward the Offender," *Journal of Criminal Law, Criminology and Police Science,* 58 (March, 1967), pp. 75–79; William P. Lentz, "Social Status and Attitudes Toward Delinquency Control,"

trayal of crime in all personal and mass communications. By such means, criminal conceptions are constructed and diffused in the segments of a society. The most critical conceptions are those held by the power segments of society. These are the conceptions that are certain of becoming incorporated into the social reality of crime. In general, then, *the more the power segments are concerned about crime, the greater the probability that criminal definitions will be created and that behavior patterns will develop in opposition to criminal definitions.* The formulation and application of criminal definitions and the development of behavior patterns related to criminal definitions are thus joined in full circle by the construction of criminal conceptions.

PROPOSITION 6 (THE SOCIAL REALITY OF CRIME): *The social reality of crime is constructed by the formulation and application of criminal definitions, the development of behavior patterns related to criminal definitions, and the construction of criminal conceptions.*

These five propositions can be collected into a composite. The theory, accordingly, describes and explains phenomena that increase the probability of crime in society, resulting in the social reality of crime.

Since the first proposition is a definition and the sixth is a composite, the body of the theory consists of the four middle propositions. These form a model, as diagrammed in Figure 1.1, which relates the propositions into a theoretical system. Each proposition is related to the others forming a theoretical system of developmental propositions interacting with one another. The phenomena denoted in the propositions and their relationships culminate in what is regarded as the amount and character of crime in a society at any given time, that is, in the social reality of crime.

Journal of Research in Crime and Delinquency, 3 (July, 1966), pp. 147–154; Jennie McIntyre, "Public Attitudes Toward Crime and Law Enforcement," *Annals of the American Academy of Political and Social Science,* 374 (November, 1967), pp. 34–46; Anastassios D. Mylonas and Walter C. Reckless, "Prisoners' Attitudes Toward Law and Legal Institutions," *Journal of Criminal Law, Criminology and Police Science,* 54 (December, 1963), pp. 479–484; Elizabeth A. Rooney and Don C. Gibbons, "Social Reactions to 'Crimes Without Victims,'" *Social Problems,* 13 (Spring, 1966), pp. 400–410.

FIGURE 1.1

Model of the
Social Reality of Crime

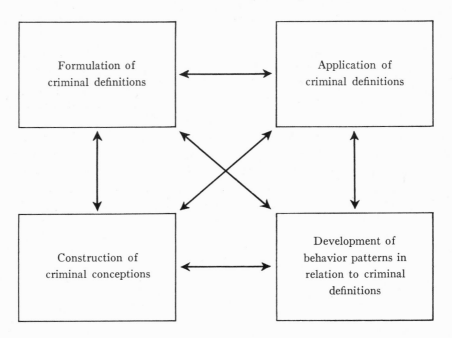

A THEORETICAL PERSPECTIVE
FOR STUDYING CRIME

The theory as I have formulated it is inspired by a change currently altering our view of the world. This change, found at all levels of society, has to do with the world that we all construct and, at the same time, pretend to separate ourselves from in assessing our experiences. Sociologists, sensing the problematic nature of existence, have begun to revise their theoretical orientation, as well as their methods and subjects of investigation.

For the study of crime, a revision in thought is directing attention to the process by which criminal definitions are formulated and applied. In the theory of the social reality of crime I have attempted to show how a theory of crime can be consistent with some revisionist assumptions about theoretical explanation and about man and society. The theory is cumulative in that the framework incorporates the diverse findings from criminology.

The synthesis has been brought about by conceiving of crime as a constructive process and by formulating a theory according to a system of propositions. The theory is integrative in that all relevant phenomena contribute to the process of creating criminal definitions, the development of the behaviors of those who are involved in criminal defining situations, and the construction of criminal conceptions. The result is the social reality of crime that is constantly being constructed in society.

The theory of the social reality of crime is used as a *theoretical perspective* throughout this book. It has allowed me to organize a considerable amount of material into a coherent framework, giving a perspective for a sociological study of crime. The theory can be useful to the extent that it helps us to understand crime as we experience it today.

2

Formulation
of Criminal
Definitions

CHAPTER TWO

Criminal Law
in Politically
Organized Society

In roughly a decade social scientists have amassed an impressive amount of research on criminal law. Yet, in spite of the research, a theory of criminal law has not developed. We are not at the moment theoretically equipped to generalize beyond the empirical studies or to formulate theoretically relevant research questions. In this chapter, I will develop a theoretical perspective to assist in these tasks. For this perspective I have elaborated on my general proposition describing how criminal definitions are formulated in the social reality of crime.[1]

THE STUDY OF
CRIMINAL LAW

Paradoxically, with law and social science gradually converging, we have no greater theoretical understanding of legal matters than we did all of half a century ago. The rapprochement that we are currently witnessing is not novel; a similar trend appeared in the United States shortly after the turn of the century. At that time social scientists, the early American sociologists in particular, were incorporating law into their scheme of things. E. A. Ross

[1] Portions of this chapter are adapted, with the publisher's permission, from the introduction to my *Crime and Justice in Society* (Boston: Little, Brown and Company, 1969), pp. 20–30.

referred to law as "the most specialized and highly furnished engine of control employed by society."[2] Lester F. Ward, an advocate of government control and social planning, foresaw a day when legislation would undertake to solve "questions of social improvement, the amelioration of the condition of all the people, the removal of whatever privations may still remain, and the adoption of means to the positive increase of the social welfare, in short the organization of human happiness."[3] The possibility of social reform, through legal means available to the state, was also emphasized by Albion W. Small.[4]

The ideas of the early sociologists directly influenced the school of legal philosophy that became a major force in American legal thought — sociological jurisprudence — in which Roscoe Pound was the principal figure. He drew from the early sociologists in asserting that law should be studied as a social institution.[5] Pound saw law as a specialized form of social control that brings pressure to bear upon each man "in order to constrain him to do his part in upholding civilized society and to deter him from anti-social conduct, that is, conduct at variance with the postulates of social order."[6] Moreover, in his theory of interests, Pound provided one of the few starting points for the study of law as a social phenomenon.

Recent writing and research have documented the role of interest groups in the political process. The techniques and tactics of interest groups, relations between the groups, their internal organization and politics, and overlapping group membership have been ex-

[2] E. A. Ross, *Social Control* (New York: Macmillan, 1922), p. 106 (originally published in 1901).

[3] Lester F. Ward, *Applied Sociology* (Boston: Ginn, 1906), p. 339.

[4] Albion W. Small, *General Sociology* (Chicago: University of Chicago Press, 1925).

[5] The relationship between early American sociologists and the development of Pound's sociological jurisprudence is discussed in Gilbert Geis, "Sociology and Jurisprudence: Admixture of Lore and Law," *Kentucky Law Journal*, 52 (Winter, 1964), pp. 267–293. Also see Edwin M. Schur, *Law and Society* (New York: Random House, 1968), pp. 17–50.

[6] Roscoe Pound, *Social Control Through Law* (New Haven: Yale University Press, 1942), p. 18. Earlier statements by Pound are found in Roscoe Pound, *An Introduction to the Philosophy of Law* (New Haven: Yale University Press, 1922); Roscoe Pound, *Outline of Lectures on Jurisprudence* (Cambridge: Harvard University Press, 1928).

amined.[7] In addition, studies have been conducted on how specific groups operate.[8] But almost no research has been directed at finding how much influence the interests have in formulating and administering law.[9] Moreover, few have attempted to revise Pound's theory of interests to reflect recent sociological developments. As it has been observed, "Sociologists to date have paid virtually no attention to Pound's doctrine, either in terms of rejecting it, refining it for their purposes, or supplementing it with sociological material of more recent vintage."[10]

[7] Donald C. Blaisdell, *American Democracy Under Pressure* (New York: Ronald Press, 1957); V. O. Key, Jr., *Politics, Parties and Pressure Groups* (New York: Thomas Y. Crowell, 1959); Earl Latham, *Group Basis of Politics* (Ithaca, N.Y.: Cornell University Press, 1952); David B. Truman, *The Governmental Process* (New York: Alfred A. Knopf, 1951); Henry W. Ehrmann (ed.), *Interest Groups on Four Continents* (Pittsburgh: University of Pittsburgh Press, 1958); Henry A. Turner, "How Pressure Groups Operate," *Annals of the American Academy of Political and Social Science,* 319 (September, 1958), pp. 63–72; Richard W. Gable, "Interest Groups as Policy Shapers," *Annals of the American Academy of Political and Social Science,* 319 (September, 1958), pp. 84–93; Murray S. Stedman, "Pressure Groups and the American Tradition," *Annals of the American Academy of Political and Social Science,* 319 (September, 1958), pp. 123–129.

[8] Robert Engler, *The Politics of Oil* (New York: Macmillan, 1961); Oliver Garceau, *The Political Life of the American Medical Association* (Cambridge: Harvard University Press, 1941); Charles M. Hardin, *The Politics of Agriculture: Soil Conservation and the Struggle for Power in Rural America* (New York: The Free Press of Glencoe, 1962); Grant McConnell, *Private Power and American Democracy* (New York: Alfred A. Knopf, 1966); Harry A. Millis and Royal E. Montgomery, *Organized Labor* (New York: McGraw-Hill, 1945); Warner Schilling, Paul Y. Hammond, and Glenn H. Snyder, *Strategy, Politics and Defense* (New York: Columbia University Press, 1962); William R. Willoughby, *The St. Lawrence Waterway: A Study in Politics and Diplomacy* (Madison: University of Wisconsin Press, 1961).

[9] Other social orientations to the law may be found among sociological jurists, among the so-called legal realists, and among current legal historians. See, in particular, Oliver Wendell Holmes, "The Path of the Law," *Harvard Law Review,* 10 (March, 1897), pp. 457–478; Thurman W. Arnold, *Symbols of Government* (New Haven: Yale University Press, 1935); Jerome Frank, *Courts on Trial* (Princeton: Princeton University Press, 1949); K. N. Llewellyn and E. Adamson Hoebel, *The Cheyenne Way: Conflict and Case Law in Primitive Jurisprudence* (Norman: University of Oklahoma Press, 1941); J. Willard Hurst, *Law and Economic Growth: The Legal History of the Lumber Industry in Wisconsin, 1836–1915* (Cambridge, Mass.: The Belknap Press, 1964).

[10] Geis, "Sociology and Sociological Jurisprudence: Admixture of Lore and Law," p. 292.

In the current movement by social scientists toward research into law and the use by lawyers of social science research, an interest approach might well help us to construct a theory of criminal law that would integrate research findings and provide direction for future research. For sociological purposes, however, Pound's approach necessarily requires reformulation and extension into a sociological theory of criminal law.

FROM SOCIOLOGICAL JURISPRUDENCE TO SOCIOLOGY OF CRIMINAL LAW

Law is not merely a complex of rules and procedures; Pound taught us that in calling for the study of "law in action." For some purposes it may be useful to think of law as autonomous within society, developing according to its own logic and proceeding along its own lines. But law also simultaneously reflects society and influences it, so that, in a social sense, it is both social product and social force. In Pound's juristic approach, however, law represents the consciousness of the total society. This *consensus* model of (criminal) law has been described in the following way: "The state of criminal law continues to be — as it should — a decisive reflection of the social consciousness of a society. What kind of conduct an organized community considers, at a given time, sufficiently condemnable to impose official sanctions, impairing the life, liberty, or property of the offender, is a barometer of the moral and social thinking of a community."[11] Similarly, Pound, formulating his theory of interests, felt that law reflects the needs of the well-ordered society. In fact, the law is a form of "social engineering" in a civilized society:

> For the purpose of understanding the law of today, I am content to think of law as a social institution to satisfy social wants — the claims and demands involved in the existence of civilized society — by giving effect to as much as we may with the least sacrifice, so far as such wants may be satisfied or

[11] Wolfgang Friedmann, *Law in a Changing Society* (Harmondsworth, England: Penguin Books, 1964), p. 143. A similar statement is found in Jerome Michael and Mortimer J. Adler, *Crime, Law and Social Science* (New York: Harcourt, Brace, 1933), pp. 2–3.

such claims given effect by an ordering of human conduct through politically organized society. For present purposes I am content to see in legal history the record of a continually wider recognizing and satisfying of human wants or claims or desires through social control; a more embracing and more effective securing of social interests; a continually more complete and effective elimination of waste and precluding of friction in human enjoyment of the goods of existence — in short, a continually more efficacious social engineering.[12]

Thus, the interests Pound had in mind would maintain and, ultimately, improve the social order. His was a *teleological* as well as consensus theory of interests: men must fulfill some interests for the good of the whole society; these interests are to be achieved through law. In Pound's theory, only the right law can emerge in a civilized society.

Jurisprudence has generally utilized a *pluralistic* model with respect to law as a social force in society. Accordingly, law regulates social behavior and establishes social organization; it orders human relationships by restraining individual actions and by settling disputes in social relations. In recent juristic language, law functions "first, to establish the general framework, the rules of the game so to speak, within and by which individual and group life shall be carried on, and secondly, to adjust the conflicting claims which different individuals and groups of individuals seek to satisfy in society."[13] For Pound, the law adjusts and reconciles conflicting interests:

> Looked at functionally, the law is an attempt to satisfy, to reconcile, to harmonize, to adjust these overlapping and often conflicting claims and demands, either through securing them directly and immediately, or through securing certain individual interests, or through delimitations or compromises of individual interests, so as to give effect to the greatest total

[12] Pound, *An Introduction to the Philosophy of Law,* pp. 98–99.
[13] Carl A. Auerbach, "Law and Social Change in the United States," *U.C.L.A. Law Review,* 6 (July, 1959), pp. 516–532. Similarly, see Julius Stone, *The Province and Function of Law* (Cambridge: Harvard University Press, 1950), Part III; Julius Stone, *Social Dimensions of Law and Justice* (Stanford: Stanford University Press, 1966), chaps. 4–8.

of interests or to the interests that weigh most in our civilization, with the least sacrifice of the scheme of interests as a whole.[14]

In Pound's theory of interests, law provides the general framework within which individual and group life is carried on, according to the postulates of social order. Moreover, as a legal historian has written, "The law defines the extent to which it will give effect to the interests which it recognizes, in the light of other interests and of the possibilities of effectively securing them through law; it also devises means for securing those that are recognized and prescribes the limits within which those means may be employed."[15] In the interest theory of sociological jurisprudence, then, law is an instrument that controls interests according to the requirements of social order.

Pound's theory of interests included a threefold classification of interests, including the individual, the public, and the social:

> Individual interests are claims or demands or desires involved immediately in the individual life and asserted in the title of that life. Public interests are claims or demands or desires involved in life in a politically organized society and asserted in the title of that organization. They are commonly treated as the claims of a politically organized society thought of as a legal entity. Social interests are claims or demands or desires involved in social life in a civilized society and asserted in the title of that life. It is not uncommon to treat them as the claims of the whole social group as such.[16]

Pound warned that the types are overlapping and interdependent and that most can be placed in all the categories, depending upon one's purpose. He argued, however, that it is often expedient to put claims, demands, and desires in their most general form; that is, into the category of social interests.

[14] Roscoe Pound, "A Survey of Social Interests," *Harvard Law Review*, 57 (October, 1943), p. 39.

[15] George Lee Haskins, *Law and Authority in Early Massachusetts* (New York: Macmillan, 1960), p. 226.

[16] Pound, "A Survey of Social Interests," pp. 1–2.

Surveying the claims, demands, and desires found in legal proceedings and in legislative proposals, Pound suggested that the most important social interest appears to involve security against actions that threaten the social group.[17] Others are interest in the security of domestic, religious, economic, and political institutions; morals; conservation of social resources; general progress, including the development of human powers and control over nature to satisfy human wants; and individual life, especially the freedom of self-assertion. According to Pound, any legal system depends upon the way in which these interests are incorporated into law.

My theoretical perspective on criminal law departs from the general tradition of the interest theory of sociological jurisprudence in a number of ways. First, my perspective is based on a special conception of society. Society is characterized by diversity, conflict, coercion, and change, rather than by consensus and stability. Second, law is a *result* of the operation of interests, rather than an instrument that functions outside of particular interests. Though law may control interests, it is in the first place *created* by interests. Third, law incorporates the interests of specific persons and groups; it is seldom the product of the whole society. Law is made by men, representing special interests, who have the power to translate their interests into public policy. Unlike the pluralistic conception of politics, law does not represent a compromise of the diverse interests in society, but supports some interests at the expense of others. Fourth, the theoretical perspective of criminal law is devoid of teleological connotations. The social order may require certain functions for its maintenance and survival, but such functions will not be considered as inherent in the interests involved in formulating substantive laws. Fifth, the perspective proposed here includes a conceptual scheme for analyzing interests in the law. Finally, construction of the perspective is based on findings from current social science research.

---

[17] Pound, "A Survey of Social Interests," pp. 1–39. Other aspects of the theory of interests are discussed by Pound in the following publications: *The Spirit of the Common Law* (Boston: Marshall Jones, 1921), pp. 91–93, 197–203; *An Introduction to the Philosophy of Law*, pp. 90–96; *Interpretations of Legal History* (New York: Macmillan, 1923), pp. 158–164; *Social Control through Law*, pp. 63–80.

LAW IN POLITICALLY
ORGANIZED SOCIETY

Authority relations are present in all social collectivities: some persons are always at the command of others. As order is established in a society, several systems of control develop to regulate the conduct of various groups of persons. Human behavior is thus subject to restraint by varied agencies, institutions, and social groupings — families, churches, social clubs, political organizations, labor unions, corporations, educational systems, and so forth.

The control systems vary considerably in the forms of conduct they regulate, and most provide means for assuring compliance to their rules. Informal means, spontaneously employed by some persons, such as ridicule, gossip, and censure, may ensure conformity to some rules. Control systems may, in addition, rely upon formal and regularized means of sanction.

The *legal system* is the most explicit form of social control. The law consists of (1) specific rules of conduct, (2) planned use of sanctions to support the rules, and (3) designated officials to interpret and enforce the rules.[18] Furthermore, law becomes more important as a system of control as societies increase in complexity. Pound wrote that "in the modern world law has become the paramount agent of social control. Our main reliance is upon force of a politically organized state."[19]

Law is more than a system of formal social control; it is also a body of specialized rules created and interpreted in a *politically organized society,* or the state, which is a territorial organization with the authorized power to govern the lives and activities of all the inhabitants. Though other types of organized bodies may possess formal rules, only the specialized rule systems of politically organized societies are regarded here as systems of law.[20]

---

[18] F. James Davis, "Law as a Type of Social Control," in F. James Davis, Henry H. Foster, Jr., C. Ray Jeffery, and E. Eugene Davis, *Society and the Law* (New York: The Free Press of Glencoe, 1962), p. 43.

[19] Pound, *Social Control through Law,* p. 20.

[20] The rule systems of societies other than those which are politically organized may be adequately referred to, for comparative purposes, in any number of quasilegal ways, such as nonstate law, primitive law, or "lawways." Perhaps, even better, such systems of rules could be described simply as "tradition," "normative system," or "custom." The concept of law is expanded to

Law, as a special kind of institution, again is more than an abstract body of rules. Instead of being autonomous within society and developing according to its own logic, law is an integral part of society, operating as a force in society and as a social product. The law is not only that which is written as statutes and recorded as court opinions and administrative rulings, but is also a method or *process* of doing something.[21] As a process, law is a dynamic force that is continually being *created* and *interpreted*. Thus, law in action involves the making of specialized (legal) decisions by various *authorized agents*. In politically organized society, human actions are regulated by those invested with the authority to make specified decisions in the name of the society.

Furthermore, law in operation is an aspect of politics — it is one of the methods by which public policy is formulated and administered for governing the lives and activities of the state's inhabitants. As an act of politics, law and legal decisions do not represent the interests of all persons in the society. Whenever a law is created or interpreted, the values of some are necessarily assured and the values of others are either ignored or negated.

THE INTEREST STRUCTURE

Modern societies are characterized by an organization of differences. The social differentiation of society, in turn, provides the basis for the state's political life. Government in a politically organized society operates according to the interests that characterize the socially differentiated positions. Because varied interests are distributed among the positions, and because the positions are differently equipped with the ability to command, public policy represents

---

include the control systems of other than politically organized society among such writers as Bronislaw Malinowski, *Crime and Custom in Savage Society* (London: Routledge and Kegan Paul, 1926); E. Adamson Hoebel, *The Law of Primitive Man* (Cambridge: Harvard University Press, 1954); William M. Evan, "Public and Private Legal Systems," in William M. Evan (ed.), *Law and Sociology* (New York: The Free Press of Glencoe, 1962), pp. 165–184; Philip Selznick, "Legal Institutions and Social Controls," *Vanderbilt Law Review*, 17 (December, 1963), pp. 79–90.

[21] For this conception of law, as applied to criminal law, see Henry M. Hart, Jr., "The Aims of the Criminal Law," *Law and Contemporary Problems*, 23 (Summer, 1958), pp. 401–441.

specific interests in the society. Politically organized society, therefore, may be viewed as a differentiated *interest structure.*

Each *segment* of society has its own values, its own norms, and
its own ideological orientations. When these are considered to be
important for the existence and welfare of the respective segments,
they may be defined as *interests.*[22] Further, interests can be categorized according to the ways in which activities are generally pursued in society; that is, according to the *institutional orders* of
society. The following may then serve as a definition of interests:
the institutional concerns of the segments of society. Thus, interests
are grounded in the segments of society and represent the institutional concerns of the segments.

The institutional orders within which interests operate may be
classified into fairly broad categories.[23] For our use, these may be
called: (1) *the political,* which regulates the distribution of power
and authority in society; (2) *the economic,* which regulates the
production and distribution of goods and services; (3) *the religious,*
which regulates the relationship of man to a conception of the
supernatural; (4) *the kinship,* which regulates sexual relations,
family patterns, and the procreation and rearing of children; (5)
the educational, which regulates the formal training of the society's
members; and (6) *the public,* which regulates the protection and
maintenance of the community and its citizens. Each segment of
society has its own orientation to these orders. Some, because of their
authority position in the interest structure, are able to have their
interests represented in public policy.

The segments of society differ in the extent to which their interests are organized. The segments themselves are broad statistical
aggregates containing persons of similar age, sex, class, status, occupation, race, ethnicity, religion, or the like. All these have *formal
interests;* those which are advantageous to the segment but which
are not consciously held by the incumbents and are not organized

[22] The view here that interests are not distributed randomly in society but are
related to one's position in society follows Marx's theory of economic production and class conflict. See Ralf Dahrendorf, *Class and Class Conflict in Industrial Society* (Stanford: Stanford University Press, 1959), especially pp. 3–35.

[23] The conception of institutional orders closely follows that of Hans Gerth
and C. Wright Mills, *Character and Social Structure* (New York: Harcourt,
Brace, 1953), especially pp. 25–26.

for action. *Active interests,* on the other hand, are manifest to persons in the segments and are sufficiently organized to serve as the basis for representation in policy decisions.[24]

Within the segments, groups of persons may become aware of and organize to promote their common interests; these may be called *interest groups.* Public policy, in turn, is the result of the success gained by these groups.

The interest structure is characterized by the unequal distribution of *power* and *conflict* among the segments of society. It is differentiated by diverse interests and by the ability of the segments to translate their interests into public policy. Furthermore, the segments are in continual conflict over their interests. Interests thus are structured according to differences in power and are in conflict.

Power and conflict are linked in this conception of interest structure. Power, as the ability to shape public policy, produces conflict among the competing segments, and conflict produces differences in the distribution of power. Coherence in the interest structure is thus ensured by the exercise of force and constraint by the conflicting segments. In the conflict-power model, therefore, politically organized society is held together by conflicting elements and functions according to the coercion of some segments by others.

The conflict-power conception of interest structure implies that public policy results from differential distribution of power and conflict among the segments of society. Diverse segments with specialized interests become so highly organized that they are able to influence the policies that affect all persons in the state. Groups that have the power to gain access to the decision-making process are able to translate their interests into public policy. Thus, the interests represented in the formulation and administration of public policy are those treasured by the dominant segments of the society. Hence, public policy is created because segments with power differentials are in conflict with one another. Public policy itself is a manifestation of an interest structure in politically organized society.

[24] The distinction between formal interests and active interests is similar to the distinction Dahrendorf makes between latent and manifest interests. See Dahrendorf, *Class and Class Conflict in Industrial Society,* pp. 173–179.

FORMULATION AND ADMINISTRATION
OF CRIMINAL LAW

Law is a form of public policy that regulates the behavior and activities of all members of a society. It is *formulated* and *administered* by those segments of society which are able to incorporate their interests into the creation and interpretation of public policy. Rather than representing the institutional concerns of all segments of society, law secures the interests of particular segments, supporting one point of view at the expense of others.

Thus, the content of the law, including the substantive regulations and the procedural rules, represents the interests of the segments of society that have the power to shape public policy. Formulation of law allows some segments of society to protect and perpetuate their own interests. By formulating law, some segments are able to control others to their own advantage.

The interests that the power segments of society attempt to maintain enter into all stages of legal administration. Since legal formulations do not provide specific instructions for interpreting law, administration of law is largely a matter of discretion on the part of *legal agents* (police, prosecutors, judges, juries, prison authorities, parole officers, and others). Though implementation of law is necessarily influenced by such matters as localized conditions and the occupational organization of legal agents, the interest structure of politically organized society is responsible for the general design of the administration of criminal justice.

Finally, the formulation and administration of law in politically organized society are affected by changing social conditions. Emerging interests and increasing concern with the protection of various aspects of social life require new laws or reinterpretations of old laws. Consequently, legal changes take place within the context of the changing interest structure of society.

INTERESTS IN
CONTEMPORARY SOCIETY

Interests not only are the principal forces behind the creation and interpretation of law, but they are changing the very nature of government. For centuries the state was the Leviathan, protector, repository of power, main source of the community's economic and social life. The state unified and controlled most of the activities of the society. In recent times, however, it is apparent that some groups and segments of society have taken over many of the state's functions:

> The question must be raised in all seriousness whether the "overmighty subjects" of our time — the giant corporations, both of a commercial and non-commercial character, the labor unions, the trade associations, farmers' organizations, veterans' legions, and some other highly organized groups — have taken over the substance of sovereignty. Has the balance of pressures and counter-pressures between these groups left the legal power of the State as a mere shell? If this is a correct interpretation of the social change of our time, we are witnessing another dialectic process in history: the national sovereign State — having taken over effective legal political power from the social groups of the previous age — surrenders its power to the new massive social groups of the industrial age.[25]

Some analysts of the contemporary scene have optimistically forecasted that checks of "countervailing power" will adequately balance the interests of the well organized groups.[26] This pluralistic conception disregards the fact that interest groups are grossly unequal in power. Groups that are similar in power may well check each others' interests, but groups that have little or no power will not have the opportunity to have their interest represented in public policy. The consequence is government by a few powerful private interest groups.

Furthermore, the politics of private interests tends to take place outside of the arena of the public governmental process. In private politics, interest groups receive their individual claims in return for allowing other groups to press for their interests.[27] Behind public politics a private government operates in a way that not only guarantees rewards to well organized groups but affects the lives of us all.

If there be any check in this contemporary condition, it is in the

[25] Friedmann, *Law in a Changing Society,* pp. 239–240.
[26] John Kenneth Galbraith, *Modern Capitalism* (Boston: Houghton Mifflin, 1952).
[27] See Theodore Lowi, "The Public Philosophy: Interest-Group Liberalism," *American Political Science Review,* 61 (March, 1967), pp. 5–24.

prospect that the "public interest" will take precedence over private interests. Interest groups, if for no other reason than their concern for public relations, may bow to the commonweal. Optimistically, the public interest may become an ideal fulfilled, no matter what the source of private power.

But the fallacy in any expectation of the achievement of the public good through the "public interest" is that the government which could foster such a condition will become again in a new age an oppressive interest in itself. That age, in fact, seems to be upon us. Increasingly, as Reich has argued, "Americans live on government largess — allocated by government on its own terms, and held by recipients subject to conditions which express 'the public interest.' "[28] While the highly organized, scientifically planned society, governed for the social good of its inhabitants, promises the best life that man has ever known, not all of our human values will receive attention, and some may be temporarily or permanently negated.

In raw form we cannot hold optimistically to either government by private interests or public interest by government largess. The future for individual man appears to lie in some form of protection from both forms of government. Decentralized government offers some possibility for the survival of the individual in a collective society. But more immediately, that protection must be sought in procedural law, a law that must necessarily be removed from the control of either the interests of private groups or public government. The challenge for law of the future is that it create an order providing fulfillment for individual values that are now within our reach, values that paradoxically are imminent because of the existence of interests from which we must now seek protection. A new society is indeed coming: Can a law be created apart from private interests which assures individual fulfillment within a good society?

[28] Charles A. Reich, "The New Property," *Yale Law Journal,* 73 (April, 1964), p. 733.

CHAPTER THREE

Interests in
the Formulation
of Criminal Laws

The perspective on criminal law in politically organized society provides the basis for understanding how particular criminal laws are formulated. Following this perspective, criminal laws — including the enactments of legislatures, court decisions, and administrative rulings — are formulated by those segments of society which have the power to shape public policy. The formulation of criminal law is thus an act of politics: Public policy is established by some for governing the lives and affairs of all inhabitants of a society. Crime, then, is a definition of human conduct that is created in the course of the political life of the community.

Lawmaking, according to this perspective, represents the translation of specific group interests into public policy. For the most part, criminal laws support particular interests to the neglect or negation of other interests, thus representing the concerns of only some members of society. Though some criminal laws may involve a compromise of conflicting interests, more likely than not, criminal laws mark the victory of some groups over others. The notion of a compromise of conflicting interests is a myth perpetuated by a pluralistic model of politics. Some interests never find access to the lawmaking process. Other interests are overwhelmed in it, not compromised. But ultimately some interests succeed in becoming criminal law, and are able to control the conduct of others.

EMERGENCE OF CRIMINAL LAW

The very emergence of criminal law is historically a political phenomenon. Because of the interests of particular social segments, criminal law was created: it has continued to operate in various social contexts for the benefit of diverse and shifting interests, including the interests of the state itself.

Early law was a private matter in that injured individuals and their families had the responsibility of securing retribution from the parties that had wronged them. The concept of criminal law developed only when the notion of private vengeance was replaced by the principle that in some instances the community was also injured when harm came to its members. Thus, the right of action arising from a wrong ceased to be restricted to the immediate victim and was granted in the case of certain offenses to all citizens, or to the politically organized society. "True criminal law," as distinguished from elementary tort and primitive law, contains several new legal concepts:

> (1) It will recognize the principle that attacks upon the persons or property of individuals, or rights thereto annexed, as well as offenses that affect the state directly, may be violations of the public peace and good order. (2) It will provide, as part of the ordinary machinery of government, means by which such violations may be punished by and for the state, and not merely by the individual who may be directly affected. (3) The protection it offers will be readily available to the entire body politic, and not restricted to particular groups or classes of citizens.[1]

Criminal law as we know it today in the Western world emerged in several different social contexts, notably, those of Greece, Rome, and England, and has shaped our conception of "criminal" in several ways. Contemporary criminal law embodies notions on (1) the public character of criminal law, (2) the state nature of criminal law, and (3) the role of political unity in criminal law. Each of these concepts in the emergence of criminal law was shaped by social interests.

[1] George M. Calhoun, *The Growth of Criminal Law in Ancient Greece* (Berkeley: University of California Press, 1927), p. 5.

Criminal Law and Democracy in Greece. The decisive step in the emergence of criminal law was taken in Athens at the beginning of the sixth century B.C. At that time, Solon, after being appointed *nomothete,* with dictatorial powers, instituted several formal enactments which gave every citizen the right of action in the prosecution of certain offenses. Greek society was in the throes of a political crisis. The enactments of Solon, which formed the basis for the development of criminal law in Greece, were part of an attempt toward solving the crisis and rehabilitating Greek government.

A number of facts surrounding the Athenian political struggle have been established.[2] At the time all functions of government were exclusively in the hands of the *eupatrids,* an hereditary class of Athenian aristocrats. The inferior orders of citizens, the peasant proprietors (the *georgi*) and the artisans (the *demurgi*), had no part in government except by attaching themselves to a member of the aristocracy. Below this level was the lowest class of freemen, the propertyless population (variously named *thetes, hectemori,* and *pelatae*), whose members had few rights and were in many cases virtually serfs. Still lower were the slaves, without rights of any kind.

The class and political structure of Athens thus consisted of an oligarchy of the wealthy and privileged that ruled over a large proletariat. The lower classes were politically subjugated and were made the object of merciless economic exploitation. The oppressiveness of the situation, accompanied by the increasing economic strength of the proletariat, eventually produced discontent among those excluded from the process of government. The ruling aristocrats reacted to the situation through compromise:

> In such a situation the alternative to revolution and perhaps tyranny was compromise, and this the ruling class, or some of them, were wise enough to see. And we must believe that these wiser men were keenly alive to the menace which confronted them in the presence of a prosperous alien population, chafing under the denial of the political rights to which their economic strength entitled them, ready at the first opportunity to fan

[2] See Calhoun, *The Growth of Criminal Law in Ancient Greece,* especially p. 44.

into the flame of revolution the smouldering discontent of the native proletariat.[3]

The political compromise that resulted from the class conflict of ancient Greece provided the beginnings for the criminal law of the Western world. The step taken toward criminal law consequently protected citizens from one another and from government itself, in this case protecting the lower classes of Athens from the aggression of the rich and powerful. Through legal reform, as an alternative to possible revolution, Solon and his council established popular courts, provided for appeal from the decisions of magistrates, and assured the right of all citizens to initiate prosecutions. It may be suggested that Greece became the "cradle of democracy" through the creation of criminal law. At least, whatever the connection may be, the foundations of democratic government and the emergence of criminal law occurred together in a relationship that was mutually supportive of both.

Criminal Law in the Roman State. The concept of criminal law developed slowly among the Romans. Although eventually a distinction was made between *civilis* and *criminalis,* law in Rome was devoted primarily to private legal matters and civil procedure. When a criminal law did develop, its principal concern was with offenses against the state and with the punishment of such offenders. The Romans were more the efficient administrators of their empire than students and practitioners of justice.

The law of the Twelve Tables — of the middle of the fifth century B.C. — was based on the idea of the right of the injured party to private vengeance. Punishment was inflicted by the state, however, for crimes which were committed directly against the commonwealth. While most of the provisions of the Twelve Tables, as codifications of Roman customary law, rested on the concept of private law, the Twelve Tables were originally created as a safeguard for a portion of the population. In effect the Twelve Tables protected the plebeians against the unfair treatment of the patricians.[4]

---

[3] Calhoun, *The Growth of Criminal Law in Ancient Greece,* p. 52.

[4] Hans Julius Wolff, *Roman Law: An Historical Introduction* (Norman: University of Oklahoma Press, 1951), pp. 54–61. Also Barry Nicholas, *An Introduction to Roman Law* (Oxford: Oxford University Press, 1962), pp. 208–209.

As Rome grew from a rural community to a powerful city-state, the "private criminal law" of the Twelve Tables proved increasingly inadequate.

> The "private criminal law" of the Twelve Tables reflected the conditions of a primitive commonwealth of modest dimensions and rustic character. It was bound to prove increasingly inadequate as Rome developed into a metropolis dominated by powerful social tensions; and the growth of the urban proletariat and of the slave population was certainly accompanied by a rise in criminality which demanded vigorous measures for the maintenance of public security.[5]

Subsequently, during the third century B.C. and the beginning of the second century, a criminal jurisdiction was established for the control of those engaged in such politically threatening activities as violence, treason, arson, poisoning, the carrying of weapons, and the theft of state property. Tribunals and courts were instituted to deal with such cases.[6]

Thus, the criminal law which did emerge late in the Roman Republic was a device created mainly for the protection of the state itself. The protection of the rights of the individual from the state was not a concept central to Roman law. Criminal law in Rome was created by the interests that could be best satisfied through the maintenance of a strongly controlled political regime.

Political Unification and the Emergence of Criminal Law in England. In England, as in any society, a criminal law could emerge only with the parallel development of national sovereignty. The history of English law is thus related to changes in the social and political structures of the country.[7] Criminal law emerged as a specific form of law when England achieved the political unity that allowed a law to be established and administered in the name of a centralized government.

[5] Wolfgang Kunkel, *An Introduction to Roman Legal History and Constitutional History* (Oxford: Oxford University Press, 1966), p. 61.

[6] Erich S. Gruen, *Roman Politics and the Criminal Courts, 149–78* B.C. (Cambridge: Harvard University Press, 1968).

[7] Clarence Ray Jeffrey, "The Development of Crime in Early English Society," *Journal of Criminal Law, Criminology and Police Science,* 47 (March–April, 1957), pp. 647–666.

The turning point in the history of English law marked also the emergence of criminal law itself. This important change in English law began in the latter part of the eleventh century and continued throughout the twelfth. Prior to that time the territory we now know as England was divided into separate units with their own laws. These legal systems could not foster the concept of criminal law.

The law of the Anglo-Saxons was originally a system of tribal justice. Each tribe, as a group of kinsmen, was controlled by its own chief and armed warriors who met and, among other things, passed laws. Any wrong was regarded as being against or by the family; and it was the family that atoned or carried out the blood-feud if an offense occurred between kinship groups.

By the tenth century England was divided into six to eight large kingdoms. Some degree of political consolidation had come about as a result of civil wars among local tribes. The acceptance of Christianity among leaders provided not only a spiritual unity but, as found in the Roman Catholic Church, a scheme of centralized control. In the reorganization, tribal chiefs were replaced by kings who became both military leaders and landlords. As feudalism changed the organization of Saxon society, between the eighth and eleventh centuries, the blood-feud was replaced by a system of compensations. Eventually the collective responsibility of the kinship group was absorbed by the kingdom. Compensation for offenses became the domain of the king, lord, or bishop, rather than the kinship group. One of Aethelred's laws, for example, made it a breach of the king's peace to resort to the feud before compensation had been demanded from the offender or his family.[8]

It was with the Norman invasion and the reign of the Norman kings that the old tribal-feudal system of law disappeared and a new system of law emerged in England. When William conquered England in 1066, he proclaimed himself the "supreme landlord" of all England. By this move, implemented by the Domesday Survey, William redistributed the land, with the Norman nobles at the top, and placed all social relationships on a land tenure basis, under his control. In addition, William took the important step of separating state law from canon law. But the most important move taken in William's time toward the emergence of criminal law was the

---

[8] See F. L. Attenborough (ed.), *The Laws of the English Kings* (Cambridge: Cambridge University Press, 1922).

unification of England under one head, the "King of England."

With their administrative abilities the Norman kings developed centralized legal institutions. In order to place law under the jurisdiction of the king's government, several courts were created by the king. Writs were devised by which cases could be carried out of baronial courts into the king's courts. Itinerant judges were sent into the various "hundreds" and "shires" to administer the king's laws. By the end of the reign of Henry II (1154–1189), the law of England was in the hands of the Crown. A court of "common law" was established for the justice of all men. A new procedure and a new conception of offenses had been created.[9] Now for the first time some offenses were regarded as clearly in violation of the peace of king and country. A criminal law had emerged in England.

To be sure, criminal law in England came about for the protection of particular interests, primarily those of the king. The criminal law placed the affairs of the king's subjects under his jurisdiction. The powerful landholders and the church could no longer freely create and administer law in their own courts. Law which affected the nation was now the king's law. As supreme overlord, the king demanded the authority of his position.

But political unification, perhaps inadvertently, also benefited the interests of the common man. Men lowly placed in the land tenure system were no longer at the complete mercy of their landlords. Justice potentially was in the reach of all. Eventually in England's history, the power of the monarch diminished and finally vanished with the creation of parliamentary goverment. Today, because of this political unification in the eleventh and twelfth centuries and because of the emergence of a criminal law at the same time, a common law survives. We need not be bothered for the moment that its justice continues to be more common for some men than for others.

CRIMINAL LAW IN COLONIES AND TERRITORIES

Once criminal law emerged as concept and fact, it became a widely used means of regulating human conduct in politically organized

---

[9] G. O. Sayles, *Medieval Foundation of England* (London: Methuen, 1966), chap. 21. Also John W. Jeudwine, *Tort, Crime and Police in Medieval Britain* (London: Williams and Norgate, 1917), especially chaps. 7 and 8.

societies. Conceivably *all* forms of human behavior have been under
the jurisdiction of criminal law, in one society or another, at one
time or other. Each criminal law specified the illegality of some specific behavior. The formulation of criminal law, therefore, depends
upon standards of some sort; otherwise formulation of substantive
criminal laws would be impossible.

Our task is to indicate the ways in which various kinds of criminal law have been shaped by social interests in their formulation.
The regulation of specific kinds of behavior will be investigated
within the various institutional orders. It will be shown that the
values of social groups acted as interests in the formulation of specific kinds of criminal law. The interests represented in each case are
those of the social segments that have had the power to translate
their values into social policy. The theory of criminal law as related
to social interests can be seen to operate in several social contexts.

The formulation of criminal law in the colonies and territories of
nations presents a special case of social interests in the formulation
of criminal law. In such situations criminal laws are either formulated directly by the imperial nation for the control of its colonies
and territories or formulated by the colonies and territories under
the close supervision of the imperial nation. The social interests of
the laws imposed, supervised, or inspired by imperial nations are
related to the political and economic order of the imperial nation.
The operation of such social interests can be seen in three settings:
(1) English common law in the American colonies, (2) British law
in India and Africa, and (3) American frontier law.

English Common Law in the American Colonies. The English
charters for the founding of settlements in the New World provided
that the laws established within the settlements should not be contrary to the laws of England. During the American colonial period,
colonial statutes which were counter to the English common law
could be disallowed by the Crown's Privy Council. In addition, the
decisions of the provincial courts were subject to appeal by the Privy
Council where any radical departure from the common law could be
corrected.[10] But in spite of these provisions for the control of the
American colonies, in accord with the political and economic interest

[10] Roscoe Pound, "The Development of American Law and Its Deviation
from English Law," *Law Quarterly Review,* 67 (January, 1951), pp. 49–66.

of the Crown and stockholders, there were instances where innovations in law would be desirable for the colonies.

Some local conditions in America made irrelevant or impractical the legal practices of England. There were even vast differences of settlement and development within colonies which would foster divergences in the legal systems of the colonies.[11] Except for England's primary political interest in control over its colonies, the colonies were in fact relatively free to develop their own legal systems.

However, the criminal laws that developed in America did not depart substantially from English common law.[12] The interests embodied in the common law of England became the interests that were instrumental in the formulation of American criminal law. Several forces were at work, beyond the standards set by the Crown, which assured the continuance of English common law in America. One important force was in the fact that the early settlers, coming from the mother country, were deeply imbued with the ideas and traditions of the common law. Another force was an adherence to the liberal ideal of democracy. The natural law conception of man's inherent rights as a human being inspired the Declaration of Independence (1776) as it had the British Bill of Rights (1689).[13] The Lockean formula of "life, liberty and property" (later broadened to include the pursuit of happiness) served as an underlying value for American law. As another force, the English common law was exalted and perpetuated in nineteenth century America through the popularity of such codifications as Sir Edward Coke's *Institutes* and Sir William Blackstone's *Commentaries on the Laws of England*. One other force that made the interests of English common law the same as those of American law was in the attempts of American lawyers to adapt the common law to American conditions.[14] While there was considerable conflict with fellow countrymen, American lawyers

[11] Julius Goebel, Jr., "King's Law and Local Custom in Seventeenth Century New England," *Columbia Law Review,* 31 (March, 1931), pp. 416–448.

[12] See Edwin C. Surrency, "Revision of Colonial Laws," *American Journal of Legal History,* 9 (July, 1965), pp. 189–202; Elizabeth Caspar Brown, *British Statutes in American Law, 1776–1836* (Ann Arbor: University of Michigan Law School, 1964).

[13] See Carl J. Friedrich, "Rights, Liberties, Freedoms: A Reappraisal," *American Political Science Review,* 57 (December, 1963), pp. 841–854; Roscoe Pound, *The Formative Era of American Law* (Boston: Little, Brown, 1938).

[14] Perry Miller, *The Life of the Mind: From the Revolution to the Civil War* (New York: Harcourt, Brace and World, 1965), pp. 99–265.

were generally successful in asserting the legal heritage of England against provincial concerns.

All these forces combined to produce an American law which incorporated the interests of English common law. Political independence did not signify new beginnings in law. Old interests in a new setting best describes America's legal development.

British Law in India and Africa. The control of foreign colonies is in sharp contrast to the American experience. The subjects of British rule in the colonies of India and Africa were not as ready to adopt the laws of an imperial power. Native customs and traditions of India and Africa were far from amenable to the principles of English common law. Furthermore, the imposition of a single English legal system on a native colony ignored the diverse local customs within the colonies.

The importation of British law to India and Africa required a change in local customs. In India the administration of English law required, and accomplished in many instances, modifications in Hindu customary law.[15] The change was mutual, in that successful administration of English law in India also brought about changes in the English law itself.

In North India, where English law did not readily accommodate to local custom, the British legal system was used in a manipulative fashion by the local inhabitants.[16] In attempting to introduce British procedural law into the Indian courts, the British presented the Indians with a situation that involved a conflict of values between the British common law, on the one hand, and Indian customary law, on the other. The British thought that by providing an impartial judge and firm rules of court procedure cases of disputes between parties, criminal and civil, could be decided in court. But such an assumption was contrary to the values underlying the Indian caste system:

> Basic to British law is the idea of equality of the individual before the law. North Indian society operates on the reverse

[15] J. Duncan and M. Derrett, "The Administration of Hindu Law by the British," *Comparative Studies in Sociology and History,* 4 (November, 1961), pp. 10–52; Marc Galanter, "The Displacement of Traditional Law in Modern India," *Journal of Social Issues* (October, 1968), pp. 65–91.

[16] Bernard S. Cohn, "Some Notes on Law and Change in North India," *Economic Development and Cultural Change,* 8 (October, 1959), pp. 79–93.

value hypothesis: men are not born equal, and they have widely differing inherent worth. This theme or value is basic to the whole social structure and is expressed most clearly in the caste system. When Indians go into court they are supposed by definition to lose their outside statuses. It is not Thakurs and Chamars who are having a dispute, but a defendant and a complainant. The adversary system has developed to equalize the persons in court. To an Indian peasant this is an impossible situation to understand. The Chamar knows he is not equal to the Thakur. He may want to be equal, but he knows he is not. The Thakur cannot be convinced in any way that the Chamar is equal, but the court acts as if the parties in the dispute were equal.[17]

The imposition of the British legal system in North India ignored the long-established caste arrangements and community relations. Under the British system a court decision was disruptive of the network of social relationships.

The extent to which a monolithic and foreign legal system inhibits national development can be seen in the new nations of Africa. The situation is, however, paradoxical in that the English legal system provided the centralization necessary for nation-building, but at the same time hindered the development of an indigenous legal system that would best meet the needs of a new nation.

The "Africanization" of African law is a phenomenon that most African nations are now experiencing. Recently the Ghanian Parliament repealed a number of its British laws.[18] In the African colonial period the British had imposed a legal system that represented metropolitan interests. For example, the British made bigamy a criminal offense in Ghana. Ghanian customary law, however, allowed polygamy. The bigamy statute was one of the laws recently repealed.

Today the British inspired courts are in flux in the African nations. Indigenous African ideas on crime and punishment are being revived and used as sources of criminal law.[19] A distinct policy has

[17] Cohn, "Some Notes on Law and Change in North India," pp. 90–91.
[18] William Burnett Harvey, *Law and Social Change in Ghana* (Princeton: Princeton University Press, 1966), especially chap. 6; A. N. Allott, "The Changing Law in a Changing Africa," *Sociologus*, 11 (No. 2, 1961), pp. 115–131.
[19] A. St. J. Hannigan, "The Imposition of Western Law Forms Upon Primitive Societies," *Comparative Studies in Sociology and History*, 4 (November, 1961), pp. 1–9.

not yet been established regarding the extent to which native custom will be incorporated into Western-inspired law. But a law which undermines and conflicts with the values and interest of local African custom is not likely to survive intact when lawmaking is in the hands of the African nations themselves.

American Frontier Law. In the expansion of the American frontier, two legal problems naturally developed. One involved the legal status and control of the first native Americans, the Indians. The second problem, which at times was related to the first, concerned legal regulation in territories not yet with their own law.

The Crown did not recognize the sovereign right of the native Indians and acknowledged only their right of occupancy in the land.[20] In other words, without existing law, any law that was to be established in America was to be a law imposed by the Crown or by the colonial settlers according to standards set by the Crown. As the law developed, any offense against the colony by Indians outside of colonial territory was administered by tribal leaders. But for those Indians who were within the territory, cases were tried in colonial courts. The Indians who were subject to colonial law were not judged by their own customary law but according to the interests of the settlers from England.

Later a new problem arose in the formulating and administering of law in the western Indian territory. The United States federal government sent agents and legal officers into the expanding territories. One such case was the attempt of the federal government to establish law and order in the Indian Nations of Oklahoma. On May 2, 1875, Judge Isaac C. Parker arrived in Fort Smith to take over the Federal District Court of the territory. His task was to control the Indians who were against the white man and to put an end to the "outlawry" of the breed of man that has since become the western folk hero. Judge Parker fast acquired the reputation of "the hanging judge." In his twenty-one years on the bench at Fort Smith, Judge Parker heard 13,490 cases and convicted 9,454 persons, of whom 344 were tried for offenses punishable by death. Of the 344

[20] W. Stitt Robinson, "The Legal Status of the Indian in Colonial Virginia," *Virginia Magazine of History and Biography,* 61 (July, 1953), pp. 247–259.

cases, 165 were convicted and 160 of these were sentenced to the gallows. Seventy-nine persons were eventually hanged, while 2 others were killed in attempting to escape and two more died in jail awaiting execution. Judge Parker saw his mission thus:

> During the twenty years that I have engaged in administering the law here, the contest has been one between civilization and savagery, the savagery being represented by the intruding criminal class. The United States government, in its treaties from the days of Andrew Jackson, stipulated that this criminal element should be kept out of the country, but the treaties have only been made to be broken. . . . Thus this class keeps on increasing; its members marry, and the criminal population keeps ever growing larger. . . . At the present time there seems to be a criminal wave sweeping over the country, the like of which I have not yet seen before.[21]

Judge Parker, according to his sympathetic biographer, "had taken pardonable pride in eradicating lawlessness from his jurisdiction. He had taught the criminal class to fear the law and respect the rights and property of peaceful citizens, and had helped the Indian advance to a higher civilization."[22]

There was also need in the fast-growing western mining camps for some kind of order to resolve the conflicts that arose between miners and the disputes that developed over land and mining rights. There were as yet no territorial or state governments to create and administer law. In this void there developed a "local law" among the miners to regulate their own self-interests.[23] In other words, a popular sovereignty was created in the mining territory, a sovereignty which formulated and administered its own form of law. The miners' customs, or local laws, spread throughout the western territories. Eventually when states were formally established, the local laws of the miners were enacted into statute law or were incorporated into

[21] Quoted in Glenn Shirley, *Law West of Fort Smith: Frontier Justice in the Indian Territory, 1834–1896* (New York: Collier Books, 1961), p. 146.
[22] Shirley, *Law West of Fort Smith*, p. 180.
[23] For one of the few studies of law in the mining territory, see Charles Howard Shinn, *Mining Camps: A Study in American Frontier Government*, originally published 1884 (New York: Harper and Row, 1965).

the legal precedents of court decisions. The interests of the miners of the nineteenth century were formulated into laws which continue to operate in the twentieth century.

PROTECTION OF THE
POLITICAL ORDER

In a sense the formulation of all criminal law is political. Formal codes and decisions are created in order that certain behaviors may be defined as criminal by groups in control of politically organized society. But, in addition, particular kinds of criminal laws are created to protect the political order of the state. These *political criminal laws* define as criminal those behaviors that are regarded as dangers or threats to the very existence of the state.

Interest in the protection of the political order is characteristic of all states. In the creation of such laws, those in positions of power attempt to preserve both the political system and their own positions within the system.

"Every political regime has its foes or in due time creates them."[24] The struggles or perceived conflicts that may take place between power holders, their foes, and the contenders for political power assume a great variety of forms. Various kinds of criminal laws may be formulated in the attempt to control or eliminate the political foe from competition. These criminal laws, as political weapons, serve to authenticate and limit the political action of those who would appear to jeopardize the stability and survival of the existing political order.

Most politically organized societies, especially those which claim to be political democracies, maintain the paradox of two opposing ideals. On the one hand, states claim the power to govern but, on the other, grant the freedom that may result in words and actions against the state. The opposing ideals are able to exist because of the unspoken agreement that "the majority agrees to tolerate the criticism and dissent of the minority (or minorities), while the minority agrees to seek power only through persuasion and political

[24] Otto Kirchheimer, *Political Justice: The Use of Legal Procedure for Political Ends* (Princeton: Princeton University Press, 1961), p. 3.

activity, not through violence."[25] Thus, in the abstract, the majority is not to persecute the minority and the minority is not to express dissent through revolution.

The boundaries and definitions of political freedom, however, are by no means constant within any society. The latitude of dissent that may be regarded as legitimate varies from one time to another. During some periods a considerable amount and degree of dissent may be tolerated, while in other periods dissent may be suppressed by means of the criminal law.

Political expression is especially restricted during periods of tension and conflict. When a political emergency is perceived, the government is likely to take actions of various sorts to protect the political order. The events that led to the American Revolution illustrate the ways in which criminal law may be used to maintain the desired political order. England as the imperial nation naturally tried to maintain its political control over the colonies. At the same time the British government was faced with other administrative problems, including administration of the territorial acquisitions elsewhere in North America and a mounting debt at home. In order to organize a more efficient administration, Britain made several demands of the colonies, such as the trade and revenue acts passed in Parliament, which resulted in a tightening of control over the colonies. Occurring simultaneously in the colonies, however, was the development of a revolutionary ideology and a new spirit of nationalism. As a result, Britain's attempt to demand more of the colonies and the Americans' growing desire for freedom of political action produced a sharp clash of interests.[26] The ultimate outcome, of course, after a series of insurrections and a war, was independence for the colonies in 1776.

One of the devices used by the British government in the colonies to establish and preserve their own political order was substantive criminal law. The British used at various times the law of treason against the colonists. The law had its origins in a statute enacted in

[25] Paul B. Horton and Gerald R. Leslie, *The Sociology of Social Problems,* 3rd ed. (New York: Appleton-Century-Crofts, 1965), pp. 632–633.
[26] This is the thesis found in Lawrence Henry Gipson, *The Coming of the Revolution, 1763–1775* (New York: Harper and Row, 1954). Also see George Adrian Washburne, *Imperial Control of the Administration of Justice in the Thirteen Colonies, 1684–1776* (New York: Columbia University Press, 1923).

the time of Edward III, making it a crime to plot or imagine the death of the king, to adhere to the king's enemies, to give them aid and comfort, or to levy war against the king. The law of seditious libel was also used to control public criticism of British efforts.

There is some debate on the question of the extent to which the British resorted to their criminal law of seditious libel to control dissent in the colonies.[27] But there is no question as to the ironical fact that each of the colonies formulated similar laws to protect its own political interests. These political criminal laws of the colonies were almost identical to the English laws that were being imposed on them.

The English common law on political crime was eventually adopted by the states and the federal government. What had seemed oppressive in the hands of the British became the law for Americans to impose on those who would appear to endanger their government. The federal government in 1798 enacted the Sedition Act, providing for the punishment of anyone who uttered or published statements against the government of the United States.[28] The law, as well as curtailing loyalty to the British, became an instrument of the Federalists in their attempt to suppress the activities (considered as pro-French) of the opposition Republican Party.[29]

The American law of treason was shaped by fears the Americans had of British loyalists during and immediately following the Revolution. Drawing upon English common law once again, the Americans formulated and utilized treason laws against those who aided the British or fled to the enemy.[30] After the Declaration of Inde-

[27] See Harold L. Nelson, "Seditious Libel in Colonial America," *American Journal of Legal History,* 3 (April, 1959), pp. 160–172; and Frederick S. Siebert, *Freedom of the Press in England, 1476–1776* (Urbana: University of Illinois Press, 1952).

[28] Leonard W. Levy, *Freedom of Speech and Press in Early American History: Legacy of Suppression* (New York: Harper and Row, 1963); James Morton Smith, "The Sedition Law, Free Speech, and the American Political Process," *William and Mary Quarterly,* 9 (October, 1952), pp. 497–511.

[29] Herbert L. Packer, "Offenses Against the State," *Annals of the American Academy of Political and Social Science,* 339 (January, 1962), pp. 77–89.

[30] See Bradley Chapin, *The American Law of Treason: Revolutionary and National Origins* (Seattle: University of Washington Press, 1964); J. Willard Hurst, "Treason in the United States," *Harvard Law Review,* 58 (December, 1944), pp. 226–272; 58 (February, 1945), pp. 395–444; and 58 (July, 1945), pp. 806–857.

pendence, the state legislatures enacted a series of anti-loyalist laws. "Test acts" compelled a declaration of loyalty from those who appeared to be indifferent or enemies of the Revolution. In addition to these acts, there were laws (1) disfranchising the loyalists or removing them from office, (2) suppressing, quarantining, and exiling loyalists, (3) providing for the crime of adhering to Great Britain, and (4) amercing, taxing, or confiscating the property and estates of loyalists.[31] In most states loyalists were legally defined as traitors.

All of the states today have criminal laws to protect subversion of the political order. Subversion, however, is not always clearly defined in the state laws, although most agree on which kinds of behavior are subversive:

> There can no doubt be general agreement that, at the very least, subversive activities include (1) the use of violent or otherwise unconstitutional means to change this country's political or economic institutions; (2) the commission of espionage, sabotage, and other crimes of stealth in behalf of foreign enemies or domestic cliques; (3) the bearing of arms against the United States, other affirmative behavior in aid of hostile forces; and (4) the entry into a conspiracy to perform these acts or the actual though unsuccessful attempt to do them. Conduct of these types is unquestionably within the reach of criminal laws in every American state.[32]

In addition to the state laws numerous federal statutes have been created to control subversive activity. The Espionage Act of 1917 made it a crime to "willfully make or convey false reports or false statements with intent to interfere with the operations or success of the military or naval forces of the United States." A 1918 amendment to the Espionage Act broadened the proscriptions in terms reminiscent of the Sedition Act of 1798. The Voorhis Act of 1940 restricted the registration of persons and organizations that act as agents of foreign powers. The Smith Act of 1940 forbade the advocacy of the overthrow of the government. The Internal Security Act of 1950 (McCarran Act) required the registration of com-

[31] Claude H. Van Tyne, *The Loyalists in the American Revolution* (New York: Macmillan, 1962), especially appendix C.

[32] Walter Gellhorn, "A General View," in Walter Gellhorn (ed.), *The States and Subversion* (Ithaca: Cornell University Press, 1952), p. 359.

munist and communist-front organizations as well as strengthened other legislation on subversion. The Immigration and Nationality Act of 1952 (McCarran-Walter Act) provided for the deportation of resident aliens because of disloyal beliefs and associates. The Communist Control Act of 1954 required the registration of Communist party members with the Attorney General. In addition to such legislation, loyalty and security programs have been initiated and black-list procedures have been established.

Political expression is an especially delicate matter in the United States. It appears that Americans, as compared to other peoples in representative governments, are particularly intolerant of social and political differences.[33] This intolerance is expressed in the denial of various civil rights to certain social and political minority groups, religious groups, racial and ethnic groups, and political dissenters of various persuasion. Numerous criminal laws have been formulated by groups in power to deal with these conditions and activities. In addition to the various acts that have been defined as subversive, recent attempts to express dissatisfaction with nuclear testing, civil defense, military build-ups, and racial discrimination have been subject to criminal action. A host of previously existing laws have been used in the suppression of dissent and protest. Demonstrators for civil rights and other causes have been arrested on such charges as disorderly conduct, breach of peace, parading without a permit, trespassing, loitering, and violation of fire ordinances. All these crimes have the common element that the offenders are pursuing values different from those of the groups that are formulating and administering criminal law.

RELIGIOUS FOUNDATIONS OF CRIMINAL LAW

Along the shores and tidewater in the vicinity of what is today Boston Harbor, a Puritan community was established in 1630. Although the Massachusetts Bay Colony was chartered as a commercial enterprise, the objectives of its settlers were clearly re-

[33] Herbert H. Hyman, "England and America: Climates of Tolerance and Intolerance," in Daniel Bell (ed.), *The Radical Right* (Garden City, N.Y.: Doubleday, 1963), chap. 12.

ligious and social. From the outset, the chief aim of the undertaking was, in Governor John Winthrop's words, the building of "a City upon a Hill," the founding of a society that would be an example of godliness to the world. Religious interests were to play a predominant role in the creation of a social and legal order in early Massachusetts.

The new colony was an extension of many of the traditions of the England from which the settlers had emigrated. But it was to be, in addition, a revision of conditions that were regarded as unjust or wrong. Puritanism itself as a religious doctrine and as a way of life had been shaped by English political ideas. Among these ideas were the beliefs that government exists to regulate imperfect man, that political leaders must be obeyed, and that the welfare of the whole is more important than that of the individual. Puritanism drew as well from the medieval imagery of piety, doom, and sin.[34] Out of these older ideas the Puritans developed a conception of the covenant. Under this conception government was viewed as originating in a compact among the people. But more than this, the power of the state was viewed as legitimate because it was a government conforming to what God had decreed. "Thus, in subjecting themselves to a state that was divinely approved, the people also subjected themselves to obedience to God."[35]

In adhering to the conception of the covenant, the word of God served as a basis for the establishment of government and society in Massachusetts Bay. The Puritans viewed themselves as being an elite chosen by God to represent Him on earth. But most important for government, they viewed the positions to which the leaders were elected in the colony as being ordained by God. Once elected, the governor and the magistrates were granted power through divine authority. As "Gods upon earth," the leaders must be obeyed in order that the covenant be kept. This idea was forcefully expressed to the Puritans when Winthrop declared that "the determination of law belongs properly to God: He is the only lawgiver, but He hath given power and gifts to man to interpret his

---

[34] See Perry Miller, *The New England Mind: The Seventeenth Century* (New York: Macmillan, 1939).

[35] George Lee Haskins, *Law and Authority in Early Massachusetts* (New York: Macmillan, 1960), p. 44.

laws; and this belongs principally to the highest authority in a commonwealth, and subordinately to other magistrates and judges according to their several places."[36] The logical conclusion of the covenant was rule by a few for the interests they deemed appropriate: "The government of Massachusetts was thus a dictatorship of a small minority who were unhesitantly prepared to coerce the unwilling to serve the purposes of society as they conceived it."[37]

The early history of Massachusetts Bay Colony was marked by a continuing problem about the place of law in a religious community.[38] The problem was resolved by the early settlers in the construction of a legal structure based upon Biblical authority. The Scriptures thus served as a most appropriate source for establishing a government according to God's word. In 1635 the General Court of the colony ordered work to begin on a legal code. By 1641 a brief bill of rights, known since as the Body of Liberties, was passed. Finally, in 1648, a comprehensive code of law, known as "Laws and Liberties," was adopted. The code — the first of its kind in the English-speaking world — consisted of a compilation of constitutional guarantees, provisions for the conduct of government, trade, military affairs, and the relations between church and state, as well as the substantive law of crime, tort, property, and domestic relations. At the beginning of the Code was the Epistle which dramatically related the laws of the colony to the religious principles of the Old Testament Scriptures:

> So soon as God had set up Political Government among his people Israel he gave them a body of laws for judgment both in civil and criminal causes. These were brief and fundamental principles, yet withall so full and comprehensive as out of them clear deductions were to be drawn to all particular cases in future times.[39]

The Code was a unique effort to order man's life and conduct in accordance with the ideals of Puritanism.

36 Quoted in Richard B. Morris, *Studies in the History of American Law*, 2nd ed. (New York: Joseph M. Mitchell, 1959), p. 35.

37 Haskins, *Law and Authority in Early Massachusetts*, pp. 44–45.

38 See Kai T. Erikson, *Wayward Puritans: A Study in the Sociology of Deviance* (New York: John Wiley, 1966), pp. 54–64. Also see Edwin Powers, *Crime and Punishment in Early Massachusetts* (Boston: Beacon Press, 1966).

39 Quoted in Haskins, *Law and Authority in Early Massachusetts*, p. 145.

The Biblical influence in the formulation of the law of the colony is most clearly observed in the provisions of the criminal (or capital) laws of the Code. The provisions, all punishable by death, included the crimes of idolatry, witchcraft, blasphemy, bestiality, sodomy, adultery, rape, man stealing, treason, false witness with intent to take life, cursing or smiting a parent, stubbornness or rebelliousness on the part of a son against his parents, and homicide committed with malice prepense, by guile or poisoning, or in anger or passion. Most of the provisions, as well as other enactments, were annotated by some chapter and verse from the Old Testament, and several incorporated Biblical phraseology. A comparison of a provision from the law to its counterpart in the Old Testament is illustrated in the provision regarding rebellion of the son:[40]

> *Code of 1648:* If a man have a stubborn or REBELLIOUS SON, of sufficient years and understanding (*viz*) sixteen years of age, which will not obey the voice of his Father, or the voice of his Mother, and that when they have chastened him will not harken unto them: then shall his Father and Mother being his natural parents, lay hold on him, and bring him to the Magistrates assembled in Court and testifie unto them, that their Son is stubborn and rebellious and will not obey their voice and chastisement, but lives in sundry notorious crimes, such a son shall be put to death.

> *Deuteronomy 21:18–21:* If a man have a stubborn and rebellious son, which will not obey the voice of his father, or the voice of his mother, and that, when they have chastened him, will not harken unto them: Then shall his father and his mother lay hold on him, and bring him out unto the elders of his city, and unto the gate of his place; And they shall say unto the elders of his city, This our son is stubborn and rebellious, he will not obey our voice; he is a glutton, and a drunkard. And all the men of his city shall stone him with stones, that he die. . . .

Other capital laws containing words, clauses, or phrases taken directly from the Old Testament have been noted:

> Thus, the witchcraft provision defined a witch as one that

---

[40] Quoted in Haskins, *Law and Authority in Early Massachusetts*, p. 146.

"hath or consulteth with a familiar spirit" in terms of Leviticus 20:27 and Deuteronomy 18:11, which speak respectively of one "that hath a familiar spirit" and of "a consulter with familiar spirits." Again, it is prescribed in Leviticus 20:15 and 16 that "if a man lie with a beast, he shall surely be put to death: and ye shall slay the beast," and a similar punishment was provided "if a woman approach unto any beast, and lie down thereto;" by comparison, the bestiality law of Massachusetts states that "If any man or woman shall LYE WITH ANY BEAST, or bruit creature, by carnall copulation; they shall surely be put to death: and the beast shall be slain, and buried, and not eaten." In the same chapter of Leviticus, 20:13, it is stated that "If a man also lie with mankind, as he lieth with a woman, both of them have committed an abomination;" the colony law against sodomy prescribes that "if any man LYETH WITH MAN-KINDE as he lieth with a woman, both of them have committed abomination. . . ." In Exodus 21:16 it is declared that "he that stealeth a man, and selleth him, or if he be found in his hand, he shall surely be put to death;" in Massachusetts law, "If any man STEALETH A MAN, or Man-kinde, he shall surely be put to death." Finally, the colonial provision that "if any child, or children . . . shall CURSE, or SMITE their natural FATHER, or MOTHER: he or they shall be put to death," is paralleled by Exodus 21:15 and 17, to the effect that "he that smitteth his father, or his mother . . . And he that curseth his father, or his mother, shall surely be put to death."[41]

There can be no doubt that the religious principles of the Old Testament provided one of the cornerstones for the criminal law of the Puritans. The authority of the Bible served as a justification for the provisions of the law. The law was God's word enacted on earth.

The purpose of law for the Puritans was the accomplishment of God's will in a society bound together by a religious and political covenant. Authority of the state was thus religiously condoned. Carried to its conclusion, this meant that the welfare of the whole, rather than that of the individual, was the chief concern of the state. Law and government, therefore, have the power to coerce individuals according to the interests of the holders of power. With

---

[41] Haskins, *Law and Authority in Early Massachusetts*, pp. 146–147.

respect to this character of Puritan law, and in relation to our law of today: "The end of law as viewed by the colonists was less alien to our own conceptions than a first impression might suggest. In politically organized society, law operates as a restraint on individual action for the benefit of some other individual or of the group as a whole."[42]

SUNDAY LAW

Since the time that Sunday became somehow different from other days of the week, interests have been effective in guarding it through criminal law. Until fairly recent times religious interests determined the legal meaning of the Sabbath. Today, however, Sunday is receiving the protection of the law because of the influence of social and economic interests.

Sunday law, or "blue law," had its origin in the command from Mount Sinai: "Ye shall keep the Sabbath therefore; for it is holy unto you: every one that defileth it shall surely be put to death" (Exodus 31:14). The command gained legal character in A.D. 321 when Constantine, after his conversion to Christianity, issued an edict requiring all work to cease on the day that was settled by law to be the Sabbath.[43] Numerous statutes in reference to the regulation of activities on Sunday were later enacted in England. In 1237 Henry III forbade attendance at markets on Sunday; the Sunday showing of wools at the staple was banned by Edward III in 1354; in 1409 Henry IV prohibited the playing of certain games on Sunday; Henry VI proscribed Sunday fairs in churchyards in 1444 and four years later he made unlawful all fairs and markets and all showings of goods or merchandise; Sunday bodily labor was disallowed by Edward VI in the mid-sixteenth century; and various Sunday sports and amusements were restricted in 1625 by Charles I. The early English Sunday laws were thus aimed at frequenting markets, participating in commercial activity, laboring, and engaging in amusements on Sunday.

[42] Haskins, *Law and Authority in Early Massachusetts*, p. 225.
[43] For a history of Sunday law, see Abram H. Lewis, *A Critical History of Sunday Legislation from 321 to 1888* A.D. (New York: D. Appleton, 1888); and George E. Harris, *A Treatise on Sunday Laws* (Rochester, N.Y.: The Lawyers' Cooperative Publishing Co., 1892).

The American colonies wasted little time in enacting Sunday laws. The colonial Sunday laws, however, were similar to the later English statute of Charles II (29 Charles II, c. 7, 1677). The law stated:

> For the better observation and keeping holy the Lord's day, commonly called Sunday; be it enacted . . . that all the laws enacted and in force concerning the observation of the day, and repairing to church thereon, be carefully put in execution; and that all and every person and persons whatsoever shall upon every Lord's day apply themselves to the observation of the same, by exercising themselves thereon in the duties of piety and true religion, publicly and privately; and that no tradesman, artificer, and workman, laborer, or other person whatsoever, shall do or exercise any worldly labor or business or work of their ordinary callings upon the Lord's day, or any part thereof (works of necessity and charity only accepted) . . . and that no person or persons whatsover shall publicly cry, show forth, or expose for sale any wares, merchandise, fruit herbs, goods, or chattels, whatsoever, upon the Lord's day, or any part thereof. . . .

The law of Charles II thus added to the earlier statutes the concept of compulsory worship and church attendance on Sunday. The concept was evident in the 1610 statute of the colony of Virginia, which made church attendance compulsory, for both the morning and afternoon services.[44] Such laws were for the benefit of the respective churches of the colonies, just as they had been for the protection of the established church in England.

Most states today have Sunday laws among their statutes. Their substance no longer relates to church attendance, but to other diversions that are likely to occur on Sunday, such as labor, amusement, and sales. The change in the substance of Sunday law is indicated in the statutes of the state of New York. The first Sabbath law of New York, included in conditions of the Burgomaster of Amsterdam of 1656, required the Scriptures to be read in public by a hired schoolmaster. Shortly after, in 1664, the "Duke of

---

[44] Sunday Laws in America are discussed in Alvin W. Johnson, "Sunday Legislation," *Kentucky Law Journal,* 23 (November, 1934), pp. 131–166; and Warren L. Johns, *Dateline Sunday: U.S.A.: The Story of Three Centuries of Sunday-Law Battles in America* (New York: Taplinger, 1967).

York laws" were issued to regulate worship on Sunday. The fore-
runner of the present Sunday law, however, was an act of 1695
which forbade labor on Sunday. The act continued in effect until
1788, when it was adopted as part of the laws under the State
Constitution. Certain revisions were made in the years 1813, 1830,
and 1909, but the body of the act remained. Today the statute
prohibits on Sunday certain acts "which are serious interruptions
of the repose and religious liberty of the community." Thus, in
New York, as in other states, there has been a shift from the law of
church attendance to a law of the restriction of work on Sunday.
Sunday law has become "closing" law.

The enforcement of Sunday law, needless to say, is not usually
taken seriously. The laws are only sporadically enforced, and then
only with considerable discretion within local settings. However
dated and obsolete these laws may seem, there has been in recent
times a revival in the formulation and administration of Sunday
law. The current situation has been succinctly described and analyzed in the following way:

> The Sunday blue laws are unfair and seem to serve no useful
> function in our society today. However, due to their antiquity,
> they are well established and widespread, although seldom
> enforced. In addition to their ages, their widespread incorpora-
> tion and continuation are due to a large degree to various pres-
> sure groups. Their incorporation probably had its basis in the
> religious pressure elements and their continuance, in the pres-
> sure groups representing the retail sellers' associations.[45]

New pressure groups with other than religious interests have been
effective in renewing Sunday laws. Interests in the formulation and
administration of Sunday laws have become secularized, economic
rather than religious, accompanied by such rationales as relaxation,
leisure, and recreation.

The action of pressure groups on Sunday legislation can be seen
in recent amendments to existing statutes. The wording of the
statutes has been altered to include the private interests of specific
groups.[46] In 1957 the Massachusetts Sunday law was amended to

---

[45] Eugene P. Chell, "Sunday Blue Laws: An Analysis of Their Position in Our
Society," *Rutgers Law Review,* 12 (Spring, 1958), p. 520.
[46] Chell, "Sunday Blue Laws," pp. 511–512.

allow frozen custard stands to operate on Sunday. The frozen custard lobby was able to have the ice cream sales clause expanded to permit on Sunday the sale of "frozen dessert mixes." Likewise, local pressure groups in Massachusetts were active in changing the Sunday statute to permit the selling of fishing bait on Sunday. Pressure groups in New York were also able to have the Sunday law expanded, allowing roadside stands to sell farm products.

In a similar fashion, through the efforts of the Automobile Dealers Association, several states have amended their Sunday laws in respect to the sale of automobiles on Sunday. The action was inspired by the increasing combination of the traditional Sunday pleasure drive with Sunday shopping on the superhighway. Sunday drivers were finding it convenient to purchase autos on Sunday from the automobile dealers located on the highways. This meant that the auto dealers within the city limits, out of range of the highways, could not compete with the highway auto dealers. Into this crisis stepped the Automobile Dealers Association, dominated by downtown dealers, to successfully lobby for the prohibition of the sale of autos on Sunday. A similar phenomenon has occurred in respect to the restriction of the sale of other kinds of merchandise in the large discount stores also located on the superhighways. Downtown businesses have been successful in local areas in having statutes amended or enforced in order to curb the competition of businesses advantageously located on the highway in easy access of the affluent Sunday driver.

It was on the basis of such a situation that the United States Supreme Court in 1960 heard an appeal from the Maryland Court of Appeals. The Maryland State Court had convicted and fined employees of a large department store on a highway in Anne Arundel County for selling on Sunday a looseleaf binder, a can of floor wax, a stapler, staples, and a toy. The Maryland State Court had ruled that the conduct of the employees was in violation of a Maryland statute which forbade the sale on Sunday of all merchandise, except the retail sale of tobacco products, confectioneries, milk, bread, fruit, gasoline, oils, greases, drugs, medicines, newspapers, and periodicals. After hearing the case the Supreme Court upheld (on May 29, 1961), in *McGowan v. Maryland,* the conviction of the Maryland State Court.

The principal argument upon which the Supreme Court based

its decision in *McGowan v. Maryland* was that while Sunday law originated for religious purposes today the law is maintained for secular purposes: "In the light of the evolution of our Sunday Closing Laws through the centuries, and of their more or less recent emphasis upon secular considerations, it is concluded that, as presently written and administered, most of them, at least, are of a secular rather than of a religious character, and that presently they bear no relationship to establishment of religion, as those words are used in the constitution of the United States."[47] Furthermore, the opinion continues, secular interests may be served on Sunday: "The present purpose and effect of most of our Sunday Closing Laws is to provide a uniform day of rest for all citizens; and the fact that this day is Sunday, a day of particular significance for the dominant Christian sects, does not bar the State from achieving its secular goals." In addition, it was argued that "the present purpose and effect of the statute here involved is not aid to religion but to set aside a day of rest and recreation." Finally, in regard to the issue of religious liberty, Chief Justice Warren, in writing the majority opinion, observed that Sunday law does not violate constitutional rights: "People of all religions and people with no religion regard Sunday as a time for family activity, for visiting friends and relatives, for late sleeping, for passive and active entertainments, for dining out, and the like."[48]

The Supreme Court in its decision has therefore recognized that "Sunday closing legislation no longer exclusively represents religious interests."[49] That Sunday law now represents economic interests is recognized in the Court's decision. The Court remarked that the recent Sunday laws of such states as New Jersey were reformulated because of the pressure of labor groups and trade associations. It was noted by the Court as well that modern Sunday legislation in England was promoted by such interest groups as the National Federation of Grocers, the National Chamber of Trade, the Drapers' Chamber of Trade, and the National Union of Shop Assistants.

The conclusion in reference to the theory of interests, therefore,

[47] *McGowan v. Maryland*, in 366 United States Reports (October term, 1960), p. 421.
[48] *McGowan v. Maryland*, pp. 451–452.
[49] *McGowan v. Maryland*, p. 435.

is that a criminal law may be intended for a particular interest at one time and then amended and implemented at another time for some other interest. Sunday law, while being in existence for hundreds of years, for religious reasons, was never officially negated, nor ever much enforced. But with changes in social conditions and with a shift in social interests, Sunday law has been revived and lives once again.

THE LAW OF THEFT

The creation of a particular criminal law must have its conception in some concrete setting of time and place. The development of the law of theft demonstrates that necessity. For prior to the fifteenth century there was no legal conception of theft as we know it today. It was during the fifteenth century in England that the modern law of theft was officially formulated into criminal law. The law of theft was shaped by changing social conditions, and especially by pressing social interests of the time. The definition of theft as a crime was a solution to a legal problem that arose within a particular social framework.

The decision that resulted in the legal concept of theft occurred in England in 1473, in what is known as the Carrier's Case. The case has been documented and interpreted by Jerome Hall in his book *Theft, Law and Society*.[50] The facts of the case are these: The defendant was hired to carry bales to Southampton. Instead of fulfilling his obligation, he carried the goods to another place, broke open the bales, and took the contents. The man was apprehended and charged with felony.

The most illustrious judges of the time discussed the case at length. While the defendant was finally held guilty by a majority of the judges, a legal problem of considerable portent developed during the proceedings. Before the case arose, the common law recognized no criminality in a person who came legally into possession and converted it to his own use. The reasoning of the common law had been that the owner of transported goods was responsible for protecting himself by employing trustworthy persons. There was, in the Carrier's Case, a legal problem of *stare decisis* in which the judges regarded themselves as bound by the common law.

[50] Jerome Hall, *Theft, Law and Society,* 2nd ed. (Indianapolis: Bobbs-Merrill, 1952).

Until the Carrier's Case it had been agreed that while trespass (the taking of property from one who is in possession of it) was an essential element of larceny, a person in possession of property could not commit a trespass upon that property. Therefore, since a bailee (an employee who is trusted with property) had possession, larceny could not technically be committed by such an employee. The judges, however, departed from precedent by introducing a new concept which could neither be found among the existing legal rules nor logically derived from them. For the judges held that "breaking bulk" terminated the bailment, that such property at once reverted to the possession of the bailor, and that the removal of it from the bales supplied the trespass. Hall thus observes: "By this refinement the door was opened to admit into the law of larceny a whole series of acts which had up to that time been purely civil wrongs."[51] Law was being made by judges in the Carrier's Case by the departure from and the renunciation of certain precedents of the common law.

An important question arises as to the forces that were active in the creation of a new legal concept. In his analysis of the case, Hall outlines the changes that were occurring in fifteenth century England. These changes coupled with the social conditions and the institutions of the period made convenient a change in the law of theft. To begin with, in the political realm, the courts were subservient to the wishes of Edward IV. This meant that the special interests of the Crown were protected by the courts. Among the interests of the king that received the favor of the courts were the royal commercial activities, including trade with merchants on the Continent. Edward himself was a merchant who carried on many private ventures.

The economic conditions of the period were especially important for the decision reached in the Carrier's Case. During this phase of the Renaissance a commercial revolution was taking place in England and Europe. The old feudal structure resting on an agricultural economy was giving way to a new order based on industry and trade. These economic conditions bear upon an interpretation of the Carrier's Case: "(1) the complainant was an alien merchant; (2) he had a covenant with the kings which provided safe passage

[51] *Ibid.,* p. 10.

for him and his goods; (3) the property taken is described as being within bales, and weighing twenty pounds; (4) the defendant was a carrier; (5) and he was to deliver the merchandise at South-ampton."[52]

Hall thus argues that the complainant was a foreign merchant (probably Italian) whose trade was desired by the Crown. Such foreign merchants were subject to special risks: There was naturally hostility by local merchants toward foreign trade. Moreover, foreign merchants were handicapped in the transport of goods because of the uncertainty of finding trustworthy carriers who would not abscond with the goods. The king attempted to relieve the situation somewhat, issuing convenants of safe conduct through the country.

The merchandise taken by the bailee of the Carrier's Case was probably wool or cloth, or both. Such goods were usually transported in bales. Also, Southampton was a principal port for shipping these goods, serving as a port for trade with Latin countries in particular. All these deductions mean that "the interests of the most important industry in England were involved in the case."[53]

The relation of the conditions of fifteenth-century England to the decision of the Carrier's Case has been concisely summarized:

> We are now in a position to visualize the case and the problem presented to the judges as a result of the legal, political and economic conditions described above. On the one hand, the criminal law at the time is clear. On the other hand, the whole complex aggregate of political and economic conditions described above thrusts itself upon the court. The more powerful forces of the time were interrelated very intimately and at many points: the New Monarchy and the *nouveau riche* — the mercantile class; the business interests of both and the consequent need for a secure carrying trade; the wool and textile industry, the most valuable, by far, in all the realm; wool and cloth, the most important exports; these exports and the foreign trade, this trade and Southampton, chief trading city with the Latin countries for centuries; the numerous and very influential Italian merchants who bought English wool and cloth inland and shipped them from Southampton. The great forces of an

[52] *Ibid.*, p. 19.
[53] *Ibid.*, p. 31.

emerging modern world, represented in the above phenomena, necessitated the elimination of a formula which had outgrown its usefulness. A new set of major institutions required a new rule. The law, lagging behind the needs of the times, was brought into more harmonious relationship with the other institutions by the decision rendered in the Carrier's Case.[54]

The Carrier's Case of 1473 vividly demonstrates the way in which changing social conditions and emerging social interests may bring about the formulation of a criminal law. The decision of the Carrier's Case provided the framework for the further development of the law of theft. Eventually, with the growth in banking and the use of paper currency, the law was expanded to include the act of embezzlement by clerks, officers, and the like. A Whig Parliament in the eighteenth century passed an embezzlement statute in order to protect mercantile interests. The legal protection of property has always been to the interest of the propertied segments of society.

ANTITRUST LAWS

Toward the end of the nineteenth century in the United States an antimonopoly movement emerged. This movement was accompanied by a body of doctrine which regarded the problem of monopoly as soluble only through the powers of government. Subsequent action of the federal government resulted in an innovation in criminal law, that is, the concept that the state had the responsibility of protecting the national economic order from private interests within that order. This departure from the traditional scope and purpose of the criminal law, a departure which meant that the criminal law not only protected private property but also assisted in the maintenance of a particular kind of economy, marked the creation of a new type of criminal law, administrative criminal law.

A tradition for antitrust legislation existed in the common law of England and America.[55] The common law precedents had established that certain commercial activities were to be restricted by law. Yet the common law doctrine as applied by the individual states was

[54] *Ibid.*, p. 33.

[55] See Hans B. Thorelli, *The Federal Antitrust Policy: Origination of an American Tradition* (Baltimore: Johns Hopkins Press, 1955), pp. 9–53.

not effective in controlling the monopolies that were developing in the United States. Broad interpretation by state courts of the interstate commerce clause of the Constitution and the first article of the Fourteenth Amendment allowed many corporations to expand greatly beyond state borders and to receive the protection of the federal government. Since there was no federal common law on the regulation of monopolies, the need for federal antitrust legislation was clear.

Opposition to trusts and monopolies was aroused in several segments of American society. Diverse groups, not always with compatible ideologies, agitated for antimonopoly legislation.[56] Some groups were gravely concerned with the ruthless exploitation of national resources by corporations that used them for their own profit-making ventures. Labor was hostile to powerful corporations, finding that it was at a distinct disadvantage in bargaining with the large corporations. Small businessmen feared possible surrender or ruin because of the concentration of wealth and facilities in gigantic corporations. Declining farm prices were attributed to the growth of large corporations. The Populist Party was active in supporting agrarian antagonism toward big business. Typical of the antimonopoly spirit of the period was the feeling expressed by a Granger, who related monopoly to the question of progress:

> Progress which the possessors of the good things of earth call innovation, progress the cardinal principle of this democracy of the people, will go on as all history shows. It must be through continual strife, for progress is but a contest still going on in spite of the death chants, the impenetrable armor, and the resisting spirit of self; a contest which has been going on through earth's long day, and will still go on until evening — until the mighty purposes of creation are accomplished, and the many are entitled to preeminence over the few in the view of the earth as they are now entitled in the eye of heaven. This is what the great democracy of the people demands. That is what the antimonopoly movement means.[57]

In the 1880's monopolies were attacked in the name of the theory

[56] Thorelli, *The Federal Antitrust Policy,* pp. 54–163.
[57] Quoted in Arthur P. Dudden, "Men Against Monopoly: The Prelude to Trust-Busting" *Journal of the History of Ideas,* 18 (October, 1957), p. 593.

and practice of laissez-faire economics. A challenge was presented to the long-ingrained classical economics. Influential also were indi-vidual radicals, such as Wendell Phillips and Peter Cooper, and the writings of Henry George, Edward Bellamy, and Henry Demarest Lloyd reached wide audiences. President Cleveland brought the is-sue to the front in a tariff message of 1887 and stressed it with even greater urgency the following year: "As we view the achieve-ments of aggregated capital we discover the existence of trusts, combinations and monopolies, while the citizen is struggling far in the rear or is trampled to death beneath an iron heel. Corporations which should be carefully restrained creatures of the law and ser-vants of the people, are fast becoming the people's masters."[58] That year the platforms of both major political parties pledged to oppose trusts and monopolies.

The result of the widespread opposition to monopolies from vari-ous sides was the enactment of the Sherman Act of 1890. The law, drafted primarily by Senator John Sherman of Ohio, declared that "(1) Every contract, combination in the form of trust or otherwise, or conspiracy, in restraint of trade or commerce among the several States, or with foreign nations is hereby declared to be illegal . . . (2) Every person who shall monopolize, or attempt to monop-olize . . . any part of the trade or commerce among the several States, or with foreign nations, shall be deemed guilty of a misde-meanor. . . ." Thus, to combine in restraint of trade and to monop-olize became public offenses. The federal government was empow-ered to proceed against violations of the law by criminal action.

In broad perspective, the interest to be protected in the law was the basic economic order of the nation. The aim of the supporters of antitrust legislation was not, for the most part, to alter the exist-ing economic order, but to protect the free enterprise system. "The interest to be protected was the maintenance of a competitive economy based on private enterprise. The State did not mean to become owner or entrepreneur, but it felt compelled to use its legis-lative, administrative, and judicial machinery for the protection of the economic well-being of the community as a whole — as conceived

[58] Quoted in Samuel Eliot Morison and Henry Steele Commager, *The Growth of the American Republic,* vol. 2 (New York: Oxford University Press, 1950), p. 143.

by a liberal economic philosophy — and to defend it against power-ful industrial and commercial interests."[59]

Further legislation and measures for the stricter enforcement of antitrust laws followed. Particular attention was given to the reg-ulation of corporations during the administration of Theodore Roosevelt. Roosevelt's intentions were clear, to work within the framework of the capitalistic system: "In dealing with the big corporations we call trusts, we must resolutely purpose to proceed by evolution and not by revolution. . . . Our aim is not to do away with corporations; on the contrary these big aggregations are an inevitable development of modern industrialism. . . . We can do nothing of good in the way of regulating and supervising these cor-porations until we fix clearly in our minds that we are not attack-ing the corporations, but endeavoring to do away with any evil in them. We are not hostile to them; we are merely determined that they shall be so handled as to subserve the public good."[60]

The legislation and actions of the New Deal added considerably to governmental planning and regulation of the economy. Yet in spite of the antitrust legislation and enforcement since the Sherman Act of 1890, it must be cautioned that the purpose was to protect the capitalistic system from abuse, rather than to create a new type of economic order. Franklin D. Roosevelt was not the socialist the public thought and feared, but was indeed a conservative. The case has been nicely presented:

> It would be a mistake to assume that this socialization was developed entirely at the expense of private enterprise. Indeed it is certain that the New Deal did more to strengthen and to save the capitalist economy than it did to weaken or destroy it. That economy had broken down in many nations abroad, and its collapse contributed to the rise of totalitarian govern-ments which completely subordinated business to the state. The system was on the verge of collapse in the United States during the Hoover administration, and it is at least conceivable that had that collapse been permitted to occur, it might have been followed by the establishment of an economy very different from that to which Americans were accustomed. Historically

[59] Wolfgang Friedmann, *Law in a Changing Society* (Harmondsworth, Eng.: Penguin Books, 1964), p. 161.

[60] Quoted in Morison and Commager, *The Growth of the American Republic*, vol. 2, p. 391.

Franklin Roosevelt's administration did for twentieth-century American capitalism what Theodore Roosevelt's and Wilson's had done for nineteenth-century business enterprise: it saved the system by ridding it of its grosser abuses and forcing it to accommodate itself to larger public interests. History may eventually record Franklin D. Roosevelt as the greatest American conservative since Hamilton.[61]

The attack upon corporations, then, beginning in the latter part of the nineteenth century and continuing to the present, has not been against business but has been inspired and led by the business interest itself. Antitrust legislation was formulated and administered by and for the interests of capitalist economics.

PURE FOOD AND DRUG LAWS

The increasing responsibility of the modern state for protecting the public's welfare is reflected in recent criminal law. Only in fairly recent times has criminal law come to embody provisions for the regulation of that which is regarded by the state as important for the health and safety of the community. Criminal laws of today thus regulate such spheres of social life as employment, housing, sanitation, traffic, and the conduct of occupations and professions. Among the concerns in the protection of the public order is that of the purity and safeness of foods and drugs. The effort to control foods and drugs through criminal law is a demonstration of how the public interest may eventually be served in spite of the private interests of individual members of society.

Through the first half of the nineteenth century the United States was chiefly an agricultural nation and the problem of purity of food and safeness of drugs rested largely with the family. During this period the principle of *caveat emptor*, or "let the buyer beware," prevailed regarding any purchases. Beginning in the industrial era following the Civil War, the economy grew in complexity. As many new products were introduced and as the consumer became further removed from the producer, the standards for a person's judgment became uncertain. Because of this situation the

[61] Morison and Commager, *The Growth of the American Republic*, vol. 2, p. 630.

older attitude of *caveat emptor* was eventually replaced by another which favored the protection of the consumer and put the blame for poor food and drug standards on the manufacturer or distributor. The new value, *caveat vendor*, became reinforced in legislation, making the producer and distributor responsible for the quality of food and drugs.

With an increasing amount of food and drugs being produced and shipped, the possibilities for spoilage, adulteration, and misrepresentation were considerable. The public gradually became aware of adulteration through various bulletins and reports, the purchase of the products, and the appearance of popular books, articles, and newspaper editorials. The Division of Chemistry of the Department of Agriculture, under the direction of Dr. Harvey W. Wiley, was especially effective in defining the abuses as a threat to public welfare. Dr. Wiley's dramatic "poison squad" experiments showed that some food preservatives were harmful and dangerous. It was also shown by the Division that a thriving interstate business was being developed in the sale of patent medicines, some of which were of questionable value.

After the public became aware of dangers in the foods and drugs they were consuming, conflicts arose over a solution.[62] Various state and federal legislative measures were proposed. Much opposition to these proposals arose because of value conflicts between several interest groups. In general the conflict was between consumer and producer. The first attempts to gain passage of legislation were instigated, in true capitalistic fashion, by those interest groups desiring to protect their respective products from what they thought was unfair competition. Consequently, the early bills that were passed were concerned chiefly with one or two specific products and did not apply to the basic problem of adulteration and misrepresentation in food and drugs.

Not until the 1880's was the first federal pure food and drug legislation introduced which would be of benefit to the public. These measures, however, were defeated. In the words of one who has documented the struggle: "It and other efforts like it were defeated by a durable alliance of quacks, ruthless crooks, pious

[62] A natural history of the social problem of food adulteration is found in Donald J. Newman, "A Study of the Criminal Nature of Pure Food Law Violations," unpublished M.A. thesis, University of Wisconsin, 1952.

frauds, scoundrels, high-priced lawyer-lobbyists, vested interests, liars, corrupt members of Congress, venal publishers, cowards in high office, the stupid, the apathetic, and the duped."[63] With interests like these not much could be hoped for in the public's interest.

Over one hundred and fifty pure food and drug bills were introduced in Congress from 1880 to 1906. Most of the measures were never heard of after their introduction, and the few that were approved were of minor significance.[64] But through continued pressure from the popular press and the opinions received from congressional constituents, the apathy of Congress was overcome, and in 1906, the Federal Food and Drug Act was passed by both the House and Senate. The act declared it unlawful to manufacture in any territory, or to introduce into any state, any adulterated or misbranded food or drug. Offending products were to be seized, and criminal penalties were provided for persons found guilty of violating the provisions of the act.

The need for revision of the act, however, became apparent shortly after its passage. The absence of adequate control over advertising provided an especially serious loophole for evasion of the spirit of the law, and labeling requirements of the law were such as to permit extravagant and unwarranted therapeutic claims for a product. Also, the 1906 act contained no provisions applying to cosmetics and failed to provide measures for safe and effective health devices. In spite of amendments in 1912 (the Sherley amendment) and 1919 (the New Weight Act), the problem of impure and unsafe foods and drugs had not been effectively reformed through law.

A renewed effort was made to regulate food and drugs. During this period further awareness of the problem was provided in such popular works as Kallet and Schlink's *100,000,000 Guinea Pigs* and Lamb's *American Chamber of Horrors*.[65] Various consumer organizations were formed and consumer research groups were es-

[63] Morton Mintz, *The Therapeutic Nightmare: A Report on Prescription Drugs, the Men Who Take Them, and the Agency That Controls Them* (Boston: Houghton Mifflin, 1965), p. 41.

[64] For these and later laws, see Stephen Wilson, *Food and Drug Regulation* (Washington, D.C.: American Council of Public Affairs, 1942).

[65] Arthur Kallet, and F. J. Schlink, *100,000,000 Guinea Pigs* (New York: The Vanguard Press, 1933); Ruth deForest Lamb, *American Chamber of Horrors* (New York: Farrar and Rinehart, 1936).

tablished. After Franklin D. Roosevelt took office in 1933 a committee was appointed to draft new legislation.

A bill to correct the deficiencies of the 1906 law was introduced
in 1933. As could be expected, planned attacks were launched
against the bill. Particularly active in the opposition to the proposal
was the organization representing the patent medicine interests, the
United Medicine Manufacturers of America. The organization attempted to block the bill by engaging in a drive which involved
"17 plans." Among the plans were to: "(1) secure cooperation of
newspapers in spreading favorable publicity; (2) enlist all manufacturers and wholesalers to instruct customers through their salesmen; (3) secure the pledge of manufacturers, wholesalers, advertising agencies, and all other interested affiliates to address letters to
Senators to gain their promise to vote against the bill; (4) line up
with other organizations, such as the Drug Institute, Proprietary
Association, National Association of Retail Druggists, to make a
mass attack on the bill; (5) enlist the help of carton, tube, bottle,
and box manufacturers; (6) ridicule organizations favoring the
bill; and (7) convey by every means available — radio, newspapers, mail, and personal contact — the alarming fact that if the
bill is adopted, the public will be deprived of the right of self-
diagnosis and self-medication."[66]

But the public interest was to succeed, at least in concept. The
Federal Food, Drug and Cosmetic Act was enacted in 1938. The
act required, among other things, more effective methods for the control of false labeling and advertising. Informative, specific labeling
was definitely required. False advertising of foods, drugs, and cosmetics was prohibited, with provision for more severe penalties for
violation of the law. In addition, authority was established for
setting standards for the identity, quality, strength, and purity of
drugs. Later, in 1951, the act was amended by the passage of the
Durham-Humphrey Amendment. The amendment placed stricter
controls on the dispensing of drugs.

In the meantime a number of other special federal laws were
enacted to govern the manufacture and marketing of particular
classes of drugs (narcotics, marihuana, biologic products). Still
other laws were passed to regulate such activities as the weighing,

[66] From Mintz, *The Therapeutic Nightmare*, pp. 45–46.

measuring, and mailing of foods and drugs.[67] The various federal laws were complemented by state laws which were also concerned with manufacturing, labeling, and advertising, but which in addition regulated the occupational activity of pharmacy.[68]

Continued interest in providing the public with safe and pure foods can be seen in the federal government's inquiry into the drug industry at the beginning of the 1960's. Presumably interested in the broad problem of administered prices, the Senate Subcommittee on Antitrust and Monopoly under the chairmanship of Estes Kefauver touched on such topics as the high cost of drugs, the large number of new drugs released each year, the multiple names for identical chemicals and compounds, advertising and promotion of drugs, safeness and efficacy of drugs, and violation of antitrust laws by drug manufacturers.[69] The hearings were highly critical of the amount of money drug manufacturers spend on advertising and promotion in comparison to what they spend for research. Upon the conclusion of the hearings, amid strong opposing pressure from the large pharmaceutical houses and their lobbying organizations, Congress passed in 1962 the Kefauver-Hart Drug Act. The act, however, was not successful in gaining the regulation of drug prices, but was successful in securing provisions for stricter control of drug testing, labeling, and advertising.

Although the drug act of 1962 was able to correct many abuses in the drug industry, other problems remain. Pharmaceutical interests, especially manufacturers and dispensers of drugs, continue to

[67] Thomas W. Christopher and Charles W. Dunn, *Special Federal Food and Drug Laws* (New York: Commerce Clearing House, 1954).

[68] David H. Vernon and Franklin M. Depew, *General State Food and Drug Laws* (New York: Commerce Clearing House, 1955). For a study of the formulation of occupational laws according to the interests of the occupations, pharmacy included, see Ronald L. Akers, "The Professional Association and the Legal Regulation of Practice," *Law and Society Review*, 2 (May, 1968), pp. 463–482.

[69] U.S. Congress, Senate, Subcommittee of the Committee on the Judiciary, *Hearings Before the Subcommittee on Antitrust and Monopoly*, 86th Congress, 1st and 2nd Sessions, Parts 14–22, 1959–1960; U.S. Congress, Senate, Subcommittee of the Committee on the Judiciary, *Report of the Committee on the Judiciary*, "Antitrust and Monopoly Activities, 1960," Report No. 167, 87th Congress, 1st Session, 1961; U.S. Congress, Senate, Subcommittee of the Committee on the Judiciary, *Report of the Committee on the Judiciary*, "Administered Prices: Drugs," Report No. 448, 87th Congress, 1st Session, 1961.

advertise and sell drugs according to their trade name, when prescription by generic name would be to the advantage of the public. Yet from a broad perspective we can see that since the end of the last century the public interest has been increasingly served, in spite of private interests.

SEXUAL PSYCHOPATH LAWS

Some criminal laws, not unlike our other social passions and conveniences, experience periods of increased popularity. The formulation of "sexual psychopath" laws is such an instance of fashion in law. Beginning in the later 1930's and extending into the 1950's, more than half the states enacted sexual psychopath laws. The statutes varied somewhat from one state to another, but generally defined the sexual psychopath as "one lacking the power to control his sexual impulses or having criminal propensities toward the commission of sex offenses."[70] From the standpoint of sanctions, the laws usually provided that a person diagnosed as a sexual psychopath be confined for an indefinite period in a state hospital for the insane. Why were these laws enacted during a particular period, and what social interests were involved in their formulation?

Sexual psychopath laws were in part a response to public anxiety about serious sex crimes. Like the earlier and somewhat comparable "habitual offender" laws that also swept the country, the sexual psychopath laws provided a partial solution to what was being defined as a social problem.[71] Consequently, characteristic to the American legal system, a law was created to solve a problem.

The problem of the sex offender, as defined by the public, was based on a series of propositions, most of which were false or at least questionable:

> Namely, that the present danger to women and children from serious sex crimes is very great, for the number of sex crimes is large and is increasing more rapidly than any other crime; that most sex crimes are committed by "sexual psychopaths" and

[70] See Alan H. Swanson, "Sexual Psychopath Statutes: Summary and Analysis," *Journal of Criminal Law, Criminology and Police Science,* 51 (July–August, 1960), pp. 215–235.

[71] Habitual Offender laws are discussed in Paul W. Tappan, "Habitual Offender Laws in the United States," *Federal Probation,* 13 (March, 1949), pp. 28–31.

that these persons persist in their sexual crimes throughout life; that they always give warning that they are dangerous by first committing minor offenses; that any psychiatrist can diagnose them with a high degree of precision at an early age, before they have committed serious sex crimes; and that sexual psychopaths who are diagnosed and identified should be confined as irresponsible persons until they are pronounced by psychiatrists to be completely and permanently cured of their malady.[72]

But once the public's concern had been aroused, partly through press coverage of a few spectacular sex crimes, and partly through the diffusion of a misinformed conception of the sex offender, sexual psychopath legislation followed as the answer to the problem.

Yet the public's concern about sex offenses could not be effective in the formulation of criminal law without the organization of action groups within the community. Concrete pressure for sexual psychopath legislation was provided in most states by the organization of committees, which in most cases were guided by psychiatrists. These committees presented sexual psychopath bills to the public and to the legislatures as the most scientific and enlightened method of protecting society against dangerous sex criminals. Thus, "the psychiatrists, more than any others have been the interest group back of the laws."[73] A committee of psychiatrists and neurologists in Chicago wrote the bill that became the sexual psychopath law of Illinois. In Minnesota all the members of the governor's committee except one were psychiatrists.

The fact that the formulation of the sexual psychopath laws was predominantly in the hands of psychiatrists accounts in large measure for the substance of the laws. Since a common assertion among psychiatrists is that serious sex crimes are the result of emotional or mental pathology, or that all psychological defectives have actual or potential sexual abnormalities, it is little wonder that the sexual psychopath laws stipulated that sex offenders be handled as psychologically disturbed persons and be treated as patients. But the psychiatric interest in the formulation of sexual psychopath laws was also a matter of private economics.

The interests of psychiatrists in sexual psychopath legislation

---

[72] Edwin H. Sutherland, "The Diffusion of Sexual Psychopath Laws," *American Journal of Sociology,* 56 (September, 1950), pp. 142–148.
[73] *Ibid.,* p. 145.

was, nevertheless, reinforced by the more general movement which promoted the treatment of all offenders. Furthermore, professionally trained persons employed in corrections have tended to believe that emotional traits are the explanation of crime. The treatment of the criminal as a patient, therefore, was consistent with the aims of those engaged in the application of the sexual psychopath laws.

In spite of the rush to enact sexual psychopath laws, there has been a tendency not to enforce the laws. There are several reasons for the lack of enforcement of the sexual psychopath laws:

> One is that the laws were passed in a period of panic and were forgotten after the emotion was relieved by this action. A second reason is that the state has no facilities for the care and custody of sexual psychopaths; the state hospitals are already crowded with psychotic patients. A third reason is that the prosecutor and judge, anxious to make records as vigorous and aggressive defenders of the community, favor the most severe penalty available and are unwilling to look upon serious sex criminals as patients. They use the sexual psychopath laws only when their evidence is so weak that conviction under the criminal law is improbable. Finally, it is reported that defense attorneys have learned that they can stop the proceedings under this law by advising their clients to refuse to talk to the psychiatrists. The psychiatrists can make no diagnosis if those who are being investigated refuse to talk.[74]

But perhaps "the greatest saving grace has been the almost uniform lack of enforcement that has followed their enactment."[75] Basically, the sexual psychopath laws depart from some of the most fundamental conceptions of criminal law. Most important, the Anglo-American legal doctrine of *nulla crimen sine lege*, prohibiting prosecution in the absence of clearly specified substantive norms, is denied by most of the sexual psychopath statutes. Since the individual may be adjudged either without a criminal charge or without a finding of guilt, merely through the diagnosis that he is a sexual psychopath, due process considerations are ignored. Furthermore, since the concept of "sexual psychopath" is so vaguely and variously defined by psychiatrists, there is a great deal of variation in diag-

---

[74] Edwin H. Sutherland, "The Sexual Psychopath Laws," *Journal of Criminal Law, Criminology and Police Science,* 40 (January–February, 1950), pp. 543–554.

[75] Paul W. Tappan, "Sex Offender Laws and Their Administration," *Federal Probation,* 14 (September, 1950), p. 33.

nosis and a considerable amount of discretion in the administration of the law.

> There appears to be no agreement as to the syndromes of aberration that justify special treatment. Indeed, hospital authorities handling cases of alleged sex psychopaths committed to them by the courts discover a wide spread of psychological types — many who are normal, along with neurotics, psychotics, epileptics, feeble-minded, alcoholics, and constitutional types. Agreement among authorities is often difficult enough to attain for purposes of classifying individuals where traditional and fairly precise clinical categories are involved; consensus is impossible in the no man's land of psychopathic personality. The hazard inherent in the substantive definitions of these statutes is manifest upon inspection; the psychopathology is defined by such nondiscriminating terminology as "impulsiveness of behavior," "lack of customary standards of good judgment," "emotional instability," or "inability to control impulse." The cases adjudicated under these criteria display varied forms of personality organization and a widely assorted sexual symptomatology, a significant proportion of which is in fact normal behavior viewed from either a biological or statistical point of view.[76]

And in some jurisdictions a person may be adjudicated — according to this imprecise status of sexual psychopath — without a criminal charge being placed against the individual and without it being established that a crime has been committed. "Thus individuals who are nonpsychotic and nondefective, against whom no charge has been laid, may be confined for long periods in hospitals that lack both the space and the treatment facilities to handle them. By the simple expedient of shifting jurisdiction to civil courts, these legislators have made it possible to commit minor deviates who are not insane to psychiatric institutions where they do not belong."[77]

There is no reason to believe that similar rashes of legislation will not recur. Law has its element of fashion. The recent enactment of a drug addiction control law in the state of New York may become an example for other states. Again certain persons could be adjudicated and confined for long periods of time in institutions without the safeguards of due process. The establishment of official

[76] *Ibid.*, p. 33.
[77] *Ibid.*, p. 34.

policies in the name of the common good, and under the guise of scientific knowledge, is always a force in the formulation of certain types of criminal law.

PROTECTION OF MORALITY
AND PUBLIC ORDER

Whether or not it is the proper business of criminal law to enforce moral principles, much of our criminal law is formulated and maintained for just that purpose. A great many of our criminal laws attempt to control personal behaviors that are contrary to the morals of some members of the community. Many of these criminal laws are kept on the books, without serious or uniform enforcement, because they reflect a popular sense of reprobation. The behaviors they prohibit are regarded, at least by some, as wrong and unworthy of the society. The criminal laws that aim to protect morality and public order include those which regulate various kinds of sexual conduct, prostitution, homosexuality, abortion, drinking, the use of drugs, and certain public behaviors defined by such names as "public nuisance," "loitering," "trespassing," and "vagrancy."[78]

Regulation of Sexual Conduct. Much of the concern for public order pertains to the control of sexual conduct. This concern, in Anglo-American society at least, is based on a fairly rigid conception of appropriate sexual expression. Our moral sense carries strong Puritan overtones. To be moral in America is to be *sexually* discreet.

The range of sexual conduct that is covered by law is so extensive that the law makes potential criminals of most of the adolescent and adult population.[79] One of the principal reasons for such complete control over the sexual behavior of the members of society is to protect a particular kind of family system. A great number of state laws seek to control acts which might otherwise endanger the chastity of women before marriage. There are the numerous laws in regard to rape (statutory and forcible), fornication, incest, and

[78] On public order crimes, see Marshall B. Clinard and Richard Quinney, *Criminal Behavior Systems: A Typology* (New York: Holt, Rinehart and Winston, 1967), pp. 247–269.

[79] See Morris Ploscowe, "Sex Offenses: The American Legal Context," *Law and Contemporary Problems,* 25 (Spring, 1960), pp. 217–225; Also, Gerhard O. W. Mueller, *Legal Regulation of Sexual Conduct* (Dobbs Ferry, N.Y.: Oceana Publications, 1961).

sexual deviance of juveniles. The criminal laws on adultery also exist to protect the family by preventing sexual relations outside the marriage bond.[80] The Puritans of Massachusetts Bay Colony placed such a value on sexual relations within the family that they made adultery a crime punishable by death. Other criminal laws today as in the past regulate sexual relations of family members. Through these laws the cherished monogamous family pattern is preserved.

Some of our criminal laws on sexual behavior were formulated to protect specific aspects of marriage and family life for very special interests. Several southern states, for instance, enacted laws to prevent marriages between Negroes and whites. In 1967, however, the Supreme Court ruled that an antimiscegenation statute of Virginia was unconstitutional. Such "slavery laws," held over from a bygone era, had been originally formulated to ensure the slavery status of Negroes and in more recent times have been used to maintain segregation of the races.

Another type of criminal law, also enacted at an early time in Virginia, pertained to bastardy among women of the lower ranks. This law was not only instituted for a moral purpose but was to ensure the maximum work from domestic servants. "Having paid a very high price for their labor, their masters, not unnaturally, were opposed to their entering a relationship which was quite certain to lead to interruptions in their field work, perhaps, at the very time their part in that work would be most valuable, if not wholly indispensable. Not only would the birth of children make it necessary for them to lie by for a month or more, but it might even result in their deaths, and the complete loss of the money invested by the planter in their purchase."[81] Also in the law of bastardy the blame for the offense could be placed on the servant woman who had been overpowered by the advances of her masters.

Criminal law has also been formulated to prevent the exposure of members of the society to that which is regarded by some as lewd or obscene. The Comstock Act of 1873 stands in American criminal law as a landmark in the control of obscenity. Before that time the

[80] Morris Ploscowe, *Sex and the Law* (Englewood Cliffs, N.J.: Prentice-Hall, 1951), pp. 136–164.
[81] Philip Alexander Bruce, *Social Life in Old Virginia* (New York: Capricorn Books, 1965, originally published in 1910), p. 45.

common law was not clear on the issue. In fact, obscenity was not considered to be a problem before the nineteenth century. By the middle of the nineteenth century a new concept of obscenity had emerged, given an identity by the Victorian Age.[82] The protection of woman and the young became a concern of several segments of the population. Finally, in 1873, with considerable pressure for a statutory law, the Comstock Law was enacted, providing for the censorship of literature and other printed matter which might come in the hands of the innocent.

Today well-organized interest groups, such as the National Organization for Decent Literature, continue to pressure courts and legislatures for statutes and decisions on the regulation of obscenity. A short time ago in New York moral interests were successful in having the cabaret code amended to prevent bar waitresses or barmaids from working with "their breasts or lower part of the torso uncovered."[83] The morning following the amendment the owner of a bar and her three topless waitresses, after being arrested during the night, appeared in court to answer summonses for "offending the public morals."

Prostitution, Homosexuality, and Abortion. The laws in regard to prostitution vary greatly from one country to another. In most states the act of solicitation is a misdemeanor punished by a fine or a jail sentence of one year. Repeated apprehensions may result in a strong charge of felony. In some states laws have been enacted to control not only solicitation by prostitutes but also the activities of the exploiters and customers of prostitutes. While prostitution may be defined as a crime, the conduct is frequent in all societies. The laws remain, however, as a representation of what some in society expect in the ideal moral order. But the Wolfenden Report of England perhaps best expressed the reasons for the continued legal regulation of prostitution:

> If it were the law's intention to punish prostitution *per se,* on the ground that it is immoral conduct, then it would be right that it should provide for the punishment of the man as well

[82] Henry H. Foster, Jr., "The 'Comstock Load'—Obscenity and the Law," *Journal of Criminal Law, Criminology and Police Science,* 48 (September–October, 1957), pp. 245–258.

[83] Reported in *The New York Times,* November 15, 1966, p. 49.

as the woman. But that is not the function of the law. It should confine itself to those activities which offend against public order and decency or expose the ordinary citizen to what is offensive or injurious; and the simple fact is that prostitutes do parade themselves more habitually and openly than their prospective customers, and do by their continual presence affront the sense of decency of the ordinary citizen. In so doing they create a nuisance which, in our view, the law is entitled to recognize and deal with.[84]

Criminal penalties for homosexual acts in the United States have tended to be severe. Some states provide penalties of ten or more years imprisonment. In actuality, however, a relatively small proportion of persons are arrested for homosexual acts and when penalties are administered they tend to be lenient. While a moral connotation is still attached to homosexuality by some segments of society, the trend is toward the removal of certain homosexual acts from the list of crimes. The Wolfenden Report, after stating that the purpose of law is to protect the citizen, asserted that it is not the function of criminal law "to intervene in the private lives of citizens, or to seek to enforce any particular pattern of behavior, further than is necessary to carry out the purpose we have outlined."[85] In England the law of homosexuality was subsequently changed to allow homosexual acts privately carried out between persons twenty-one years of age and over. Similar legal reforms are currently under consideration in the United States.

Abortion has long been defined as a crime. Though a few states today allow the termination of pregnancy on broad medical grounds, most prohibit abortion except when the life of the mother is in danger. Understandably the taking of a life is a moral offense, but the question of whether or not life is taken when an abortion is performed is subject to debate. Various groups have exerted pressure to have their views represented in an appropriate abortion law.[86] Legal reform has taken place in England in part through the well-organized activities of the Abortion Law Reform Association. Similar reform proposals have been advanced in the United States.

[84] The Wolfenden Report, *Report of the Committee on Homosexual Offenses and Prostitution* (New York: Stein and Day, 1963), pp. 143–144.

[85] *Ibid.*, p. 81.

[86] See Edwin M. Schur, *Crimes Without Victims* (Englewood Cliffs, N.J.: Prentice-Hall, 1965), pp. 11–66.

The Planned Parenthood Federation has called for the drafting and adoption of a law that would recognize therapeutic abortion for psychological, eugenic, and humanitarian purposes. The American Law Institute has proposed a model abortion code with similar provisions. Such legalization schemes have been opposed primarily by the Roman Catholic Church. A solution to the problem of abortion is by no means clear. But any legal solution that will be achieved will represent the aims of the most powerful interest groups in society.

Drinking and Drunkenness. Although drinking itself is not a crime, being drunk in public view may result in a criminal arrest. Criminal laws have been formulated to handle persons who openly disturb the public order.[87] The person who drinks excessively may be apprehended simply because he is disturbing the community's sense of propriety or because his being intoxicated may lead to other acts of public nuisance or disturbance. To become intoxicated and exuberant in one's own home is proper middle class behavior. But to be drunk in public is to violate the Puritanical standards of moral strength and personal discipline.

The likelihood exists that public drunkenness will not be treated as crime in the future. A legal change has occurred already in the United States. In 1966 the United States Court of Appeals for the District of Columbia ruled that a chronic alcoholic cannot be convicted of the crime of public drunkenness. Since the defendant to a drunkenness charge "has lost the power of self-control in the use of intoxicating beverages," the court held, the defendant thus lacks necessary criminal intent to be guilty of a crime and cannot therefore be punished under the criminal law. Similar rulings and legislative measures may eventually eliminate a vast portion of criminal offenses.

The current trend in the law associated with drinking and drunkenness is in part an extension of the forces that operated in the repeal of the Eighteenth Amendment. The repeal of the constitu-

[87] Such offenders are discussed in Irwin Deutscher, "The Petty Offender: A Sociological Alien," *Journal of Criminal Law, Criminology and Police Science,* 44 (January–February, 1954), pp. 592–595; David J. Pittman and C. Wayne Gordon, *Revolving Door* (New York: The Free Press of Glencoe, 1958); and Earl Rubington, "The Chronic Drunkenness Offender," *Annals of the American Academy of Political and Social Science,* 315 (January, 1958), pp. 65–72.

tional amendment in 1933 marked the end of the "great experiment" known as Prohibition, which had been established through the Volstead Act and ratified through the Eighteenth Amendment in 1920. It has been observed that the movement to place a ban on drinking and the liquor trade was an assertion of the rural Protestant mind against the urban culture that had emerged at the end of the nineteenth century and the beginning of the twentieth.[88] Prohibition meant for a significant portion of the population the stamping out of sin in an evil society. The rural element was temporarily successful, in the enactment of prohibition legislation, but succumbed within thirteen years to the inevitable.

Within a generalized context of resentment against drinking and what it represented, specific interest groups were active in the movement that led to prohibition legislation. The Prohibition party was founded in 1869 as a third political party to deal with the problem of drinking. Later such organizations as the Anti-Saloon League and the Woman's Christian Temperance Union were founded to crusade against alcohol and the saloon. The lobbying efforts of these groups were effective in bringing about the enactment of state and local temperance legislation. The "dry" lobby groups exerted great pressure against legislators. For example, in the case of the Anti-Saloon League: "With the menace of thousands of votes cast at the next election against any legislator who dared to vote against a dry measure, the League could make the representatives of the people vote against their personal wet convictions."[89] The activities of the dry interest groups accompanied with other forces in American society at the time resulted in the formal enactment of prohibition:

> In this way, the Eighteenth Amendment and the Volstead Act became the law of the land. Through the many roots of prohibition — rural mythology, the psychology of excess, the exploited fears of the mass of the people, the findings of science and medicine, the temper of reform, the efficiency of the dry pressure groups, their mastery of propaganda, the stupidity and self-interest of the brewers and distillers, the necessary trimming of politicians, and the weakness of the elected representatives of the people — through all these channels the sap

[88] Andrew Sinclair, *Era of Excess: A Social History of the Prohibition Movement* (New York: Harper and Row, 1964).
[89] *Ibid.*, p. 105.

of the dry tree rose until the legal prohibition of the liquor trade burst out new and green in the first month of 1920. The roots had been separate; yet they were all part of a common American seed. They combined and contributed to the strength of the whole. The Anti-Saloon League, bent on its particular reform, was the heir and beneficiary of many interactions in American life. As the drys stood on the threshold of victory at the opening of the twenties, they could see manifest destiny in the success of their cause. They seemed to be the darling army of the Lord. Behind them appeared to lie one mighty pattern and purpose. Before them hung the sweet fruits of victory.[90]

But prohibition was to fail as law as it was to fail as a noble experiment. An outdated morality could not be enforced through criminal law. Rural interests were replaced by the interests of a new social order. "The old order of the country gave way to the new order of the cities. Rural morality was replaced by urban morality, rural voices by urban voices, rural votes by urban votes. A novel culture of skyscrapers and suburbs grew up to oust the civilization of the general store and Main Street. A technological revolution broadcast a common culture over the various folkways of the land. It is only in context of this immense social change, the metamorphosis of Abraham Lincoln's America into the America of Franklin Roosevelt, that the phenomenon of national prohibition can be seen and understood. It was part of the whole process, the last hope of the declining village. It was less of a farce than a tragedy, less of a mistake than a proof of changing times."[91]

The Use of Drugs. The Harrison Act passed by Congress in 1914 had the effect of defining users of certain drugs as criminals. In technical language the Harrison Act required that all drug-handlers be registered and that the fact of securing drugs be made a matter of record.[92] But through the interpretation of the act, the court rulings in specific cases, and the enactment of supplementary laws,

[90] *Ibid.*, p. 170.

[91] *Ibid.*, pp. 5–6. Laws, such as that of prohibition, are discussed as responses to the lack of consensus on norms in Joseph R. Gusfield, "Moral Passage: The Symbolic Process in Public Designations of Deviance," *Social Problems*, 15 (Fall, 1967), pp. 175–188.

[92] Alfred R. Lindesmith, *The Addict and the Law* (Bloomington: Indiana University Press, 1965), chap. 1.

criminal sanctions were provided for the unauthorized possession, sale, or transfer of drugs. In addition to the federal statutes and rulings, the states have enacted their own antinarcotic laws. In the United States, penalties for violation of drug laws have become more severe in recent years. The possession of narcotics, for example, is now a felony instead of a misdemeanor.

Drug laws have not only defined users as criminals but have created a generalized public suspicion and fear of drug users and addicts. Today the use of any type of drug among a segment of the population — be the drug addictive or not, a narcotic drug, marihuana, or a psychedelic drug — produces a public response that almost certainly results in the call for repressive legislation. Much of this atmosphere has been created by the actions of the Federal Bureau of Narcotics. The Bureau has, in particular, been responsible for administrative decisions which have served as the basis for most of the drug legislation.[93] The Bureau of Narcotics has defined its interests as total restriction of drugs and complete enforcement of the law. These interests have become the standards by which the public now views and officially acts upon the use of drugs.

In sharp contrast to the American drug policy is the policy of Great Britain. In England drug addiction is considered a medical rather than a legal problem. The addict, therefore, is not regarded as a criminal. The Dangerous Drug Act of 1920 defined the addict as a patient who may receive drugs upon the medical discretion of a physician.[94] As a result, drug addicts in England do not have to engage in criminal activities to maintain a drug supply. Because of the British approach to drug addiction, it is now being argued, primarily by academicians, that the American policy on drug use is unsound and that in order to deal more effectively with the drug problem official policy on drugs should be changed.[95] Lindesmith

[93] See Alfred R. Lindesmith, "Federal Law and Drug Addiction,". *Social Problems*, 7 (Summer, 1959), pp. 48–57; Howard S. Becker, *Outsiders: Studies in the Sociology of Deviance* (New York: The Free Press, 1963), pp. 135–146; Donald T. Dickson, "Bureaucracy and Morality: An Organizational Perspective on a Moral Crusade," *Social Problems*, 16 (Fall, 1968), pp. 143–156.

[94] Alfred R. Lindesmith, "The British System of Narcotics Control," *Law and Contemporary Problems*, 22 (Winter, 1957), pp. 138–154; Edwin M. Schur, *Narcotic Addiction in Britain and America: The Impact of Public Policy* (Bloomington: Indiana University Press, 1962).

[95] Lindesmith, *The Addict and the Law;* Schur, *Narcotic Addiction in Britain and America.*

has made several proposals: (1) antinarcotic laws should be written so that addicts do not have to violate them solely because they are addicts; (2) drug users are admittedly handicapped by their habits but they should nevertheless be encouraged to engage in productive labor even when they are using drugs; (3) cures should not be imposed upon narcotics victims by force but should be voluntary; (4) police officers should be prevented from exploiting drug addicts as stool pigeons solely because they are addicts; and (5) heroin and morphine addicts should be handled according to the same principles and moral precepts applied to barbituate and alcohol addicts because these three forms of addiction are basically similar.[96] Greater understanding of drug use and addiction is being gained. Efforts are being made to handle drug addiction as a disease and not as a criminal problem. The danger that accompanies this trend is the formulation of programs that may be both as punitive and unsuccessful as current legal practices.

The Law of Vagrancy. Vagrancy has been a crime in virtually every state in the United States. Since the state statutes have had their heritage in English law, the common law meaning of the term "vagrancy" is either stated or implied in the statutes. Accordingly, a vagrant is an idle person, beggar, or person wandering without being able to give a good account of himself. Most important to the vagrancy concept, then, is the nature of the person. "Vagrancy is the principal crime in which the offense consists of being a certain kind of person rather than in having done or failed to do certain acts."[97]

Vagrancy laws are widely used on the community level to detain various kinds of questionable and suspicious persons. The vagrancy laws and their enforcement thus are aimed at potential criminals, are used sometimes in lieu of other charges, and often are the means to rid the community of those who do not meet the standards of the respectable members.

The crime of vagrancy has been derived from early English laws

---

[96] Lindesmith, *The Addict and the Law,* p. 270.

[97] Forrest W. Lacey, "Vagrancy and Other Crimes of Personal Condition," *Harvard Law Review,* 66 (May, 1953), p. 1203. Also see Caleb Foote, "Vagrancy-Type Law and Its Administration," *University of Pennsylvania Law Review,* 104 (March, 1956), pp. 603–650.

which came into existence during the fourteenth century in response to changing social conditions.[98] The first full-fledged vagrancy law was enacted in 1349. The statute made a crime of giving alms to able-bodied, unemployed persons and established that such persons would be criminally punished. The law and supplementary statutes were formulated, after the Black Death and the flight of workers from landowners, for the purpose of supplying needed labor: "There is little question that these statutes were designed for one express purpose: to force laborers (whether personally free or unfree) to accept employment at a low wage in order to insure the landowner an adequate supply of labor at a price he could afford to pay."[99]

Changing social conditions in England made it unnecessary to enforce the vagrancy statutes. But by the sixteenth century, with increased emphasis on commerce and industry, vagrancy law was revived. However, because of changes in the social structure, there was a shift in the focal concern of the law from the regulation of labor to the control of criminal activities. The following summarizes the development of the law of vagrancy in early English society:

> The foregoing analysis of the vagrancy laws has demonstrated that these laws were a legislative innovation which reflected the socially perceived necessity of providing an abundance of cheap labor to landowners during a period when serfdom was breaking down and when the pool of available labor was depleted. With the eventual breakup of feudalism the need for such laws eventually disappeared and the increased dependence of the economy upon industry and commerce rendered the former use of the vagrancy statutes unnecessary. As a result, for a substantial period the vagrancy statutes were dormant, undergoing only minor changes and, presumably, being applied infrequently. Finally, the vagrancy laws were subjected to considerable alteration through a shift in the focal concern of the statutes. Whereas in their inception the laws focused upon the "idle" and "those refusing to labor" after the turn of the sixteenth century an emphasis came to be upon "rogues," "vagabonds," and others who were suspected of being engaged in

[98] William J. Chambliss, "A Sociological Analysis of the Law of Vagrancy," *Social Problems*, 12 (Summer, 1964), pp. 67–77. Also see George Rusche and Otto Kirchheimer, *Punishment and Social Structure* (New York: Columbia University Press, 1939), pp. 32–41.

[99] Chambliss, "A Sociological Analysis of the Law of Vagrancy," p. 69.

criminal activities. During this period the focus was particularly upon "roadmen" who preyed upon citizens who transported goods from one place to another. The increased importance of commerce to England during this period made it necessary that some protection be given persons engaged in this enterprise and the vagrancy statutes provided one source for such protection by re-focusing the acts to be included under these statutes.[100]

In other words, the formulations and changes in the vagrancy statutes were the result of the efforts of powerful interest groups. "The vagrancy laws emerged in order to provide the powerful landowners with a ready supply of cheap labor. When this was no longer seen as necessary and particularly when the landowners were no longer dependent upon cheap labor nor were they a powerful interest group in society the laws became dormant. Finally a new interest group emerged and was seen as being of great importance to the society and the laws were then altered so as to afford some protection to this group."[101]

With only minor variations the vagrancy statutes remained essentially the same through the seventeenth and eighteenth centuries. The statutes were adopted by American colonies and states to serve the same purposes they were performing in English society. Today the vagrancy laws continue to provide a source of control of persons and activities regarded as undesirable in the community.

However, the vagrancy laws are currently being evaluated and questioned. One writer has stated, "The time is surely at hand to modernize the vagrancy concept or, better yet, to abandon it altogether for statutes which will harmonize with notions of a decent, fair, and just administration of criminal justice, and which will at the same time make it possible for police departments to discharge their responsibilities in a reasonable manner."[102] Along these lines, a significant change in vagrancy law has been made in the state of New York. In 1967 the New York Court of Appeals ruled unconstitutional a statute of 1788 that provided for the arrest of persons with no visible means of support.[103] The court ruled that

100 *Ibid.*, p. 76.
101 *Ibid.*, p. 77.
102 Arthur H. Sherry, "Vagrants, Rogues, and Vagabonds—Old Concepts in Need of Revision," *California Law Review*, 48 (October, 1960), p. 567.
103 Reported in *The New York Times*, July 8, 1967, pp. 1 and 9.

the law "constitutes an overreaching of the proper limitations of the police power." Furthermore, the court said that the statute has little use "other than, perhaps, as a means of harassing, punishing or apprehending suspected criminals in an unconstitutional fashion." The old statute was declared unconstitutional on the ground that it interfered with the liberty of a citizen to conduct himself as he sees fit as long as he does not interfere with the rights of others. Such repeal, which is likely to occur in other states as well, will end the use of laws of the vagrancy type to enforce community interests. Perhaps other means of maintaining public order, legal or extralegal, will be substituted for vagrancy law. But in this case at least, the forces that would protect individual rights have triumphed over those forces that would at the same time control individuals in the protection of public order.

3

Application of Criminal Definitions

CHAPTER FOUR

Enforcement
of Criminal
Law

Once human conduct has been abstractly defined as criminal in the criminal law, criminal definitions are concretely applied by agents of the law. Moreover, criminal definitions are applied to situations, persons, and behavior at a number of legal stages. The stages include the enforcement of the law, prosecution, court proceedings, sentencing, and finally the release of cases from the legal system. Shown in Figure 4.1 are the specific stages of the American legal system and the movement of criminal cases through the system. As indicated, the police observe or have reported to them instances which are regarded as violations of the criminal law. An arrest may then be made and a charge may be entered. During prosecution a decision is made whether to continue a case or to drop it. Through bargaining the defendant may plead guilty to a charge or may stand trial. Upon conviction the accused is sentenced. Following the completion of the sentence, cases are processed out of the legal system. The most striking feature of the legal system is the great number of alternatives available in the enforcement and administration of the criminal law.

This chapter is devoted solely to the sociology of law enforcement. Enforcement will be construed narrowly as the *arrest* of persons suspected of committing a crime. Arrest is here regarded as a distinct operational step which involves decisions to interfere with the freedom of persons suspected of criminal conduct.[1] It is one of the stages

[1] See Wayne R. LaFave, *Arrest: The Decision to Take a Suspect into Custody* (Boston: Little, Brown, 1965).

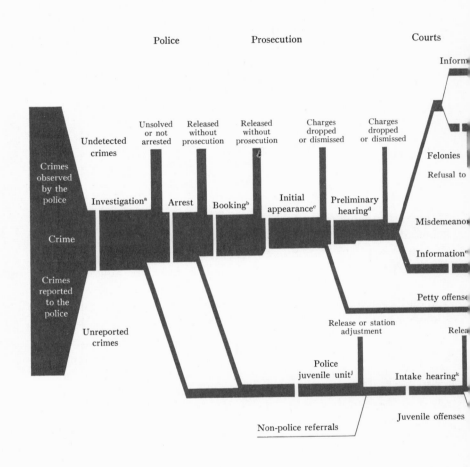

| Police | Prosecution | Courts |

[a] May continue until trial.

[b] Administrative record of arrest. First step at which temporary release on bail may be available.

[c] Before magistrate, commissioner, or justice of peace. Formal notice of charge, advice of rights. Bail set. Summary trials for petty offenses usually conducted here without further processing.

[d] Preliminary testing of evidence against defendant. Charge may be reduced. No separate preliminary hearing for misdemeanors in some systems.

[e] Charge filed by prosecutor on basis information submitte by police or citizens Alternative to grand jury indictment; ofte used in felonies, almo always in misdemeanors.

FIGURE 4.1

The American
Legal System

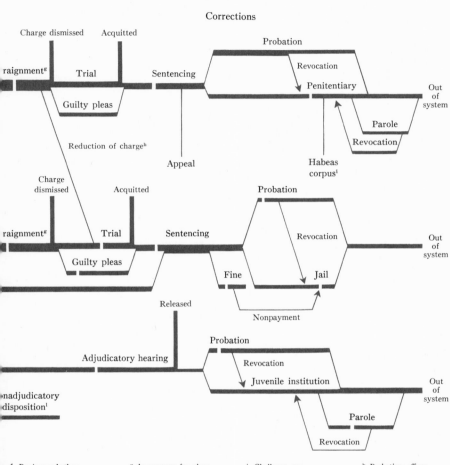

Corrections

Charge dismissed   Acquitted

raignment[g]   Trial   Sentencing   Probation

Guilty pleas   Revocation   Penitentiary   Out of system

Reduction of charge[h]   Parole   Revocation

Appeal   Habeas corpus[i]

Charge dismissed   Acquitted   Probation

raignment[g]   Trial   Sentencing   Revocation   Out of system

Guilty pleas   Fine   Jail

Released   Nonpayment

Probation

Adjudicatory hearing   Revocation

Juvenile institution   Out of system

nadjudicatory disposition[l]   Parole

Revocation

---

[f] Reviews whether government evidence sufficient to justify trial. Some states have no grand jury system; others seldom use it.

[g] Appearance for plea; defendant elects trial by judge or jury (if available); counsel for indigent usually appointed here in felonies. Often not at all in other cases.

[h] Charge may be reduced at any time prior to trial in return for plea of guilty or for other reasons.

[i] Challenge on constitutional grounds to legality of detention. May be sought at any point in process.

[j] Police often hold informal hearings, dismiss or adjust many cases without further processing.

[k] Probation officer decides desirability of further court action.

[l] Welfare agency, social services, counseling, medical care, etc., for cases where adjudicatory handling not needed.

at which persons and behaviors may be defined as criminal. The application of criminal definitions beyond arrest — in the course of prosecution, conviction, and sentencing — will be covered in Chapters 5 and 6.

POLICE DISCRETION

The criminal code does not provide specific instructions for the enforcement of the law. How the law is enforced is largely a matter of *discretion*. Yet it is commonly assumed that the police can and should fully enforce the criminal law by arresting all persons who violate the law. The ideal of *full enforcement* is preserved officially in formal law as well as in popular conception.[2] Criminal statutes are so stated as to imply that the duty of the police is to faithfully enforce all the laws, against everyone, in all circumstances, at all times. The common stereotype of the policeman is that of the ministerial officer whose function it is to detect crime, gather evidence, and make arrests. Police themselves tend to reinforce this conception by denying that decisions are involved in their work or that informal standards exist for making their decisions.

Full enforcement of criminal law, however, is not a realistic expectation. Numerous limitations and circumstances preclude the possibility of enforcing the law to the fullest extent. First, *procedural* restrictions prohibit the enforcement of the law beyond the lawful rights of the individual citizen. Second, *interpretational* latitude, resulting primarily from ambiguity in the wording of many statutes, permits considerable discretion as to what constitutes a criminal offense. Third, *technical* difficulties confound law enforcement, such as limitation of police time, personnel, and equipment in the detection and investigation of crime. Fourth, *organizational* demands of local police departments provide guides for both the enforcement and nonenforcement of criminal law. Fifth, *ideological* orientations or values of policemen provide a basis for selective law enforcement. Sixth,

---

[2] Joseph Goldstein, "Police Discretion Not to Invoke the Criminal Process: Low Visibility Decisions in the Administration of Justice," *Yale Law Journal*, 69 (March, 1960), pp. 543–594; Sanford H. Kadish, "Legal Norm and Discretion in the Police and Sentencing Processes," *Harvard Law Review*, 75 (March, 1962), pp. 904–931; Edward L. Barrett, Jr., "Police Practices and the Law— From Arrest to Release of Charge," *California Law Review*, 50 (March, 1962), pp. 11–55.

numerous *societal* pressures prevent full enforcement of some criminal laws. Included in this last category of reasons for partial enforcement are such factors as the lack of correspondence between particular criminal statutes and current norms, the failure of victims and the public to report offenses, and the harmful social consequences that might follow the enforcement of certain criminal laws. Whatever the reasons, law enforcement is a matter of decision-making. Discretion is the principal characteristic of law enforcement.

Police discretion rarely becomes known to the public. Most persons have little idea of the extent of discretionary decisions in law enforcement and little knowledge of the ways in which discretion operates. There is instead a generalized public feeling that since discretion involves personal decisions on the part of police, the operation of such discretion is totally improper in a democratic society. Solutions such as the following are currently being suggested in regard to the problem of the discretionary power of police:

> The first step is to elevate police discretion from the sub-rosa position it now occupies; the role of police as decision-makers must be expressly recognized. Then, as has been found possible with respect to other administrative agencies, the areas in which discretion properly may be exercised must be delimited, principles to govern its exercise must be established, and effective means of control must be discovered.[3]

No matter what solutions may be proposed and implemented, for our immediate purpose it is sufficient to recognize that discretion does exist and that it is basic to law enforcement. From a sociological standpoint, the purpose is to understand the operation of police discretion. At a crucial stage in the legal process persons are defined as criminal because police act in certain ways rather than in other ways.

LEGAL REGULATION OF LAW ENFORCEMENT

Law enforcement takes place within a tenuous framework of social control and legal regulation. The issue of the control of police prac-

---

[3] Wayne R. LaFave, "The Police and Nonenforcement of the Law," *Wisconsin Law Review,* 1962 (January–March, 1962), p. 239. Also see LaFave, *Arrest,* p. 153.

tices lays bare one of the fundamental problems of modern society: "A democracy, like all other societies, needs order and security, but it also and equally requires civil liberty. This complexity of need creates difficult theoretical and practical problems."[4] Any resolution of the conflicting demands of order and freedom can be, at best, one in which the demands are maintained in a state of tension.

The policeman is placed in the middle of the control-freedom dilemma. He is charged with the enforcement of a multitude of criminal laws and is at the same time expected to observe the rights of the individual. His decision to invoke the law is basically a decision to restrict the individual. Yet the policeman's function of control is itself regulated to ensure that the suspect receives his *legal* rights once his freedom has been restricted. That police are often charged with brutality and lawlessness reflects the difficulty of both attempting to control human conduct and providing for the protection of the rights of the individual.

Most of the law that regulates police behavior has developed from specific cases in which defendants have questioned the procedures used in their criminal convictions. Thus courts, in contrast to legislatures and executive agencies, have been the principal law-givers in the regulation of law enforcement. In recent years, primarily by default, the Supreme Court has sought to provide legal guarantees for the protection of the person against the actions of the state. Court rulings have been made in reference to a number of issues directly related to law enforcement. Decisions have been made in respect to such related matters as arrest warrants, search and seizure, interrogation, confessions, wiretapping and eavesdropping, the use of informers, and the right of counsel. As a result of the active role of the court in these matters the charge is being made that the courts are moving beyond their proper function. Courts are also being accused of laying down rules that impede law enforcement. The more enlightened criticism, however, would be that other lawmaking institutions are neglecting their function and, most of all, that the conduct of those who enforce the criminal law must be adequately regulated in a free society.[5]

---

[4] Jerome Hall, "Police and Law in Democratic Society," *Indiana Law Journal*, 28 (Winter, 1953), p. 162.

[5] See Herbert L. Packer, "Policing the Police," *The New Republic* (September 4, 1965), pp. 17–21.

The Supreme Court decisions on law enforcement are founded on three provisions of the Constitution. The Fourth Amendment provides: "The right of the people to be secure in their persons, houses, papers, and effects, against unreasonable searches and seizures, shall not be violated, and no warrants shall issue but upon probable cause, supported by oath or affirmation, and particularly describing the place to be searched, and the persons or things to be seized." The Fifth Amendment provides that "no person . . . shall be compelled in any criminal case to be a witness against himself, nor be deprived of life, liberty, or property, without due process of law." And the Fourteenth Amendment provides that "no state shall . . . deprive any person of life, liberty, or property without due process of law, nor deny to any person within its jurisdiction the equal protection of the laws." A number of Supreme Court decisions, particularly in recent years, have resulted from the review of criminal cases in which these constitutional guarantees have been jeopardized.[6]

One of the first constitutional tests of law enforcement practices confronted by the Supreme Court was in the *Weeks v. United States* case of 1914. In establishing the "exclusionary rule" in that case, the Court ruled that evidence obtained by illegal means must be excluded from criminal procedure. With the *McNabb v. United States* case in 1943 the Supreme Court ruled that confessions are inadmissible if obtained by federal officers during an unlawful detention. The Mc-Nabb decision was elaborated upon in 1957 in *Mallory v. United States*. The Court ruled in this case that confessions are inadmissible when they are obtained from an arrestee who has not been properly brought before a magistrate. In 1961 the Court ruled in *Mapp v. Ohio* that evidence obtained through unreasonable searches and seizures must be excluded from state and federal criminal trials. The *Gideon v. Wainwright* decision of 1963 ensured the right of counsel for defendants. The right of counsel was further specified in 1964 in

[6] Supreme Court decisions on law enforcement are discussed by, among others, Richard C. Donnelly, "Police Authority and Practices," *Annals of the American Academy of Political and Social Science,* 339 (January, 1962), pp. 90–110; David Robinson, Jr., "Massiah, Escobedo, and Rationales for the Exclusions of Confessions," *Journal of Criminal Law, Criminology and Police Science,* 56 (December, 1965), pp. 412–431; Bernard Weisberg, "Police Interrogation of Arrested Persons: A Skeptical View," *Journal of Criminal Law, Criminology and Police Science,* 52 (May–June, 1961), pp. 21–46; "A Symposium on the Supreme Court and the Police: 1966," *Journal of Criminal Law, Criminology and Police Science,* 57 (September, 1966), pp. 237–311.

Massiah v. United States and *Escobedo v. Illinois.* The decisions of
1964 provide that the accused in custody may not be questioned until the request for legal counsel has been complied with. Specific
guidelines for law enforcement and minimum procedural safeguards
were established in 1966 in *Miranda v. Arizona.* Cases such as these
will continue to be decided by the courts as the divergent values on
control and freedom continue to be defined and balanced. Moreover,
legislative action as well as decisions by the courts will add to the
controversial issues involved in the legal regulation of law enforcement.

Ultimately the regulation of law enforcement must come from
sources other than governmental agencies. In democratic society the
police themselves bear part of the responsibility for safeguarding the
rights of the citizen and at the same time maintaining peace and
order in the society. Police must develop a professional orientation
that is sensitive to individual rights. Efficient enforcement of the law
is not the sole end of the police function. Police are also responsible
for a humane law enforcement policy. An argument for the development of a *legal* professionalism among police has been strongly presented:

> The needed philosophy of professionalism must rest on a set
> of values conveying the idea that the police are as much an in-
> stitution dedicated to the achievement of legality in society as
> they are an official social organization designed to control mis-
> conduct through the invocation of punitive sanctions. The
> problem of police in a democratic society is not merely a mat-
> ter of obtaining newer police cars, a higher order technical
> equipment or of recruiting men who have to their credit more
> years of education. What must occur is a significant alteration
> in the ideology of police, so that police "professionalization"
> rests on the values of a democratic legal order, rather than on
> technological proficiency.[7]

LAW ENFORCEMENT SYSTEMS

Globally and historically law enforcement assumes numerous forms.
Even within some contemporary societies the forms of police sys-

---

[7] Jerome H. Skolnick, *Justice Without Trial: Law Enforcement in Democratic
Society* (New York: John Wiley and Sons, 1966), pp. 238–239.

tems are varied. One of the most important distinguishing characteristics of law enforcement systems is the degree to which they are
centralized within their respective states. With some obvious exceptions, democratic countries usually permit local autonomy in police
administration and authoritarian states tend to centralize police
control. England, Wales, and Scotland have scores of local police
forces. Belgium has dual police systems for the national and local
levels. In Denmark all police activities are administered by func-
tionaries of the crown. For the most part, European countries have
tended to follow the French pattern of a national police charged with
overall law enforcement, maintenance of public order, and investigation of major crimes. In such countries a branch of the national police
performs local duties, but routine matters are principally the responsibility of locally recruited forces. Law enforcement systems in the
United States and Canada, on the other hand, consist of parallel national, state, and local police forces.

The most centralized of law enforcement systems are those organized explicitly for the purpose of political control. Governments
which have maintained such systems have been known in their time
as "police states." Notable examples include the Nazi Gestapo, Mus-
solini's ORVA, and the Soviet Union's NKVD. The FBI in the
United States is actually maintained in part as a political police
force, enforcing laws on subversion, espionage, and sedition.

Outside of the FBI, and a number of federal quasi-judicial agencies
with law enforcement powers, the approach to law enforcement in the
United States has been to avoid a centralized police force. There
never has been a federal system for the control of local law enforcement. While the FBI suggests a uniform method for the reporting
of crime statistics, the control of police behavior is a matter of state
and local authority.

Although the British police system today is controlled to a considerable extent by the national government, whereas the American
system is locally autonomous, law enforcement in the United States
has its origins in English legal institutions. The organization of a
police force for the purpose of detecting and arresting law violators,
protecting the innocent, preventing crime, and maintaining order in
the community can be traced to the development of various kinds of
peace officers in England.[8] In early England, local citizens were mu-

---

[8] See Leon Rodzinowicz, *A History of English Criminal Law and Its Admin-*

tually responsible, through the "pledge" system, for the maintenance of law and order. Eventually local noblemen appointed constables to enforce the law. When the local areas, known as "hundreds," were grouped to form "shires," the office of the "shire-reeve" came into being. During the reign of Edward I (1272–1307) the first official police forces were established in the large towns of England. These "watch and ward" officers were charged with protecting property and arresting offenders between sunset and daybreak. In 1326 Edward II created the office of the justice of the peace to assist the sheriff in policing the country. The constable, however, remained the primary law enforcement officer in all the towns throughout England.

As long as England was a rural country the existing offices of law enforcement were adequate. But by the middle of the eighteenth century, with the growth of fairly large towns and cities, innovations in law enforcement were needed. One of the most important experiments in law enforcement was Henry Fielding's appointment of a foot patrol (later known as the "Bow Street Runners") in the Bow Street magistracy of London. However, such a small local force could not meet the law enforcement needs of the urban area. So critical had the situation become at the close of the eighteenth century that committees of the House of Commons called for a better system of protecting the public. Finally in the early years of the nineteenth century a committee of the Commons issued a report that investigated the increase in crime and urged a change in the method of policing the metropolis. Sir Robert Peel, the person responsible for the establishment of the committee, and Home Secretary, introduced a police reform bill which was passed by Parliament in 1829.[9] The Metropolitan Police Act of 1829 thus established for London a police force separate from the old constabulary system and served as the model for other cities in Great Britain.

The American colonies in the seventeenth and eighteenth centuries

istration from 1750 (London: Stevens & Sons, 1956), vols. 2 and 3; Alwyn Solmes, *The English Policeman 1871–1935* (London: George Allen & Unwin, 1935); William Alfred Morris, *The Medieval English Sheriff to 1300* (Manchester: University Press, 1927).

[9] J. L. Lymon, "The Metropolitan Police Act of 1829: An Analysis of Certain Events Influencing the Passage and Character of the Metropolitan Police Act in England," *Journal of Criminal Law, Criminology and Police Science,* 55 (March, 1964), pp. 141–154.

adopted the contemporary law enforcement offices of England.[10] American villages and rural areas had their night-watchmen, constables, sheriffs, and justices of the peace. Following the creation of police forces in the English cities in the early nineteenth century, American cities established their own forces. London's police plan was adopted by New York in 1844. During the next ten years similar police systems were organized in Chicago, Boston, and Philadelphia.[11] By the early 1900's most cities in the United States had unified police forces of their own.

Law enforcement in the United States today cannot be viewed as a single system. Although some 420,000 persons are employed in approximately 40,000 law enforcement agencies, the law enforcement duties vary considerably. There are at least five types of law enforcement systems in the United States, conforming roughly to the major levels of government: (1) the police agencies of the federal government; (2) the state police forces and criminal investigation agencies of the fifty states; (3) the sheriffs and deputy sheriffs in over 3,000 counties, plus a few county police forces which either duplicate the sheriffs' police jurisdiction or virtually displace it; (4) the police of a thousand cities and over 20,000 townships or New England towns, to which must be added an unknown number of magisterial districts and county districts in the south and west; and (5) the police of 15,000 villages, boroughs, and incorporated towns, together with a small number of forces serving public quasi-corporations and ad hoc districts.[12] These systems of law enforcement are interrelated in their functions and at times overlap in their jurisdictions.

Even within the various systems of law enforcement there are specific police agencies. On the federal level, for example, there are such agencies with law enforcement powers as the Federal Bureau of Investigation, the Secret Service, the Bureau of Narcotics, Post Office Inspectors, the Bureau of Internal Revenue, the Bureau of Customs,

[10] Cyrus Harreld Karreker, *The Seventeenth-Century Sheriff: A Comparative Study of the Sheriff in England and Chesapeake Colonies* (Chapel Hill: University of North Carolina Press, 1930); Julius Goebel and T. Raymond Naughton, *Law Enforcement in Colonial New York* (New York: The Commonwealth Fund, 1944).

[11] For a history of the evolution of the police force in Boston, see Roger Lane, *Policing the City: Boston, 1822–1885* (Cambridge: Harvard University Press, 1967).

[12] Bruce Smith, *Police Systems in the United States*, 2nd rev. ed. (New York: Harper, 1960).

the Immigration Border Patrol, and the Alcohol Tax Unit of the Department of the Treasury. In addition, the federal government maintains the United States Marshal as a law enforcement agent whose duty it is to preserve order in the courtroom, handle subpoena and summons, seize goods, transport prisoners, and serve as a disbursing officer.[13]

Law enforcement on the state level was not established in the United States until the first part of this century. In 1905 Pennsylvania organized the first state police force. By World War II, all states had their own police forces. Today the state police forces perform such varied functions as highway patrol, fire investigation, liquor inspection, juvenile offender arrest, and property inspection.[14] State police also provide a number of services to local police forces, including criminal identification, laboratory services, and communication services.

Outside the framework of civil law enforcement is a type of law enforcement usually obscured from public view: the *private police*. Private police agencies, such as Pinkerton's National Detective Agency, came into being in the middle of the last century when private companies desired protection that could not be afforded them by civil police. Railroads, coal companies, and iron ore companies in particular employed their own police forces to control theft and robbery, and in some cases to prevent and break strikes of workers against the companies.[15] Today private police are employed by numerous kinds of businesses, industries, and institutions. They are used by firms to guard property, apprehend thieves, investigate offenses, and to detect fraud and embezzlement. Several hundred national and local agencies are engaged in the private enforcement of criminal law. Although private police do not usually make arrests, suspects they apprehend may be turned over to civil police for official arrest and prosecution.

The discussion of law enforcement in this chapter will be devoted principally to civil law enforcement on the local level. Not only has

[13] Rita W. Cooley, "The Office of United States Marshal," *Western Political Quarterly,* 12 (March, 1959), pp. 123–140.

[14] Jack J. Preiss and Howard J. Ehrlich, *An Examination of Role Theory: The Case of the State Police* (Lincoln: University of Nebraska Press, 1966).

[15] J. P. Shalloo, *Private Police: With Special Reference to Pennsylvania* (Philadelphia: American Academy of Political and Social Science, Monograph No. 1, 1933).

most sociological research been concentrated on *local police activity*, but the majority of persons defined as criminal receive their special status from the police of the villages, towns, and cities. The principal imposers of criminal definitions at the law enforcement stage of the legal process are the police of local communities.

COMMUNITY CONTEXT OF
LAW ENFORCEMENT

In a sense there are as many systems of law enforcement as there are communities. Each police department must operate within a community. To a considerable degree, then, the differences in law enforcement can be attributed to the concrete social setting in which police operate.

The role of the police in the community in relation to the duties of law enforcement has always been the source of a major dilemma. The dilemma is brought on by the issue of whether the police are to be involved in community affairs, or whether they are to be isolated from the community. Too much involvement might negate the possibilities of fulfilling the ideal of fair and impartial handling of cases, while too much isolation removes the police from an understanding of the needs of the community. A delicate balance of the alternatives is all that can be expected at best.

Certain natural forces, because of the requirements of law enforcement, contribute to the isolation of the police in any community.[16] Much of police activity involves intrusion into the private interests of the citizen. To separate from one's daily life those who are charged with the detection and arrest of one's person is a rather logical reaction to the police. This reaction is reinforced by the traditional public conception of fear and mistrust of the police. The police, in addition, provide the public with a constant reminder of the deviant aspects of human behavior. The actions of the police represent the social sanctions and degradations that may be a consequence of deviation within the community.

One other factor that tends to isolate the police is found in the organization and procedure of police work itself. The requirements

[16] John P. Clark, "Isolation of the Police: A Comparison of the British and American Situations," *Journal of Criminal Law, Criminology and Police Science,* 56 (September, 1965), pp. 307–319.

of patrol, investigation, surveillance, and the like necessitate a clear-cut separation of the police from the public in order that the functions may be fulfilled. Most of the operating policies of the police are beyond public scrutiny; that is, they are secretive and known only to the police themselves. Some forced community isolation seems necessary, because of what is expected of the police.

To view police activity solely from the standpoint of law enforcement is perhaps to miss the crux of the role of the police in the community. It may be argued that the principal function of the police is to promote peace in the community.[17] All communities operate and survive through the resolution of internal tension and conflicts. The police serve as one of the agencies that assist in maintaining some community integration and order. Through their various activities, the police bring discipline to personal disputes that arise from more basic value conflicts in the various parts of the community.

Thus, in his day-to-day activity, the policeman is both a "law officer" and a "peace officer." In a sense, however, the two functions cannot be separated. The policeman in his attempt to maintain peace in the community decides whether or not to invoke the law on the basis of the actual situation.[18] In some situations "peace keeping" may best be achieved by not making an arrest. In others an arrest may appear to be the most appropriate means of maintaining order in the community.

In part, maintaining peace in the community involves giving support to some members of the community. Many disputes that arise require human support. Even in controlling one member of the community, the policeman may be lending support to another. The supportive role of the police has been documented in a study of the calls received at the desk of a metropolitan police department.[19] In an analysis of the telephone calls, it was found that nearly half of the calls were requests for support of some kind. The calls for support were concerned with personal problems and consisted of requests for

[17] Michael Banton, *The Policeman in the Community* (London: Tavistock, 1964), p. 127.

[18] Egon Bittner, "The Police on Skid-Row: A Study of Peace Keeping," *American Sociological Review*, 2 (October, 1967), pp. 699–715. Also see James Q. Wilson, *Varieties of Police Behavior* (Cambridge: Harvard University Press, 1968), pp. 16–56.

[19] Elaine Cumming, Ian Cumming, and Laura Edell, "Policeman as Philosopher, Guide and Friend," *Social Problems*, 12 (Winter, 1965), pp. 276–286.

health services (such as ambulance escorts, investigation of accidents, suicide attempts), children's problems (complaints about trespassing or destructive behavior), and the behavior of incapacitated persons. Other calls consisted of requests for assistance regarding personal disputes and quarrels, violence or protection from potential violence, and requests for assistance regarding missing persons and the behavior of youths. The policeman thus performs many actions that are not directly related to enforcement of the law per se, but are instead supportive of other aspects of the welfare of the community.

One of the most important sources of variation in the actions of police is found in the *expectations* of law enforcement in different kinds of communities. First, communities differ from one another in regard to the kinds of behavior that should receive criminal sanction. The correspondence between the criminal law and what is actually condemned may vary considerably from one community to another. Within one community, or a segment of a community, arrest of a violent spouse may be expected, while such an arrest would be entirely inappropriate in another community or segment. Second, communities differ in their norms on the seeking of assistance from the police. While one community may prescribe that complaints be made to the police, another may restrict the citizen's use of the police. Third, community attitudes toward the police vary considerably. In the villages of Great Britain the policeman is perceived as an individual known for his personal characteristics.[20] On the other hand, in the bigger towns policemen are seen more as members of a social category. Also, in some British working class neighborhoods the police are identified with the propertied classes and are at times viewed as enemies. These feelings appear to be even more marked in the industrial regions of the west of Scotland. Such community variations in attitudes toward the police have their effect both upon the use of the police by community members and upon the way in which police respond to situations in which law breaking may be involved.

Perhaps the most significant characteristic that accounts for community differences in law enforcement is the extent to which the community is homogeneous in such matters as cultural values, social class, race, and occupation. A homogeneous community tends to have fairly well defined expectations in regard to appropriate community

[20] Banton, *The Policeman in the Community*, p. 210.

behavior. The consequence for law enforcement is that the police in a homogeneous community operate as an integral part of the community, enforcement of the law being guided by the way such enforcement relates to the order of the community.

In a heterogeneous community, in comparison, the police must operate more by the formal law than by community expectations. The police in a homogeneous community may detect more law violations than those in a heterogeneous community, but the police in a homogeneous community handle the cases informally rather than through the formality of an arrest. Furthermore, in a homogeneous community, violators of the law may be referred back to the community for disposition rather than to the legal process. Invocation of the law may be the only means of maintaining order in the heterogeneous community. Thus, in the homogeneous community a wide scope of law-violating behavior is handled informally by the police, while in the heterogeneous community criminal sanctions are more readily applied to the same behaviors.

The relationship between community homogeneity and law enforcement is found in a study of the handling of juvenile cases by police in four different communities in the Pittsburgh area.[21] The research consisted of an investigation of the differential selection by the police of juvenile offenders for court appearance. It was found that there were clear differences in the rates of juvenile arrests and court referrals between the four different kinds of communities. The large industrial community ("Steel City") had a juvenile arrest rate of 37.3 per 1,000 juvenile population, in comparison to a rate of 12.4 in the residential and commercial community ("Trade City"), 34.8 in the small industrial community ("Mill Town"), and 49.7 in the well-to-do residential community ("Manor Heights"). Through the further analysis of police records and a series of interviews with police, Goldman concluded that there were indeed community differentials in the handling of juvenile cases by the police.

Several patterns of handling cases of juvenile offenders in the four communities were distinguished in the above research. The patterns appeared to be a function of the relations between the police and the community. In general, the police attempted in each community to

[21] Nathan Goldman, *The Differential Selection of Juvenile Offenders for Court Appearance* (New York: National Council on Crime and Delinquency, 1963).

reflect what they considered to be the attitudes of the community toward delinquency. Differentials in arrests according to the type of relation between the police and the community were summarized as follows: (1) "Where there exists an objective, impersonal relation between the police and the public, court referral rates will be high and there will be little discrimination with respect to seriousness of offense, race, and sex of the offender"; (2) "Where there exists a personal face-to-face relation between the police and the public, there will be more discriminations with respect to court referral of an arrested juvenile."[22] The research thus showed that law enforcement is associated with the role of the police in the specific community. Differences in the relation between the community and the police explain some of the differences in law enforcement from one community to another.

Law enforcement in rural areas seems to be especially affected by the expectations of the community and the role of law enforcement officers in the community. A study of the social role of the county sheriff has documented the nature of law enforcement in a rural area.[23] In "Star County," in southern Illinois, the sheriff was permitted (or expected) to use a great amount of discretion in law enforcement. His primary function was to conserve the peace, and peace was not always best preserved by the making of an arrest. The rule of thumb in enforcement was the principle of public safety. The conclusion that may be drawn is that a community organized on informal relations resorts to official sanctions only when other means are exhausted or are for some reason inappropriate. In rural communities, whenever possible, informal controls tend to be used in place of law enforcement. Or, law enforcement in rural communities takes place with a maximum of discretion.

In the final analysis, no matter how the community is organized, the police attempt to accomplish their job within the context of their community. This means that the police tend to select law violators not according to legal prescriptions alone but also according to how closely enforcement approximates the expectations of the commu-

[22] Goldman, *The Differential Selection of Juvenile Offenders for Court Appearance*, p. 129.

[23] T. C. Esselstyn, "The Social Role of the County Sheriff," *Journal of Criminal Law, Criminology and Police Science*, 44 (July–August, 1953), pp. 177–184.

nity.[24] Although some isolation between police and community is inevitable, the police would rather avoid public criticism and gain local acceptance. The handling of cases, the defining of persons as criminal, is more a matter of informal community relations than it is the following of abstract principles of law enforcement.

POLICE ORGANIZATION AND
LAW ENFORCEMENT

The behavior of the police is greatly influenced by the organization of police departments. The application of criminal definitions in law enforcement takes place within the context of locally organized police forces. Organizational considerations are, therefore, always involved when a decision is made to enforce the criminal law.

One of the most significant organizational aspects of law enforcement is the bureaucratization of the police.[25] The bureaucratic, and quasi-military, organization of the police is characterized by a system of subordination and by a chain of command. However, although still bureaucratic, modernized police departments tend to be organized according to a centralized command system. The communications center, as the core of the modern metropolitan police department, provides the principal source of organizational structure. That is, each police department is divided into a number of separate units. These units differ from one another in the specialized occupational roles they incorporate, and are necessary because of the variety of cases dealt with by the police.

The functional divisions of police departments have been divided according to the different kinds of activities handled by the police: (1) traffic patrol and other patrol of structural disorder, involving enforcement of regulations which do not entail the moral turpitude of those who break the law; (2) street patrol (including radio cars), especially in downtown areas, to control individual offenses in public places; (3) investigative work, generally involving complaints; (4) undercover work, in which fraud is used to get inside situations

[24] William J. Chambliss and John T. Liell, "The Legal Process in the Community Setting," *Crime and Delinquency*, 12 (October, 1966), pp. 310–317.

[25] David J. Bordua and Albert J. Reiss, Jr., "Command, Control and Charisma: Reflections on Police Bureaucracy," *American Journal of Sociology*, 72 (July, 1966), pp. 68–76.

otherwise protected by the institutions of privacy; and (5) quasi-military action, in which the problem is to apply coercion to control public riot.[26] The implication of the differentiated structure within police departments is that the criminal law is selectively enforced according to the organization and normative expectations of the separate units within the police department. Each division develops and perpetuates its own unique system of law enforcement.

The "effectiveness" of the police in enforcing the law corresponds closely to the organization of police departments.[27] As documented in a study of a non-professionalized police department in an east coast city and a professionalized police department in a west coast city, the arrest rates reflect the nature of the organization of police departments.[28] Wilson found that in the non-professionalized department the members had no strong sense of urgency about police work and, hence, there were low rates of official actions with regard to offenders. In the professionalized department, however, infractions of the law were more likely to be detected and offenders were more likely to be arrested, producing a higher crime rate in the city with the professionalized police force.

The extent to which police organization and procedure can affect the rate of reported crime is also illustrated in the yearly change of crime rates within particular cities. The annual fluctuations are at times an obvious result of changes in law enforcement policy. For various reasons policy changes occur within police departments in such matters as the recording of crime. In the course of organizational change in the New York City Police Department in 1966, it was decided to change the procedure of recording crime statistics. The newly appointed Chief Inspector suggested that under the old system of recording a great number of offenses either went unrecorded or were "downgraded" in the official reports. He estimated that roughly 60 per cent of the complaints involving burglary had in the previous year been officially recorded as lesser crimes, such as

[26] Arthur L. Stinchcombe, "Institutions of Privacy in the Determination of Police Administrative Practice," *American Journal of Sociology,* 69 (September, 1963), pp. 158–159.

[27] Robert Edward Mitchell, "Organization as a Key to Police Effectiveness," *Crime and Delinquency,* 12 (October, 1966), pp. 344–353.

[28] James Q. Wilson, "The Police and the Delinquent in Two Cities," in Stanton Wheeler (ed.), *Controlling Delinquents* (New York: John Wiley, 1968), pp. 9–30; also see Wilson, *Varieties of Police Behavior,* pp. 83–139.

petty larceny, or had been given a non-criminal label, such as lost property. In order "to insure factual recording of crime statistics," the Inspector ordered that "there should be no discretion with regard to reporting a crime and no ambiguity with regard to categorizing a crime."[29] Needless to say, the burglary rate the following year climbed considerably. A new policy had been established in regard to imposing and recording criminal definitions by the police.

POLICE IDEOLOGY AND LAW ENFORCEMENT

As a result both of the role played by the police in society and the organization that comes into being in relation to that role, a special occupational ideology develops among the police:

> The policeman finds his most pressing problem in his relationships to the public. His is a service occupation but of an incongruous kind, since he must discipline those whom he serves. He is regarded as corrupt and inefficient by, and meets with hostility and criticism from, the public. He regards the public as his enemy, feels his occupation to be in conflict with the community, and regards himself to be a pariah. The experience and the feeling give rise to a collective emphasis on secrecy, an attempt to coerce respect from the public, and a belief that almost any means are legitimate in completing an important arrest. These are for the policeman basic occupational values. They arise from his experience, take precedence over his legal responsibilities, are central to an understanding of his conduct, and form the occupational concepts within which violence gains its meaning.[30]

Each policeman learns to behave appropriately according to the ideology of his occupation. During his training, the recruit gradually adopts an outlook on his work and a justification for using certain procedures and methods in the line of "duty." Furthermore, socialization of police recruits into the occupation is affected to some extent by their backgrounds. A study of the training of policemen for entry into the New York City Police Department found that police candidates tend to be drawn primarily from the lower middle class

[29] *The New York Times,* March 15, 1966, pp. 1 and 26.
[30] William A. Westley, "Violence and the Police," *American Journal of Sociology,* 59 (July, 1953), p. 35.

segment of the population.[31] The recruits considered their new source of employment to be an upward step, but at the same time were convinced that police work, in relation to other occupations, was not assigned high prestige by the general population. Because of backgrounds similar in socioeconomic status and career expectations, the recruits adapted similarly to their training. They eventually displayed, in particular, a common lack of ability to handle enforcement situations impersonally. In addition, the recruits shared the belief, which increased during their training, that the police lack the basic legal authority to effectively carry out their work.

Upon completion of academy training and assignment to a local precinct, the police rookie is called upon to face the challenge of actual duty. "His reputation is made in the next few weeks and will shadow him for the rest of his police career: no matter where or when he is transferred, a phone call will precede his arrival, reporting the evaluation that was made of his handling of his first few important cases."[32] The principal challenge to the new patrolman is the dilemma of choosing between the professional ideal of police work learned in the academy and the pragmatic approach of the precinct. The "lock-them-up" philosophy of the precinct contradicts the professional orientation toward police work learned in the academy.

> In the case of the young policeman the choice between professionalism and pragmatism is apt to depend largely on the circumstances of the case. It is, for example, no great feat for a policeman working in an upper-class neighborhood to protect the rights of his white clientele. It is much more difficult in a lower-class community. In a slum area the professional ethic loses most of the time; the civil rights of lower-class individuals do not count as much as the necessity to accomplish a staggering amount of police work as expeditiously as possible. Shifting from idealism to pragmatism, the newcomer to a lower-class precinct house enters a new reference group whose members are a little contemptuous of all the Academy represents.[33]

[31] John H. McNamara, "Uncertainties in Police Work: the Relevance of Police Recruits' Backgrounds and Training," in David J. Bordua (ed.), *The Police: Six Sociological Essays* (New York: John Wiley, 1967), pp. 163–252.

[32] Arthur Niederhoffer, *Behind the Shield: The Police in Urban Society* (Garden City, N.Y.: Doubleday, 1967), p. 52.

[33] *Ibid.*, p. 54.

It becomes obvious to the new policeman that every law on the book cannot be enforced. The rookie realizes as well that the laws are, in fact, to be enforced with considerable discretion according to the norms of his department and neighborhood.

The occupational ideology learned by the policeman is closely related to two characteristics of his day-to-day work: danger and authority. These two characteristics can lead to a description of the "working personality" of the policeman:

> The element of danger seems to make the policeman especially attentive to signs indicating a potential for violence and law-breaking. As a result, the policeman is generally a "suspicious" person. Furthermore, the character of the policeman's work makes him less desirable as a friend, since norms of friendship implicate others in his work. Accordingly, the element of danger isolates the policeman socially from that segment of the citizenry which he regards as symbolically dangerous and also from the conventional citizenry with whom he identifies.
>
> The element of authority reinforces the element of danger in isolating the policeman. Typically, the policeman is required to enforce law representing puritanical morality, such as those prohibiting drunkenness, and also laws regulating the flow of public activity, such as traffic laws. In these situations the policeman directs the citizenry, whose typical response denies recognition of his authority, and stressed his obligation to danger. The kind of man who responds well to danger, however, does not normally subscribe to codes of puritanical morality. As a result, the policeman is unusually liable to the charge of hypocrisy. That the whole civilian world is an audience for the policeman further promotes police isolation and, in consequence, solidarity. Finally, danger undermines the judicious use of authority.[34]

The combination of danger and authority in police work frustrates any possibility of procedural regularity in law enforcement.

Through socialization and experience within the occupation, the policeman develops other personal attributes. As shown in a study of policemen in the New York City Police Department, policemen after appointment to the force tend to become cynical. "When they succumb, they lose faith in people, society, and eventually in themselves.

[34] Skolnick, *Justice Without Trial*, p. 44.

In their Hobbesian view the world becomes a jungle in which crime, corruption, and brutality are normal features of the terrain."[35] Cynicism is part of the occupational ideology of the police and is learned in the course of socialization into the occupation. Furthermore, the policeman, in addition to becoming cynical, tends to acquire an authoritarian personality during his police career. "The police occupational system is geared to manufacture the 'take charge guy,' and it succeeds in doing so with outstanding efficiency. It is the police system, not the personality of the candidate, that is the more powerful determinant of behavior and ideology."[36]

The occupational ideology of the police ultimately affects the defining of persons as criminal. While the activities of the police are governed officially by procedural law, their actual behavior conforms to their own occupational code. The policeman's view of the effect of the exclusionary rule, for example, is not that the rule has guaranteed greater protection of freedom for the citizen, but rather that it has unnecessarily complicated the task of detecting and apprehending criminals.[37] Similarly, many practices of the police are in opposition to the guarantee of due process. Actual police practices are minimally affected by legalistic considerations:

> When he (the policeman) sees a black girl and a white serviceman enter a hotel together, he assumes an act of prostitution is in the offing. To him, these are not constitutionally protected citizens, but predictable actors whose misbehavior he usually judges correctly. Sometimes, to be sure, he may be in error. The probabilities, however, are so strong, he feels, that his judgment is rarely going to be wrong.[38]

For the policeman, "due process of law is, therefore, not merely a set of constitutional guarantees for the defendant, but also a set of working conditions which, under increasingly liberal opinions by the courts, are likewise becoming increasingly arduous."[39]

Thus, because of the particular role of the police in society, specific kinds of occupational values exist among the police. As part of the occupational structure, they provide the rationale for the use of

[35] Niederhoffer, *Behind the Shield,* p. 9.
[36] *Ibid.,* p. 151.
[37] Skolnick, *Justice Without Trial,* pp. 211–219.
[38] *Ibid.,* p. 202.
[39] *Ibid.,* p. 202.

harsh and oftentimes illegal methods by the police.[40] Furthermore, and with justification, the police believe that the public supports their use of such methods. The public, especially in the United States, provides the police with an implicit directive on the use of violence and other expedient methods to accomplish police goals. It may be the fate of democratic society that harsh and illegal law enforcement practices will always be supported by the public belief in submission to popular sovereignty.

THE ENCOUNTER BETWEEN POLICE AND CITIZENS

The making of an arrest takes place within a complex of social relations and personal perceptions. That which is defined as criminal is not so much behavior in obvious violation of a specific criminal law as it is a definition of circumstances that occur in the encounter between interacting parties in a concrete situation. In few cases of law enforcement is there clear evidence that a particular person is the "criminal." Usually it is only in the totality of the encounter that a decision is made to apply the label "criminal" to a person and his behavior.

The encounter can take place only when the police have been mobilized. The police tend to be mobilized through the actions of private citizens, rather than through police initiative. Thus the police may be mobilized in several ways:

> Police departments refer to incidents or complaints that originate by mobilizing police units through the communication center as *"calls-for-service," "dispatches,"* or *"runs,"* the first term referring to the citizen's call or complaint and the latter terms to the fact that a mobile unit is radio-dispatched to take the complaint. A request for police action made by a citizen personally appearing at the police station is referred to as a *"sta-*

---

[40] Albert J. Reiss, Jr., "Police Brutality — Answers to Key Questions," *Trans-Action,* 5 (July–August, 1968), pp. 10–19; Ellwyn R. Stoddard, "The Informal 'Code' of Police Deviancy: A Group Approach to 'Blue-Coat Crime'," *Journal of Criminal Law, Criminology and Police Science,* 59 (June, 1968), pp. 201–213. Police misconduct and brutality are documented in David Burnham, "Misconduct Laid to 27% of Police in 3 Cities' Slums," *The New York Times,* July 5, 1968, pp. 1 and 28; David Burnham, "Police Violence: A Changing Pattern," *The New York Times,* July 7, 1968, pp. 1 and 34.

tion complaint" or a *"citizen station mobilization."* All incidents arising in a field setting are commonly referred to as *"on-view"* incidents, but a distinction can be made among them. A direct, in-the-field, citizen request for police action, usually by flagging a patrol car or a call to an officer on the beat, is sometimes referred to as a *"field complaint"* or a *"citizen field mobilization."* When an officer initiates contact and reports on an incident that occurs in his presence, it is referred to as an *"on-view"* mobilization. Any law violation occurring in an officer's presence that leads to an arrest with the officer as complainant is an *"on-view arrest."*[41]

In respect to these types of police mobilization, it was found in a study of 5,360 mobilization situations in Boston, Chicago, and Washington, D.C., that 81 per cent of the mobilizations were dispatches, 14 per cent were on-views; and the remaining 5 per cent were citizen field mobilization. Most important, nearly three-quarters of the mobilizations consisted of some kind of police-citizen interaction.[42] In a great majority of cases, then, the police are involved in criminal defining situations because of the reporting of offenses by citizens.

The encounter of police and citizens in a situation that may potentially be defined as criminal involves playing a number of social roles. In addition to the policeman, eight citizen roles may be distinguished in the encounter: complainant, member of complainant group, offender, member of offender group, victim, member of victim group, informant, and bystander.

> A *complainant* is a person who wants police action in response to what he sees as an "offense" of some kind; e.g., a man whose car has been stolen or a woman who complains about a noisy party is a complainant. A *member of a complainant* group is a person who supports or stands with the central complainant. An *offender* is either a person who is seen or treated as a possible violator of the law or as a person who is not fulfilling role obligations or expectations that the complainant regards as "legal."

---

[41] Donald J. Black and Albert J. Reiss, Jr., "Patterns of Behavior in Police and Citizen Transactions," in the President's Commission on Law Enforcement and Administration of Justice, *Studies in Crime and Law Enforcement in Major Metropolitan Areas*, vol. 2, Field Surveys III (Washington, D.C.: U.S. Government Printing Office, 1967), pp. 4–5.

[42] Black and Reiss, "Patterns of Behavior in Police and Citizen Transactions," p. 17.

The first kind of offender is represented by a person accused of a larceny, the second by a man whose wife thinks he has been negligent in fulfilling his obligations as husband or head of the household. A *member of an offender group* is a person who supports or stands with the offender. A citizen is called a *victim* who needs or requests help or a service from the police in a situation that does not involve an "offense" or possible criminal violation of any kind, e.g., a sick or accidentally injured person. A *member of a victim group* is a person who supports or is behaviorally concerned about a victim. The *informant* is a participant who gives information relative to the nature of any situation or incident but who does not support or stand with any of the more involved participants; he is, however, more than a mere guide or person who gives information only about the location of a situation. The *bystander* is nothing more than an onlooker.[43]

The outcome of the playing of these roles may be a criminal arrest.

Of the various social roles involved in the situations that may become defined as criminal, the most important are those of the policeman, the suspect, and the victim. The role of the victim in the creation of crime is not only in being the object of an offense. The *victim*, for the purpose of an arrest, may be the only person who is able to report the offense to the police. It was found in the studies for the President's Commission on Law Enforcement and Administration of Justice that in only about half the cases of victimization did the victim report the offense to the police.[44] The tendency to report or not to report varied, of course, according to the type of offense and the characteristics of the victim. But in general, victims did not report offenses to the police for several reasons. The most frequently cited reason was a resigned belief that the police could not do anything about the incident, would not catch the offender, or would not want to be bothered. Many other nonreporting victims believed that the incident was not a police matter. These victims either did not want the offender to be known to the police or thought that the incident was a private affair. Other victims simply did not want to get in-

[43] *Ibid.*, pp. 53–54.

[44] Philip H. Ennis, *Criminal Victimization in the United States: A Report of a National Survey*, President's Commission on Law Enforcement and Administration of Justice, Field Surveys II (Washington, D.C.: U.S. Government Printing Office, 1967), pp. 41–51.

volved with the police. They did not want to take the time or the trouble to report the offense. Still other victims were afraid of possible reprisal from the offender and his friends or some other kind of loss. Finally, some did not notify the police because of their own uncertainty of what ought to be done. It is not always clear whether a criminal offense has been committed or what is the proper procedure for reporting an offense. For all these reasons, possible criminal defining situations do not come to the attention of the police.

The ultimate encounter that may lead to a criminal definition is between the *policeman* and the *suspect*. The possible encounter is guided by a conflict of two opposing interests: (1) those of a person who wants to carry out certain behaviors (some of which may conceivably be in violation of the criminal law), and (2) those of the policeman who wants to prevent criminal violations and apprehend criminals. These opposing interests are responsible for the development of sets of strategies by both parties.[45] The strategies are formulated on the basis of what the one party expects of the other. Each attempts to predict the behavior of the other, at the same time attempting to reduce the opponent's ability to predict his own moves.

Once the encounter has taken place, the conflicting interests of the policeman and the suspect continue to be important in the relationship. The concern now, however, becomes not the matter of whether the two parties are to have a face-to-face encounter, but how that encounter will be conducted. It is during this confrontation that the policeman makes the decision on whether or not to impose a criminal definition through the act of arrest.

Many factors beyond the principal reason for the encounter between the policeman and the suspect enter into the arrest decision. The policeman, using a *probabilistic* model of law enforcement, looks for personal characteristics that may be indicative of criminal behavior. The outward appearance and demeanor of the suspect are obviously of interest to him in a possible arrest situation. A study of the disposition of juvenile cases showed that the decision of whether or not to bring a boy to the station — and the decision made at the station — "were based largely on cues from which the officer

---

[45] The game-like conception of police-suspect relations is found in Dean R. Smith, "Random Patrol: An Application of Game Theory to Police Problems," *Journal of Criminal Law, Criminology and Police Science,* 53 (June, 1962), pp. 258–263.

inferred the youth's character."[46] The cues included the youth's group affiliations, age, race, grooming, and dress. Members of known delinquent gangs, older boys, Negroes, and youths with well-oiled hair, black jackets, and soiled denims or jeans tended to receive the more serious dispositions.

But the most important cue found to be used by the police in handling juveniles was a youth's demeanor. The patrolmen themselves stated that the demeanor of apprehended juveniles was the major determinant of their decisions for 50 to 60 per cent of the cases they processed. Youths who were perceived by the police as being uncooperative were more likely to be dealt with severely than youths who were perceived as being cooperative. The researchers made the following conclusion on the demeanor of juveniles and the decisions of the police:

> The cues used by police to assess demeanor were fairly simple. Juveniles who were contrite about their infractions, respectful to officers, and fearful of the sanctions that might be employed against them tended to be viewed by patrolmen as basically law-abiding or at least "salvageable." For these youths it was usually assumed that informal or formal reprimand would suffice to guarantee their future conformity. In contrast, youthful offenders who were fractious, obdurate, or who appeared nonchalant in their encounters with patrolmen were likely to be viewed as "would-be tough guys" or "punks" who fully deserved the most severe sanction: arrest.[47]

The policeman, then, uses various symbols and behavioral cues in applying criminal definitions. The policeman maintains an image of the kind of person who is a "troublemaker" or who is likely to be a law-breaker. When the suspect lives up to this expectation, he increases the possibility of his own arrest. Furthermore, the attitude the person assumes in his relation with the policeman has consequences for the outcome of the encounter. Persons who behave antagonistically toward the police are more likely to be treated in a hostile, authoritarian, or belittling manner by the police than are other citizens.[48] The encounter between police and citizen is, indeed,

[46] Irving Piliavin and Scott Briar, "Police Encounters with Juveniles," *American Journal of Sociology,* 70 (September, 1964), p. 210.

[47] Piliavin and Briar, "Police Encounters with Juveniles," pp. 210–211.

[48] Black and Reiss, "Patterns of Behavior in Police and Citizen Transactions," pp. 33–37.

a crucial moment of interaction and assessment. Both parties are involved in jockeying for their personal fates. The result of the encounter may be the creation of a crime.

THE OFFENSE SITUATION AND SELECTIVE LAW ENFORCEMENT

The encounter of policeman and citizen takes place in a specific offense situation. The outcome is affected not only by the interactions, perceptions, and reactions of the parties, but also by the larger setting of the encounter. Offense situations may thus vary in such matters as the racial context, the objectives of the police and community in the enforcement of certain laws, and the nature of the offense. Differences in law enforcement can be affected by variations in these situations.

The Racial Context of Arrest. Considerable evidence suggests that the police have long had differential arrest policies in regard to race.[49] It is apparent that police have tended to arrest Negroes on slight evidence in comparison to the amount of evidence required to arrest whites. Furthermore, Negroes have been exposed more than others to the misuses of police power. The attitudes and policies of the police in regard to race were dramatically described by a police captain some time ago, in a Southern town, when he told a writer: "In this town there are three classes of homicide. If a nigger kills a white man, that's murder. If a white man kills a nigger, that's justifiable homicide. If a nigger kills a nigger, that's one less nigger."[50]

Official police statistics reveal that Negroes are arrested between three and four times more frequently than whites.[51] While Negroes comprise about one-tenth of the population, they constitute nearly one-third of the persons arrested for all offenses. From such figures as these it is obvious that the status of being Negro entails a greater risk of being arrested than does the status of being white. The differences in arrest rates are not, however, due entirely to the fact that

---

[49] See Guy B. Johnson, "The Negro and Crime," *Annals of the American Academy of Political and Social Science*, 271 (September, 1941), pp. 93–104.

[50] Cited in Banton, *The Policeman in the Community*, p. 173.

[51] See the discussion on Negro crime rates in Margin E. Wolfgang, *Crime and Race: Conceptions and Misconceptions* (New York: Institute of Human Relations Press, 1964).

Negroes may be involved more than whites in law-violating behavior, but that in similar situations Negroes are more likely than whites to be apprehended.

Selective enforcement according to racial factors results in part from long-held prejudices of individual policemen.[52] But also important is the fact that the Negro tends to fit the stereotype that police have of the criminal.[53] Through the use of certain cues, a probabilistic model of law violation, and their past experiences, the police are more likely to arrest the Negro than the white man in a similar offense situation. The extent to which police use a Negro image of the offender was shown in a survey of police officers in Philadelphia: 75 per cent of the policemen overestimated the percentage of arrests involving Negroes made in the districts to which they were assigned.[54] With such conceptions of events and offenders, a differential in law enforcement according to the racial context of the situation is to be expected.

Police and Community Objectives in the Arrest Situation. In order to accomplish certain objectives, possibly known only to the police and various community members, an arrest may be made. The situation may be such that an arrest may solve a problem that seemingly could not be resolved in any other fashion. A policeman might arrest a person who ordinarily would not be arrested in order to maintain respect for the police system.

> A police patrol stopped a car that had been traveling at 39 m.p.h. in a 30 m.p.h. zone. They decided prior to leaving the squad car that they would only issue a warning. When the deputies approached, the driver said in a sarcastic tone, "What in hell have I done now?" Because of his belligerent attitude the driver was placed under arrest.[55]

Another instance of the use of arrest to accomplish extralegal objectives is in the arrest of a person in order to maintain an image of

[52] For documentation of anti-Negro attitudes among police, according to race of police and racial composition of the police precinct, see Black and Reiss, "Patterns of Behavior in Police and Citizen Transactions," pp. 132–139.

[53] Piliavin and Briar, "Police Encounters with Juveniles," pp. 212–213.

[54] William M. Kephart, *Racial Factors and Urban Law Enforcement* (Philadelphia: University of Pennsylvania Press, 1957), pp. 88–93.

[55] LaFave, *Arrest*, p. 146.

full enforcement. This form of arrest often occurs when an offense not usually handled by arrest comes to public attention:

> The police were aware of the operation of a private card game in which there was no house "cut." Since this operation therefore qualified as mere social gambling, no action was taken against the offenders. However, the operators of the game made no attempt to conceal the operation, and it was soon apparent to the general public that the police must be aware of it. Realizing this, the police arrested the gamblers.[56]

Once an offense is widely publicized, an arrest becomes imminent.

An arrest may on occasion be made in order to detain or punish a person suspected of other criminal activity.

> The police learned of a minor property theft. As the victim was not interested in prosecution, the police, in accord with their usual policy, decided not to arrest. However, when they learned that the offender was known to the police department as a "bad actor," and that the police had been unsuccessful in obtaining his conviction for other, more serious offenses, they arrested him.[57]

In addition, an arrest may be made for a minor offense when the police suspect that a person is responsible for a relatively serious offense, but they need more time to gather sufficient evidence in order to successfully prosecute the case.

> Officers had reasonable grounds to believe that a particular man was responsible for a recent homicide. However, desiring an opportunity to conduct a prolonged in-custody investigation, they arrested him on a vagrancy charge. He was then convicted for vagrancy, and the murder investigation was continued while he served his sentence.[58]

In some situations offenders may be arrested to ensure their own safety. The drunk, in particular, may be arrested in order to protect him from the cold, because he has injured himself, or because he is likely to become a criminal victim.[59] In such a case, the person will probably be released the next morning.

[56] *Ibid.*, p. 147.
[57] *Ibid.*, p. 149.
[58] *Ibid.*, p. 151.
[59] *Ibid.*, pp. 439–449.

Arrest charges that are often used to accomplish a multitude of extralegal objectives are those of vagrancy and disorderly conduct. These arrests are not usually made for the enforcement of the respective laws but for such purposes as the banishment of unwanted persons, the prevention and control of other offenses, and the clearing of public areas.[60] Police departments may even conduct drives at certain times of the year, in the name of the enforcement of the vagrancy and disorderly conduct statutes, to get "undesirables" out of town.

Public Morals and Law Enforcement. Some forms of private conduct on occasion become the concern of the police. Criminal laws created primarily for purposes of reprobation are subject to a great amount of discretion in their enforcement. The laws are enforced only occasionally, and then only under particular circumstances. Thus, in the appropriate situational contexts the police are expected to enforce public morals through the arrest of private citizens.

In general the police are not called upon to enforce laws that regulate private conduct. Although there are laws based on moral behavior, they are not usually enforced as long as the conduct is unharmful to the persons involved and as long as the participating parties consent to the behavior. Enforcement is likely to take place however, when personal violence erupts and also when conduct becomes defined by the community as a public nuisance. Therefore, solicitation by homosexuals and prostitutes in public places may bring the police into action in the enforcement of laws on homosexuality and prostitution.[61]

Since the behavior of homosexuals in public is likely to be offensive to a large segment of the community, numerous complaints may be registered with the police. The responsibility of the police, then, becomes not so much the full enforcement of the law but the assurance of a public order that satisfies the sensibilities of community members. The public demands that the police provide the community with an inoffensive environment.

Prostitutes are usually arrested for purposes other than prosecution. The prostitutes who tend to be arrested, however, are those who

[60] Caleb Foote, "Vagrancy-Type Law and Its Administration," *University of Pennsylvania Law Review,* 104 (March, 1956), pp. 603–650.

[61] See LaFave, *Arrest,* pp. 465–470.

come to public attention, the street walkers rather than the call girls. While prostitution may be condoned in the community, as long as it does not recruit our wives and daughters, community members do not like to be reminded of the behavior. Therefore, the police are required to crack down on the girls who publicly solicit for their favors. Furthermore, the police may obtain information about other criminals from the arrest of prostitutes.[62] Most of the time, however, the objective of such arrests is the harassment of prostitutes. The harassment program may unwittingly force such prostitutes to develop, as it were, undercover techniques that are less obvious and offensive to the public.

The Enforcement of Dormant Laws. A great many of our criminal laws were created to support values that have since ceased to be important. Although the laws have remained on the books, they have in essence become dormant. On occasion, however, these laws have been enforced for brief periods. In most cases, the revival of these laws has been for purposes other than those intended in the original legal formulations. The sporadic enforcement of dormant laws represents the ultimate use of discretion in law enforcement.

The enforcement of Sunday closing laws provides one of the best examples of the sporadic enforcement of a dormant law. Sunday laws were enacted early in the history of our states, and their enforcement usually has been the responsibility of local authorities. Thus, Sunday laws are enforced according to particularistic objectives.

Furthermore, within local communities, Sunday laws, when enforced, have been enforced for diverse reasons. In New York City sporadic attempts in the enforcement of the Sunday law have been guided by different objectives. In this century alone there have been several instances of organized efforts to enforce the law on Sunday closing of business establishments. In each case, the reasons for the enforcement of the dormant law were different.

In 1924 the number of police actions in regard to Sunday closing rose 77 per cent in New York over the previous year. Responsible for the sudden enforcement policy was the agitation of a group of citizens known as the Lord's Day Alliance. The Alliance crusaded for the enforcement of Sunday law primarily on religious grounds. The

[62] Skolnick, *Justice Without Trial*, pp. 96–109.

following year the arrest rate for being open on Sunday declined to its regular low level. Then in 1938 another campaign for the enforcement of Sunday law was launched in the Flatbush section of Brooklyn. The campaign, under the direction of the Flatbush Chamber of Commerce, was motivated by the civic interests of local businessmen in keeping a law-abiding image for the community.

The increased enforcement of the Sunday law in 1954 in the Bedford-Stuyvesant area of Brooklyn was prompted by a campaign for better working conditions. A union, the American Federation of Retail Kosher Butchers, began the campaign in an attempt to abolish forced work on Sunday by management. In the next year, this time on Manhattan's West Side, the police responded to pressures by unions which were organizing the car wash industry in the area. The police reacted by acting upon any business establishment that was open on Sunday. One of the last police crackdowns on Sunday openings was in August of 1962 in the upper Broadway area. Behind the drive, which lasted one week, was the attempt of the large chain-store supermarkets to have the small neighborhood stores closed on Sundays.

The enforcement of Sunday closing laws illustrates the extent to which discretion is used in enforcing dormant laws. Furthermore, their enforcement is prompted by pressure on police by diverse interests to accomplish various objectives.

Political Protest and Law Enforcement. One other example of law enforcement in a particular context is the role of the police in situations involving political protest. In such situations the police are used by those who hold power to resolve value conflicts in favor of the dominant interests of the society. The use of the police to control political protest clearly shows the extent to which the police are the representatives of the powerful interests of the society. Law enforcement in this context consists of the selective application of criminal definitions on those who protest against the established government in ways that are regarded by the government as illegitimate. Behavior that is regarded by the government as illegitimate may, consequently, be defined as criminal.

The very emergence of the police in the last century was a response to conditions of unrest and mass protest. In several democratic countries in the nineteenth century the elite were able to organize police for the purpose of protecting their interests.[63] The police were able not only to control the various forms of protest against politically organized society, but served as well to divert the hostility of the protesters from the elites to the police themselves. Protest in many cases, as today, was deflected from the original issues to protests against the power of the police. In this fashion, the interests of the powerful in society are not only protected but are also given support by the existence of the police.

Political protest almost by definition is regarded as a threat and danger to the existing government. The police become involved in such situations not only for the express purpose of maintaining peace, but also to preserve the status quo of the government. Actions of the police in such situations serve to punish the protesters as much as to keep order. In fact, police intimidation and brutality have been evident in many instances of political protest by citizens. In the "race riots," in particular, much of the violence that has occurred has been either prompted or initiated by the police.[64] In many other cases of protest and in demonstrations of various kinds, the only violence has been that which the police have inflicted on the participants. The only illegalities in situations of protest may be those committed by the police themselves.[65] But since criminal definitions are imposed by the police, they are not likely to be the ones defined as criminals.

The federal government, especially, resorts to the use of the police to protect its own interests. In the name of national security, laws have been created and enforced in order to protect the government from perceived threats. The scare of communism in this century in the United States resulted in the arrest of thousands of persons under a host of laws especially enacted for that purpose or under laws that may be conveniently enforced for the same purpose.[66] Whether

[63] Allan Silver, "The Demand for Order in Civil Society: A Review of Some Themes in the History of Urban Crime, Police, and Riot," in Bordua (ed.), *The Police*, pp. 1–24.

[64] Allen D. Grimshaw, "Actions of Police and the Military in American Race Riots," *Phylon*, 24 (Fall, 1963), pp. 271–289.

[65] See Joseph C. Mouledoux, "Political Crime and the Negro Revolution," in Marshall B. Clinard and Richard Quinney, *Criminal Behavior Systems: A Typology* (New York: Holt, Rinehart and Winston, 1967), pp. 217–231.

[66] See Robert K. Murray, *Red Scare: A Study of National Hysteria, 1919– 1920* (Minneapolis: University of Minnesota Press, 1965); William Preston,

dubious methods such as harassment have been used or whether arrests have been made, police have been used to protect and help preserve the interests of the government and the interests of those who benefit from the status quo.[67] In situations of political protest the police are required to enforce the law according to the interests of those in power. Such is to be expected, since the police are, after all, agents of the government.

Jr., *Aliens and Dissenters: Federal Suppression of Radicals, 1903–1933* (Cambridge: Harvard University Press, 1963).

[67] See Jerome H. Skolnick, *The Politics of Protest* (New York: Ballantine, 1969), especially pp. 241–292.

CHAPTER FIVE

Administration
of Criminal
Justice

Justice is an ideal that abstractly pervades the value systems of most human societies. The American colonists, imbued with the liberal thought of the European enlightenment, made justice the basis of democratic government. The Massachusetts Bill of Rights of 1780 captured the essence of the ideal: "It is essential to the preservation of the rights of every individual, his life, liberty, property, and character, that there be an impartial interpretation of the laws and the administration of justice." A similar notion of justice was written into the Declaration of Independence and the Bill of Rights.

In symbolic form, justice weighs all men impartially on her scales. She represents our ideal of equality between all parties and classes. Law is thus to be administered according to an ideal, not according to the experiences of everyday life. Yet the administration of justice is full of devices for individualizing the application of criminal law. The complicated machinery of the judicial system involves a series of mitigating practices whereby cases are necessarily individualized according to numerous extralegal factors.[1] However, the very structure of the judicial system tends to obscure from public view the operation of the criminal law. Partly by design, the decision-making activities of the judicial system are hidden behind the "purple curtain" of the law. The fiction of

[1] Roscoe Pound, *An Introduction to the Philosophy of Law* (New Haven: Yale University Press, 1954), chap. 3.

judicial objectivity is obscured by a system that administers the law according to its own rules.

From an idealistic standpoint, it is useful to analyze the administration of criminal law in reference to the concept of justice. Even from a standpoint of scientific inquiry, the concept of justice is appropriate. Whether or not we always maintain an explicit image of the good and the beautiful, our sociological interest in the administration of criminal law is directed to a goal that is consistent with — and aided by — considerations of justice: How is the criminal law actually administered? From personal experience we know that the criminal law is not administered uniformly. To understand the processes involved in the administration of the criminal law is thus our immediate interest. Nevertheless, in our moments of idealism, we are investigating the differentials in the administration of justice. Whether we use the phrase "administration of criminal law" or "administration of justice," our interest is a sociological investigation of the processes that result in the application of criminal definitions.

POLITICALITY OF JUSTICE

The administration of justice, contrary to common belief, is not "above politics" but is by its very nature political. That is, the administration of criminal law is political in that public policy is being made. The political nature of the judiciary is inherent in government itself. Wherever decisions are made — and that is what the judiciary is about — politics necessarily serves as the basis of the process.

In addition to being political in the general sense of policy making, the judicial system is a creature of the political community in more specific ways. The courts, for instance, are an essential part of the local political structure. To begin with, the kinds of criminal cases that enter the courts are influenced by the character of community politics. The prosecuting attorney, an elected official and often the key figure in the local political machine, determines according to his discretion what law is being violated. His actions result in either the release of suspects or their indictment; and if suspects are indicted, the prosecutor decides the character of the charge. Still later in the process, the fate of the accused depends upon the discretion of the judge, also an appointed or locally elected official. The extent to which the local political system and the administration of criminal laws are related is indicated in conclusions reached by two political scientists:

> Thus, elected officials sensitive to the political process charge, prosecute, convict, and sentence criminal defendants. This means that such decisions are made in response to cues from the political structure; thereby the political system provides channels by which local claims and local interests can influence judicial outcomes. In this way, the judiciary helps create the conditions necessary for the re-election of court officials or for their frequent promotion to higher offices in the state or nation. In short, criminal prosecutions provide opportunities for the political system to affect judicial decisions and for the judicial process to provide favors which nourish political organizations.[2]

The politicality of local criminal justice is shaped considerably by the structure of the American party system. Political leadership in the country is dispersed among the political parties. Because of the decentralized nature of the parties, local politics is influenced by party considerations. Party leaders use the judiciary as a source of patronage. Elected judges usually owe their office to favors rendered to a political party. Specific party concerns inevitably enter into the content of public policy, including the decisions made in respect to criminal matters.

Since the judiciary is the focus of significant power, it is one of the principal points at which the claims of interest groups are aimed.[3] Because courts serve as the arena where the conflicting claims of diverse groups are presented and resolved, some control over the courts is desired by the interest groups affected by judicial decisions. Interest groups utilize every resource at their command to ensure that decisions of the courts are made in the protection of their interests.

Because the judiciary operates within a fairly routinized legal

[2] Herbert Jacob and Kenneth Vines, "The Role of the Judiciary in American State Politics," in Glendon Schubert (ed.), *Judicial Decision-Making* (New York: The Free Press of Glencoe, 1963), p. 250.

[3] David B. Truman, *The Governmental Process* (New York: Alfred A. Knopf, 1951), chap. 15; Harmon Zeigler, *Interest Groups in American Society* (Englewood Cliffs, N.J.: Prentice-Hall, 1964), chap. 11.

structure, interest groups must rely primarily upon indirect means to gain access to the decision-making process. These indirect methods may be classified into three categories: (1) those influencing the selection of judges, (2) those influencing the content of decisions, and (3) those maximizing or minimizing the effects of decisions as they are implemented.[4] By such methods, interest groups are able to have criminal statutes interpreted in their favor. The application of criminal definitions at the judicial level is largely a matter of selective interpretations of the law that favor the interests of some while negating the interests of others. Under the adversary system of justice, there is little compromise: someone wins while someone else loses.

The politicality of justice is by no means the sole result of the conflict between diverse interest groups. The political nature of the administration of criminal law is also affected by the interests of the government itself. In every society the wielders of governmental power use the criminal law to legitimate their assertions and the criminal courts to maintain their domination. Opposing political viewpoints and actions may be suppressed through the use of the courts by the government. Through various forms of the *political trial,* political foes may be eliminated from political competition.[5] In addition, the judicial system may be used by governments to repress certain groups in the society. Judges in the American south, for example, have tended to consistently make decisions that would maintain the domination of the white man over the black. In South Africa, the ruling minority has been able to successfully subjugate the rest of the population in large part by their use of the criminal courts. In these cases and others, the judiciary maintains the interests of the established government.

DISCRETION AND DECISION-MAKING IN THE JUDICIAL PROCESS

Justice is political because the administration of criminal law involves making decisions. Furthermore, whenever decisions are

[4] Jack Peltason, *Federal Courts in the Political Process* (New York: Doubleday, 1955), p. 29.
[5] Otto Kirchheimer, *Political Justice: The Use of Legal Procedure for Political Ends* (Princeton: Princeton University Press, 1961), p. 46.

made, discretion necessarily occurs. Judicial decision-making without the exercise of discretion is inconceivable.

Within the judicial process a number of types of decisions are made at various stages. Once a case is admitted to the judicial system, after an arrest, a series of decisions are made regarding the fate of the suspect. Some cases, on the basis of the decision reached during the first judicial appearance, may be removed entirely from the judicial system. The other cases, however, move sequentially from one stage to another before going out of the system. At each stage, the decision reached by certain officials limits the alternatives for the decisions in the subsequent stages.

Following the arrest, then, the suspect is usually brought before a court official (the magistrate) to determine the nature of the case. A preliminary hearing may follow to establish "probable cause." A decision is also made on the detention of the suspect, including the possible setting of bail. Between the time of the first judicial appearance and the indictment, the prosecution decides what charges to press or whether to press charges at all. Once formal charges are made, pretrial proceedings are established during the arraignment. Decisions are reached regarding such matters as the time of trial, the use of the plea, challenge of the formal charge, the nature of the evidence, and the defendant's mental or physical capacity. If a trial takes place, rather than a settlement through guilty plea proceedings, decisions are made by judge and jury in the courtroom. In arguing their cases, the prosecuting attorney and the lawyer for the defense make innumerable strategic decisions. The decision to convict the accused and the decision to impose a particular sentence are the consequences of the decisions made from the time of the arrest.

The fate of the convicted person is still problematic to some extent, however, in that an appellate review may alter previous decisions. But most likely the convicted person must continue within the judicial system until the time when officials make decisions regarding his release. From the time the suspect enters the judicial process, the decisions of others determine whether or not he will be defined as criminal.

As in the use of discretion by the police, the boundaries of discretion in the administration of criminal law are not clearly defined. Obviously judicial decisions are not made uniformly. Decisions are made according to a host of extralegal factors, including the age of the offender, his race, and social class.

Perhaps the most obvious example of judicial discretion occurs in the handling of cases of persons from minority groups. Negroes, in comparison to whites, are convicted with lesser evidence and sentenced to more severe punishments. In a study of 821 homicides in several counties of North Carolina between 1930 and 1940, it was found that the fewest indictments were made when whites killed Negroes and the highest proportion when Negroes killed whites.[6] The courts tended to regard the slaying of a white by a Negro as almost prima facie evidence of guilt, while the murder of a Negro by a white was believed to require mitigating circumstances such as provocation. Furthermore, prisoner statistics show that in most states Negroes are committed to prison longer than are whites for the same types of offenses.[7]

Another source of variation in judicial decision-making is found in the great variety of judicial systems. In the United States there are fifty-two separate court jurisdictions, consisting of the judicial systems of the fifty states, the District of Columbia, and the federal government. Furthermore, within the state jurisdictions there are several forms of courts, variously known as "police" courts, "special sessions" courts, and "quarter" courts. Some courts deal with minor criminal violations of local laws and ordinances and others with more serious offenses. While these courts have specialized functions, considerable confusion results from the overlapping of their jurisdictions.

The federal judicial system is also composed of several types of courts with diversified activities and functions. In addition, there are the federal circuit courts which are divided according to the geographical areas of the country. Because of the complexity and diversity of the judiciary in the United States, variations in judicial

---

[6] Harold Garfinkel, "Research Note on Inter- and Intra-Racial Homicides," *Social Forces*, 27 (May, 1949), pp. 369–381. Also see Thorsten Sellin, "Race Prejudice in the Administration of Justice," *American Journal of Sociology*, 41 (September, 1935), pp. 212–217.

[7] *National Prisoner Statistics*, "State Prisoners: Admission and Releases, 1964" (Washington, D.C.: Federal Bureau of Prisons, 1965). Also see Henry Allen Bullock, "Significance of the Racial Factor in the Length of Prison Sentence," *Journal of Criminal Law, Criminology and Social Science*, 339 (January, 1962), pp. 411–417.

decision-making are to be expected. The administration of the criminal law cannot be uniform, but necessarily involves the use of localized discretion in the course of individualized justice.

PROSECUTION AND NONTRIAL ADJUDICATION

By popular conception, the focal point of the administration of justice consists of the court trial, where the fate of the accused is decided by twelve of his peers. Not only is this conception incorrect about the *way* in which persons are convicted, but it is misleading in the implication that adjudication consists *only* of the decision of the judge or jury to convict or acquit. As we have seen, several judicial stages necessarily precede a trial. But it is most significant that in these pretrial proceedings the majority of criminal cases never reach the stage of the criminal trial. The decision to impose a criminal definition is usually made in the *pretrial* proceedings by *nontrial* adjudication.

Upon arrest, or following the issuance of a summons or on-the-spot citation, the suspect is supposed to be brought promptly before a magistrate, who reads the warrant to the suspect.[8] If the offense is a minor one, triable by the magistrate, a summary trial may be held immediately. If the offense is more serious, not triable by the magistrate, the purpose of the initial appearance is more limited. The suspect will be given the opportunity of having a preliminary hearing to determine if there is sufficient evidence to justify being held for possible trial. If he waives a preliminary hearing, he is then bound over to a court of trial jurisdiction.

The principal function of the first judicial appearance is not, however, to determine whether there is sufficient evidence for trial. Neither the prosecuting attorney nor the defense lawyer is ready at this point to determine whether probable cause exists. The principal function of the first appearance is to provide for the defendant's release, pending further judicial proceedings. While release is a constitutional right, the bail procedure of temporarily forfeiting money for freedom has resulted in a number of unjust practices.

[8] See Frank W. Miller and Frank J. Remington, "Procedures Before Trial," *Annals of the American Academy of Political and Social Science,* 339 (January, 1962), pp. 111–124.

Ideally the only criterion for the determination of the amount of bail is the amount necessary to ensure the reappearance of the defendant. In practice, however, the bail system discriminates against those who cannot afford to pay the bail fee, fosters a shady bail-bond business, and promotes the use of questionable judicial procedures in the setting of bail.[9] Recent alternatives to the bail system, such as pretrial parole, are eliminating the deficiencies of bail, at the same time providing for both the constitutional release of the defendant and the assurance of his return for subsequent judicial processing.[10]

Arraignment and the Plea. In some jurisdictions the suspect is arraigned immediately after being booked at the police station, thus bypassing the appearance before a magistrate. Whether arraignment is the first judicial appearance or a later one, the arraignment proceeding consists of an appearance before a judge of the trial court. There the judge reads the charge to the defendant and informs him of his right to counsel. The initial charge is based either upon the "information" or "indictment," depending upon the procedures used in the jurisdiction. Some jurisdictions rely upon a grand jury to return an indictment for felony cases with charges for misdemeanors being based on information filed by the prosecuting attorney.

Whatever procedure is used for reaching a charge, the judge then asks the defendant to plead to the charge. The defendant may plead guilty, not guilty, or may stand mute. With the permission of the judge, he may also have the option of pleading *nolo contendere,* which is the same as a plea of guilty except that it cannot be used as an admission in subsequent civil suits. If the defendant pleads guilty, the judge will ordinarily enter a judgment of conviction, postponing the sentence until a presentence investigation can be made by the probation department. If the defendant stands mute, the judge will enter a plea of not guilty, and a trial will follow. If

[9] Caleb Foote, "The Bail System and Equal Justice," *Federal Probation,* 23 (September, 1959), pp. 43–48; Frederic Suffet, "Bail Setting: A Study of Courtroom Interaction," *Crime and Delinquency,* 12 (October, 1966), pp. 318–331; Ronald Goldfarb, *Ransom: A Critique of the American Bail System* (New York: Harper and Row, 1965).

[10] Charles E. Ares, Anne Rankin, and Herbert Sturz, "The Manhattan Bail Project: An Interim Report on the Use of Pre-Trial Parole," *New York University Law Review,* 38 (January, 1963), pp. 67–95.

the plea of the defendant is not guilty, the judge asks whether the defendant desires a jury trial or whether he prefers to be tried by the judge without the presence of a jury. A plea of not guilty places the burden on the state to prove every element of the offense beyond a reasonable doubt.

Guilty Plea Negotiation. Important as the trial is as an ideal in the administration of justice, it is far from the most commonly used method of convicting and acquitting defendants. Roughly 90 per cent of criminal convictions are based on pleas of guilty which are adjudicated without a trial.[11] Estimates on the percentage of cases disposed of by guilty pleas, however, are difficult to establish because of such matters as variations in use from one jurisdiction to another, fluctuations from time to time, and variations according to the kinds of crime being tabulated. Nevertheless, the statistics in Table 5.1 indicate the extent to which guilty plea convictions are used in the general trial jurisdictions of several states.

TABLE 5.1
Guilty Plea Convictions in Several States
(1964 statistics unless otherwise indicated)

State	Total convictions	Guilty pleas	
		Number	Percentage
California (1965)	30,840	22,817	74.0
Connecticut	1,596	1,494	93.9
District of Columbia (yr. end. June 30, 1964)	1,115	817	73.3
Hawaii	393	360	91.5
Illinois	5,591	4,768	85.2
Kansas	3,025	2,727	90.2
Massachusetts (1963)	7,790	6,642	85.2
Minnesota (1965)	1,567	1,437	91.7
New York	17,249	16,464	95.5
U.S. District Courts	29,170	26,273	90.2
Average			87.0

Source: President's Commission on Law Enforcement and Administration of Justice, *Task Force Report: The Courts,* Washington, D.C.: U.S. Government Printing Office, 1967, p. 9.

[11] See Donald J. Newman, *Conviction: The Determination of Guilt or Innocence Without Trial* (Boston: Little, Brown, 1966), pp. 3–4.

Our judicial system has come to depend upon the use of the guilty plea. If all criminal cases were to receive a trial upon a plea of not guilty, the courts simply could not handle the case load. There are not enough, and conceivably could never be enough, judges, prosecutors, and defense attorneys to operate a system in which most defendants would go to trial.

The judicial necessity of guilty pleas has given rise to the practice commonly known as "plea bargaining." A substantial portion of guilty pleas result from negotiations between the prosecutor and defense lawyer or between the prosecutor and the defendant. In addition to managing the case load, the negotiated plea accomplishes other purposes.

> As the term implies, plea negotiation involves an exchange of concessions and advantages between the state and the accused. The defendant who pleads guilty is treated less severely than he would be if he were convicted of the maximum charge and assessed the most severe penalty. At the same time, he waives his right to trial, thereby losing his chance, no matter how slight, for outright acquittal. The state, at the relatively small cost of charge reduction leniency, gains the numerous administrative advantages of the guilty plea over a long, costly, and always uncertain trial. In this way the negotiated plea in a real sense answers two important objectives of criminal justice administration: the individualization of justice and the maintenance of the guilty plea system.[12]

The negotiated guilty plea is thus a compromise conviction reached by the state and the accused for the benefit of both.

Having studied this informal conviction process, Newman reported in an article that plea bargaining occurred in more than half the felony cases studied.[13] During the process the accused, directly or through an attorney, offered to plead guilty providing the charge was reduced in kind or degree, or exchanged for a specific type or length of sentence. The subsequent conviction agreements followed several patterns according to the types of bargains involved:

[12] *Ibid.*, p. 77.
[13] Donald J. Newman, "Pleading Guilty for Considerations: A Study of Bargain Justice," *Journal of Criminal Law, Criminology and Police Science*, 46 (March–April, 1956), pp. 780–790.

1. *Bargain Concerning the Charge.* A plea of guilty was entered by the offenders in exchange for a reduction of the charge from the one alleged in the complaint. This ordinarily occurred in cases where the offense in question carried statutory degrees of severity such as homicide, assault, and sex offenses. This type was mentioned as a major issue in twenty percent of the cases in which bargaining occurred. The majority of offenders in these instances were represented by lawyers.

2. *Bargain Concerning the Sentence.* A plea of guilty was entered by the offenders in exchange for a promise of leniency in sentencing. The most commonly accepted consideration was a promise that the offender would be placed on probation, although a less-than-maximum prison term was the basis in certain instances. All offenses except murder, serious assault, and robbery were represented in this type of bargaining process. This was by far the most frequent consideration given in exchange for guilty pleas, occurring in almost half (45.5 percent) of the cases in which any bargaining occurred. Again, most of these offenders were represented by attorneys.

3. *Bargain for Concurrent Charges.* This type of informal process occurred chiefly among offenders pleading without counsel. These men exchanged guilty pleas for the concurrent pressing of multiple charges, generally numerous counts of the same offense or related violations such as breaking and entering and larceny. This method, of course, has much the same effect as pleading for consideration in the sentence. The offender with concurrent convictions, however, may not be serving a reduced sentence; he is merely serving one sentence for many crimes. Altogether, concurrent convictions were reported by 21.8 percent of the men who were convicted by informal methods.

4. *Bargain for Dropped Charges.* This variation occurred in about an eighth of the cases who reported bargaining. It involved an agreement on the part of the prosecution not to press formally one or more charges against the offender if he in turn pleaded guilty to (usually) the major offense. The offenses dropped were extraneous law violations contained in, or accompanying, the offense alleged in the complaint such as auto theft accompanying armed robbery and violation of probation where a new crime had been committed. This informal method, like bargaining for concurrent charges, was reported

chiefly by offenders without lawyers. It occurred in 12.6 percent of cases in which bargaining was claimed.[14]

Although most of the remainder of the sample pleaded guilty without considerations, in many of these cases the attorneys probably
bargained, or attempted to bargain, without successfully achieving
a conviction compromise.

The interactions and perceptions of the prosecutor and the defense are critical in the negotiation of a guilty plea. A student of the
guilty plea process observed that the prosecutor (district attorney)
and the defense (public defender) develop during their interactions
a common orientation to the alteration of charges.[15] The negotiators
are not able, for purposes of a suitable reduction in charge, to refer
to a statutory definition of a particular offense, since the penal code
does not provide the reference for deciding the correspondence
between the conduct of the offender and the legal category. In the
charge of burglary, for example, the prosecutor and defense nego-
tiate about a nonstatutory type of "burglar." The reduction of a
burglary charge to a charge of petty theft is accomplished because
the negotiators are able to regard the reduction as reasonable and
consistent with the kinds of behaviors that are normally associated
with the specific charge. During their interaction and repeated
negotiations, then, the prosecutor and defense develop unstated
guides for reducing original charges to lesser charges.

Plea bargaining takes place between the prosecutor and the accused or his defense for reasons more immediate than those of the
individualization of justice and the maintenance of the judicial
system.[16] The decision to reduce the charge is often made because
the prosecutor realizes that his evidence is probably insufficient for
conviction at trial. In other cases reduction may be necessary because of the reluctance of complainants, victims, or witnesses to
testify. The prosecutor at other times may suggest a reduction in
charge because he believes that the judge or jury is unlikely to
convict the defendant. Judges themselves in some cases may favor

[14] *Ibid.*, p. 787.
[15] David Sudnow, "Normal Crimes: Sociological Features of the Penal Code
in a Public Defender Office," *Social Problems,* 12 (Winter, 1965), pp. 255–276.
[16] Newman, *Conviction,* pp. 67–75, 105–130, 177–187.

charge reduction to avoid the necessity of imposing the mandatory sentence (either maximum or minimum) associated with the original charge. A parole sentence may only be possible if the original charge is reduced to a lesser charge. On the other hand, whatever the bargaining agreement, the judge may acquit the defendant for a number of reasons that grow out of an interest in individualized justice and judicial maintenance. Acquittals are made because (1) the conduct is regarded as a minor violation, (2) the offender is viewed as unaccountable for his behavior, (3) the conduct is considered normal to the subculture of the defendant, (4) the conduct is a matter of private morality, (5) specialized treatment may be deemed more appropriate than punishment, (6) restitution is otherwise made to the victim, and (7) the judge disagrees with the purpose of the law or with the law enforcement effort.[17]

Whether the judge convicts according to the plea negotiated by the prosecutor and defense or acquits the defendant, he obviously has a personal interest in the outcome of each case. Technically the judge is not supposed to enter into the bargaining. However, by subtle cues and not so subtle demands, the judge has an influence on the negotiation of pleas. The advantages of plea negotiation for the judge have been indicated in a study of "Metropolitan Court":

> According to the ideology of the law, the judge is required to be not only impartial but active in seeking out and preserving the rights of all offenders. Nevertheless, he also has a vested interest in a high rate of negotiated pleas. He shares the prosecutor's earnest desire to avoid the time consuming, expensive, unpredictable snares and pitfalls of an adversary trial. He sees an impossible backlog of cases, with their mounting delays, as possible public evidence of his "inefficiency" and failure. The defendant's plea of guilty enables the judge to engage in a social-psychological fantasy — the accused becomes an already repentant individual who has "learned his lesson" and deserves lenient treatment. Indeed, as previously indicated, many judges give a less severe sentence to a defendant who has negotiated a plea than to one who has been convicted of the same offense after a trial.[18]

[17] *Ibid.*, pp. 152–172, 188–196.
[18] Abraham S. Blumberg, *Criminal Justice* (Chicago: Quadrangle Books, 1967), p. 65.

Whatever may be the reason for the negotiation of a guilty plea, be it the vested interest of the prosecutor, the defense, the judge, or an interest further removed, the resulting conviction is a criminal definition. Guilty plea negotiation ultimately amounts to the creation of crime.

THE CRIMINAL LAWYER IN THE ADVERSARY SYSTEM

Underlying the administration of criminal justice in the United States is the adversary principle. In the adversary system of criminal justice, opposing parties — the state and the accused — are engaged in a public battle. The game is one of black and white; one side must be entirely correct and the other all wrong. One side wins when the judgment is made in its favor. Furthermore, there are rules and procedures to guide the battle throughout its course. The adversary principle is a basic part of the American system of criminal justice.

The adversary system requires a number of specific occupational roles for its functioning. As such, criminal justice is bureaucratically organized.[19] That is, the system of criminal justice is composed of distinct legal work roles with specified duties and obligations. Each position is defined in itself and in relation to the others. Expectations of performance in respect to the administration of criminal law regulate the occupational behavior of persons that occupy the work roles. The principal roles in the organization of the judicial system are those of the prosecutor, the defense attorney, and the judge. In separate ways, each is engaged in a process which results in the defining of persons and behaviors as criminal.

The judge acts on the basis of evidence and arguments presented by the prosecuting and the defense attorneys. He finds the defendant guilty or innocent, sometimes by referring to the decision of a jury, and then imposes a sentence. The prosecutor's role, how-

---

[19] *Ibid.* For other observations on the social organization of the administration of criminal justice, see Jerome H. Skolnick, "Social Control in the Adversary System," *Journal of Conflict Revolution,* 11 (March, 1967), pp. 52–70. On the juvenile court, see Aaron V. Cicourel, *The Social Organization of Juvenile Justice* (New York: John Wiley, 1968).

ever, is more critical in the early stages of the judicial process. As the representative of the state, the prosecutor has the authority to determine whether an alleged offender should be charged and the authority to obtain a conviction through guilty plea negotiation. He has the responsibility of presenting the state's cases in court, that is, of prosecuting the accused. His skill as a trial lawyer is important in the conviction of the defendant. The prosecutor also has an influence on the arrest practices of the police, the volume of cases in the courts, and the number of offenders referred to the correctional system.[20] By definition of his legal role, the prosecutor is engaged in a continuous battle against the accused and their defending lawyers.

Legal Representation of the Accused. The right of the accused to be represented by legal counsel has been assured in the Sixth Amendment to the Constitution, and is essential to the adversary system of criminal justice. An individual forced to answer to a criminal charge needs the assistance of one who understands the legal system and who will protect the defendant's legal rights. The defendant is not likely to understand the legal system, largely because of its planned obscurity. In order for a judicial system to be effective and efficient, counsel for the defendant is necessary. Furthermore, an adversary system of justice depends upon vigorous challenges to the state's accusations.

When and how to assure or provide legal counsel for the accused has been the vital issue in the adversary system. Through the establishment of various procedures, in part inspired by rulings of state supreme courts and the United States Supreme Court, defendants are either entitled or required to have legal counsel from the moment of arrest. Likewise, through a recent Supreme Court decision in the *Gault* case, the jurisdictional rights of counsel have been expanded to include juvenile delinquency proceedings.

In providing for counsel, several schemes have been instituted to ensure (in theory at least) that defendants are represented by

[20] For a discussion of the responsibilities of the prosecutor as outlined in state statutes, see Duane R. Nedrud, "The Career Prosecutor," *Journal of Criminal Law, Criminology and Police Science,* 51 (September–October, 1960), pp. 343–355. Also see President's Commission on Law Enforcement and Administration of Justice, *Task Force Report: The Courts* (Washington, D.C.: U.S. Government Printing Office, 1967), pp. 72–79.

legal counsel.[21] The types of legal representation include (1) court appointed counsel, as in the legal aid system, (2) the public defender system, whereby the state provides permanent lawyers to defend the accused, and (3) lawyer reference plans, in which private or public agency lawyers are made known to defendants. The availability of these and other forms of legal representations varies from one jurisdiction to another. Also, and most important for the conviction process, the outcome of cases depends to some extent on the kind of legal counsel the defendant receives.[22]

That criminal justice is differently administered according to social class is at least vaguely realized by most persons. Since the poor are accused of criminal behavior more often than members of other classes, their dependence upon legal service is crucial. However, legal services are the most inadequate for the class which requires legal assistance the most. The poor are least likely to use lawyers; when they do they usually have access to the least competent lawyers, and the legal counsel with which they are provided is generally of limited character. Surveys from several states indicate that about two out of three lower class families have never employed a lawyer, compared with about one out of three upper class families.[23] The few private attorneys who are available to the poor tend to be the least well trained and, because of the insecurity of their practice, are likely to succumb to temptations to exploit clients.[24]

To supplement private legal representation, special agencies and procedures, such as legal aid societies and the defender system,

[21] Albert P. Blaustein and Charles O. Porter, *The American Lawyer: A Summary of the Survey of the Legal Profession* (Chicago: University of Chicago Press, 1954), pp. 64–96.

[22] Differences in the outcomes of criminal cases according to type of legal representation are reported in Lee Silverstein, *Defense of the Poor in Criminal Cases* (Chicago: American Bar Foundation, 1965); Dallin H. Oaks and Warren Lehman, "Lawyers for the Poor," *Trans-Action*, 4 (July–August, 1967), pp. 25–29; Laura Banfield and C. David Anderson, "Continuances in the Cook County Criminal Courts," *University of Chicago Law Review*, 35 (Winter, 1968), pp. 259–316. Differences in juvenile cases are reported in Edwin M. Lemert, "Legislating Change in the Juvenile Court," *Wisconsin Law Review* (Spring, 1967), pp. 421–448.

[23] Jerome E. Carlin and Jon Howard, "Legal Representation and Class Justice," *UCLA Law Review*, 12 (January, 1965), pp. 382–383.

[24] Jerome E. Carlin, *Lawyers' Ethics: A Survey of the New York City Bar* (New York: Russell Sage Foundation, 1966), pp. 71–73.

have extended legal services to the poor. Nevertheless, it appears that indigents are not provided with legal services adequate to their needs. The ultimate result is higher rates of conviction and severer sentences for the poor.

> With respect to the representation of criminal defendants, there is considerable evidence to suggest that neither the assigned counsel nor public defender system as now constituted is capable of providing adequate service to the indigent accused. A large proportion of poor defendants (particularly in misdemeanor cases) are not represented at all. Moreover, when counsel is provided he frequently has neither the resources, the skill nor the incentive to defend his client effectively; and he usually enters the case too late to make any real difference in the outcome. Indeed, the generally higher rate of guilty pleas and prison sentences among defendants represented by assigned counsel or the public defender suggest that these attorneys may actually undermine their clients' position.[25]

Career Patterns in the Practice of Criminal Law. Lawyers who represent criminal defendants on a private basis tend to be engaged in a particular type of legal practice. They also tend to have distinct career patterns. Both tendencies affect the way in which such lawyers handle criminal cases.

More than half the lawyers practicing in cities in the United States are self-employed. The other half are either employed in firms or as lawyers in corporations, governmental legal departments, and legal aid societies.[26] The individual practitioner (or "solo" lawyer) differs sharply from those engaged in the other types of legal practice. It was found in a comparison of individual practitioners and firm lawyers in Detroit that solo lawyers more often came from minority, religious-ethnic, entrepreneurial, and working class homes, had inferior educations, and experienced chaotic work histories.[27] In addition to their special backgrounds, individual practitioners tend to restrict their practices to those residual matters that the large law

[25] Jerome E. Carlin, Jon Howard, and Sheldon L. Messinger, "Civil Justice and the Poor: Issues for Sociological Research," *Law and Society Review,* 1 (November, 1966), p. 56.

[26] 1958 Supplement to *Lawyers in the United States: Distribution and Income* (Chicago: American Bar Foundation, 1959), pp. 54–55.

[27] Jack Ladinsky, "Careers of Lawyers, Law Practice, and Legal Institutions," *American Sociological Review,* 28 (February, 1963), pp. 47–54.

firms have not pre-empted. Their practice, as found in Chicago, includes the following matters:

> (1) matters not large enough or remunerative enough for the large firms to handle — most general work for small to medium-sized businesses and corporations, the smaller real estate transactions (for individuals or small businesses), and estate matters for middle-income families; (2) the undesirable cases, the dirty work, those areas of practice that have associated with them an aura of influencing and fixing and that involve arrangements with clients and others that are felt by the large firms to be professionally damaging. The latter category includes local tax, municipal, personal injury, divorce, and criminal matters.[28]

Thus, the lawyers who privately handle the criminal cases of lower and working class defendants tend to be individual practitioners. Moreover, they are likely to be engaged in a diversified legal practice in which the handling of criminal cases is only an occasional affair. Their practice of law generally centers around the local police court or the traffic court and tends to be ethnic and neighborhood oriented. The following quotation from a solo lawyer in Chicago illustrates the way in which diverse legal matters are related for the individual practitioner:

> I handle some small criminal cases. This year I had one case, an indictment in felony court, a bench trial. The rest would be either police court — up to the preliminary hearing, getting charges reduced to misdemeanors, and so on — assault and battery, domestic problems, mostly drunks and disorderlies, assaults, etc. Neighborhood stuff. So many domestic relations cases come out of the police court; after representing them in the police court, you get them dismissed for divorce.[29]

The individual practitioners who do specialize in criminal law practice must maintain regular sources of case referral. These lawyers depend upon close relations with bondsmen, policemen, and community leaders for business. The competition for criminal cases among solo lawyers who specialize in criminal law produces a legal

---

[28] Jerome E. Carlin, *Lawyers on Their Own: A Study of Individual Practitioners in Chicago* (New Brunswick, N.J.: Rutgers University Press, 1962), pp. 17–18.
[29] *Ibid.*, pp. 105–106.

practice that is based more on sharp business practices than the pursuance of criminal justice.

The difference between lawyers with criminal practices and those with civil practices has been documented in a study of the careers of a sample of lawyers in five cities.[30] This study compared criminal lawyers and civil lawyers on such characteristics as social origins, choice of legal career, preparation for law, adjustment to legal practice, and reasons for entering the particular field of legal practice. It was found that the criminal lawyers, in comparison to the civil lawyers, tended to have relatively low socioeconomic backgrounds, had less professional training, had difficulty getting established, were solo practitioners engaged in an entrepreneurial career, and were not especially satisfied with criminal practice.

On the basis of the characteristics of the criminal lawyers, the study distinguished between two types of criminal law careers. In the first type,

> the attorney did not choose to enter criminal law, but rather he accepted criminal cases as they came his way in the process of establishing a practice or as a supplement to a meager practice in civil law. From the standpoint of the legal profession, these lawyers are among the least successful, and accordingly one may judge their morale to be correspondingly low. The second type of criminal lawyer is one who often chose this field, but in any case he enjoys the drama and thrill of those accused of crime. He may achieve considerable success; lacking this, he is compensated by his intense absorption in the work.[31]

Only about one-fourth of the criminal lawyers can be placed in the second type of criminal law career. Of course, some criminal lawyers do not fit into either of the two types, including the successful ones who do not have a welfare orientation and those who strongly identify with the welfare of their clients but whose careers may be described as failures. Nevertheless, the majority of practitioners of criminal law can be described as either those who have failed to establish a successful practice and therefore accept criminal cases as a way of enlarging a legal practice, or those who relish the excite-

[30] Arthur Lewis Wood, *Criminal Lawyer* (New Haven: College & University Press, 1967), pp. 34–67.
[31] *Ibid.*, p. 238.

ment of criminal work and feel that their practice secures justice for those accused of crime.

Behavior and Ethics of Criminal Lawyers. All lawyers are subject to the normative controls of their occupation. Among these controls are standards that proscribe behavior considered unethical by society in general, such as cheating, bribery, and stealing. Additional standards deal with professional problems, such as relations among colleagues, methods of obtaining business, and conflicts of interests. Lawyers differ in the extent to which they conform to these standards. Ultimately the legal assistance the client receives is influenced by the behavior and ethics of the lawyer that handles the case.

On the ethical conduct of lawyers, in a study of a sample of New York City bar members it was found that various characteristics of the lawyers' practice influence violation of professional standards.[32] Among other things, it revealed that because of the instability of their practice, lawyers with low status clients are subject to far more temptations, opportunities, and client pressure to violate professional ethics than are lawyers with high status clients. Also influencing the ethical conduct of the lawyers is the court setting in which the lawyer operates and the constraints provided by the lawyer's work group. Conformity to professional norms and ethics thus depends greatly on the location of the lawyer within the structure of the legal profession.

For the lawyer engaged in criminal practice, professional norms cover several areas: "(1) confidentiality of the attorney-client relationship; (2) affective or emotional neutrality with respect to the merits of the case, while at the same time service in the interests of the client; and (3) participation in procedures in which a professional as opposed to a personal relationship is maintained with other participants — the police, the bondsman, the prosecutor and the judge."[33] The behavior of the defense lawyer is especially complicated by the fact that he is confronted with conflicting claims. Because of his legal role, the defense attorney must act as a mediator between the client and judicial agents. The professional conduct of the criminal lawyer, therefore, is related to the way in which he

[32] Carlin, *Lawyers' Ethics*, pp. 165–182.
[33] Wood, *Criminal Lawyer*, p. 93.

manages the conflicting claims imposed by the adversary system of justice.

The great majority of defendants handled by criminal lawyers are actually guilty of some offense. Because of his precarious position, the defendant is subject to considerable manipulation by his attorney, and his case tends to become guided by the personal interests of the lawyer. Finally, the lawyer's handling of the defendant's case is affected by the bureaucratic structure of the court: "In the sense that the lawyer in the criminal court serves as a double agent, serving higher organizational rather than professional ends, he may be deemed to be engaged in bureaucratic rather than private practice."[34] In this way, criminal law practice is actually bureaucratic practice, because of the enmeshment of the lawyer and his client in the authority and discipline of the judicial system. Strategies and decisions affecting the application of criminal definitions are made within the boundaries established by the adversary system of justice.

THE CRIMINAL TRIAL AND THE JURY

The adjudication of the accused may eventually take place in a criminal trial. When negotiation between the various legal agents has failed to result in the defendant's plea of guilty, or when the defendant pleads not guilty without any attempt at bargaining, a criminal trial will provide the setting for the further enactment of the drama of imposing a criminal definition. While variations occur in the operation of a trial, a trial generally follows a number of steps.[35] The arraignment and plea may be followed by: (1) the selection of the jury, (2) the prosecutor's and defense's opening statements, (3) presentation of the state's and the defense's evidence, (4) prosecutor's and defense's arguments to the jury, (5) prosecutor's rebuttal, (6) judge's instructions on the law, (7) rendition of the jury verdict, and (8) imposition of a sentence.

[34] Abraham S. Blumberg, "The Practice of Law as Confidence Game: Organizational Cooptation of a Profession," *Law and Society Review,* 1 (June, 1967), pp. 15–39.
[35] Robert E. Knowlton, "The Trial of Offenders," *Annals of the American Academy of Political and Social Science,* 339 (January, 1962), pp. 125–141.

It is obvious that not all of these steps are included in any trial. It may be decided that the defendant will be tried before a judge or panel of judges, rather than by a jury. Various motions for change in procedure may be entered during the trial. Decisions may be made in regard to the waiving of statements, evidence, and testimony. Motions may be made by the defense for a new trial or to hold immediate judgment. Following the sentence, the case may be appealed to a higher court, or upon a charge of the denial of due process there may be further litigation. In other words, the final conviction depends upon a host of decisions and actions once the defendant reaches the trial stage.

Extralegal Considerations in the Criminal Trial. According to popular conception the criminal trial is symbolic of justice in America. This conception is based on the notion that justice is rationally dispensed. The assumption is that persons involved in the judicial process — lawyers, defendants, witnesses, jurors, judges — base their statements, arguments, and judgments on facts and according to the rules of law. All parties are supposedly engaged in pursuit of the "truth" about the case. Such a conception of the criminal trial ignores both the nature of the actions of men and the organizational constraints imposed by the judicial system itself. The criminal trial may be most profitably analyzed as a system of human actions that entails perceptions and behaviors the like of which are found in any social situation. The persons involved in the trial are acting according to their own pasts, their present perspectives, and their future expectations; and their actions are oriented to the behavior of others.

> In a sense the courtroom may be viewed as a microcosm of the larger social world in which human beings exist, act, and interact. That the action reconstructed in court and the action-process of reconstruction are meaningful and purposive, that they involve subjective as well as objective meanings, and that they significantly hinge on human goals, purposes and motives becomes at once apparent. If some juridical writers envisage a mere mechanical application of formalized law, the participants in the ordinary court trial of a criminal case are involved in more mundane practices.[36]

[36] Edwin M. Schur, "Scientific Method and the Criminal-Trial Decision," *Social Research*, 25 (Summer, 1958), p. 178.

The combative nature of the criminal trial ensures that judicial actions are social and extralegal rather than logical deductions from abstract principles. As a substitute for private brawls, the modern criminal trial places parties in opposing camps. The adversary system of justice promotes a "fight" method rather than a "truth" method of trying cases.[37]

In other words, the criminal trial nominally is a process of constructing a reality — a social reality. Objective facts are not gathered in a criminal trial, but decisions are reached on "evidence" that is meaningful to the interacting and conflicting participants. Subjectivity enters into the arguments of the attorneys, the testimony of the witnesses, the deliberations of jurors, and the actions of the judge. All the actors involved in the drama are reacting subjectively to the actions of each other. The decisions reached during the trial, including the decision that ultimately defines the defendant as a convicted criminal, are made by men as social beings. That is to say, though the criminal trial is not an exercise in fact finding and logical deduction, it is a product of human action. Could something else be expected?

Testimony and Witnesses. The testimony of various types of witnesses is used by both sides — the prosecution and the defense — to argue the merits of their respective positions. Of particular concern to the defense attorney is the decision on whether or not to put the defendant on the stand as a witness in his own behalf. The decision of the defense is usually based on speculation about how the jury will react to the performance of the defendant. Also, the defense will be reluctant to place a defendant on the witness stand who has a prior criminal record.[38] Though procedurally a previous conviction should not be considered as evidence of guilt on another charge, the defendant with a previous conviction is especially vulnerable to probing by the prosecuting attorney. The use of the defendant as a witness is of strategic importance in the criminal trial.

Both the prosecution and defense will utilize any witness who may favorably shape the opinions of the judge and jury members.

[37] Jerome Frank, *Courts on Trial: Myth and Reality in American Justice* (Princeton: Princeton University Press, 1949), chap. 6.

[38] Arnold S. Trebach, *The Rationing of Justice* (New Brunswick, N.J.: Rutgers University Press, 1964), pp. 172–173.

Such witnesses, however, tend to be placed in an insecure position.[39] In spite of procedures to guarantee his protection, the witness is subject to pressures from the public, the press, and personal contacts. He may eventually suffer repercussions from his testimony. The witness is most dramatically subjected to harassment during the opposition's cross-examination in the courtroom. Little wonder that the "facts" provided by witnesses are selective and subjective, rather than objective as commonly supposed.

Among the testimony that may be included in the adjudication of the accused is the testimony of the so-called "experts." Criminal procedure today relies especially upon the testimony of the psychiatrist. Most states provide for observation of defendants suspected of mental disorders. On the basis of a judge's decision to accept evidence provided by a psychiatrist, the accused may be judged incompetent to stand trial and then be committed indefinitely to a mental hospital.

During the criminal trial, the psychiatrist, in responding to the *M'Naghten* test of insanity, is asked to make a judgment as to the responsibility and, in essence, the guilt or innocence of the defendant.[40] In jurisdictions that have rules of the *Durham* type, the psychiatrist may describe the mental state of the defendant entirely in psychiatric language. The psychiatrist thus has a crucial role in the criminal trial of today because of the information he can supposedly provide in regard to the legal concept of the defendant's responsibility.

The power of the psychiatrist in the criminal trial, because of the questionable nature of his practice, has been seriously criticized in recent years. A person charged with a criminal offense may be denied the right to trial as a result of the pretrial psychiatric examination.[41] In other words, psychiatrists are engaged in putting people away without the guarantee of a trial. Such "putting away" may

[39] See Rudolph E. Morris, "Witness Performance Under Stress: A Sociological Approach," *Journal of Social Issues,* 13 (November 2, 1957), pp. 17–22; Israel Gerver, "The Social Psychology of Witness Behavior With Special Reference to Criminal Courts," *Journal of Social Issues,* 13 (November 2, 1957), pp. 23–29.
[40] Seymour L. Halleck, "A Critique of Current Psychiatric Roles in the Legal Process," *Wisconsin Law Review* (Spring, 1966), pp. 379–401. Also see Abraham S. Goldstein, *The Insanity Defense* (New Haven: Yale University Press, 1967).
[41] Thomas S. Szasz, *Psychiatric Justice* (New York: Macmillan, 1965).

actually be inspired by adversaries who do not want the would-be defendant around.

To illustrate this point, Szasz describes the case of a filling station operator in Syracuse, New York, who had been pressed by real estate developers to sell his property for the development of a shopping center on the site. When agents of the developers attempted to erect a sign on the property, the enraged operator fired warning shots from a rifle into the air. He was arrested but was never brought to trial. On the recommendation of the prosecuting attorney, the filling station operator was ordered to undergo psychiatric examination to determine his fitness to stand trial. He was held incapable and was committed to a state mental hospital. Still in a hospital after ten years, the filling station operator had already served more time than he would have spent in prison had he been tried and convicted. Whatever criticism one wants to direct at the use of psychiatric evidence, the fate of the defendant may be directly affected by the testimony of "experts."

Trial by Jury. Trial by a jury stands as the cornerstone of American criminal justice. In practice, trial by jury in the United States accounts for about 80 per cent of criminal jury trials in the world today.[42] However, the jury trial is the mode of conviction for only a small fraction of criminal prosecutions in the United States. Of those cases which are tried, nearly half are tried without a jury. Only about one in seven felony prosecutions ends in a trial by jury.

The relatively small use of the jury trial for criminal conviction is accounted for by (1) legal restrictions on the right of trial by jury, (2) the decision of the prosecution and defense to settle by guilty plea conviction, and (3) the choice of the defendant to be tried before a judge without a jury.[43] Although the Sixth Amendment to the Constitution guarantees the right to trial by jury, the states specify the kinds of offenses that will be tried by a jury. Under the laws of most states, a jury trial may be denied for such minor offenses as traffic violation, disorderly conduct, petty gambling, public drunkenness, and prostitution.

Beyond the stipulations of the state laws, trial by jury is a choice

[42] Harry Kalven, Jr. and Hans Zeisel, *The American Jury* (Boston: Little, Brown, 1966), p. 13.
[43] *Ibid.*, pp. 14–17.

that is left open to the defendant. Whether to be prosecuted without a trial or to be tried with the waiver of a jury, depends upon the strategy worked out by the defendant and the various legal actors. The decision to avoid a jury trial varies considerably according to the nature of the offense and local custom. About 90 per cent of forgeries are prosecuted through guilty pleas, but only about 30 per cent of murders are prosecuted in such a way. When trials are used for murder, the jury is waived only about 15 per cent of the time, whereas for forgery the jury is waived about 50 per cent of the time. Furthermore, local variations in the waiver of jury are marked. In Wisconsin, the jury is waived in approximately three-fourths of criminal cases; in Utah it is waived in only about 5 per cent of the cases.[44]

While the jury trial is not used as frequently as commonly assumed, it nevertheless exerts an important influence on American criminal justice. The trial operates as a control on the judicial administration of cases that are not tried by a jury.

> It has become something of a commonplace to read the statistics on the impact of guilty pleas and jury waivers as gravely reducing the significance of the jury and transferring its power largely to the prosecuting attorney in the bargaining over guilty pleas. But we saw at every stage of this informal process of pre-trial dispositions that decisions are in part informed by expectations of what the jury will do. Thus, the jury is not controlling merely the immediate case before it, but the host of cases not before it which are destined to be disposed of by the pre-trial process. The jury thus controls not only the formal resolution of controversies in the criminal case, but also the informal resolution of cases that never reach the trial stage. In a sense the jury, like the visible cap of an iceberg, exposes but a fraction of its true volume.[45]

Once the decision has been made to try the defendant before a jury, numerous social factors enter into the way in which the jury operates in arriving at a decision on the defendant's guilt or innocence. The prosecutor and defense are well aware that jurors' backgrounds and personal characteristics influence the way in which jurors respond to the evidence and arguments presented in the trial.

[44] *Ibid.*, pp. 19–30.
[45] *Ibid.*, pp. 31–32.

In selecting the jury, during the *voir dire* examination, the attorneys attempt to choose jurors who will make decisions favorable to the respective sides of the case. For each attorney, a trial may be won or lost during the empaneling of the jury. The composition of the jury is thus an important factor in determining the kind of definition that will be imposed on the defendant.

Defendants are supposedly tried by a representative body of the citizenry, at least such is the stereotype. However, social and economic biases are present in the methods by which jurors are selected. The result is that the lower occupational groups tend to be systematically excluded from juries in the United States.[46] Furthermore, and important for our purpose, the unrepresentative character of the jury affects the way in which juries deliberate and arrive at decisions about the innocence or guilt of the defendant.

The sources of bias in jury deliberation have been commented on in several studies of jury behavior. On the basis of a study of mock jury deliberations, it was found that foremen tend to be selected according to their social position in the larger community.[47] The incidence of selection was three and a half times as great among proprietors as among laborers. In addition, only one-fifth as many women were made foremen as would be expected by chance. The role of foreman is particularly important in jury deliberation because of the foreman's opportunity to change the opinion of the individual jurors according to his own views.[48]

The social status and sex of the individual jurors appear to be related to the extent to which they participate in jury deliberations and influence the overall decision of the jury. From the studies of mock juries it has been found that men and persons of higher social status, in comparison to women and persons of lower social status, have higher participation rates and greater influence in jury deliberations.[49] Men of the upper occupational groups tend to act more

[46] W. S. Robinson, "Bias, Probability, and Trial by Jury," *American Sociological Review,* 15 (February, 1950), pp. 73–78.

[47] Fred L. Strodtbeck, Rita M. James, and Charles Hawkins, "Social Status in Jury Deliberations," *American Sociological Review,* 22 (December, 1957), pp. 713–719.

[48] William Bevan, Robert S. Albert, Pierre R. Loiseaux, Peter N. Mayfield, and George Wright, "Jury Behavior as a Function of the Prestige of the Foreman and the Nature of His Leadership," *Journal of Public Law,* 7 (Fall, 1958), pp. 419–449.

[49] Strodtbeck, James, and Hawkins, "Social Status in Jury Deliberations,"

in jury deliberation than any other type of juror. Women and persons of the lower occupational groups, on the other hand, when they do participate, tend to react to the contributions of the others.

Thus, the ability of jury members to influence the decisions of others is in part a function of the social status and sex of the jurors. Furthermore, jurors also differ according to the kinds of things they focus on during the deliberation. In general, as found in another mock jury study, jurors spend about half their time exchanging experiences and opinions either directly or indirectly related to the trial. About a quarter of the time is spent on procedural matters, about 15 per cent is spent on review of the facts of the case, and about 8 per cent on the court instructions.[50] The more educated give relatively more emphasis to procedure and instructions, the less educated place greater emphasis on testimony, personal and daily life experiences, and opinions based on the trial rather than on procedure and instruction. The same researcher found that in insanity trials lower class jurors are more likely to favor the defendant. Women jurors, on the other hand, are more sympathetic toward the defendant than men, but are likely to qualify their verdict according to the nature of the offense.[51]

In the end, the verdict reached by the jury may not be the same as the one the trial judge would have rendered. The extent to which the verdicts of juries and judges differ has been extensively researched.[52] This study investigated and analyzed a sample of 3,576 cases of actual jury verdicts and the matching hypothetical verdicts of the judges involved in the cases. The major finding of the research was that the judge and jury *agreed* in 75.4 per cent of the trials. More specifically, the judges and juries agreed to acquit in 13.4 per cent of the cases and to convict in 62.0 per cent. In the trials in which the judges and juries disagreed, the disagreement was predominantly in one direction: the jury was more likely than the judge to acquit. The jury acquitted when the judge would have convicted in 16.9 per cent of the cases. In contrast, the jury con-

---

pp. 713–719; also see Fred L. Strodtbeck and Richard D. Mann, "Sex Role Differentiation in Jury Deliberations," *Sociometry,* 19 (March, 1956), pp. 3–11.

[50] Rita M. James, "Status and Competence of Jurors," *American Journal of Sociology,* 64 (May, 1959), pp. 536–570.

[51] Rita James Simon, *The Jury and the Defense of Insanity* (Boston: Little, Brown, 1967), pp. 98–119.

[52] Kalven and Zeisel, *The American Jury,* esp. pp. 55–65.

victed when the judge would have acquitted in 2.2 per cent of the cases. In other words, the juries were more lenient that the judges in 16.9 per cent of the cases and less lenient than the judges in 2.2 per cent of the cases. Practically, this means that when the defense decides to bring the case before a jury, the defendant fares better on the average 14.7 per cent of the times than he would have in a bench trial. The defense strategy in reference to the type of trial, in other words, plays an important part in determining the probability of a criminal conviction.

JUDICIAL SENTENCING

Following the conviction of the defendant, a decision must be made regarding the sanction that will be attached to the newly ascribed status of "criminal." The specification of the sanction, a process known as *sentencing*, involves the manipulations and discretions of a number of persons. In some jurisdictions the type and length of sentence are determined by the jury. In other jurisdictions sentencing is the responsibility of an administrative board. But in most jurisdictions in the United States the judge assigns the sentence.[53]

However, even when sentencing is the province of the judge, other persons participate in the decision-making process. Many states provide for a presentence investigation of the convicted defendant. The decision to proceed with such an investigation depends upon the discretion of the defense attorney and to some extent upon the maneuvers of the prosecutor and the judge. The presentence investigation is then made by persons in the probation department attached to the court. The report, which covers the defendant's personal and social background, his criminal record, and his mental and physical condition, includes the probation department's recommendations for sentencing. With the report and recommendations in hand, the judge imposes a sentence. But as shown in a study of the relation between presentence reports and dispositions, in most cases judges sentence according to the recommendations of the probation department.[54] Although the final sen-

[53] See Paul W. Tappan, "Sentencing Under the Model Penal Code," *Law and Contemporary Problems*, 23 (Summer, 1958), pp. 528–543.

[54] Robert M. Carter and Leslie T. Wilkins, "Some Factors in Sentencing Policy," *Journal of Criminal Law, Criminology and Police Science*, 58 (De-

tencing decision may belong to the judge, the decisions of others are crucial in the actual disposition.

The sentence imposed by the judge must fall within the limits provided by the penal law. The codes of penal law contain an elaborate classification of crimes with corresponding penalties graded according to seriousness of the crime. Within the boundaries of penal law, however, judges may exercise a great deal of discretion in deciding upon a sentence. A range of alternative sentences and lengths of sentences are available to the judge for any given crime.

Furthermore, recent legal innovations, especially the indeterminate sentence and probation, have increased the discretionary possibilities of sentencing. In addition, the movement toward individualizing treatment has provided both a rationale and justification for the use of discretion in sentencing convicted offenders.

The fact that sentencing practices of judges vary is easy to illustrate with sentencing statistics. A study of sentences assigned in nearly 7,500 criminal cases handled by six judges over a ten-year period in a county in New Jersey reported that the judges differed considerably in the frequency, length, and types of sentences they assigned to convicted offenders.[55] The diversity of the sentencing tendencies of the judges was even more marked when the sentences were analyzed according to the type of crime.

An explanation for the varied sentencing practices may be found in the backgrounds and attitudes of the judges. Some indication of the relation of various background and attitudinal characteristics of judges to their decisions is provided in research on the judicial decisions of a sample of state and federal supreme court judges.[56]

---

cember, 1967), pp. 503–514. Also see Robert M. Carter, "The Presentence Report and the Decision-Making Process," *Journal of Research in Crime and Delinquency*, 4 (July, 1967), pp. 203–211; Trebach, *The Rationing of Justice*, pp. 178–187.

[55] Frederick J. Gaudet, "The Difference Between Judges in Granting Sentences of Probation," *Temple Law Quarterly*, 19 (April, 1946), pp. 471–484; Frederick J. Gaudet, "Individual Differences in Sentencing Tendencies of Judges," *Archives of Psychology*, 32 (1938); Frederick J. Gaudet, G. S. Harris, and C. W. St. John, "Individual Differences in Penitentiary Sentences Given by Different Judges," *Journal of Applied Psychology*, 8 (October, 1934), pp. 675–680.

[56] Stuart S. Nagel, "Judicial Backgrounds and Criminal Cases," *Journal of Criminal Law, Criminology and Police Science*, 53 (September, 1962), pp. 333–339.

TABLE 5.2

Average Sentences in Months, by Offense and Judicial
Circuit, of Federal Prisoners Received from
the Courts into Federal Prison

(fiscal year ended June 30, 1966)

Judicial circuit	Narcotics laws	Forgery	Immigration	Liquor laws	Stolen motor vehicles	Other offenses
1st Circuit (Me., Mass., N.H., R.I., P.R.)	45.8	13.7	13.7	4.0	26.5	31.8
2nd Circuit (Conn., N.Y.)	64.2	18.2	9.2	14.9	25.2	23.8
3rd Circuit (Del., N.J., Penn., V.I.)	33.1	24.8	12.0	25.8	36.2	51.7
4th Circuit (Md., N.C., S.C., Va., W. Va.)	51.6	20.4	24.0	15.0	34.1	34.3
5th Circuit (Ala., Fla., Ga., La., Miss., Tex.	63.9	28.7	12.2	14.0	32.6	36.2
6th Circuit (Ken., Mich., Ohio, Tenn.)	69.6	24.4	17.6	16.2	30.4	49.3
7th Circuit (Ill., Ind., Wis.)	58.6	33.7	18.3	14.8	35.4	45.1
8th Circuit (Ark., Iowa, Minn., Mo., Neb., N.D., S.D.)	66.5	32.7	5.2	16.1	35.0	45.1
9th Circuit (Alaska, Ariz., Cal., Hawaii, Idaho, Mont., Nev., Ore., Wash., Guam)	58.7	31.3	8.2	8.4	40.9	53.0
10th Circuit (Colo., Kans., N.M., Okla., Utah, Wyo.)	73.9	36.0	7.4	19.4	37.5	45.4

Source: Figures from U.S. Department of Justice, Federal Bureau of Prisons, *Statistical Report Fiscal Year 1966* (Washington, D.C., 1967), pp. 46–47.

Each judge was given a decision score representing the proportion of times he favored the defense. Judges who tended to be more defendant-minded were likely to be Democrats rather than Republicans, non-members rather than members of the American Bar Association, non-former prosecutors rather than former prosecutors, Catholics rather than Protestants, and relatively liberal as measured by off-the-bench attitudes. Therefore, because of certain attributes, judges tend to make particular kinds of judicial decisions.

The decisions of judges also vary on a geographical basis. Ecological variations in sentencing statistics seem to indicate that the sentencing behavior of judges is normatively regulated and that the normative patterns differ from one region to another. In Table 5.2 are shown the average sentences assigned to persons convicted of federal crimes and committed to federal institutions. Even federal judges appear to be bound by local customs in sentencing persons who violate federal laws. For the convicted offender, the sentence he receives depends to some extent on the sentencing patterns of the jurisdiction in which he is tried and sentenced.

To show that judges differ in their sentencing practices is not necessarily to criticize judicial sentencing. The principal matter for our purpose is that defendants are differently defined and handled according to a process that consists of factors beyond the behavior of those who are criminally defined. Sentencing itself must be regarded as a process in which a series of decisions are made, decisions that are necessarily based on the operation of discretion by various legal agents.

These sentencing decisions probably are made within the framework provided by the law, including the nature of the crime and the offender's prior criminal record.[57] Nevertheless, within the boundaries of the law there is the opportunity for decisions to be made on the basis of social or extralegal considerations. The criminal sanctions that are ultimately imposed on the convicted defendant are influenced by such extralegal matters as the nature of the judges who assign the sentences, the norms that regulate sentencing, the social organization of the judiciary, the activities of the attorneys, and the responses and cues provided by the defendant himself. Sentencing could not take place any other way. Sentencing, like all social actions, is a human endeavor.

[57] Edward Green, *Judicial Attitudes in Sentencing* (London: Macmillan, 1961).

CHAPTER SIX

Penal and
Correctional
Administration

The application of criminal definitions is not completed with the sentencing of the convicted offender. Once a sentence has been decided upon, it must be administered. The administration of the sentence involves the same types of processes that operate in all other stages of applying criminal definitions. Thus, administration of the sentence is influenced by such community and organizational factors as community expectations, public reaction, and the occupational organization and ideology of the legal agents. Ultimately, within this social and cultural framework, the fate of the criminally defined is determined by the evaluations of those assigned the task of administering criminal sentences.

Conceptually and practically the administration of the criminal sentence can be divided into orientations that emphasize either the punishment or the treatment of offenders. The legal policies themselves provide a general orientation to the administration of sentences, and differ from one jurisdiction to another in the relative emphasis placed on penal and correctional objectives. It is in the administration of sentences that the fulfillment of these orientations becomes evident.[1]

A major development in the system of criminal justice in the United States has been the growing emphasis on correction. Over

[1] Research on the punishment-treatment orientation of several jurisdictions is found in Norman S. Hayner, "Correctional Systems and National Values," *British Journal of Criminology*, 3 (October, 1962), pp. 163–175.

the last fifty years probation and parole have been used increasingly, the juvenile court was created, treatment and prevention programs were developed, and treatment was established within the prison. All these signal the rise of "the rehabilitative ideal."[2] However, the results of this rise have not been as humanitarian in outcome as intended. In fact, the schemes resulting from the rehabilitative ideal have often led to an increase in penal measures. Many of the original aims of the ideal have been debased and practices have been instituted which conflict with individual rights. As a consequence, in the administration of criminal sentences the separate orientations of punishment and treatment have not been as disparate as might have been expected.

Whatever the general objectives of penal and correctional policy, the criminal sentence may be served and completed in a number of ways. The convicted offender may be placed on probation, imprisoned, given therapy, educated, executed, or paroled. Or attempts may be made to prevent criminal offenses through the establishment of community prevention programs. These efforts will be discussed in relation to the social reality of crime.

ORGANIZATION AND SUPERVISION OF PROBATION

The sentencing of an offender may consist of a prescribed period of probation supervised by agents of the state. The satisfactory completion of the probationary period depends on the offender's "good behavior" and conformity to the stipulated conditions of probation. The removal of the convicted offender from the status of "criminal" depends in the end on the actions and recommendations of the probation officer.

The decisions of probation officers are made within the broader context of the organization of the probation system. Currently the administration of probation is "involved in a transitional period of organizational conflict as a consequence of moving from a politically

---

[2] Francis A. Allen, "Criminal Justice, Legal Values and the Rehabilitative Ideal," *Journal of Criminal Law, Criminology and Police Science,* 50 (September–October, 1959), pp. 226–232. For a discussion of the possible infringement of the constitutional and civil rights of prisoners who are made to participate in therapy programs, see David Sternberg, "Legal Frontiers in Prison Group Psychotherapy," *Journal of Criminal Law, Criminology and Police Science,* 56 (December, 1965), pp. 446–449.

oriented to a professionally career-oriented service."[3] Increasingly, officers with a professional orientation are being drawn from the field of social work. These more recent workers contrast with the older, politically oriented officers. Though the professionally oriented workers are humanitarian and liberal in ideology, recognizing the dignity of the human personality, the older workers, drawing ideological support from a conservative middle-class philosophy of life, act as paternal counselors to the offender. The professionally oriented officers, trained in the casework approach, believe in promoting the welfare of the community by aiding the offender, while the politically oriented officers, relying on their own common sense and experience, attempt to protect the community from the offender.

The administration of probation, therefore, is beset by a conflict between the different types of officers and a subsequent struggle for the control of probation agencies. Moreover, the *decisions* of the probation officers are affected by these organizational problems. Because of several incompatible role obligations in his occupation, the officer has difficulty in making consistent and satisfactory decisions. The officer trained in social work finds that his acquired skills have not equipped him to deal with authoritative and punitive demands. These officers demonstrate a great deal of disagreement and confusion about the proper way to supervise cases.[4] Many regard some surveillance and enforcement activities as inappropriate responsibilities. The officer without training in social work, on the other hand, discovers that he lacks the knowledge and ability to understand the personal needs of the offenders he is supervising. Most probation officers, therefore, whatever their occupational orientation, experience some kind of conflict in their work.

Aside from the personal inconveniences that the officers experience, those who are ultimately affected by the organization of probation are the persons on probation. The divergent orientations to probation work directly affect the ways in which probationers

[3] Lloyd E. Ohlin, *Sociology and the Field of Corrections* (New York: Russell Sage Foundation, 1956), p. 45.

[4] See Lloyd E. Ohlin, Herman Piven, and Donnell M. Pappenfort, "Major Dilemmas of the Social Worker in Probation and Parole," *National Probation and Parole Journal,* 11 (July, 1956), pp. 211–225; Dale E. Van Lanengham, Merlin Taber, and Rita Dimants, "How Adult Probation Officers View Their Job Responsibilities," *Crime and Delinquency,* 12 (April, 1966), pp. 97–108; Seymour Z. Gross, "Biographical Characteristics of Juvenile Probation Officers," *Crime and Delinquency,* 12 (April, 1966), pp. 109–116.

are handled. "Competing philosophies and working principles within the agency result in the inconsistent handling of cases and produce frustrations on the part of the workers which, in turn, affect the counseling and disposition of problem cases."[5] As has been true for the offender throughout the processing of his case, his fate is decided as much by the problems and actions of others as by his own volitions.

In maintaining surveillance over the offender, the probation officer makes crucial decisions about the probationer's behavior. Probation can be successfully completed only when the terms stipulated in the sentence have been met to the satisfaction of the probation officer — or of any other legal agents who may come in contact with the probationer. If the probationer should be suspected of violating the terms of probation, his probationary status can be revoked. When such a case occurs, the probation officer recommends whether or not probation should be revoked. In many jurisdictions the decision is made during a judicial hearing.[6] At that time the probation officer can testify that the probationer has violated probation and can, in addition, offer an appropriate course of action. Officers tend to differ among themselves in the kinds of decisions they make in revocation proceedings.[7] The differences in recommendations are related to the personal characteristics and orientations of the officers, the extenuating circumstances of the cases, the role relations of the officers and the offenders, and the involvement of other legal agents in the cases. Again, decisions that directly determine the offender's future are made by others, and are influenced by extralegal considerations.

SOCIAL ORGANIZATION
OF PENAL CUSTODY

However diverse the rationale, the "prison exists as a dramatic symbol of society's desire to segregate the criminal."[8] And once the

[5] Ohlin, *Sociology and the Field of Corrections*, p. 47.

[6] Ronald B. Sklar, "Law and Practice in Probation and Parole Revocation Hearings," *Journal of Criminal Law, Criminology and Police Science*, 55 (June, 1964), pp. 175–198.

[7] John P. Reed and Charles E. King, "Factors in the Decision-Making of North Carolina Probation Officers," *Journal of Research in Crime and Delinquency*, 3 (July, 1966), pp. 120–128.

[8] Gresham M. Sykes, *The Society of Captives: A Study of a Maximum Security Prison* (New York: Atheneum, 1965), p. 18.

prisons are populated with criminals, the primary task becomes that of custody. To provide for the secure maintenance of inmates is thus the major objective in the administration of the prison.

> The prison wall, that line between the pure and the impure, has all the emotional overtones of a woman's maidenhead. One escape from the maximum security prison is sufficient to arouse public opinion to a fever pitch and an organization which stands or falls on a single case moves with understandable caution. The officials, in short, know on which side their bread is buttered. Their continued employment is tied up with the successful performance of custody and if society is not sure of the priority to be attached to the tasks assigned the prison, the overriding importance of custody is perfectly clear to the officials.[9]

The internal order of the prison is maintained by the strict control of inmates and the rigid satisfaction of all functions and personnel within the prison. The prison, as a "system of total power," is an organization unto itself, an organization that is relatively unaffected by external events and in which social control is paramount.[10] A distinct caste-like division is maintained between those who rule and those who are ruled. Furthermore, operation of the prison requires several, often contradictory, internal hierarchic organizations.

> The structure of prisons provides for three principal hierarchies — devoted to *keeping, using,* and *serving* inmates — but not for the integration of their divergent purposes. The separate organizations concerned with keeping and with serving inmates, for example, are not merely overlapping, but have entirely different and partly contradictory purposes.[11]

Each type of organization, in turn, promotes a particular kind of relationship between the staff and the inmates and a specific pattern of authority, communication, and decision-making. However, the

[9] *Ibid.,* p. 18.
[10] See Erving Goffman, "On the Characteristics of Total Institutions," in Donald R. Cressey (ed.), *The Prison: Studies in Institutional Organization and Change* (New York: Holt, Rinehart and Winston, 1961), pp. 15–106; Sykes, *The Society of Captives,* pp. 40–62.
[11] Donald R. Cressey, "Limitations on Organization of Treatment in the Modern Prison," in Richard A. Cloward, *et al., Theoretical Studies in Social Organization of the Prison* (New York: Social Science Research Council, 1960), pp. 79–80.

persons most affected by the divergent organizations of the prison are the inmates. Differences in the handling of the inmates' affairs are in large measure the result of the organizational problems inherent in the prison.

Administration of the prison can be best understood if we recognize the pressures exerted by groups that are attempting to achieve conflicting objectives. These "correctional interest groups" determine the ways in which prison policy is established and administered.[12] Among these interest groups are some that operate within the prison, such as the groups that make up the staff (administrative staff, custodians, professional workers) and the inmate population. Interest groups that operate outside of the prison include welfare agencies, educational groups, religious organizations, various kinds of legal agents, and leaders of political parties. The numerous inconsistencies and contradictions in prisons are due to the activities of these groups. The unique organization that is the prison is a result of the convergence of competing groups that define their interests according to the ways in which prisons are operated.

The objective of custody creates its own form of communication and decision-making within the prison. In an authoritarian fashion, a social order is imposed upon the inmates by the administrators. The conditions of such an order are maintained by a rigid system of communication. A massive body of regulations from above is passed on to those below. Decision-making occurs at the top of the administrative structure and is communicated through well defined channels of authority. At the bottom of the chain of command, that is, among the inmates, decision-making is kept at a minimum. "Inmates are officially permitted to make only those types of decisions which prior study by administrators has shown to be of no danger to community safety."[13]

The requirements of a custodial regime present the inmate with a personally frustrating situation. Being used to achieving goals, the prisoner finds that it is virtually impossible to realize these goals

[12] Lloyd E. Ohlin, "Conflicting Interests in Correction Objectives," in Cloward, et. al., *Theoretical Studies in Social Organization of the Prison*, pp. 111–129.

[13] Donald R. Cressey, "Prison Organizations," in James G. March (ed.), *Handbook of Organizations* (Chicago: Rand McNally, 1965), p. 1044. Also see Richard McCleary, "Communication Patterns as Bases of Systems of Authority and Power," in Cloward, *et al.*, *Theoretical Studies in Social Organization of the Prison*, pp. 49–77.

within the prison. The inmate is deprived of basic liberties, goods and services, heterosexual relationships, and autonomy.[14] Imprisonment is painful. Not only are the physical deprivations overwhelming, but the withdrawal of the many commonly assumed freedoms is an attack against the foundations of the prisoner's sense of being.

The pains of imprisonment cannot be easily removed by the inmate:

> Unable to escape either physically or psychologically, lacking the cohesion to carry through an insurrection that is bound to fail in any case, and bereft of faith in peaceful innovation, the inmate population might seem to have no recourse but the simple endurance of the pains of imprisonment. But if the rigors of confinement cannot be completely removed, they can at least be mitigated by the patterns of social interaction established among the inmates themselves. In this apparently simple fact lies the key to our understanding of the prisoner's world.[15]

The social world of prisoners, however imperfect that society may be, is an uneasy solution to the rigors of penal custody.

The inmate society is composed of a number of related social roles, which are structured by the ideology of the inmate code. The chief tenets of the code are, roughly: (1) Do not interfere with the interests of other inmates; (2) Refrain from arguments and quarrels with fellow inmates; (3) Do not exploit or take advantage of one another; (4) Maintain integrity in the face of privation; and (5) Do not side with the custodial authorities.[16] Inmate society, in prison argot, orders and classifies inmates by their orientations to the maxims of the code. The *rat* is an inmate who violates the norm proscribing the betrayal of a fellow inmate; the *merchant* exploits his fellows by manipulation; and the *tough* quarrels with other prisoners. The *square John* or *center man* makes the mistake of allying with officials. The role that most nearly fulfills the norms of the inmate code is that of the *right guy*, the *real con*, or the *real man*. This epitomizes what it is to be the ideal inmate, as judged

---

[14] Sykes, *The Society of Captives*, pp. 63–83.

[15] *Ibid.*, p. 82.

[16] Gresham M. Sykes and Sheldon L. Messinger, "The Inmate Social System," in Cloward, *et al.*, *Theoretical Studies in Social Organization of the Prison*, pp. 5–9.

by fellow inmates. But all the social roles are important for an understanding of the inmate society, for they establish patterns of social interaction among inmates.[17] Only by this interaction, within a society of the inmates' own creation, can the rigors of imprisonment be made bearable.

The extent to which prisoners conform to the inmate culture and oppose the expectations of the prison staff varies according to a number of factors. An early study observed that most inmates gradually assimilate aspects of the prison culture.[18] This assimilation has been called "prisonization," suggesting that inmates increase their commitment to the prison culture with the *length* of time they serve in the prison. Using another temporal conception, it was more recently found that conformity to expectations of the prison staff also depends on the length of time *remaining* to be served.[19] Wheeler showed that inmates tend to follow an adaptive U shaped pattern of conformity. That is, in the early and late phases of incarceration inmates conform to staff expectations, whereas those in the middle phase deviate from such expectations. Further research by others has specified these relationships. It has been found that the temporal effect of the inmate code on administrative expectations varies according to the social characteristics of the inmate, the type of crime committed by the offender, the experiences the inmate has had prior to imprisonment, and the social role the inmate plays in the inmate society.[20] Also, there is evidence that inmates in a prison oriented primarily to custody are less likely to become committed to prison objectives than inmates who are in a treatment-oriented prison.[21] All these findings support the position

[17] Sykes, *The Society of Captives*, pp. 84–108.

[18] Donald Clemmer, *The Prison Community* (New York: Rinehart, 1940), pp. 294–320.

[19] Stanton Wheeler, "Socialization in Correctional Communities," *American Sociological Review*, 26 (October, 1961), pp. 697–712.

[20] See, in particular, Peter G. Garabedian, "Social Roles and Processes of Socialization in the Prison Community," *Social Problems*, 11 (Fall, 1963), pp. 139–152; Daniel Glaser, *The Effectiveness of a Prison and Parole System* (Indianapolis: Bobbs-Merrill, 1964), pp. 548–583; Charles Wellford, "Factors Associated with Adoption of the Inmate Code: A Study of Normative Socialization," *Journal of Criminal Law, Criminology and Police Science*, 58 (June, 1967), pp. 197–203.

[21] David Street, "The Inmate Group in Custodial and Treatment Settings," *American Sociological Review*, 30 (February, 1965), pp. 40–55.

taken here, namely that the social organization of custody affects the administration of penal and correctional policy.

A final consideration in this administrative setting involves the relationship between inmates and the prison staff. Although the social organization of the prison is composed of an inmate system and an administrative system, prison organization also contains an informal system of inmate-staff relations. Both inmates and staff find it necessary to establish patterns of interaction in order to secure their separate interests. Successful operation of the inmate society requires a certain amount of cooperation from the staff. Likewise, the interests of the prison staff can be achieved only with the cooperation of the inmates. In a sense, there is a "corruption of authority" among the members of the prison staff.[22] The guard, for example, under pressure to maintain a smoothly running cell block, ignores breaches of prison rules in return for manageable conduct by the inmates. The informal inmate-staff system is thus a response to the insurmountable difficulties of maintaining strict control in a custodial institution. Informal patterns, not specified in prison regulations, are essential to the administration of penal and correctional policy within the confines of custody.

ADMINISTRATION OF INSTITUTIONAL TREATMENT

The modern prison is based on a paradox: it is designed to punish inmates and at the same time reform them by nonpunitive measures. The paradox is a logical outcome of earlier practices.

> Even the first prison used some nonpunitive measures believed to have a reformative effect on prisoners, such as haphazard religious and secular education, and exhortations in the name of God, mother, and country. An important characteristic of Elmira, the first American "reformatory," established in 1876, was provision of educational classes and vocational training, which were believed to be reformative. Yet this reformatory was constructed as a maximum-security *penal* institution, and the educational and vocational efforts at rehabilitation were made in that setting. The conflicting punitive and treat-

[22] Gresham M. Sykes, "The Corruption of Authority and Rehabilitation," *Social Forces*, 34 (March, 1956), pp. 257–262.

ment conceptions of reformation thus became institutionalized, for almost all prisons in the United States have followed the Elmira pattern.[23]

Because of the basic incompatibility of punishment and treatment, rehabilitating the offender within the punitive setting is either difficult, at best, or impossible. The inherent contradictions in the achievement of both goals are many.[24] From the standpoint of the inmate, it is contradictory to put an offender into a custodial institution against his own will, and, at the same time, expect him to be willing to enthusiastically participate in a treatment program. Similarly, there is the difficulty of expecting staff members of an institution to enforce and administer conflicting goals. Furthermore, the implementation of punishment and treatment requires diverse kinds of organizational arrangements. And theoretically, punitive restriction is incompatible with rehabilitation theory. Attempts at treatment, nevertheless, continue to be pursued vigorously within the prison.

Some of the most important concrete problems that arise in institutional treatment involve the relation of staff members to one another, the relationships of the inmates, and the interaction between staff members and inmates. The staff in charge of treatment is faced with the problem of getting the respect of the inmates while the inmates are also being required by other staff members to obey elaborate regulations. The regulations themselves are restrictive, and their violation results in penalties and even harsher restrictions. The therapeutic staff must maintain the restrictions while simultaneously offering the potential for inmate self-expression. This hypocritical behavior on the part of the therapeutic staff understandably receives little respect from the inmates. Further, the attempts of the therapeutic staff to administer treatment conflicts with the objectives of the custodial staff.[25] Not only are the goals

[23] Cressey, "Limitations on Organization of Treatment in the Modern Prison," pp. 85–86.

[24] See Donald R. Cressey, "Contradictory Directives in Complex Organizations: The Case of the Prison," *Administrative Science Quarterly*, 4 (June, 1959), pp. 1–19; Johan Galtung, "Prison: The Organization of Dilemma," in Cressey (ed.), *The Prison*, pp. 107–145.

[25] See Gene G. Kassebaum, David A. Ward, Daniel M. Wilner, and Will C. Kennedy, "Job Related Differences in Staff Attitudes Toward Treatment in a Women's Prison," *Pacific Sociological Review*, 5 (Fall, 1962), pp. 83–88; Joseph C. Mouledoux, "Organizational Goals and Structural Change: A Study of the

of the therapeutic staff and the custodial staff contradictory, but the implementation of their goals requires divergent actions. The therapeutic and custodial staffs view one another's daily activities as being at cross-purposes.

> Custodial workers are concerned with maintaining control and this concern is reflected in their priorities of action in a given situation as well as in the considerations they express in planning and supervising inmates' activities. On the other hand, treatment personnel tend to be concerned with mitigating the psychological or interpersonal problems of inmates. Conflict engendered by these different priorities is exacerbated because custodial and treatment workers, by virtue of their different responsibilities, are also frequently confronted in a different manner by inmates. These workers thus develop different conceptions of the inmates and each staff group becomes convinced of the correctness of its view and derides that of the other.[26]

In addition, the relationships that the inmates develop among themselves affect the implementation of treatment programs. As we have seen, inmates are forced to form their own social system in response to the pains of imprisonment. This inmate system, in turn, affects the way in which treatment is administered. In particular, the participation of inmates in treatment programs is influenced by their involvement in the inmate system. Inmates who are highly committed to the inmate system are less likely to participate meaningfully in a treatment program.[27] Imprisonment makes an inmate

---

Organization of a Prison System," *Social Forces,* 41 (March, 1963), pp. 283–290; George H. Weber, "Conflicts Between Professional and Non-Professional Personnel in Institutional Delinquency Treatment," *Journal of Criminal Law, Criminology and Police Science,* 48 (June, 1957), pp. 26–43; Stanton Wheeler, "Role Conflict in Correctional Communities," in Cressey (ed.), *The Prison,* pp. 229–259; Mayer W. Zald, "Power Balance and Staff Conflict in Correctional Institutions," *Administrative Science Quarterly,* 7 (June, 1962), pp. 22–49.

[26] Irving Piliavin, "The Reduction of Custodian-Professional Conflict in Correctional Institutions," *Crime and Delinquency,* 12 (April, 1966), pp. 125–134.

[27] See Daniel Glaser and John R. Stratton, "Measuring Inmate Change in Prison," in Cressey (ed.), *The Prison,* pp. 381–392; Clarence Schrage, "A Preliminary Criminal Typology," *Pacific Sociological Review,* 4 (Spring, 1961), pp. 11–16; Charles R. Tittle and Drollene P. Tittle, "Structural Handicaps to Therapeutic Participation: A Case Study," *Social Problems,* 13 (Summer, 1965), pp. 75–82.

system necessary, and the inmate system creates its own problems for the administration of institutional treatment.

The ability of a treatment program to be administered with any success in an institutional setting varies according to the ideology and structure of the prison. Although all prisons are punitive in that their inmate populations are confined against their wills, coupled with the fact that physical confinement produces social and psychological deprivations, prisons do differ in the manner in which they balance punitive and treatment goals. Some prisons are primarily oriented and arranged for the rehabilitation of the inmates, while other prisons devote most of their attention to the punitive custody of prisoners.

There is considerable evidence to indicate that the ideological orientation and structure of the prison determine the administration of institutional treatment programs. In one study, the organization of six institutions for male delinquents was examined.[28] The institutions differed in the relative emphasis placed on punishment and treatment. The findings showed that the treatment-oriented institutions varied systematically from those which were custodial-oriented in such characteristics as power distribution, departmental structure, role definition, organizational conflict, and systems of social control. It was also found that the staff attitudes toward inmates differed in the two types of institutions. All these factors were shown to influence the effectiveness of treatment within the institutions. Similarly, other research has shown that in treatment-oriented institutions inmates are more positive toward the prison goals and that inmate leaders often serve as coordinators and interpreters for administrative policies.[29] Whether the institution is basically oriented to treatment or custody determines the potential for the administration of treatment programs.

[28] David Street, Robert D. Vinter, and Charles Perrow, *Organization for Treatment* (New York: The Free Press, 1966). Also see Mayer N. Zald, "Organization Control Structures in Five Correctional Institutions," *American Journal of Sociology,* 68 (November, 1962), pp. 335–345.

[29] Bernard B. Berk, "Organizational Goals and Inmate Organization," *American Journal of Sociology,* 71 (March, 1966), pp. 522–534. Also see Street, "The Inmate Group in Custodial and Treatment Settings," pp. 40–55; Richard M. Stephenson and Frank R. Scarpitti, "Argot in a Therapeutic Correctional Milieu," *Social Problems,* 15 (Winter, 1968), pp. 384–395.

Whatever the orientation of the prison, some form of treatment is usually attempted. A host of treatment "techniques" have been designed and administered with the aim of changing criminals into noncriminals. The punitive-oriented prisons have tended to rely on clinical techniques, working with individual inmates in some form of counseling or psychotherapy. Treatment-oriented prisons, on the other hand, have tended to implement programs based on a group-relations principle, attempting to change the attitudes and behavior of inmates through the manipulation of social relationships.[30] Recent developments in institutional treatment have involved a modification of the custodial setting in which treatment is administered. Included in these recent developments are work release programs outside of the prison, halfway houses where offenders receive residential treatment while they also work or attend school, and community treatment centers where offenders attend daily sessions but live at home.[31]

Nevertheless, the effectiveness of institutional treatment is questionable: "Prisons are highly successful as a means of incapacitating persons for a period of time, but their successes in deterring them from becoming recidivists or repeaters is much less."[32] Others have similarly reached the conclusion that "the success of imprisonment as a means of reformation is very slight."[33] After a review of

[30] The theoretical background of the "group-relations principle," is discussed in Donald R. Cressey, "Social Psychological Foundations for Using Criminals in the Rehabilitation of Criminals," *Journal of Research in Crime and Delinquency,* 2 (July, 1965), pp. 49–59. For a discussion of specific programs, see Lloyd W. McCorkle, "Group Therapy in the Treatment of Offenders," *Federal Probation,* 16 (December, 1952), pp. 22–27; Lloyd W. McCorkle and Richard Korn, "Resocialization Within Walls," *Annals of the American Academy of Political and Social Science,* 293 (May, 1954), pp. 88–98.

[31] Arthur Pearl, "The Halfway House: The Focal Point of a Model Program for the Rehabilitation of Low Income Offenders," in Frank Reisman, Jerome Cohen, and Arthur Pearl (eds.), *Mental Health for the Poor* (New York: The Free Press, 1964), pp. 497–508; Lamar T. Empey and Jerome Rabow, "The Provo Experiment in Delinquency Rehabilitation," *American Sociological Review,* 26 (October, 1961), pp. 679–695; President's Commission on Law Enforcement and Administration of Justice, *Task Force Report: Corrections* (Washington, D.C.: U.S. Government Printing Office, 1967), pp. 38–44.

[32] Marshall B. Clinard, *Sociology of Deviant Behavior,* 3rd ed. (New York: Holt, Rinehart and Winston, 1968), p. 792.

[33] Edwin H. Sutherland and Donald R. Cressey, *Principles of Criminology,* 7th ed. (Philadelphia: J. B. Lippincott, 1967), p. 542.

several sources of available statistics, it was observed that a large proportion of prisoners return to prison.[34] Furthermore, and more specifically, approximately 55 per cent of persons received into state and federal prisons and reformatories have had previous experience with institutional rehabilitation. More recent evidence shows, however, that the prison may be more effective in rehabilitation than previously indicated. An analysis of several follow-up studies of inmates released from various prisons reaches the conclusion that reimprisonment rates actually vary between 20 and 40 per cent for different correctional systems.[35] In addition, it is argued, the criminal career of the offender is reversed during prison experience and at least 90 per cent of the inmates released from the federal prison system seek legitimate careers for a month or more after they leave prison.[36]

Some of the variations in reimprisonment rates can be accounted for by the ways in which treatment programs are implemented in various prisons. Variations are also influenced by the structure of the respective inmate populations, the selective use of probation, and the policies of probation and parole officers.[37] In regard to differences in prison populations, some persons have strongly presented the case that some types of prisoners are better risks for rehabilitation than others. Treatment methods used with one type of inmate could be less effective with others.[38] More recently, an elaborate typology of criminal careers was proposed, along with associated treatment strategies for each type.[39] Group therapy or milieu forms of therapy are recommended for semiprofessional property offenders, drug addicts, joyriders, aggressive rapists, and certain other types. Intensive psychiatric treatment is suggested for nonviolent sex offenders, incest cases, male homosexuals, violent sex offenders, and psychopathic assaultists. A program of minimal treatment is recommended for statutory rapists and for "one-time loser" property or

[34] George B. Vold, "Does the Prison Reform?" *Annals of the American Academy of Political and Social Science,* 293 (May, 1954), pp. 42–50.
[35] Daniel Glaser, *The Effectiveness of a Prison and Parole System* (Indianapolis: Bobbs-Merrill, 1964), pp. 13–35.
[36] *Ibid.,* pp. 475–487.
[37] *Ibid.,* pp. 13–35.
[38] George B. Vold, *Theoretical Criminology* (New York: Oxford University Press, 1958), pp. 296–304.
[39] Don C. Gibbons, *Changing the Lawbreaker: The Treatment of Delinquents and Criminals* (Englewood Cliffs, N.J.: Prentice-Hall, 1965), pp. 228–282.

personal offenders. The implication is that inmate recidivism rates will be lowered when treatment programs are related to the needs of particular types of offenders.

Another reason for the inconclusive evidence on recidivism is the lack of systematic postrelease information and reliable follow-up studies of inmates, which results in part from the underdevelopment of rehabilitation theories. Correctional workers, in addition, have not been trained in the skills necessary for evaluative research. But more important, persons engaged in administering institutional treatment have vested interests which foster particular kinds of programs. A negative evaluation of a program might mean personal loss for those associated with the program.

> Precise research on the "success" of either general programs of crime control or more specific methods of correction furnishes information which is the basis for public esteem and professional reputation, as well as information about the correctional technique being evaluated. These two are very different. Personal and organizational needs supplement the societal needs being met by administration and utilization of various correctional techniques. For example, by utilizing or advocating use of particular techniques in correctional work, a person may secure employment and income, good professional reputation, prestige as an intellectual or scholarly authority, the power stemming from being the champion of a popular ideology, and many other personal rewards. An agency organized around administration of a technique may fill such needs for dozens, even hundreds, of employees, and may itself have more general, organizational needs for survival. Hence, evaluative research results which would show that the technique is ineffective and would, thereby, seriously threaten the agency or the personnel must be avoided if possible.[40]

Regardless of the variations in the effectiveness of institutional treatment, we are left with the question of why some inmates *do not* return to prison. The argument usually advanced is that those who do not return have been rehabilitated *because of* specific treatment they have received in prison. But perhaps some persons do not return to prison *in spite of* institutional treatment. It might be

[40] Donald R. Cressey, "The Nature and Effectiveness of Correctional Techniques," *Law and Contemporary Problems*, 23 (Autumn, 1958), p. 758.

suggested that some ex-prisoners never return because of circumstances they encounter upon their release. This is the basis of the argument that most of those who return to prison have not been able to find legitimate opportunities during the first crucial weeks of their release.[41] Those who remain outside of prison most often find themselves in situations where it is no longer necessary to engage in criminally defined activity or are able to avoid criminal definitions in some other way. If this is so, the prison is virtually useless as a rehabilitative agency. Rather, it serves as a holding device while the inmate ages and society changes. Time itself can create new circumstances for the offender. Following this argument, the prison should at least be a humane place of caretaking. But, as implied above, custody (by definition) cannot be humane. Meaningful community and personal activity, much of it not currently regarded as "work," would be a much better alternative to penal custody and institutional treatment. "Rehabilitation" as an explicit objective would be better relegated to penological history.

ADMINISTRATION OF
CAPITAL PUNISHMENT

Several administrative means are used for releasing inmates from the prison. The original sentence may be modified by the executive in the form of pardon, commutation, or amnesty. Other prisoners are released merely through the expiration of their sentences. In such cases, the expiration date is fixed by the legislature, or on an indeterminate sentence, an administrative board decides upon the date of release within the minimum and maximum limits established by the court.

But the final and fatal solution to the removal of the prisoner is either by execution or by death from other causes while in prison. Some prison deaths are the result of the mistreatment of inmates. These deaths aside, primarily because the public has little knowledge about them, the administration of capital punishment can be considered as the most consequential aspect of the application of criminal definitions.

That death, as a legal sentence, is subject to human discretion

[41] Glaser, *The Effectiveness of a Prison and Parole System,* pp. 487–496.

seems rather absurd. But, since the death sentence is a provision of law and an administrative action, discretion operates in decision-making. To begin with, variations are found in the decision to make capital punishment a sentencing alternative. At the end of 1967 capital punishment was legally provided for in all but nine jurisdictions.[42] Among these jurisdictions variations occur in the number and types of crimes that are subject to the death penalty. In addition, states differ in their stipulations as to whether the death penalty is mandatory upon conviction.[43] Alabama provides capital punishment for sixteen offenses, with the mandatory sentence for assault by a person serving a life sentence. California has provisions for six capital crimes, with the mandatory sentence for train wrecking, assault by a lifer, perjury, and treason. More generally, most of the states with capital punishment provisions specify murder and kidnaping as capital offenses. Rape and treason are subject to the death penalty in about half the capital punishment states. Other states have scattered capital provisions for such offenses as robbery, arson, dueling, illegal use of explosives, attempt on the life of the executive, and lynching. Most of the variations result from differences in regional and local customs. Although it may be true that death is a private affair, legally lives are taken by the wills and actions of others.

The extent of discretion involved in the administration of capital punishment is obvious from a view of execution statistics. Historically, the number of executions has been decreasing. Between 1900 and 1966 there have been approximately 7,126 executions in the United States.[44] But since 1930, when statistics began to be systematically compiled, executions have declined from an annual average of 167 during the 1930's to an annual average of 27 during the

---

[42] Bureau of Prisons, "Executions 1930–1967," *National Prisoner Statistics,* No. 42, Washington, D.C., 1968, pp. 30–32.

[43] See Robert H. Finkel, "A Survey of Capital Offenses," in Thorsten Sellin (ed.), *Capital Punishment* (New York: Harper & Row, 1967), pp. 22–31; Leonard D. Savitz, "Capital Crimes as Defined in American Statutory Law," *Journal of Criminal Law, Criminology and Police Science,* 46 (September–October, 1955), pp. 355–363.

[44] Bureau of Prisons, "Executions 1930–1967," p. 8; and Hugo Adam Bedua, "Introduction: The Laws, the Crimes, and the Executions," in Hugo Adam Bedua (ed.), *The Death Penalty in America* (Garden City, N.Y.: Doubleday, 1964), p. 35. Also see Thorsten Sellin, "Executions in the United States," in Sellin (ed.), *Capital Punishment,* pp. 31–35.

first seven years of the 1960's. Though there were 199 executions
in 1935, there were 15 executions in 1964, 7 in 1965, and only 2 in
1967. Nevertheless, even with the decrease in executions, at the end
of 1967, 435 persons were under sentence of death waiting time in
the death rows of state and federal prisons.

There have always been regional variations in executions. As
shown in Table 6.1, approximately 60 per cent of the executions
between 1930 and 1967 occurred in the south.[45] Of the executions
between 1930 and 1967, 2,306 were in the southern states, 608 in the
northeastern states, 509 in the western states, and 403 in the north
central states. These regional variations are also evident according
to executions for *types* of offenses. Of the 455 executions for rape,
443 took place in the south. Less than 1 per cent of the executions
in the northeastern region were for rape, whereas rape accounted
for 15 per cent of the executions in the southern region.

Execution patterns also prevail regarding the *race* of execution
victims. Review of the execution statistics for the years 1930–1967
shows that 54 per cent of those executed were Negroes.[46] For rape,
in particular, the vast majority of those executed, 89 per cent, were
Negroes. These figures indicate that capital punishment is highly
discriminatory. Although the disproportional percentage of Negroes
executed, compared to the proportion of Negroes in the general
population, reflects lower class and racial involvement in violence,
this disproportion *also* indicates the greater willingness of jurisdictions to apply the death penalty to Negroes than to whites convicted
of similar crimes. Lower class persons from the discriminated-
against racial and ethnic groups have a greater risk of being executed than their counterparts in crime.

The discriminatory (or discretionary) character of execution
operates at several stages preceding the final execution. Not only
are Negroes and lower class persons more likely than others to be
convicted for committing similar crimes, but they are more likely
to be given a death sentence rather than some alternative sentence.
Further, once Negroes and lower class persons are placed on death
row, their sentences are less likely to be commuted.

The person or group of persons responsible for commutation of
execution sentences have grave discretionary powers. The authority

[45] Bureau of Prisons, "Executions 1930–1967," pp. 10–11.
[46] *Ibid.*, p. 10.

TABLE 6.1
Executions in the United States, 1930–1967

Region and state	All offenses	Murder	Rape	Armed robbery	Kid-naping	Other offenses
UNITED STATES	3,859	3,334	455	25	20	25
NORTHEAST	608	606	—	—	2	—
N.H.	1	1	—	—	—	—
Vt.	4	4	—	—	—	—
Mass.	27	27	—	—	—	—
Conn.	21	21	—	—	—	—
N.Y.	329	327	—	—	—	2
N.J.	74	74	—	—	—	—
Penn.	152	152	—	—	—	—
NORTH CENTRAL	403	393	10	—	—	—
Ohio	172	172	—	—	—	—
Ind.	41	41	—	—	—	—
Ill.	90	90	—	—	—	—
Iowa	18	18	—	—	—	—
Mo.	62	52	10	—	—	—
S.D.	1	1	—	—	—	—
Neb.	4	4	—	—	—	—
Kan.	15	15	—	—	—	—
SOUTH	2,306	1,824	443	23	5	11
Del.	12	8	4	—	—	—
Md.	68	44	24	—	—	—
D.C.	40	37	3	—	—	—
Va.	92	71	21	—	—	—
W. Va.	40	36	1	—	3	—
N.C.	263	207	47	—	—	9
S.C.	162	120	42	—	—	—
Ga.	366	299	61	6	—	—
Fla.	170	133	36	—	1	—
Ky.	103	88	10	5	—	—
Tenn.	93	66	27	—	—	—
Ala.	135	106	22	5	—	2
Miss.	154	130	21	3	—	—
Ark.	118	99	19	—	—	—
La.	133	116	17	—	—	—
Okla.	60	54	4	1	1	—
Tex.	297	210	84	3	—	—
WEST	509	496	—	—	7	6
Mont.	6	6	—	—	—	—
Idaho	3	3	—	—	—	—
Wyo.	7	7	—	—	—	—
Colo.	47	47	—	—	—	—
N.M.	8	8	—	—	—	—
Ariz.	38	38	—	—	—	—
Utah	13	13	—	—	—	—
Nev.	29	29	—	—	—	—
Wash.	47	46	—	—	1	—
Ore.	19	19	—	—	—	—
Cal.	292	280	—	—	6	6

Source: Adapted from Bureau of Prisons, "Executions 1930–1967," *National Prisoner Statistics,* No. 42, Washington, D.C., 1968, pp. 10–11.

and procedures for granting clemency vary considerably from one jurisdiction to another. They can be generally classified as:

> (1) a board alone; (2) a board alone, with the governor sitting as a member; (3) a board alone, the governor sitting as a member with grant, conditional on his being in the majority; (4) the governor, empowered to act only if a board makes a favorable recommendation (governor can overrule, denying commutation); (5) the governor with the advice and consent of an executive council, an elected body. Under the Federal Constitution the President alone has the power to abrogate a death sentence, derived from the power to grant reprieves and pardons.[47]

These pardoning authorities, in turn, hold differing philosophies about their responsibilities and use various criteria in making their decisions. Among the facts that these authorities consider are the nature of the crime, the character of the trial, the mental and physical condition of the offender, and rehabilitation possibilities.[48] But also important in their decisions are such extralegal considerations as the publicity surrounding the case, political pressures, precedents in other cases, and personal views on capital punishment. Once a person is placed in death row, life is dependent upon the personal problems of others.

The operation of selective factors in commutation and execution has been documented in research. Examination of the records for capital offenders in North Carolina showed that of the persons committed to North Carolina's death row since 1909, the sentences of whites were commuted more often than the sentences of Negroes. Sixty-two per cent of the Negroes committed to death row were executed, compared to 43.8 per cent of the whites waiting for execution. Also, inmates who went to the death chair tended to have less education and more menial jobs than those who were granted clemency.[49]

Similarly, it was found that of condemned inmates executed in Pennsylvania since 1914, significantly more Negroes than whites

[47] Solie M. Ringold, "The Dynamics of Executive Clemency," in Sellin (ed.), *Capital Punishment*, p. 227.

[48] See Elkan Abramowitz and David Paget, "Executive Clemency in Capital Cases," *New York University Law Review*, 39 (January, 1964), pp. 136–189.

[49] Elmer H. Johnson, "Selective Factors in Capital Punishment," *Social Forces*, 36 (December, 1957), pp. 165–169.

were included.[50] After finding that certain characteristics distinguished the executed inmates from those who had their execution orders commuted, such as the kind of counsel received during the trial, the researchers established that the race of the offender was the most important factor determining whether or not a person waiting execution was executed or granted clemency. It was concluded that "Negroes have not received equal consideration for commutation of the death penalty."[51] Such findings and conclusions illustrate not only that research in the administration of penal and correctional policy can uncover and explain the workings of the law, but also that such research has implications for legal reform.

Despite questions raised in the administration of capital punishment, popular arguments continue to be advanced for retaining statutory provisions for the death penalty. The principal arguments refer to (1) the death penalty as a deterrent to crime, (2) the certainty of punishment when the death penalty is prescribed, and (3) the financial economy of capital punishment.[52] On the first argument, the preponderance of evidence indicates that capital punishment does not act as a deterrent. This conclusion is based on a number of observations and researches that have demonstrated, first, that murder rates have remained constant despite trends away from the use of capital punishment; second, that where one state has abolished capital punishment and another has not, the murder rate is no higher in the abolition state than in the retention state; and, third, that the possible consequences of the act of murder are not considered by the murderer at the time of the offense.[53]

---

[50] Marvin E. Wolfgang, Arlene Kelly, and Hans C. Nolde, "Comparison of the Executed and the Commuted Among Admissions to Death Row," *Journal of Criminal Law, Criminology and Police Science,* 53 (September, 1962), pp. 301–311.

[51] *Ibid.*, p. 311.

[52] Sutherland and Cressey, *Principles of Criminology,* pp. 346–353.

[53] William J. Chambliss, "Types of Deviance and the Effectiveness of Legal Sanctions," *Wisconsin Law Review* (Summer, 1967), pp. 704–707. Evidence substantiating these conclusions is presented in Frank E. Hartung, "Trends in the Use of Capital Punishment," *Annals of the American Academy of Political and Social Science,* 284 (November, 1952), pp. 8–19; Leonard D. Savitz, "A Study in Capital Punishment," *Journal of Criminal Law, Criminology and Police Science,* 49 (December, 1958), pp. 338–341; Karl F. Schuessler, "The Deterrent Influence of the Death Penalty," *Annals of the American Academy of Political and Social Science,* 284 (November, 1952), pp. 54–62; Thorsten Sellin, "Capital Punishment," *Federal Probation,* 15 (September, 1961), pp. 3–11; Thorsten Sellin, *The Death Penalty* (Philadelphia: The Amercian Law Institute, 1959).

The second major argument in favor of capital punishment, the certainty of punishment, is negated by the fact that the death penalty is seldom imposed. Witnesses are less willing to testify and juries are less willing to convict when the penalty is the possibility of death rather than some other.[54] In regard to the third argument, the financial economy of the death penalty, the fact is that the per capita cost for execution is more than that for imprisonment.[55] Trials of capital cases tend to be more costly and time consuming than trials for other cases. In addition, the maintenance costs for inmates in death row are higher than for inmates in the rest of the prison. Thus capital punishment does not perform the functions claimed by its most vociferous advocates.

Although the capital punishment debate continues, the demise of the death penalty as a provision and as an actuality is imminent. Capital punishment is "an archaic custom of primitive origin that has disappeared in most civilized countries and is withering away in the rest."[56]

> If an intelligent visitor from some other planet were to stray to North America, he would observe, here and there very rarely, a small group of persons assembled in a secluded room who, as representatives of an all-powerful sovereign state, were solemnly participating in deliberately and artfully taking the life of a human being. Ignorant of our customs, he might conclude that he was witnessing a sacred rite somehow suggesting a human sacrifice. And seeing our great universities and scientific laboratories, our mental hospitals and clinics, our many charitable institutions, and the multitude of churches dedicated to the worship of an executed Savior, he might well wonder about the strange and paradoxical workings of the human mind.[57]

PAROLE DECISIONS
AND SUPERVISION

But the major form of release from prison is parole. Sixty-five per cent of the inmates released from state and federal institutions are

[54] Herbert B. Ehrmann, "The Death Penalty and the Administration of Justice," *Annals of the American Academy of Political and Police Science,* 284 (November, 1952), pp. 73–84.

[55] Sutherland and Cressey, *Principles of Criminology,* pp. 352–353.

[56] Thorsten Sellin, "The Inevitable End of Capital Punishment," in Sellin (ed.), *Capital Punishment,* p. 253.

[57] *Ibid.,* p. 253.

discharged by parole or some form of mandatory supervision.[58] In principle, parole is the conditional release of an offender who has served a portion of his sentence in a penal or correctional institution. The parole decision is made by the members of a parole board. Such boards may be staffed by personnel of an institution or by members of a statewide board of parole. In some jurisdictions the parole boards have the authority to administer parole as well as to grant it.

The wide range of discretion in the paroling of offenders is made obvious by a review of the statistics on parole releases from state prisons. As shown in Table 6.2, the differences in the use of parole by the various states are vast. To take the extremes, 100 per cent of the first releases from New Hampshire and Washington were by parole, whereas only 12.3 per cent of the first releases from Wyoming were by parole. The variations result from differences in both state penal laws and in the organization and administration of parole within the states.

The person most obviously affected by variations in parole practice is the offender. His future is settled by the decisions made by others. And as the President's Commission on Law Enforcement and Administration of Justice has argued, the decisions are not made adequately and fairly:

> Except for sentencing, no decision in the criminal process has more impact on the convicted offender than the parole decision, which determines how much of his maximum sentence a prisoner must serve. This again is an invisible administrative decision that is seldom open to attack or subject to review. It is made by parole board members who are often political appointees. Many are skilled and conscientious, but they generally are able to spend no more than a few minutes on a case. Parole decisions that are made in haste and on the basis of insufficient information, in the absence of parole machinery that can provide good supervision, are necessarily imperfect decisions. And since there is virtually no appeal from them, they can be made arbitrarily or discriminatorily.[59]

[58] See Bureau of Prisons, "Prisoners in State and Federal Institutions for Adult Felons, 1966," *National Prisoner Statistics,* No. 43, Washington, D.C., 1968, p. 28.

[59] President's Commission on Law Enforcement and Administration of Justice, *The Challenge of Crime in a Free Society* (Washington, D.C.: U.S. Government Printing Office, 1967), p. 12.

Application of Definitions

TABLE 6.2

Inmates Released on Parole from State Prisons, 1966
(Includes conditional releases under mandatory supervision)

State	Total releases	Percentage of total releases	Percentage 0–100
N.H.	117	100.0	
Wash.	1,391	100.0	
Kan.	1,199	98.2	
Utah	337	93.5	
Ohio	4,642	93.4	
Cal.	7,766	90.7	
Wis.	1,866	89.0	
Hawaii	168	88.7	
N.Y.	7,602	87.3	
Mich.	4,108	85.2	
Penn.	2,633	84.7	
Nev.	234	84.2	
N.J.	2,918	83.1	
Conn.	1,114	80.7	
Ind.	2,186	78.8	
Me.	587	78.5	
Vt.	237	78.5	
N.D.	152	78.3	
Colo.	1,612	76.5	
W. Va.	678	76.0	
Ill.	3,396	73.9	
Minn.	974	72.5	
Ark.	1,123	71.0	
Mass.	1,327	66.6	
U.S.	87,640	65.8	
D.C.	693	65.7	
Idaho	241	63.5	
La.	1,741	63.1	
Ia.	1,085	61.4	
Mont.	435	59.8	
Ga.	2,728	51.3	
N.M.	457	51.2	

TABLE 6.2
(continued)

State	Total releases	Percentage of total releases	Percentage
Ariz.	633	50.1	
Ala.	2,198	47.5	
Va.	1,827	47.3	
Miss.	863	45.0	
N.C.	2,722	44.5	
R.I.	127	44.1	
Fla.	2,899	42.5	
Ken.	1,340	42.3	
S.D.	411	41.8	
Del.	204	39.7	
Ore.	1,030	38.7	
Tenn.	1,558	37.2	
Tex.	5,824	35.7	
Md.	4,190	35.5	
Mo.	1,955	35.5	
S.C.	1,323	32.8	
Neb.	780	27.7	
Okla.	1,822	17.3	
Wyo.	187	12.3	

Source: Adapted from Bureau of the Prisons, "Prisoners in State and Federal Institutions for Adult Felons, 1966," *National Prisoner Statistics*, No. 43, Washington, D.C. 1968, pp. 28-29.

To say the least, decisions to release prisoners on parole are not always made according to the interests of the offender. Though much descriptive and predictive information is available on prospective parolees, decisions are often made intuitively. In addition, parole boards develop informal procedures for processing cases.[60] These procedures provide guides for decision-making. Parole decisions thus tend to be based on such characteristics as the original length of sentence rather than the individualities of each case. Inmates, when they are paroled, are likely to be released according to

[60] Some information on parole board decision-making is found in Don M. Gottfredson and Kelley B. Ballard, Jr., "Differences in Decisions Associated with Decision Makers," *Journal of Research in Crime and Delinquency*, 3 (July, 1966), pp. 112–119.

decisions made early in the prisoner's incarceration rather than in respect to the inmate's prognosis for a successful parole. Such procedures, combined with the nature of parole board compositions and the haste with which decisions must be reached, are the basis for the decision to parole prisoners.

Once parole has been granted, the satisfactory completion of the parole period is related to variations in the regulation and supervision of parole. Nationally, the average parole period for offenders is 29 months. Regionally the variations are considerable: 31 months in the east and northeast, 20 months in the midwest and plains, 28 months in the border south, 37 months in the south, and 24 months in the west.[61] Furthermore, state averages for the parole period range from less than 12 months to over 84 months.

The administration of parole is not dependent on regional variations alone. Parole supervision is also influenced by the relationship between the parolee and the parole officer. One of the principal duties of the parole officer is to observe the parolee's behavior, especially to determine if the parolee is violating the conditions of parole or any other regulations and laws.[62] Such parole conditions generally forbid unauthorized association with persons having a criminal record, and seek to control behavior in such areas as drinking, employment, and mobility. Parolees usually must obtain permission to change their residence, to travel to another area, to marry, or to purchase certain items. In practice the parole officer

[61] President's Commission on Law Enforcement and Administration of Justice, *Task Force Report: Corrections,* p. 187.

[62] Considerable research exists on the violation of parole and parole prediction, primarily from the standpoint of the characteristics and behavior of the parolee. See, for example, Dean V. Babst, Don M. Gottfredson, and Kelley B. Ballard, Jr., "Comparison of Multiple Regression and Configural Analysis Techniques for Developing Base Expectancy Tables," *Journal of Research in Crime and Delinquency,* 5 (January, 1968), pp. 72–80; Robert E. Clark, "Size of Parole Community as Related to Parole Outcome," 57 (July, 1951), pp. 43–47; Daniel Glaser, "A Reconsideration of Some Parole Prediction Factors," *American Sociological Review,* 19 (June, 1954), pp. 335–341; Lloyd E. Ohlin, *Selection for Parole: A Manual of Parole Prediction* (New York: Russell Sage Foundation, 1951); Jerome H. Skolnick, "Toward a Developmental Theory of Parole," *American Sociological Review,* 25 (August, 1960), pp. 542–549. For a discussion of some of the problems and issues in parole prediction, see Charles W. Dean and Thomas J. Duggan, "Problems in Parole Prediction: A Historical Analysis," *Social Problems,* 15 (Spring, 1968), pp. 450–459.

uses a great deal of discretion in supervising the parolee. But ultimately decisions made during the interaction between the officer and the parolee determine when, whether, and how parole will be completed.

The parole officer has a difficult role to perform.[63] He is expected to supervise and assist the parolee and, at the same time, to protect the community from the ex-prisoner. He must fulfill the authoritarian function of representing the state, but must simultaneously be oriented to the rehabilitation of the offender. As a middleman, or as a person who plays the role of "stranger," the parole officer must elicit the participation of the parolee and of the members of the community in integrating the parolee into community life. The role that the parole officer plays is both a handicap and a resource in accomplishing these diverse tasks.

The dual considerations of protecting the public and helping the parolee have given rise to different types of performance by parole officers, oriented in various degrees to these demands.[64] Some parole officers emphasize both control and assistance (the "paternal" officers), while others pay little attention to either (the "passive" officers). Others emphasize assistance but not control (the "welfare" officers). Finally, some emphasize control but not assistance (the "punitive" officers). Each officer style has a different way of perceiving and evaluating parolees. The fate of the offender is thus determined to a large extent by the type of parole officer who happens to be assigned to him.

PREVENTION PROGRAMS
IN THE COMMUNITY

Some programs attempt to prevent or reduce the occurrence of crime and delinquency. Such approaches are generally directed toward the larger environment. Instead of dealing with the individuals, circumstances and conditions beyond individuals are the focus of attention. Or, when individuals are considered, they are dealt

[63] Elmer H. Johnson, "The Parole Supervisor in the Role of Stranger," *Journal of Criminal Law, Criminology and Police Science,* 50 (May–June, 1959), pp. 38–43.

[64] Glaser, *The Effectiveness of a Prison and Parole System,* pp. 429–442.

with according to their larger social environment. Prevention programs, therefore, are usually located within community or neighborhood. Most of these have been directed toward preventing juvenile offenses. The administration of such programs is related to the scope and comprehensiveness of environmental change.

One of the first community-centered prevention programs, and the most limited in scope, was the Cambridge-Somerville Youth Study.[65] In the late 1930's in that area of Boston, 325 boys under twelve years of age were selected to receive preventive treatment. A matched group of the same size was selected as a control. Several community agencies cooperated in the program. The general program consisted of counseling, guidance for the family, medical and academic assistance, and recreational activities. The control group was given none of these services. At the end of the experimental period, in 1945, the two groups were compared for their contact with legal authorities. It was found, to the chagrin of the many persons involved, that the offense records of the two groups were similar; 27.7 per cent of the treatment group members had appeared in court for offenses, compared to 26.1 per cent of the control group. Still later, in 1956, a follow-up study traced the adult lives of the two groups.[66] As before, it was found that as many treated boys as control boys had been convicted of crimes in later years. The number of crimes committed was also similar for the two groups. The study can be commended for testing an assumption about the potentialities of one kind of prevention program, but the results are not pleasant for those who would change individuals through only limited change in social conditions.

A step beyond the casework approach to prevention are the programs that involve participant work with *street corner groups.* Such efforts are sometimes referred to as "detached worker" programs, indicating that a social worker is detached from the local agency. Workers are assigned to make contact with gangs in the community with the ultimate objective of changing the attitudes and behavior patterns of the members.

[65] Edwin Powers and Helen L. Witmer, *An Experiment in the Prevention of Delinquency—the Cambridge-Somerville Youth Study* (New York: Columbia University Press, 1951).

[66] Joan and William McCord, "A Follow-up Report on the Cambridge-Somerville Youth Study," *Annals of the American Academy of Political and Social Science,* 322 (March, 1959), pp. 89–96.

One of the earliest projects of this kind was conducted in New York.[67] From 1947 to 1950 trained workers were attached to several street gangs in central Harlem. In their association with the gangs, the workers attempted, with some reported success, to redirect the activity of gangs from fighting, stealing, sex offenses, marihuana smoking, and so forth to organized athletics, block parties, movie programs, camping trips, and the like. This approach was expanded by the New York City Youth Board to include work with gangs in several of the city's high delinquency areas.[68] A more recent but similar project was the YMCA-sponsored program in Chicago.[69] The success of the program is uncertain, but the research associated with it has been rewarding.

A project somewhat wider in scope operated in Boston from 1954 to 1957.[70] Attempting to reduce juvenile offenses in a lower class area, the Boston Delinquency Project included efforts to improve the coordination of community agencies and to improve the family system. But the primary objective was shifting the values of street corner groups from an emphasis on law-violating behavior to an emphasis on law-abiding behavior. In attempting to accomplish this goal, project field workers established and maintained contact with approximately 400 youths who were members of some 21 corner groups. The evaluative results of the project are mixed. Apparently the project had a "negligible impact" on the law-violating behavior of the gang members.[71] Nevertheless, it was successful in other ways. In particular, local community organization was improved. It is even possible that the project will have delayed effects in preventing delinquency.

Instituting a prevention program within an area of the city usually creates or brings to the surface conflict among city agencies. A post-mortem of the prevention project in Boston documented the

[67] Paul L. Crawford, Daniel I. Malamud, and James R. Dumpson, *Working with Teen-age Gangs* (New York: Welfare Council of New York City, 1950).

[68] New York City Youth Board, *Reaching the Fighting Gang* (New York: New York City Youth Board, 1960).

[69] James F. Short, Jr., and Fred L. Strodtbeck, *Group Process and Gang Delinquency* (Chicago: University of Chicago Press, 1965).

[70] Walter B. Miller, "Preventive Work with Street-Corner Groups: Boston Delinquency Project," *Annals of the American Academy of Political and Social Science,* 322 (March, 1959), pp. 97–106.

[71] Walter B. Miller, "The Impact of a 'Total-Community' Delinquency Control Project," *Social Problems,* 10 (Fall, 1962), pp. 168–191.

conflicts that occurred in the administration of the project.[72] About a dozen public and private organizational groups maintained an interest in the city's handling of crime and delinquency. The principal public agencies were the municipal government, the recreation department, the police department, the courts, the public schools, and the state youth corrections division. The major private groups were medical and psychiatric clinics, social work agencies, churches, universities, and various special cause groups, such as ethnic associations and crime prevention societies. Each of these groups had its own philosophy on such matters as the etiology of delinquency, the appropriate disposition of the delinquent, the proper organization and procedures for prevention, and the necessary qualifications for personnel in delinquency programs. Conflicts in these areas took place both *between* and *within* the agencies, resulting in a lack of coordination and a blocking of efforts in the administration of the city's prevention program. The respective agencies, in other words, acted as special interest groups to have their vested interests satisfied. Hence, prevention programs tend to have as a major (unstated) objective the satisfaction of the interests of those who administer the programs.

But some prevention programs do include within their scope the reorganization and development of the whole *community*. The rationale of such programs is that criminally defined behavior is a reflection of the larger social and cultural milieu and that in order to bring about change in behavior patterns the structure of the entire community must be altered. Furthermore, a basic procedure for implementing these programs is encouraging the leadership and participation of the people in the community. In other words, instead of outsiders' imposing their will and techniques upon the inhabitants, the residents themselves determine or help determine what changes are to be made in their community. Finally, the success of these programs does not necessarily depend upon the reduction of delinquent and criminal activity. Behavior patterns may eventually be changed. But in the meantime, improvements in the

[72] Walter B. Miller, "Inter-Institutional Conflict as a Major Impediment to Delinquency Prevention," *Human Organization*, 17 (Fall, 1958), pp. 20–23. Further documentation of the various groups involved in delinquency prevention is found in Robert M. MacIver, *The Prevention and Control of Delinquency* (New York: Atherton Press, 1966).

lives of the residents and in the social climate of the community are much more important.

The Chicago Area Project, beginning about 1930, has been the best known of these programs in community development.[73] The project began in three slum areas in Chicago and eventually expanded to other areas of the city. Under the direction of Clifford R. Shaw, the Area Project was based on sociological assumptions of human behavior and community organization. Basically, the implementation of the project was founded on the observation that people support and participate in only those enterprises in which they have a meaningful role. The first phase of the project required a knowledge of the area and its population. Local residents were encouraged to become the developers and administrators of the programs. Following this, residents developed services and organizations to meet the welfare needs of the community. The aims and methods of the Chicago Area Project were summarized as follows:

> (1) It emphasizes the development of a program for the neighborhood as a whole. (2) It seeks to stress the autonomy of the local residents in helping to plan, support, and operate constructive programs which they may regard as their own. (3) It attaches special significance to the training and utilization of community leaders. (4) It confines the efforts of its professional staff, in large part, to consultation and planning with responsible neighborhood leaders who assume major roles in the actual development of the program. (5) It seeks to encourage the local residents to utilize to the maximum all churches, societies, clubs, and other existing institutions and agencies, and to coordinate these in a unified neighborhood program. (6) Its activities are regarded primarily as devices for enlisting the active participation of local residents in a constructive community enterprise, for creating and crystallizing neighborhood sentiment on behalf of the welfare of the children and the social and physical improvement of the community as a whole. (7) It places particular emphasis upon the importance of a continuous, objective evaluation of its effective-

[73] Solomon Kobrin, "The Chicago Area Project — A 25-Year Assessment," *Annals of the American Academy of Political and Social Science*, 322 (March, 1959), pp. 19–29.

ness as a device for reducing delinquency, through constructive modification of the pattern of community life.[74]

From all evaluations of the Area Project, it is evident that residents of low-income areas have been able to organize themselves to promote their own communal interests.[75] Also, though precise measurement is not possible, apparently delinquent and criminal activity has been reduced through efforts in community development. But more essential, whatever has been accomplished has been primarily by self-determination and democratic participation.[76]

For some time Saul Alinsky has argued that the prevention of crime and delinquency is part of a larger program of institutional reorganization.[77] His program is not aimed specifically at prevention, but toward the eradication of unemployment, disease, inadequate housing, demoralization, and other aspects of social deterioration. Alinsky advocates the formation of "people's organizations" in the community. His program, variously known as Back of the Yards Project, People's Organization, and Industrial Areas Foundation, differs from the Chicago Area Project in several important ways:

> First, the membership is wider; each local organization, such as a church, a union, an industry, a club, is represented. Second, the primary purpose is the development of groups composed of persons who are interested in their own welfare and are organized for political action to improve their welfare. Third, the ultimate aim is the development of a nation-wide federation of people's organizations, involving millions of people; through such a federation powerful political influence could be exerted.[78]

[74] Clifford R. Shaw and Jesse A. Jacobs, "The Chicago Area Project: An Experimental Community Program for Prevention of Delinquency in Chicago," Chicago: Institute for Juvenile Research, undated. Quoted in Clinard, *Sociology of Deviant Behavior,* p. 738.

[75] Kobrin, "The Chicago Area Project — A 25-Year Assessment"; Anthony Sorrentino, "The Chicago Area Project After 25 Years," *Federal Probation,* 23 (June, 1959), pp. 40–45; Helen L. Witmer and Edith Tufts, *The Effectiveness of Delinquency Prevention Programs,* U.S. Children's Bureau Publication No. 350 (Washington, D.C.: U.S. Government Printing Office, 1954), pp. 11–17.

[76] The community development approach has since been expanded and applied in the Delhi Project, by Marshall B. Clinard, *Slums and Community Development: Experiments in Self-Help* (New York: The Free Press, 1966).

[77] Saul D. Alinsky, *Reveille for Radicals* (Chicago: University of Chicago Press, 1946).

[78] Sutherland and Cressey, *Principles of Criminology,* p. 697.

It is the element of political power in the hands of the people that makes this program more radical than most others. Because government officials must approve programs and appropriate funds, such programs have tended to remain as proposals.

Through the years, as we have seen, prevention programs have gradually evolved into ideas based on community development, institutional reorganization, and political involvement. The project that best represents the culmination of these ideas is Mobilization for Youth, a project located in a 67 block area on the Lower East Side of New York. Beginning in the early 1960's, Mobilization for Youth was founded on the theoretical proposition that obstacles to economic and social betterment are chiefly responsible for crime and delinquency among low-income groups.[79] The stated objectives of the project were "(1) to increase the employability of youths from low-income families, (2) to improve and make more accessible training and work preparation facilities, (3) to help young people achieve employment goals equal to their capacities, (4) to increase employment opportunities for the area's youth, and (5) to help minority group youngsters overcome discrimination in hiring."[80]

A number of fairly orthodox remedies were designed to implement job training and work projects for the unemployed youth and young adults. Specific programs included a youth job center, an urban youth service corps, on-the-job training, reading clinics, preschool education, and guidance counselors. But the rest of the project, the community action portion, has been devoted to more unorthodox procedures. Among these are a staff of lawyers for welfare clients, a housing unit which collects data on landlord violations, and a group of organizers who advise and assist the poor to collectively change their lives.

Thus, Mobilization for Youth is distinguished from many other contemporary programs by the organization of the poor for social protest and human betterment. The main hope of the project, according to one of the principal staff members, is to "organize the unaffiliated — to overturn the status quo and replace it with a higher

---

[79] See Richard A. Cloward and Lloyd E. Ohlin, *Delinquency and Opportunity: A Theory of Delinquent Gangs* (New York: The Free Press, 1960).

[80] *Action on the Lower East Side,* Program Report: July, 1962–January, 1964 (New York: Mobilization for Youth, Inc., 1964).

level of stability, without delinquents, alcoholism or drug addiction."[81] It is this political aspect that has gotten the project into trouble with government officials. The FBI has conducted an investigation of those who have engaged in organized action; newspapers have charged the project with subversion; the files of the project have been confiscated; and federal and local funds have been questioned and altered. To provide the poor with services and assistance from above has been the traditional way of doing things. It is regarded as subversive when the poor attempt to change the social pattern of their poverty. Welfare is legitimate oppression, political action by the poor is anarchy.

Fear of the more radical aspects of Mobilization for Youth is also imbedded in the potential of a widespread movement among the poor. Such a movement could alter the American economic system.

> If a movement of welfare recipients should, in fact, take form and gather strength, the ghetto and the slum will have yielded up a new political force. And it is conceivable that such a force could eventually be turned to the objective of procuring federal legislation for new programs of income redistribution (such as a guaranteed minimum income) to replace a welfare system that perpetuates poverty while it strips men of their fundamental rights as citizens.[82]

Indeed, programs of crime and delinquency prevention today have wide and significant implications.

REMOVAL OF CRIMINAL
DEFINITIONS

The law giveth, and the law taketh away. Because of the criminal law and its administration, persons are defined as criminal. Crime as a definition of one's status, then, can be withdrawn just as it is given — by legal means. For most who have been convicted and sentenced,

[81] Quoted in Murray Kempton, "When You Mobilize the Poor," *The New Republic* (December 5, 1964), p. 12.

[82] Richard A. Cloward and Richard M. Elman, "Advocacy in the Ghetto," *Trans-Action*, 4 (December, 1966), p. 33. Also see Richard A. Cloward and Frances Fox Piven, "The Weight of the Poor: A Strategy to End Poverty," *The Nation* (May 2, 1966), pp. 510–517.

punished, or treated, criminal status is temporary. The decisions that others eventually make will officially convert the criminal into a non-criminal.

No matter what legal means are used, removal of the criminal definition from the offender is not usually completely accomplished. Even when the legal definition of criminal is removed, the repercussions of once being defined as criminal linger on in many ways. Upon conviction for a crime, an offender automatically loses a variety of rights and privileges. Unless these rights and privileges are restored by some formal procedure upon release from the legal system, they may be permanently forfeited. In addition, the criminal record of the offender will be with him for the rest of his life.

Hence, convicted persons are subject to numerous disabilities and disqualifications quite apart from the sanction imposed in the sentence.[83] A number of civil rights — rights possessed by other persons by fact of citizenship — are lost by those persons convicted of felonies and certain misdemeanors. Most state statutes and constitutions provide for deprivation of some rights upon criminal conviction. Some states provide for the blanket loss or suspension of civil rights, including the right to vote, to hold public office, to sue, to enter into contracts, to inherit property, to testify, and to serve as a juror. Where statutes make provisions for the restoration of rights, it is often unclear what rights are restored and what disabilities and disqualifications remain. Moreover, the period of time for which rights are to be forfeited may depend upon the sentence. The law is complex and confusing in such matters.

In addition to the loss of numerous civil rights, convicted persons are usually prohibited from participating in other activities regulated by the government. They may be barred from obtaining professional, occupational, and business licenses, or from other kinds of employment. The procedures for restoring such privileges are not always clear. The restoration statutes usually restore only certain rights, leaving restoration of particular privileges to the discretion of various regulatory agencies.

In spite of legal efforts to remove the definition of "criminal" from the convicted person, and regardless of the provisions for restoring rights and privileges, the effects of a criminal conviction

[83] See President's Commission on Law Enforcement and Administration of Justice, *Task Force Report: Corrections*, pp. 82–92.

are likely to be felt throughout the lifetime of a person. The application of a criminal definition may in fact have the ultimate effect of creating within the person self-definitions by which he lives the rest of his life. The defining of persons as criminal may provide the definers with behaviors that may be similarly defined in the future. But for the time being, the application of a criminal definition is the creation of a crime.

4

Development of
Behavior Patterns
in Relation to
Criminal Definitions

CHAPTER SEVEN

Societal Organization and the Structuring of Behavior Patterns

No behavior is criminal until it has been so defined through recognized procedures of the state. In this sense, "criminal behavior" differs from "noncriminal behavior" only according to the definition that has been created by others. It is not the quality of the behavior, but the nature of the action taken against the behavior that gives it the character of criminality.

All behavior may be understood in reference to the organization of society. Depending on the structural location in society, certain behaviors may at times be defined as criminal, may be regarded some of the time as law-abiding, or may be the behavior that is involved in defining others as criminal. Although the contents of the actions differ, all the behaviors represent the *behavior patterns* of certain segments of society. Hence, persons who create criminal definitions and persons who become defined as criminal act in reference to *normative systems* learned in relative social and cultural settings.

The task is to provide a perspective of society that allows an understanding of crime in relation to the organization of society, a perspective that includes the behaviors of both those who are defined as criminal and those who do the defining. Basic to such a perspective are the assumptions that, first, behavior becomes structured in a segmented society and that, second, some segments impose their order on others by formulating and applying criminal definitions. That which is defined as criminal in any society is relative to particular behavior patterns within the society and to the segments of society that formulate and apply the criminal definitions.

SEGMENTAL ORGANIZATION
OF SOCIETY

The organization of society may be conceived according to two fundamentally different principles of social organization. The subsequent types of organization are based on the homogeneity and the heterogeneity of society.

> In the homogeneous type, a common system of values possesses it members, so that they tend to behave similarly in similar situations. In the heterogeneous type this common system still maintains its hold upon individuals. But free standing groups have developed, which are largely emancipated from the common conscience in respect to conditions with which they are especially concerned. The groups develop a value system specific to themselves and eccentric to the common system. There is thus a societal condition in which all persons tend to behave similarly in certain similar situations, and differently in certain other situations.[1]

Analyses of crime have usually been based on the homogeneous conception of society. The lack of consensus, consequently, has been regarded as a condition of "social disorganization" in society. Crime, following this conception, has been viewed simultaneously as an indicator and a product of social disorganization. However, when crime is viewed from the heterogeneous perspective, a very different theoretical approach develops.

The theory of the social reality of crime is formulated according to the assumption that society is characterized by a heterogeneity of organization. Underlying this theory of crime is a conception which, for consistency, I will refer to as the *segmental organization of society.* This conception is in sharp contrast to the *singular,* one-value system, conception of society. The two opposing conceptions are diagrammed in Figure 7.1. It can be seen that in addition to the homogeneous and heterogeneous assumptions of organization, the singular and segmental conceptions of social organization refer to the formulation and application of criminal definitions in society.

In the singular conception of society, crime must necessarily occur

[1] Frank E. Hartung, "Common and Discrete Values," *Journal of Social Psychology,* 38 (August, 1953), p. 3.

FIGURE 7.1

The Singular and
Segmental Conceptions of
the Organization of Society

The segmental society

The singular society

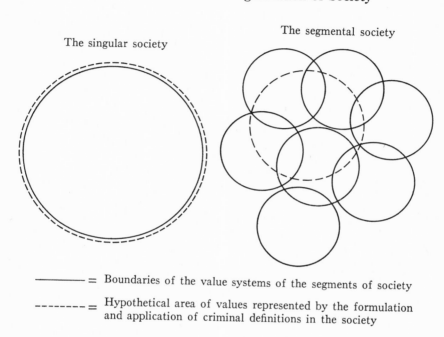

——————— = Boundaries of the value systems of the segments of society

- - - - - - - - = Hypothetical area of values represented by the formulation
and application of criminal definitions in the society

outside of any value system, since all persons within the society by
definition conform to one value system. Furthermore, the singular
conception is static, not allowing for conflict or change within the
system. But most important, the singular conception assumes that
the criminal definitions of the society represent the entire system
rather than any part of it. Any occurrence outside of the singular
society must be either deviant or criminal.

According to the segmental conception of society, on the other
hand, crime as a phenomenon occurs within a society and is, indeed,
an integral part of the organization of that society. The numerous
segments of society, each with its own value system, are variously
related to the criminal definitions of the society. For example, some
values of a segment may be incorporated into some of the criminal
laws, whereas other values are not represented in criminal laws. In

some segments all the values are represented by all the criminal laws. Some segments have none of their values represented in the formulation, enforcement, and administration of criminal laws in the society.

Finally, in their relationship to one another, the segments of such a society may or may not have overlapping values. But since few segments have complete mutual agreement on all their values, most are in conflict with one another to some extent. Therefore, the criminal laws of the society and their enforcement and administration are a consequence of the conflict and associated distribution of power between the segments. The segmental society is thus a dynamic society and, it may be added, one that provides for a meaningful explanation of crime.

BEHAVIOR PATTERNS AND PROBABILITY OF CRIMINAL DEFINITIONS

All persons, whether or not they are at times defined as criminal, act in reference to normative patterns learned in their social and cultural settings. Since society is segmentally organized, a variety of normative systems may serve as points of reference for personal behavior. Yet, because persons are differentially located in society in reference to the various segments, learning of behavior is selective. The content of one's learning is dependent to a great extent upon his position in society. Each segment of society provides its own patterns for appropriate behavior. Therefore, learning of behavior is structured and selective, or there are *differential learning structures* in segmentally organized society.

In the search for an understanding of criminal behavior, Sutherland may be credited with the most systematic formulation of the learning of behavior patterns.[2] His argument was that persons acquire patterns of criminal behavior in the same way in which they acquire patterns of lawful behavior — by interaction with other persons in a process of communication. The content of the learning includes techniques of committing offenses as well as the specific direction of motives, attitudes, and rationalizations. The specific di-

[2] Edwin H. Sutherland, *Principles of Criminology*, 3rd ed. (Philadelphia: J. B. Lippincott, 1939).

rection of motives and rationalizations, in turn, is learned in reference to favorable or unfavorable definitions of the law. It follows, from Sutherland's proposition of "differential association," that a person becomes delinquent or criminal because of an excess of definitions favorable to violation of the law over those unfavorable to violation of the law. In composite form, the theory of differential association postulates that "criminal behavior has as its necessary and sufficient conditions a set of criminal motivations, attitudes, and techniques, the learning of which takes place when there is exposure to criminal norms in excess of exposure to corresponding anticriminal norms during symbolic interaction in primary groups."[3]

The learning of criminal behavior patterns is not random, but is structured according to a person's selective exposure to situations in which both criminal and anticriminal behavior patterns are present. *Rates* of criminal behavior can thus be explained by Sutherland's concept of "differential social organization."

> . . . [I]n a multi-group type of social organization, alternative and inconsistent standards of conduct are possessed by various groups, so that an individual who is a member of one group has a high probability of learning to use legal means for achieving success, while an individual in another group learns to accept the importance of success and to achieve it by illegal means. Stated in another way, there are alternative educational processes in operation, varying with groups, so that a person may be educated in either conventional or criminal means of achieving success.[4]

Therefore, the likelihood that a person will engage in criminal behavior is dependent upon his relative exposure to various kinds of norms and, similarly, the extent to which categories of persons engage in criminal behavior is related to the structure of criminal and anticriminal behavior patterns in an area or portion of society.

This theory of the learning of criminal behavior has been described more recently as differences in access to types of "opportunity"

[3] Melvin L. De Fleur and Richard Quinney, "A Reformulation of Sutherland's Differential Association Theory and a Strategy for Empirical Verification," *Journal of Research in Crime and Delinquency*, 3 (January, 1966), p. 7.

[4] Donald R. Cressey, "Epidemiological and Individual Conduct: A Case from Criminology," *Pacific Sociological Review*, 3 (Fall, 1960), p. 55.

structures. In the formulation, persons are located in two opportunity structures — legitimate and illegitimate. Such opportunities are conceived of as both learning and performance:

> Our use of the term "opportunities," legitimate or illegitimate, implies access to both learning and performance structures. That is, the individual must have access to appropriate environments for the acquisition of the values and skills associated with the performance of a particular role, and he must be supported in the performance of the role once he has learned it.[5]

Accordingly, the learning and performance of the criminal role, as with the conventional role, depends upon patterned relationships through which values and skills are transmitted.

Whenever criminal behavior has been viewed according to learning structures, whether in the theory of differential association or in the reformulations, it has been assumed that there are behavior patterns which are objectively "criminal." Such an assumption is fallacious when held up against the theory of the social reality of crime, since according to this theory, behaviors and behavior patterns are neither criminal nor noncriminal. All behaviors are commonly *social,* and they become criminal only when they have been officially defined as such by authorized agents of the state. Without such defining, all behaviors are in a sense "criminal," since all could conceivably be prosecuted under some law.

In the theory of the social reality of crime we may refer, however, to the *probability* that particular behaviors may be defined as criminal by legal agents. Similarly, considering particular behavior patterns, we may refer to the probability that when they are followed they will lead to the application of a criminal definition.

Because society is segmentally organized, because criminal laws represent the values of only some segments in society, and because learning structures differ in the content of behavior patterns, persons and behaviors are subject to differentials in the probability of being defined as criminal. Only a *probability terminology* allows us to speculate about the likelihood that particular persons or behaviors will become criminal, that is, become defined as criminal. It may be

[5] Richard A. Cloward and Lloyd E. Ohlin, *Delinquency and Opportunity: A Theory of Delinquent Gangs* (New York: The Free Press of Glencoe, 1960), p. 148.

suggested that persons who learn the behavior patterns of the segments of society not represented in the formulation and application of criminal laws are more likely to act in ways that will be defined as criminal than those who learn the behavior patterns of the segments that formulate and apply criminal definitions. All behaviors are *social*, with varying probabilities that they will become defined as criminal, depending on their location in the segmental organization of society.

STRUCTURING OF
BEHAVIOR PATTERNS

So the problem is not explaining "criminal behavior," but explaining the development of behavior patterns that have relative probabilities of being defined as criminal. The question raised by the problem is: What are the structural sources of such behaviors? Generally, all structural sources are important to the extent that criminal definitions will be imposed on the behaviors produced by the sources.

The bulk of criminology consists of research and writing on the causes of "criminal behavior." For my purpose, this material can be reinterpreted as the *structural sources of the behaviors that may become defined as criminal*. A host of sources might be considered, but I will concentrate on what may be conceptualized as three general types of social structures that serve as the basis for patterning criminally defined behavior: (1) the age-sex structure, (2) the social class structure, and (3) the ethnic-racial structure. All three are related to the segmental organization of society. The probability that particular behaviors will both exist and be defined as criminal depends on the location of persons in the various structures of society.

Age-Sex Structure. In the official statistics on crime, contact with agents of the law follows a fairly consistent pattern according to the age and sex of the persons who are defined as criminal. The following questions may be asked: What are the behavioral variations according to age and sex status? How do behaviors become structured according to age and sex? And how are criminal definitions related to these behaviors?

For all categories of criminal offenses, taken collectively, the age of maximum criminality is in later adolescence and young adulthood. The largest proportion of persons arrested by the police are between

the ages of 18 and 24. In regard to the sex factor, males become involved in offenses several times as often as females. The rate of arrest
of males is now about ten times that for females.[6] In general, then,
the risks of being defined as criminal are much higher for young persons and for males.

The differences in criminal liability according to age and sex can
be viewed as the behavioral variations of those defined as criminal.
Persons under 25 years of age, when arrested, tend to be charged
with vandalism, auto theft, burglary, arson, larceny, liquor law violations, robbery, buying and receiving stolen property, and forcible
rape. On the other hand, arrests for drunkenness, gambling, driving
under the influence of alcohol, fraud, embezzlement, and vagrancy
tend to be among persons over 25 years of age. The percentage of
persons under 25 who are arrested thus varies considerably from one
offense charge to another. For the year 1967, 90 per cent of the arrests for vandalism involved persons under 25, while only 15.2 per
cent of the arrests for gambling consisted of persons under 25 years
of age.[7]

The difference in criminal liability according to sex is similarly
striking when we consider the kinds of offenses. Some are dispropor-
tionately male offenses and others are much less likely to involve
males. In accordance with the arrest figures for offenses in general,
for the year 1965, 7.4 males were arrested for every woman arrested.
In the same year, the sex ratios (number of men for every woman)
for selected offenses varied as follows: a sex ratio of 25.9 for burglary, 23.1 for auto theft, 18.1 for robbery, 15.4 for vandalism, 11.8
for gambling, 9.5 for vagrancy, 6.8 for disorderly conduct, 5.7 for
sex offenses, 4.7 for murder, 3.9 for fraud, 3.5 for larceny, and 1.1
for runaways.[8]

To what extent can we assume that these arrest situations reflect
behavioral variations according to differences in age and sex? Do
official criminal statistics reflect the behavioral variations of the age
groups and the sexes, or are the statistics only indicators of selective
law enforcement? Studies of the self-reporting of behavior provide a

[6] For the variations in arrest statistics according to such characteristics as sex
and race, see Federal Bureau of Investigation, *Uniform Crime Reports — 1967*
(Washington, D.C.: United States Government Printing Office, 1968).

[7] Federal Bureau of Investigation, *Uniform Crime Reports — 1967*, p. 123.

[8] Walter C. Reckless, *The Crime Problem,* 4th ed. (New York: Appleton-
Century-Crofts, 1967), pp. 99–100.

partial answer. Of juveniles, it has been found that (1) self-reported delinquency is extensive and variable, (2) the variations in the kinds of reported delinquencies are similar to variations in the official arrest figures, (3) boys report a much higher proportion of delinquencies than girls, and (4) institutionalized juvenile delinquents rank much higher than high school students in seriousness of involvement in delinquent behavior.[9] In a similar fashion, studies of the self-reporting of behavior among adults indicate that the general population is engaged in activities that could be defined as criminal and that, in addition, men are involved in behaviors that could be criminally defined more than are women.[10] The issue, therefore, becomes one of understanding the structuring of behavioral variations according to age and sex. Related to this is the ultimate matter of accounting for the defining of the behaviors as criminal according to age and sex in segmentally organized society.

The behavioral patterns of youth are in large measure the result of the very location of youth in the age structure. Though social class accounts for some of the variations in behavior among youths, the fact of growing up in relation to elders has a considerable influence on the kinds of behavior pursued by youths. Adolescent gangs, which engage in many activities that may be defined as delinquent or criminal, can be explained as an attempt by adolescents to gain the status not granted them by adults.[11] As a consequence of age grading in the larger society, gang membership and associated activities fill the status gap between childhood and adulthood. Delinquent activity naturally results when a society does not provide meaningful functions for adolescents.[12] Activities that have a high probability of being defined as delinquent or criminal are to be expected when an age group is not provided with any other meaningful means of involvement and fulfillment.

Since adolescence is a time for experimentation, for establishing an identity, activities of a high delinquency or criminal potential may

[9] James F. Short, Jr. and F. Ivan Nye, "Extent of Unrecorded Juvenile Delinquency: Tentative Conclusions," *Journal of Criminal Law, Criminology and Police Science,* 49 (November–December, 1958), pp. 296–302.

[10] James S. Wallerstein and Clement J. Wyle, "Our Law-Abiding Law-Breakers," *Probation,* 25 (April, 1947), pp. 107–112.

[11] See Herbert A. Bloch and Arthur Niederhoffer, *The Gang: A Study of Adolescent Behavior* (New York: Philosophical Library, 1958).

[12] Paul Goodman, *Growing Up Absurd* (New York: Random House, 1960).

be the only solution available for establishing that identity.[13] Although such problems of identity are critical for both sexes, they are qualitatively different for boys and girls. Some adolescent version of the adult male role must be achieved by the young male adolescent, whereas girls must attempt some kind of a solution that corresponds to the adult female role. Both the male and female attempts at identity result in different patterns of adolescent behavior. Hence, boys tend to steal, destroy property, or engage in fighting in an attempt to achieve power, prestige, and wealth. On the other hand, girls tend to become involved in those illicit sexual and related activities that are possible given the nature of the female role.[14] The sex roles of the adult world thus serve as general models for the creation of youthful activities that may, in turn, become defined as delinquent or criminal by adults.

As juveniles advance in the age structure of society, they learn to behave in more "adult" ways. The behavior patterns learned and pursued in adulthood have varying probabilities of being defined as criminal. The extent to which the behaviors become in fact so defined depends to a considerable degree on the careers developed by the respective adults, which will be examined in Chapter 8. The development of "criminal" careers is in part a function of personal experiences in contact with agents of the law.

A good part of the difference between adult male and female involvement in criminally defined activity is a consequence of the generalized adult sex roles in society. Men are expected to be active and aggressive; women are expected to be more passive. Each role leads to differing kinds and amounts of behavior that may be criminally defined. Furthermore, men are afforded greater opportunity to engage in the forms of activity — including the making of a gainful living — which may result in behaviors that have high potentials of being defined as criminal.

[13] See Erik H. Erikson, *Childhood and Society* (New York: W. W. Norton, 1950); Edgar Z. Friedenberg, *The Vanishing Adolescent* (New York: Dell & Company, 1962).

[14] Delinquency in relation to sex roles is discussed in Ruth Morris "Female Delinquency and Relational Problems," *Social Forces*, 43 (December, 1964), pp. 82–89; Albert J. Reiss, Jr., "Sex Offenses: The Marginal Status of the Adolescent," *Law and Contemporary Problems*, 25 (Spring, 1960), pp. 309–334; John C. Ball and Nell Logan, "Early Sexual Behavior of Lower-Class Delinquent Girls," *Journal of Criminal Law, Criminology and Police Science*, 51 (July–August, 1960), pp. 209–214.

Whatever the nature or amount of particular behaviors, the reason that they are criminal is that they are so defined by others. While the behaviors that provide the objects for criminal definition can be explained by the location of persons in the age-sex structure of society, the application of criminal definitions must be explained by the location of the persons and behaviors in reference to the expectations of the segments that enforce and administer the criminal law. Those behaviors that violate the sensibilities and interests of the powerful segments of society are the behaviors that have a high probability of being defined as criminal.

Social Class Structure. The official statistics on crime consistently indicate an over-representation of persons from the lower class. Studies of American communities have likewise shown that the lower class is most vulnerable to law enforcement and judicial action. In one New England town it was found that the lower classes accounted for about 90 per cent of the arrests over a seven-year period.[15] From such figures, it can be safely concluded that members of the lower class, in comparison to members of the middle and upper classes, have the greatest probability of being arrested and convicted for their behaviors.

Some recent evidence has accumulated to question, among juveniles at least, the existence of a disproportionate amount of illegal activity in the lower class. In one study comparing institutionalized juveniles and the self-reported behavior of a sample of high school students, it was found that 50 per cent of the boys in a training school for delinquents were from the lowest of four categories of socioeconomic status; however, when the high school boys reported their behaviors, only 13 per cent of delinquent activities were reported among boys of the lowest socioeconomic status.[16] Such studies tend to show that behavior that may be defined as criminal is more

[15] W. Lloyd Warner and Paul S. Lunt, *The Social Life of a Modern Community* (New Haven: Yale University Press, 1941). Similarly, see August B. Hollingshead, *Elmtown's Youth* (New York: John Wiley, 1949).

[16] F. Ivan Nye, James F. Short, Jr., and Virgil J. Olson, "Socio-economic Status and Delinquent Behavior," *American Journal of Sociology*, 63 (January, 1958), pp. 381–389. For related findings, see Ronald L. Akers, "Socio-Economic Status and Delinquent Behavior: A Retest," *Journal of Research in Crime and Delinquency*, 1 (January, 1964), pp. 38–46; Robert A. Bentler and Lawrence J. Monroe, "Social Correlates of Early Adolescent Theft," *American Sociological Review*, 26 (October, 1961), pp. 733–743.

evenly distributed throughout the class structure than is indicated by the official statistics on juvenile delinquency.

Therefore, it may be argued that such conduct is distributed throughout the social class structure, but that the lower class nevertheless has the greatest risk of officially being defined as delinquent or criminal. Furthermore, I contend that lower class members, in comparison to members of the other classes, are involved in behavior patterns that automatically have a greater probability of being officially handled as criminal. Lower class persons are more likely to engage in activities that result in charges of drunkenness, assault, disorderly conduct, burglary, and robbery. Middle and upper class persons, on the other hand, tend to be involved in activities that, although they may conceivably be defined as criminal, are not traditionally dealt with through criminal sanction. Although criminal laws cover such middle class behaviors as fraud, falsification of records, evasion of taxes, misuse of funds, malpractice, and so forth, these behaviors are not usually handled by traditional criminal procedures. Thus, I argue that the behavior patterns of the social classes are qualitatively different and that these patterns are subject to differing probabilities of being defined as criminal. How, then, can the varying behavior patterns of the social classes be explained in relation to criminal definitions?

The behavior patterns of each social class are learned during the childhood of each member. In addition to the behavior patterns associated with each class, the members of some social classes develop behavior patterns in response to the problems of growing up in a class structure. Some, depending upon their experiences in early life, their later circumstances, and their confrontation with the law, continue in a style of life that includes behaviors that have a high probability of being defined as criminal. For some other persons, a "criminal" career may be the culmination of a personal history that took shape in the class structure.

For the *lower class* child, especially for the boy, growing into adulthood involves gradually learning the cultural traditions of the lower class. The problem for the boy in the "hard core" lower class, however, is that as he matures, he has to cope with a female dominated household.[17] The adolescent street gang, accordingly, is the social mechanism for becoming a male adult in the lower class.

[17] Walter B. Miller, "Lower Class Culture as a Generating Milieu of Gang Delinquency," *Journal of Social Issues,* 14 (November 3, 1958), pp. 5–19.

The learning of the lower class structure involves an emphasis on the "focal concerns" of trouble, toughness, smartness, excitement, fate, and autonomy. In following these cultural patterns, within the context of the adolescent gang, lower class boys engage in activities that may well become defined as delinquent or criminal. Thus, lower class behavior readily and automatically becomes criminal in reference to the legal standards that embody the cultural patterns of another class.

Growing up in the *working class,* a cut above the lower class, presents its own problems for the working class boy, who is faced with the problem of adjusting to middle class standards.[18] Working class boys have learned the cultural patterns of one class but are assessed, particularly in the schools, by middle class standards that emphasize ambition, self-reliance, postponement of immediate satisfaction, good manners, wholesome recreation, control of physical aggression, and respect for property. Since working class boys do not fare well when assessed according to the "middle class measuring rod," they seek a solution by creating a "delinquent subculture." The "subculture" that they form or join may be in opposition to middle class values.[19] The solution for the working class boy then consists of a way of life that, being in opposition to the standards of the middle class, prescribes behaviors that have a good probability of being defined as delinquent or criminal.

For *middle class* youths, activity that can be defined as delinquent or criminal may result from following the practices of the middle class itself. Some of the behaviors of middle class youths, which may be in conflict with the law, are in fact a logical extension of values held by most middle class adults. Some middle class youths make use of the "subterranean values" of the middle class, allowing these values to serve as a code for everyday behavior rather than reserving them only for leisure-time activity.[20] For most persons growing up in

---

[18] Albert K. Cohen, *Delinquent Boys: The Culture of the Gang* (New York: The Free Press of Glencoe, 1955).

[19] Critiques of the theory of the "delinquent subculture" are found in David J. Bordua, "Delinquent Subcultures: Sociological Interpretations of Gang Delinquency," *Annals of the American Academy of Political and Social Science,* 338 (November, 1961), pp. 119–136; John I. Kitsuse and David C. Dietrick, "Delinquent Boys: A Critique," *American Sociological Review,* 24 (April, 1959), pp. 208–215.

[20] David Matza and Gresham M. Sykes, "Juvenile Delinquency and Subterranean Values," *American Sociological Review,* 26 (October, 1961), pp. 712–719.

the middle class, the values of the middle class need not necessarily be rejected in order to permit their violation. Rather, "techniques of neutralization" may be learned as motivation and rationalization for behavior that is at odds with middle class (and usually legal) standards.[21] At any rate, middle class youths, and also youths of the upper class, engage in behaviors that may be defined as delinquent or criminal, but the probability that such behavior will ever appear in the official statistics of delinquency and crime is relatively slight.

The conclusion about the interaction of social class, the structuring of behavior patterns, and criminal definitions is clear. Each social class has or develops its own behavior patterns, many of which may be defined as delinquent or criminal. But, since the formulation, enforcement, and administration of criminal law are based on a particular conception of appropriate behavior, primarily the standards of the middle class, official rates of delinquency and crime differ considerably from one social class to another. The probability that a person will be defined as criminal, therefore, is affected by his location in the class structure.

Ethnic-Racial Structure. The statistics on race and crime indicate that, in accordance to their proportion in the population, Negroes are arrested between three and four times as frequently as whites. Although Negroes comprise about one-tenth of the population in the United States, they account for nearly a third of the arrests for all offenses.[22] Similarly, drawing from judicial and prison statistics, Negroes have higher rates of conviction and imprisonment than whites. Hence, the status of being a Negro, in comparison to being white, involves a much greater risk of being arrested, convicted, and imprisoned. The probability of being defined as criminal thus varies according to one's location in the racial structure.

Also see Ralph W. England, Jr., "A Theory of Middle Class Juvenile Delinquency," *Journal of Criminal Law, Criminology and Police Science,* 50 (March–April, 1960), pp. 535–540; Harold L. Myerhoff and Barbara G. Myerhoff, "Field Observations of Middle Class 'Groups,'" *Social Forces,* 42 (March, 1942), pp. 328–336.

[21] Gresham M. Sykes and David Matza, "Techniques of Neutralization: A Theory of Delinquency," *American Sociological Review,* 22 (December, 1957), pp. 664–670.

[22] See Marvin E. Wolfgang, *Crime and Race: Conceptions and Misconceptions* (New York: Institute of Human Relations Press, 1964), pp. 31–35.

Furthermore, there are differences in the kinds of behaviors for which Negroes and whites are arrested. Of all the arrests in 1967 for the various offense categories, Negroes absolutely outnumbered whites in arrests for the offenses of murder, forcible rape, robbery, aggravated assault, prostitution, and gambling.[23] Likewise, Negro arrests made up more than half of the arrests for such offenses as stolen property, other assaults, carrying weapons, and possession of narcotics. Whites, on the other hand, tended to approach their proportion in the population only for such offenses as negligent manslaughter, arson, fraud, embezzlement, vandalism, drunkenness, drunken driving, disorderly conduct, and vagrancy. Thus, not only are the crime rates of Negroes higher than those of whites, the offenses for which Negroes and whites are arrested vary widely.

Differences in the crime rates of various ethnic and nationality groups are also evident.[24] And, as with the variations according to race, differences in the rate of crime are found in the types of offenses among different ethnic groups. Italian immigrants in the United States have had high rates of homicide and low rates of drunkenness, whereas Irish immigrants have tended to have lower rates of homicide and much higher offense rates for drunkenness. Also, though the immigrants themselves have tended to have offense patterns similar to those of the home country, their children have tended to be arrested for offenses characteristic of the areas in which they have settled. In addition, the extent to which the crime rate of the ethnic and nationality groups conforms to that of the native whites varies with the time the groups have been in the United States.[25] Finally, younger members of ethnic and racial groups take on the crime rates of the native whites more than do the older members.

Location in the ethnic-racial structure, therefore, presents a man with different perspectives. On the one hand, he is provided with the behavior patterns of his ethnic, nationality, or racial group. On

[23] Federal Bureau of Investigation, *Uniform Crime Reports — 1967*, pp. 126–128.

[24] For a discussion of these rates, see Donald R. Cressey, "Crime," in Robert K. Merton and Robert A. Nisbet (eds.), *Contemporary Social Problems*, 2nd ed. (New York: Harcourt, Brace and World, 1966), pp. 153–155.

[25] C. C. Van Vechten, "The Criminality of the Foreign-Born," *Journal of Criminal Law, Criminology and Police Science*, 32 (July–August, 1941), pp. 139–147.

the other hand, he confronts the behavior patterns of the other groups. Consequently, the respective groups respond to the normative patterns of their own group, but also assimilate the behavior patterns of the areas in which they reside. Furthermore, especially among Negroes, a person's behavior may be shaped by his reaction to the position he has been assigned. Much of the behavior of Negroes represents a reaction to subordination, economic insecurity, denial of employment opportunities, restricted participation, and discrimination.[26] That which becomes defined as criminal may be an honest attempt to create an existence that, ideally, is assured in the American dream.

Each group, then, develops its own behavior patterns in reference to its position in the ethnic-racial structure of society. While the behavior patterns consequently differ from one position to another, their criminality is determined not by the nature of the behavior itself but by the fact that persons in other positions, through the use of the legal resources of the state, define the behavior as criminal.

ECOLOGY OF BEHAVIOR PATTERNS
AND CRIMINAL DEFINITIONS

When rates of crime and delinquency are viewed according to their geographical or ecological distribution, regularities become apparent. In general, although there are variations from one offense category to another, crime rates in the United States tend to be higher in some states than in others, higher in urban areas than in rural areas, higher in larger cities than in smaller cities, and higher in the center of cities than in the areas further removed from the center.[27] Moreover, the high rates of crime and delinquency tend

[26] See Guy B. Johnson, "The Negro and Crime," *Annals of the American Academy of Political and Social Science,* 271 (September, 1941), pp. 93–104; Earl R. Moses, "Differentials in Crime Rates Between Negroes and Whites Based on Comparisons of Four Socio-Economically Equated Areas," *American Sociological Review,* 12 (August, 1947), pp. 411–420.

[27] For a discussion of such variations in offense rates, see Edwin H. Sutherland and Donald R. Cressey, *Principles of Criminology,* 7th ed. (Philadelphia: J. B. Lippincott, 1966), pp. 183–199. Critiques of the ecological approach in criminology can be found in Terrence Morris, *The Criminal Area* (London: Routledge & Kegan Paul, 1958); Judith A. Wilks, "Ecological Correlates of Crime and Delinquency," in President's Commission on Law Enforcement and Administration of Justice, *Crime and Its Impact — An Assessment* (Washington, D.C.: U.S. Government Printing Office, 1967), pp. 138–156.

to be found in areas characterized by lower class, non-white populations living under substandard physical conditions.

Though such regularities can be explained in any number of ways, I argue that ecological areas serve as structures for learning behavior patterns and for pursuing particular behaviors. Whether or not these behaviors are criminal, however, depends upon the decisions of others. Therefore, crime rates are ecologically distributed in accordance to the probability that certain behaviors, learned and pursued within the respective areas, will be criminally defined. The geographical variations in offense rates may thus be investigated in terms of the ecology of behavior patterns and criminal definitions.

Regional Variations. The amounts and types of crime vary considerably from one region to another in the United States. An early study found that particular offenses displayed a gradient pattern throughout the country.[28] It was found that murder was concentrated in the southeastern states, with a gradient to the north and west, and that robbery was concentrated in the mid-central states, with decreasing rates on either side of an axis running through the center of the United States. Essentially the same patterning of offenses was found several years later.[29] In the later study, it was found that some offenses show more of a regional concentration.

The regional variation in crime rates can be readily observed in the annual reports of offenses known to the police in the United States. On the basis of the 1967 report, the East South Central region had the lowest total crime rate, and the Pacific region had the highest.[30] In the specific offense categories, the South Atlantic region had the highest murder rate (9.6 per 100,000 population) and the highest aggravated assault rate (191.1). The Pacific region had the highest rate of forcible rape (21.8) and burglary (1308.4), while the Middle Atlantic region had the highest robbery rate (141.5) and New England had the highest auto theft rate (471.5). On the other hand, New England had the lowest rates in

[28] Stuart Lottier, "Distribution of Criminal Offenses in Sectional Regions," *Journal of Criminal Law, Criminology and Police Science,* 29 (September–October, 1938), pp. 329–344.

[29] Lyle W. Shannon, "The Spatial Distribution of Criminal Offenses by States," *Journal of Criminal Law, Criminology and Police Science,* 45 (September–October, 1954), pp. 264–274.

[30] Federal Bureau of Investigation, *Uniform Crime Reports — 1967,* pp. 62–67.

the country for murder (2.4), forcible rape (6.3), robbery (37.0), and aggravated assault (58.1), and the East South Central region had the lowest rates of burglary (532.3), larceny (334.9), and auto theft (192.4).

Variations in these regional crime rates can be explained by different structuring of behavior patterns, with relative probabilities of being defined as criminal, according to regions of the country. There are, first, regional variations in normative systems and behavior patterns. In the south a tradition of violence, including prescriptions on the use of weapons, accompanied by a code of personal honor, provides the background for behavior patterns that have a good chance of being defined as criminal.[31] In addition, the relation of whites and blacks in the south leads to personal conflict both within the two segments and between blacks and whites.

Second, opportunity for certain activities varies according to region. The high rate of property offenses in the west is in part a result of the casual style of living, the openness of the region, and the availability of property.[32] Opportunities for activities that may be variously defined as burglary, robbery, larceny, and theft thus vary from one region to another. Finally, regions differ in expectations of enforcement and administration of criminal law. Behavior patterns vary regionally, therefore, in both the conduct that may be criminally defined and the behaviors that result in the defining of conduct as criminal.

Community Variations. One of the most consistent findings in the ecology of crime is that overall crime rates are higher for urban than rural areas and that overall rates tend to increase with size of city.[33] Urban areas usually have higher rates for all major offenses, with the exception of murder. Hence, the greatest differences in rates between rural and urban areas are for crime against property, with the differences being less apparent for crimes against the person. The rates for all categories of offenses tend to increase progressively with each category of city size.

---

[31] See Walter C. Reckless, *The Crime Problem,* 3rd ed. (New York: Appleton-Century-Crofts, 1961), pp. 69–70.

[32] See Wilks, "Ecological Correlates of Crime and Delinquency," pp. 150–151.

[33] See Federal Bureau of Investigation, *Crime in the United States — 1967,* pp. 100–101.

Differences in offense rates between rural and urban areas can be accounted for by basic differences in the learning and opportunity structures of the two areas. In rural areas, as observed in several studies, there is a comparative absence of behavioral norms and social processes that are conducive to the development of behaviors that may be defined as criminal.[34] Similarly, gang activity in rural areas is relatively limited. The possibilities for learning techniques and motivations for committing criminally defined activities are not as readily available in rural areas as in urban areas.

Furthermore, opportunities for carrying out such property offenses as robbery, burglary, larceny, and auto theft are much greater in urban than in rural areas, and they become even more prevalent in large cities. In such ways, then, urban areas (especially the larger cities) provide the cultural and structural environments for the development of behavior patterns that may result in criminally defined activities.

Variations Within Cities. Studies over several decades have documented fairly consistent patterns in crime and delinquency rates within the boundaries of American cities. Research by members of the "Chicago school," in particular, established that the highest offense rates generally occur in the low rent areas near the center of the city and that the rates decrease with increasing distance from the city center.[35] In addition, such studies have shown that the relative rates of crime and delinquency tend to be maintained within the respective areas of the city in spite of changes in the population of the areas.

[34] Marshall B. Clinard, "The Process of Urbanization and Criminal Behavior," *American Journal of Sociology,* 48 (September, 1942), pp. 202–213; William P. Lentz, "Rural and Urban Differentials in Juvenile Delinquency," *Journal of Criminal Law, Criminology and Police Science,* 47 (September–October, 1956), pp. 331–339; Theodore N. Ferdinand, "The Offense Patterns and Family Structures of Urban, Village, and Rural Delinquency," *Journal of Criminal Law, Criminology and Police Science,* 55 (March, 1964), pp. 86–93; John P. Clark and Eugene P. Wenninger, "Socio-Economic Class and Area as Correlates of Illegal Behavior Among Juveniles," *American Sociological Review,* 27 (December, 1962), pp. 826–834; Richard Quinney, "Structural Characteristics, Population Areas, and Crime Rates in the United States," *Journal of Criminal Law, Criminology and Police Science,* 57 (March, 1966), pp. 45–52.

[35] Clifford R. Shaw and Henry D. McKay, *Delinquent Areas* (Chicago: University of Chicago Press, 1929); Clifford R. Shaw and Henry D. McKay, *Juvenile Delinquency and Urban Areas* (Chicago: University of Chicago Press, 1942).

The distribution of offense rates tends to be related to social characteristics of areas within cities. From several sources we conclude that offense rates of areas are related to the economic, family, and racial composition of the areas. In Baltimore, it was found that delinquency rates of census tract areas were associated with the percentage of owner-occupied housing and the ratio of nonwhites to whites.[36] Similar findings have emerged from studies of the distribution of offense rates in Washington, D.C., Detroit, and Indianapolis.[37] Using somewhat different modes of analysis and theoretical assumptions, others have found similar variables to be related to the ecology of crime and delinquency in Seattle, San Diego, and Lexington, Kentucky.[38] While such findings continue to accumulate, it is important to account for the relationships between social characteristics of areas and their offense rates. One meaningful explanation may be the different kinds of learning and opportunities in the areas. The learning of and the opportunity to engage in behavior patterns differ from one area to another.

Behavior patterns that may be in conflict with legal definitions necessarily develop within ecological areas of the city. Initially such behavior among adolescents may be inspired by no more insidious purpose than that of adventure and recreation. Thrasher found some time ago in his classic studies of gangs in parts of Chicago that children, in forming play groups, engage in activities that may be defined as illegal.[39] In time, conflict with other groups in the neighborhood and contact with other values may bring the

[36] Bernard Lander, *Toward an Understanding of Juvenile Delinquency* (New York: Columbia University Press, 1954).

[37] Charles V. Willie and Anita Gershenovitz, "Juvenile Delinquency in Racially Mixed Areas," *American Sociological Review*, 29 (October, 1964), pp. 740–744; David J. Bordua, "Juvenile Delinquency and Anomie," *Social Problems*, 6 (Winter, 1958–1959), pp. 230–238; Ronald J. Chilton, "Continuity in Delinquency Area Research: A Comparison of Studies for Baltimore, Detroit and Indianapolis," *American Sociological Review*, 29 (February, 1964), pp. 71–83.

[38] Calvin F. Schmid, "Urban Crime Areas: Part II," *American Sociological Review*, 25 (October, 1960), pp. 655–678; Kenneth Polk, "Juvenile Delinquency and Social Areas," *Social Problems*, 5 (Winter, 1957–1958), pp. 214–217; Richard Quinney, "Crime, Delinquency and Social Areas," *Journal of Research in Crime and Delinquency*, 1 (July, 1964), pp. 149–154.

[39] Frederick M. Thrasher, *The Gang* (Chicago: University of Chicago Press, 1927). Also see William F. Whyte, *Street Corner Society* (Chicago: University of Chicago Press, 1943).

members to engage in a variety of activities including stealing from stores, robbery, and aggressive acts against other gangs.[40] Violent gang activity may become a collective response of adolescents in lower class slums to the problems of living in such areas of the city.

The diversity of cultural traditions within ecological areas, and the juxtaposition of the traditions, appears to be important in the development of the types and amounts of criminally defined activities. In an area where adult activity is fairly stable and organized, adolescent behavior tends to take on the same qualities.[41] On the other hand, where adult patterns are not so integrated, juvenile activities (some of which may be defined as delinquent) tend to be unorganized and more violent.

In an extension of this formulation, it has been suggested that different types of adolescent "subcultures" emerge in relation to the integration of "criminal" and "noncriminal" patterns of the neighborhood.[42] Where adult patterns are integrated, the subcultures of adolescents will be "criminal" and the gangs will engage in theft, extortion, and similar activities in order to achieve status and income. In unintegrated areas, characterized by transiency and instability, "conflict" subcultures develop. Where neither criminal nor noncriminal traditions are available to youth, a "retreatist" subculture centering on drug use and sensual experiences will emerge. Whatever the utility of such a conceptualization, different behavior patterns develop within areas of the city according to the social and cultural structure of those areas.[43]

[40] Lewis Yablonsky, *The Violent Gang* (New York: The Free Press of Glencoe, 1962); Harold W. Pfantz, "Near-Group Theory and Collective Behavior: A Critical Reformulation," *Social Problems*, 9 (Fall, 1961), pp. 167–174.

[41] Solomon Kobrin, "The Conflict of Values in Delinquency Areas," *American Sociological Review*, 16 (October, 1951), pp. 653–661.

[42] Cloward and Ohlin, *Delinquency and Opportunity*, pp. 161–186.

[43] For further empirical works to support this position, see Irving Spengel, *Racketville, Slumtown, Haulburg: An Exploratory Study of Delinquent Subcultures* (Chicago: University of Chicago Press, 1964); Irving Spengel, "Male Young Adult Criminality, Deviant Values, and Differential Opportunities in Two Lower Class Negro Neighborhoods," *Social Problems*, 10 (Winter, 1963), pp. 237–250; Albert J. Reiss, Jr. and Albert Lewis Rhodes, "The Distribution of Juvenile Delinquency in the Social Class Structure," *American Sociological Review*, 26 (October, 1961), pp. 720–732. For an example of cross-cultural variations, see Lois B. De Fleur, "Ecological Variables in the Cross-Cultural Study of Delinquency," *Social Forces*, 45 (June, 1967), pp. 556–570.

Areas within the city differ in their structuring of behavior patterns and in the presence of opportunities for engaging in behaviors that may be criminally defined. Thus, crime rates tend to vary from neighborhood to neighborhood, depending on the opportunities for the pursuit of particular activities.[44] The opportunities for committing each type of crime depend on the availability of such targets as safes, cash registers, personal possessions, and other persons and are reflected in the rates for each type of offense. Rates for burglary, robbery, and larceny are highest in areas that have a high proportion of business and commercial activity. Likewise, rates of auto theft are highest where a great deal of space is devoted to parking. Rates of forcible rape are highest in areas with a high proportion of resident females, and rates of murder and assault are highest where many personal victims are available.

All behavior patterns, then, develop within concrete ecological areas. However, the patterns that develop are relative to one another not only in content but also in the probability that they will be defined as criminal. According to the perspective provided here, the forms and amounts of crime in any community are the product of the conflict between the behavior patterns of the community and the patterns represented by those who are formulating and applying criminal definitions. And, since the nature and extent of this conflict varies ecologically, rates of crime are differentially distributed according to ecological areas.

GENERAL CULTURAL THEMES
IN SEGMENTAL SOCIETY

In spite of the variations in normative systems and behavior patterns from one social or ecological segment to another, some *general cultural themes* pervade all segments. Diversity in a society does not mean that no cultural themes will be shared by all segments. Any society, in a sense, contains its own prescriptions for crime. Although laws may define some activities as criminal, the same society may contain cultural themes that are conducive to the violation of these laws. Such themes are evident in American

[44] Sarah L. Boggs, "Urban Crime Patterns," *American Sociological Review*, 39 (December, 1965), pp. 899–908.

society, making some behavior patterns that may be defined as criminal a consistent part of the American way of life.

Conformity to the law has never been an overwhelming obsession in America. Local laws were established for governing the conduct of the members of the early settlements, but behavior outside the settlements was largely a matter of personal discretion. The frontier experience called for an individuality that made each man a law unto himself. The western frontier, especially, became a haven for activities which, if pursued elsewhere, would probably have been dealt with by means of the criminal law.[45] But the frontier became an area of "lawlessness" not so much because of the definitions imposed on the conduct but because there was no law to enforce and administer. The behavior patterns that developed in the frontier context and the corresponding attitudes toward authority that supported the behavior patterns remain today as part of our cultural heritage.

The dynamic character of the American experience produced a "criminogenic" culture in still other ways. Although they certainly do not explain variations in specific behavior patterns, with varying probabilities of criminal definition, cultural themes that appeared in America did stress success, power, status, prestige, competition, and exploitation.[46] Success in the competitive struggle came to be evaluated in terms of money and material wealth. Pecuniary success was established as the measure of most men, being extolled as the major goal throughout the population, with less emphasis being placed on the means by which the goal was to be achieved.[47] The choice of paths to success, however, continues to depend upon differences in the normative systems of the respective segments of society.

At the same time that an open society was creating cultural themes conducive to law violation, other values were being affirmed that were in opposition to those which might lead to criminally defined activity. A basic American hypocrisy thus became en-

---

[45] See Mabel A. Elliott, "Crime and the Frontier Mores," *American Sociological Review*, 9 (April, 1944), pp. 185–192.

[46] Donald R. Taft, *Criminology*, 3rd ed. (New York: Macmillan, 1956), pp. 336–343. Milton L. Barron, *The Juvenile in Delinquent Society* (New York: Alfred A. Knopf, 1960), pp. 199–221.

[47] Robert K. Merton, *Social Theory and Social Structure* (New York: The Free Press, 1957), pp. 131–160.

grained. On the one hand, a Puritan ethic prohibited indulgence in certain activities, such as gambling, drinking, prostitution, and drug use, and on the other, a way of life grew around those who appreciated such indulgences. The contradiction and paradox today has been described as follows:

> It would seem that the vast majority of Americans today would like to have their proverbial cake and eat it, too, by theoretically affirming values which they hold dear, and, at the same time, reserving for themselves a certain leeway in realizing wishes which may not always correspond to these values. As a result, law and a high degree of lawlessness exist side by side, and moralists and gangsters complement each other.[48]

Not only have illicit behaviors been made illegal by criminal law, but criminal organizations have been established to satisfy the activities that we want both prohibited and fulfilled.

The economic system that developed in America also contains its own cultural themes conducive to particular kinds of behavior patterns. A capitalist economy, based on competition and free enterprise, promotes an ethic that stresses the rightness of any activity that is pursued in the interest of one's business or occupational activity. Consequently, otherwise "respectable" members of society engage in activities that have been criminally defined by various laws, but which are not considered by them or most of the public as criminal.[49] Such business and occupational activities as misrepresentation in advertising, fraudulent financial manipulations, illegal rebates, misappropriation of public funds, fee splitting, and fraudulent damage claims are regarded as little more than the American way of doing business. In spite of recent legislation and administrative rulings, that which is done in the name of business

[48] Robert K. Woetzel, "An Overview of Organized Crime: Mores Versus Morality," *The Annals of the American Academy of Political and Social Science,* 347 (May, 1963), p. 8.

[49] See, in particular, Edwin H. Sutherland, *White Collar Crime* (New York: Holt, Rinehart and Winston, 1949); Marshall B. Clinard, *The Black Market: A Study of White Collar Crime* (New York: Holt, Rinehart and Winston, 1952); Richard Quinney, "The Study of White Collar Crime: Toward a Reorientation in Theory and Research," *Journal of Criminal Law, Criminology and Police Science,* 55 (June, 1964), pp. 208–214; Gilbert Geis, "White Collar Crime: The Heavy Electrical Equipment Antitrust Cases of 1961," in Marshall B. Clinard and Richard Quinney, *Criminal Behavior Systems: A Typology* (New York: Holt, Rinehart and Winston, 1967), pp. 139–151.

and gainful employment tends to be beyond public and legal reproach.

The rationale for one of the most entrenched criminal activities in the United States, organized crime, is consistent with the free enterprise system of business. Organized crime, like legitimate business, attempts to achieve maximum returns with a minimum of expenditure by efficient organization and management. It is therefore an integral part of our culture, being closely tied to such factors as the profit motive, indifference to public affairs, general disregard for law, laissez-faire economics, and questionable political practices.[50] Furthermore, organized crime has become a normal way of achieving success for members of a number of groups in society. It has served as an appropriate activity for late-arriving immigrant groups and has become closely associated with the neighborhood politics of these groups.[51] Organized crime thus receives considerable support in the United States because of its relationship with legitimate business patterns.

> One basic fact stands out from the details of this discussion, namely that organized crime must be thought of as a natural growth, or as a development adjunct to our general system of private profit economy. Business, industry, and finance all are competitive enterprises within the area of legal operations. But there is also an area of genuine economic demand for things and services not permitted under our legal and social codes. Organized crime is the system of business function in the area. It, too, is competitive, and hence must organize for its self-protection and for control of the market.[52]

Although the formulation and enforcement of criminal laws may assist in the control of such crime, the integration of organized crime into American culture prevents any serious control of the activity.

The relationship between cultural themes and criminally defined activities can also be seen in the American emphasis on violence. The

[50] Alfred R. Lindesmith, "Organized Crime," *Annals of the American Academy of Political and Social Science*, 217 (September, 1941), pp. 76–83.
[51] Daniel Bell, "Crime as an American Way of Life," *Antioch Review*, 13 (June, 1953), pp. 131–154; Digby Baltzell, *The Protestant Establishment* (New York: Random House, 1964), pp. 49, 215–216.
[52] George B. Vold, *Theoretical Criminology* (New York: Oxford University Press, 1958), p. 240.

emphasis, though considerable, is nevertheless characterized by ambivalence.[53] We are afraid of violence, protecting ourselves by whatever means possible, yet we are fascinated by it, supporting its coverage in the mass media and condoning it when applied to others in our own interest or in the interest of our group or nation. That violence is qualified does not negate it as an important American cultural theme. Violence that becomes defined as criminal is obviously distributed unevenly throughout society.[54] Violence that occurs in the interest of the dominant segments of society is, however, legitimized violence. Assault and murder used on others in war, in military operations, in policing riots, and in the controlling of actions conceived as politically subversive are not defined as criminal.[55] Such uses of violence are patriotic and as American, as one black leader has noted, as cherry pie. Violence, wherever it originates and however it is promoted in our society, becomes culturally diffused throughout the society as a cultural theme that affects the lives of us all.

Finally, we must recognize that the general cultural themes are *mediated* by the respective segments of society. The effects of the cultural themes consequently vary from one segment to another.

[53] William A. Westley, "The Escalation of Violence through Legitimation," *Annals of the American Academy of Political and Social Science,* 364 (March, 1966), p. 125.

[54] See Robert C. Bensing and Oliver Schroeder, *Homicide in an Urban Community* (Springfield, Ill.: Charles C Thomas, 1960); Henry Allen Bullock, "Urban Homicide in Theory and Fact," *Journal of Criminal Law, Criminology and Police Science,* 45 (January–February, 1955), pp. 565–575; Gilbert Geis, "Violence and Organized Crime," *Annals of the American Academy of Political and Social Science,* 364 (March, 1966), pp. 86–95; Thomas F. Pettigrew and Rosalind B. Spier, "Ecological Structure of Negro Homicide," *American Journal of Sociology,* 67 (May, 1962), pp. 621–629; David P. Pittman and William Handy, "Patterns in Criminal Aggravated Assault," *Journal of Criminal Law, Criminology and Police Science,* 55 (December, 1964), pp. 462–470; Austin L. Porterfield, *Cultures of Violence* (Fort Worth, Texas: Leo Potishman Foundation, 1965); Marvin E. Wolfgang and Franco Ferracuti, *The Subculture of Violence: Towards an Integrated Theory in Criminology* (London: Tavistock, 1967).

[55] Allen D. Grimshaw, "Actions of Police and Military in American Race Riots," *Phylon,* 24 (Fall, 1963), pp. 271–289; Philips Taft, "Violence in American Labor Disputes," *Annals of the American Academy of Political and Social Science,* 364 (March, 1966), pp. 127–140; Westley, "The Escalation of Violence Through Legitimation," pp. 120–126; Marvin E. Wolfgang, "A Preface to Violence," *Annals of the American Academy of Political and Social Science,* 364 (March, 1966), pp. 1–7.

The general themes have different influences among the segments because, first, the themes are more strongly shared by some segments, and second, the normative systems and opportunity structures of the segments provide varying possibilities for fulfilling the cultural themes. The general culture is thus mediated in a segmental society.

Nevertheless, behavior patterns themselves are neither criminal nor noncriminal. They are merely behavior patterns, and their criminality is determined by the actions of others, who act according to other behavior patterns. Criminality is a construct, beyond the quality of specific behaviors, that is formulated and applied by the power segments of society. The observer, knowing the organization of the society, may evaluate behavior patterns by their relative probability of being defined as criminal. However, the behaviors themselves are criminal only when they are so defined by those who represent other patterns of behavior. Crime is created in a segmental society.

CHAPTER EIGHT

Action Patterns of
the Criminally Defined

Behavior becomes patterned only by the conduct of individual persons. But once behavior patterns have become established with some regularity within the segments of society, individuals are provided with a framework for personal action. That framework is, nevertheless, tenuous, since behavior patterns and associated normative systems are never static but are always emerging and changing. Yet it is within such a context that individuals construct their own patterns of meaningful social action. These *personal action patterns*, though continually developing, provide a source of personal identity and serve as the basis for social behavior. In short, personal action patterns are the essence of a life that is both human and social.

The development of action patterns gives behavior a substance in relation to criminal definitions. The following questions are thus raised in an investigation of the action patterns of the criminally defined: What is the role of the self in the development of personal action patterns? How are these patterns socially acquired? How do they develop in response to criminal definition? And, finally, how are the personal action patterns of the criminally defined organized into systems of behavior? All these questions refer to the probability that persons will be defined as criminal in a segmental society.

ACHIEVEMENT OF SELF

Each person is an object unto himself. That is, man has a conception of himself, communicates with himself, and acts toward himself.[1] By regarding himself as a separate and distinct entity, a person is able to act in a world that he simultaneously creates, confronts, and interprets. He thus acts on the basis of how he experiences his world. Action, then, is conduct that is personally constructed by the actor. For each person, action is pursued according to the personal meaning attached to that action and, furthermore, according to the personal interpretation of the actions of others.

A person's self-conception, as an image of what he means to himself and how he acts with reference to himself, is always in a process of formation. In this process, persons place themselves into categories with which they can identify, such as age, sex, occupation, ethnic group, and social class.[2] Moreover, actions themselves give an identity to a person. On the basis of his own constructions and decisions, man is ever becoming.

The achievement of any sense of self, however temporary, is crucial to all human beings. But the ease with which self-conceptions can be formed varies from one time to another and from one contemporary social situation to another. For men in some situations at particular times, the achievement of self-identity is especially problematic.

> In every age men ask in some form the questions: Who am I? Where do I belong? The degree of awareness and the kind of emphasis with which these questions are asked vary at different periods. Times of swift change and social dislocation bring them to the fore, against the background of whatever personal hopes and social harmonies an earlier period has cultivated.[3]

Hence, the achievement of self is critical for persons confronted with external environments that defy ready interpretation. Similarly, situations that frustrate expectations and aspirations promote

[1] George H. Mead, *Mind, Self, and Society* (Chicago: University of Chicago Press, 1934); Herbert Blumer, "Sociological Implications of the Thought of George Herbert Mead," *American Journal of Sociology,* 71 (March, 1966), pp. 535–544.

[2] Tamotsu Shibutani, *Society and Personality: An Interactionist Approach to the Social Psychology* (Englewood Cliffs, N.J.: Prentice-Hall, 1961), pp. 224–225.

[3] Helen M. Lynd, *On Shame and the Search for Identity* (New York: Harcourt, Brace and World, 1958), p. 13.

a crisis in self-identity. But since each man seeks a meaningful existence, some solution must be achieved.

Situations that persons find undesirable or difficult of interpretation may lead to the formation of self-conceptions that take as their reference opposition to the established order. It may not be unusual, therefore, to find that actions that result from such attitudes become defined by those in power as criminal. A great deal of the traditionally defined criminal behavior has been a response of individuals and groups to situations regarded as inadequate for the attainment of specific aspirations.[4] Calculated violation of the law may be a rational solution to socially structured and perceived problems. Protest and resistance against unjust conditions and policies may be most appropriately pursued through activities that violate criminal laws.[5]

Today, especially, violation of the law represents more than mere social deviance. Much of criminally defined activity is actually *political* behavior. Actions against the law are becoming ideological in orientation, being directed to the restructuring of the social and political order. When persons and groups of persons attempt to achieve desired goals by means of actions against the established order, the representatives of that order are likely to respond by formulating and applying criminal definitions.

Actions are a part of the process of the development of a self,

[4] On delinquency, for example, see Albert K. Cohen, *Delinquent Boys* (New York: The Free Press of Glencoe, 1955); Harold W. Pfantz, "Near-Group Theory and Collective Behavior: A Critical Reformulation," *Social Problems,* 9 (Fall, 1961), pp. 167–194; John P. Clark and Eugene P. Wenninger, "Goal Orientations and Illegal Behavior Among Juveniles," *Social Forces,* 42 (October, 1963), pp. 49–59; Delbert S. Elliott, "Delinquency and Perceived Opportunity," *Sociological Inquiry,* 32 (Spring, 1962), pp. 216–227; Judson R. Landis and Frank R. Scarpitti, "Perceptions Regarding Value Orientation and Legitimate Opportunity: Delinquents and Non-Delinquents," *Social Forces,* 44 (September, 1965), pp. 83–91; Gerald Maxwell, "Adolescent Powerlessness and Delinquent Behavior," *Social Problems,* 14 (Summer, 1966), pp. 35–47.

[5] Marshall B. Clinard and Richard Quinney, *Criminal Behavior Systems: A Typology* (New York: Holt, Rinehart and Winston, 1967), pp. 177–189; Irving Louis Horowitz and Martin Liebowitz, "Social Deviance and Political Marginality: Toward a Redefinition of the Relation Between Sociology and Politics," *Social Problems,* 15 (Winter, 1968), pp. 280–296; Richard Quinney, "A Conception of Man and Society for Criminology," *Sociological Quarterly,* 6 (Spring, 1965), pp. 119–127.

and, during this process, actions become patterned. For many, the action patterns that are formed have a fairly high probability of being defined by others (and perhaps by self) as criminal. But in expressing such actions, persons develop self-conceptions. Criminally defined behavior, like any other behavior, has meaning to the actors and is pursued in the achievement of self.

The role of the self in the development of action patterns which may be defined as criminal or delinquent has been explored in an investigation that extended over several years. The researchers examined the *self-concepts* of young teen-age boys to determine whether or not variations in conceptions of self account for specific patterns of behavior. The initial study consisted of an exploration and description of the responses of 125 "good" boys, nominated by their teachers and substantiated by official records as nondelinquent, to a battery of self-evaluation items. The researchers reported that the 125 boys portrayed themselves as law-abiding and obedient.

> Specifically, the vast majority defined themselves as being stricter about right and wrong than most people, indicated that they attempted to keep out of trouble at all costs and further indicated that they tried to conform to the expectations of their parents, teachers, and others. The nominees did not conceive of themselves as prospects for juvenile court action or detention, and they stated that their participation in such activities as stealing had been minimal and that their friends were either entirely or almost completely free of police and juvenile court contact.[6]

In subsequent research the authors reported that the "bad" boys had self-concepts that consisted of perceptions of getting into trouble, having friends who were in trouble, disliking school, expecting to go to jail, and so on.[7] Follow-up studies of the "good" and "bad" boys indicated that the earlier self-conceptions were predictive of later behavior, a much greater proportion of boys with "poor" con-

---

[6] Walter C. Reckless, Simon Dinitz, and Ellen Murray, "Self Concept as an Insulator Against Delinquency," *American Sociological Review*, 21 (December, 1956), p. 745.

[7] Walter C. Reckless, Simon Dinitz, and Barbara Kay, "The Self Component in Potential Delinquency and Potential Non-Delinquency," *American Sociological Review*, 22 (October, 1957), pp. 566–570.

cepts of self having juvenile court records than boys with "good" self-conceptions.[8] On the basis of these findings the authors have proposed that the nature of the concept of self insulates youths in high delinquency areas from involvement in delinquency.

> In our quest to discover what insulates a boy against delin- quency in a high delinquency area, we believe we have some tangible evidence that a good self-concept, undoubtedly a prod- uct of favorable socialization, veers slum boys away from delinquency, while a poor self-concept, a product of unfavora- ble socialization, gives the slum boy no resistance to deviancy, delinquent companions, or delinquent subculture. We feel that components of the self-strength, such as a favorable concept of self, act as an inner buffer or inner containment against deviancy, distraction, lure, and pressures.[9]

Such research clearly supports the position that self-conceptions and action patterns are interdependent.[10] Yet, the research noted above requires some reinterpretation to take into account the theory of the social reality of crime. I argue that *both* those who engage in behavior that is not usually defined as criminal or delinquent ("good" boys) and those who engage in behavior that has a high probability of being defined as criminal or delinquent ("bad" boys) are involved in meaningful social actions. Their respective self-conceptions and actions are personally appropriate. Only from the perspective of the standards of others can self-conceptions and actions be evaluated positively or negatively, as "appropriate" or "inappropriate," "good" or "bad." A boy's affirmative answer to a question such as the possi-

8 Frank R. Scarpitti, Ellen Murray, Simon Dinitz, and Walter C. Reckless, "The 'Good' Boy in a High Delinquency Area: Four Years Later," *American Sociological Review,* 25 (August, 1960), pp. 555–558; Simon Dinitz, Frank R. Scarpitti, and Walter C. Reckless, "Delinquency Vulnerability: A Cross Group and Longitudinal Analysis," *American Sociological Review,* 27 (August, 1962), pp. 515–517.
9 Walter C. Reckless and Simon Dinitz, "Pioneering with Self-Concept as a Vulnerability Factor in Delinquency," *Journal of Criminal Law, Criminology and Police Science,* 58 (December, 1967), pp. 515–523.
10 Other research on self-conceptions of offenders includes Leon F. Fanin and Marshall B. Clinard, "Differences in the Conception of Self as a Male Among Lower and Middle Class Delinquents, *Social Problems,* 13 (Fall, 1965), pp. 205–214; John W. Kinch, "Self-Conceptions of Types of Delinquents," *Socio- logical Inquiry,* 32 (Spring, 1962), pp. 228–234; James F. Short, Jr. and Fred L. Strodtbeck, *Group Process and Gang Delinquency* (Chicago: University Press, 1965), pp. 140–184.

bility that he will appear in juvenile court is not necessarily the basis of an "inappropriate" or a "poor" self-concept, but is more a personal prediction of future events based on past experience.[11] From the perspective of each person, all action patterns, no matter how others evaluate the patterns, are personally meaningful. Behavior that may become defined as criminal by others is behavior that is pursued in the process of the achievement of self.

ASSOCIATION, IDENTIFICATION, AND COMMITMENT

Each person constructs his own "reality world," his own view of himself and all that is about him. However, it is only as he participates in the worlds of others that he is able to develop his own world. In other words, by occupying space with others in a social setting, we share a common symbolic environment.

> While the reality world of each individual is his and his alone, it does, of course, have many aspects in common with the reality worlds of other people. The extent to which our reality worlds are alike seems to depend on the extent to which we have shared similar experiences and similar purposes.[12]

Shared meanings are provided for most persons by membership in some kind of social group. According to *reference group* terminology, social groups furnish members with a frame of reference for the organization of perceptions and experiences.[13] Persons act, then, in reference to the perspectives of their groups. Furthermore, the actions of persons are in part an attempt to preserve and enhance social status within their groups. Consequently, an explanation of variations in the behavior of persons may be sought in the context of group experiences.

[11] See Michael Schwartz and Sandra S. Tangri, "A Note on Self-Concept as an Insulator Against Delinquency," *American Sociological Review*, 30 (December, 1965), pp. 922–926; Sandra S. Tangri and Michael Schwartz, "Delinquency Research and the Self-Concept Variable," *Journal of Criminal Law, Criminology and Police Science*, 58 (June, 1967), pp. 182–190.

[12] Hadley Cantrel, *The Politics of Despair* (New York: Basic Books, 1958), p. 17.

[13] See, for example, Tamotsu Shibutani, "Reference Groups as Perspectives," *American Journal of Sociology*, 60 (May, 1955), pp. 562–569; Ralph H. Turner, "Role Taking, Role Standpoint, and Reference Group Behavior," *American Journal of Sociology*, 61 (January, 1956), pp. 316–328.

The theory of *differential association* provides such an explanation of "criminal" behavior.[14] In this view, all persons acquire their behavior during associations with others. Some, however, become criminal because the substance of their associations involves an excess of definitions favorable to the violation of the law. The theory of differential association is thus an extension of the basic theoretical perspective of the socialization process that occurs in the context of primary groups.[15] The learning of "criminal" behavior patterns is not fundamentally different from other socialization during which the individual is differentially exposed to various norms regarding some socially significant form of behavior.

The problem in the theory of differential association, however, has been not so much theoretical as empirical. Few systematic guides are provided for empirical verification of the theory. Moreover, the theory was formulated at such a high level of abstraction that it has not been possible to test it with empirical data. At best, it has been subject only to partial testing through research on the variables of association, including the frequency, duration, priority, and intensity of association. On the basis of these limited studies, nevertheless, it has been shown that persons who associate with delinquents (however defined) report more or engage in more alleged delinquent behavior than those who associate with others.[16]

Although the general principle of differential association probably holds for much of what is defined as delinquent and criminal, variations in the theory can be expected in concrete situations. In order to explore and explain these variations, the theory can be reformulated according to the logical and explanatory relations of such conceptual units as "criminal behavior," "symbolic interaction,"

[14] Edwin H. Sutherland, *Principles of Criminology*, 4th ed. (Philadelphia: J. B. Lippincott, 1947), pp. 1–9.

[15] See Melvin L. De Fleur and Richard Quinney, "A Reformulation of Sutherland's Differential Association Theory and a Strategy for Empirical Verification," *Journal of Research in Crime and Delinquency*, 3 (January, 1966), pp. 1–22.

[16] See Albert J. Reiss, Jr. and A. Lewis Rhodes, "An Empirical Test of Differential Association Theory," *Journal of Research in Crime and Delinquency*, 1 (January, 1964), pp. 5–18; James F. Short, Jr., "Differential Association and Delinquency," *Social Problems*, 4 (January, 1957), pp. 233–239; James F. Short, Jr., "Differential Association as a Hypothesis: Problems of Empirical Testing," *Social Problems*, 8 (Summer, 1960), pp. 14–25; Harwin L. Voss, "Differential Association and Reported Delinquent Behavior: A Replication," *Social Problems*, 12 (Summer, 1964), pp. 78–85.

"primary groups," "selective pattern of exposure," "crime-related learning," and so on.[17] In turn, if the theory is to be empirically tested, each unit must be divided into further subclasses of elements. Testable hypotheses can then be derived from the possible relations between the various subclasses of the conceptual units. That is, separate hypotheses of differential association can be derived and tested regarding such matters as the nature of the offense, the kind of interaction involved, the characteristics of the primary groups, and the type of normative exposure. I suspect that when some of the derived hypotheses are empirically tested, the role of association in development of personal action patterns in relation to criminal definitions will not only be supported, but will be strengthened by specification according to different types of social situations.

As the above strategy indicates, there is more to the learning of criminally defined behavior than simple association with other persons. Not only are other processes involved, but association itself is a complex process. Recognizing the complexity of the association process, the theory has been reconceptualized by an imagery of role playing.[18] The concept of differential association must first be replaced by that of *differential identification*. All persons, accordingly, identify with others, that is, view their own behavior from the perspective of other persons. Moreover, most persons identify with both "criminal" and "noncriminal" persons, by direct association, by reference to criminal roles portrayed in mass media, or as a negative reaction to forces opposed to crime. "The theory of differential identification, in essence, is that a person pursues criminal behavior to the extent that he identifies himself with real or imaginary persons from whose perspective his criminal behavior seems acceptable."[19] Thus, in the reconceptualization, persons who engage in criminally defined behavior identify with and consequently direct

[17] This strategy for empirical verification is proposed in De Fleur and Quinney, "A Reformulation of Sutherland's Differential Association Theory and a Strategy for Empirical Verification," pp. 17–21.
[18] Daniel Glaser, "Criminality Theories and Behavioral Images," *American Journal of Sociology*, 61 (March, 1956), pp. 433–444.
[19] Glaser, "Criminality Theories and Behavioral Images," p. 440. Empirical support for the theory of differential identification is found in Victor Matthews, "Differential Identification: An Empirical Note," *Social Problems*, 15 (Winter, 1968), pp. 376–383.

their actions toward persons who are behaving similarly. All factors are important in the theory of differential identification to the extent that they affect the choice of the others from whose perspective one views his own behavior. Our choices vary, and so accordingly do our behaviors.

According to the perspective developed thus far, the individual engages in behavior, some of which may be defined as criminal or delinquent, rationally and voluntarily. In any situation the individual acts according to his own evaluation of the situation and according to his reference to others. In the language of learning theory, social actions may be conceptualized as *operant* behavior, that is, behavior which is emitted in the presence of given conditions and maintained by its consequences. In other words, the behavior is stimulated by the expectation of a particular response. Most social behaviors are operant in nature, ranging from such forms as handshaking and sexual behavior to wearing clothing and driving a car. Social relations are maintained by the consequences they produce for the interacting parties. So it is that criminally defined behavior is also operant behavior. "Criminal behavior is maintained by its consequences, both material and social."[20] The criminally defined behaves in order to produce a personally desired effect, whether it is the acquisition of money, sexual gratification, or the removal of another person.

The concept of operant behavior as it applies to criminally defined behavior has been employed in a thorough revision of the theory of differential association.[21] Each proposition of the theory was reformulated according to the principle that behavior is a function of its past and current environmental consequences. Furthermore, the authors employed the related concept of *reinforcement* — that actions are repeated on the basis of the consequences of the behavior to the actor. They suggest, among other things, that criminal behavior is learned according to the principles of operant conditioning and that a person engages in those behaviors which have been most highly reinforced in the past. Consequently, some persons engage in criminally defined behavior because such behavior has been

[20] C. R. Jeffery, "Criminal Behavior and Learning Theory," *Journal of Criminal Law, Criminology and Police Science,* 56 (September, 1965), p. 300.

[21] Robert L. Burgess and Ronald L. Akers, "A Differential Association-Reinforcement Theory of Criminal Behavior," *Social Problems,* 14 (Fall, 1966), pp. 128–147.

more highly reinforced than other behavior. Personal action patterns, some of which may be defined as criminal, thus develop in reference to the responses of others. Actions are utilitarian, being pursued and repeated for their personal consequences.

The decision of whether or not to engage in behavior that has a high probability of being defined as criminal is based on the person's consideration of the likely consequences of his course of action. When confronted with a situation that may be resolved through actions that may be criminally defined, a person may evaluate the consequences of one form of action over another. Among the considerations that affect a person's decision to act in a particular way is his *commitment* to contingency interests.[22] That is, he may consider the consequences of some line of action for interests only indirectly associated with the present situation. Acting persons may have "commitments to conformity": ". . . not only fear of the material deprivations and punishments which might result from being discovered as an offender but also apprehension about the deleterious consequences of such a discovery on one's attempts to maintain a consistent self-image, to sustain valued relationships, and to preserve current and future statuses and activities."[23] Thus persons with strong commitments to law-abiding behavior are not likely to engage in actions that have a high probability of being defined as criminal. The consequences would not be to their advantage.

But for most, commitment to the legal code, specific laws in particular, is not a stable and constant matter. Persons tend to vary in their commitments during their lives and, furthermore, qualify their commitments according to the immediate context of their actions. Delinquents *drift* between various standards of conduct. "The delinquent transiently exists in a limbo between convention and crime, responding in turn to the demands of each, flirting now with one, now the other, but postponing commitment, evading decision. Thus, he drifts between criminal and conventional action."[24]

Flexibility in commitment to standards represented by the law is

[22] Howard S. Becker, "Notes on the Concept of Commitment," *American Journal of Sociology,* 66 (July, 1960), pp. 32–40.
[23] Scott Briar and Irving Piliavin, "Delinquency, Situational Inducements, and Commitment to Conformity," *Social Problems,* 13 (Summer, 1965), p. 39.
[24] David Matza, *Delinquency and Drift* (New York: John Wiley, 1964), especially pp. 27–30.

possible through the *neutralization* of legal norms. Delinquents, especially, temporarily employ "techniques of neutralization" to lessen the control of legal norms on their actions.[25] Persons violating the law are thus able at the same time to maintain some commitment to the standards of the law. Hence, actions defined as either criminal or delinquent do not necessarily represent commitment to violation itself, but are more likely episodic actions that are calculated to produce certain consequences for the actors.

Persons behave then, in reference to the anticipated consequences of their actions. The consequences that they desire are those which are socially learned. It is in the context of group association and identification that they act. Their commitments to some group rather than others, and their shifts in such commitments, are always problematic. But given one's past behavior, his present concerns, and future hopes, all actions are rationally conceived for their possible ramifications. Whether the actions may become defined as criminal by others may or may not be one of the considerations of the person when he acts in a concrete situation.

PERSONAL ACTION PATTERNS
AS RESPONSES TO
CRIMINAL DEFINITION

Personal actions are symbolic both for the actors and the respondents. As interaction continues between parties, or as the actor confronts similar situations, the meanings of personal actions become more firmly established. Eventually persons develop patterns of actions in reference to their interactions with others. An important process in the development of such patterns consists of the *social reactions* of others. It is in the reactions of others that one learns to regard himself in a particular way. What a person becomes, including how he behaves, will depend in large measure on the way he has been and continues to be assessed and defined by others.

The reactions of others are directed in large measure toward the

25 Gresham M. Sykes and David Matza, "Techniques of Neutralization: A Theory of Delinquency," *American Sociological Review*, 22 (December, 1957), pp. 664–670.

control of personal actions.[26] These social reactions to behavior come from various sources. Generally, social reaction is found, on the one hand, in the informal judgments of others in face-to-face encounters and, on the other hand, in the organized formal control of private or public agencies. Both forms of reaction provide social definitions of a situation. The actions of some persons are singled out for special consideration by others during social reaction.

Although social reaction operates as social control, it is at the same time a source of *definitional conferral* that produces in persons the actions that are the object of control. That is to say, as others react negatively to the actions of a person, that person begins to take unto himself the definitions the others have conferred upon him. This self-definition according to the definitions of others was pointed out some time ago in a discussion of community reactions to juvenile behavior. A community may react to a juvenile's adventurous behavior by eventually defining the boy himself as bad. The boy then responds by accepting the definition and acting in reference to it.

> From the community's point of view, the individual who used to do bad and mischievous things has now become a bad and unredeemable human being. From the individual's point of view there has taken place a similar change. He has gone slowly from a sense of grievance and injustice, of being unduly mistreated and punished, to a recognition that the definition of him as a human being is different from that of other boys in his neighborhood, his school, street, community. This recognition on his part becomes a process of self-identification and integration with the group which shares his activities. It becomes, in part, a process of rationalization; in part, a simple response to a specialized type of stimulus. The young delinquent becomes bad because he is defined as bad and because he is not believed if he is good. There is a persistent demand for consistency in character. The community cannot deal with people whom it cannot define. Reputation is this sort of public definition.[27]

[26] See Edwin M. Lemert, *Social Pathology* (New York: McGraw-Hill, 1951), pp. 54–72; Alexander L. Clark and Jack P. Gibbs, "Social Control: A Reformulation," *Social Problems*, 12 (Spring, 1965), pp. 398–415.

[27] Frank Tannenbaum, *Crime and the Community* (New York: Columbia University Press, 1938), pp. 17–18.

In such fashion, a person tends to become the thing he is described as being.

Defining a person in negative terms, therefore, plays a part in the person's definition of himself and in his subsequent actions. A person may channel his efforts toward behaviors that have a high potential of criminality because he has been defined as being deviant in some way. Accordingly, much of the research and writing on the physical characteristics of offenders can be reinterpreted as social definitions. The various physical stereotypes of the criminal, for example, may in many instances characterize specific offenders, but the relationship is not so much genetic as it is a self-fulfillment of others' perceptions and definitions. It may well be that some offenders conform to Lombroso's "stigmata" of overly small or large head, asymmetry of face, ears of unusual size, receding chin, and so forth.[28] However, persons with such characteristics are not savage "throwbacks," but are more likely than persons with "normal" characteristics to be defined by others as deviant (both physically and socially), more likely to be officially defined as criminal, and more likely to engage in the behaviors consistent with the status they have been assigned.

Similarly, an overly high proportion of the noted outlaws of the west may have had red hair.[29] Yet, being red-headed did not genetically make such men criminals. Rather the social definitions of others prescribed red-headed men as deviant, thus making the consequences true. In the same way we may accept the findings that delinquents tend to be mesomorphs (muscular, athletic, and aggressive).[30] Boys of such appearance and temperament are probably more likely than other boys to be recruited into juvenile gangs and to engage in behaviors that may readily be defined as delinquent. Physical characteristics are first socially defined, then

[28] Cesare Lombroso, *Crime: Its Causes and Remedies* (Boston: Little, Brown, 1911). Also see E. A. Hooton, *Crime and the Man* (Cambridge: Harvard University Press, 1937). For more recent research and interpretation, see Raymond J. Corsini, "Appearance and Criminality," *American Journal of Sociology*, 65 (July, 1959), pp. 49–51.

[29] Hans von Hentig, "Redhead and Outlaw," *Journal of Criminal Law, Criminology and Police Science*, 38 (May–June, 1947), pp. 1–6.

[30] William H. Sheldon, *Varieties of Delinquent Youth: An Introduction to Constitutional Psychiatry* (New York: Harper & Row, 1949). Also see Sheldon and Eleanor T. Glueck, *Physique and Delinquency* (New York: Harper & Row, 1956).

self-defined in relation to social reactions, and subsequently shape the patterning of personal actions. The whole interacting process of physical characteristics, social reactions, and personal action is dramatically illustrated in the case of Richard Speck, the slayer of eight Chicago nurses in the summer of 1966. When finally arrested, Speck, who had been described as physically and personally unattractive, was identified through the tattoo on his arm — which read, "Born to raise hell."

The extent to which personal action patterns develop in response to the social reactions of others depends on the degree to which the person accepts and adjusts to his assigned role. The concept of "secondary deviation" is useful in conceptualizing the transition that may occur in a person's self-conception and behavior as he is confronted with social reactions. According to the concept, the deviance imputed to a person remains "primary deviation" to that person as long as it is rationalized or otherwise dealt with as a socially acceptable role. As a person continues his actions, and as social reactions are repeated and strengthened, deviation becomes secondary.

> Secondary deviation refers to a special class of socially defined responses which people make to problems created by the societal reaction to their deviance. These problems are essentially moral problems which revolve around stigmatization, punishments, segregation, and social control. Their general effect is to differentiate the symbolic and interactional environment to which the person responds, so that early or adult socialization is categorically affected. They become central facts of existence for those experiencing them, altering psychic structure, producing specialized organization of social roles and self-regarding attitudes. Actions which have these roles and self attitudes as their referents make up secondary deviance.[31]

The person develops such a stance toward himself and others because his identity and actions are organized around the facts of the deviance that others have imputed to him.

The definition of a person as "criminal" is the extreme form of stigmatization. Criminal conviction — even confrontation with the police and judicial prosecution — produces modifications in a man's identity and actions. The "criminalization of deviance" may thus

[31] Edwin M. Lemert, *Human Deviance, Social Problems, and Social Control* (Englewood Cliffs, N.J.: Prentice-Hall, 1967), pp. 40–41.

force those engaged in particular kinds of behavior to redefine themselves and their actions.[32] Furthermore, such public branding tends
to lead a person to new situations and activities. The development
of a new style of life, in turn, increases the probability of further
criminal definition. It is through social reaction, then, in the form
of criminal definition, that crime is again created and perpetuated.

BEHAVIOR SYSTEMS OF THE
CRIMINALLY DEFINED

Within the legal structure of society and the relation of the segments of society to that structure, personal action patterns develop
with different probabilities of criminality. For *analytical* purposes,
these criminality-related action patterns may be divided into *types
of behavior systems*. The task thus becomes one of describing and
analyzing specific forms of action patterns that develop in the course
of criminal definition.

The division of criminally defined behavior into types of behavior
systems is based on various aspects of the person and his behavior.
The characteristics of behavior systems most important for our
study are the *career* of the person in regard to criminally defined
activity and the *group support* he receives from his actions. The
career of the offender consists of the extent to which criminally defined behavior is a part of his life organization. Also included are
his conception of self, his identification with crime, and his progression in activities that may be defined as criminal. Group support
consists of the extent to which the person's criminally defined behavior is supported by the norms of the group or groups to which
he belongs. Included are the differential association of the person
with behavior patterns that have varying probabilities of being
defined as criminal, his social roles, and his integration into various
social groups.

On the basis of such characteristics, a typology of behavior systems in relation to criminal definitions has been constructed.[33] It is
composed of eight types of "criminal" behavior systems: (1) vio-

---

[32] See Edwin M. Schur, *Crimes Without Victims* (Englewood Cliffs, N.J.:
Prentice-Hall, 1965), pp. 5–7.

[33] The following typology of behavior systems was constructed in Clinard
and Quinney, *Criminal Behavior Systems: A Typology*.

lent personal, (2) occasional property, (3) occupational, (4) political, (5) public order, (6) conventional, (7) organized, and (8) professional. Each behavior system contains behavior patterns that have a fairly high probability of being defined as criminal, because of the legal structure. The action patterns of persons that may be criminally defined can be analyzed according to these eight types of behavior systems.

Violent Personal Offense Behavior. Most who engage in acts that that may be defined as murder, assault, or forcible rape do not immediately identify themselves as criminals or regard crime as a part of their lives. Their actions tend, rather, to be the consequence of a social encounter in which two or more parties conceive of violence as an appropriate solution to an interpersonal problem. But since criminal sanctions for such actions are relatively certain and severe, persons convicted of a violent personal offense are likely, in time, to conceive of themselves as criminal.

Persons who act in a personally violent way in a specific situation are not likely to be involved with the law in other parts of their lives.[34] Of those offenders who do have an arrest record, a large proportion have been arrested for actions against another person. One study, in fact, concluded that "the analysis of crimes of violence according to their factual substance shows that most of the crime is not committed by criminals for criminal purposes but is rather the outcome of patterns of social behavior among certain strata of society."[35] Therefore, we conclude from extensive evidence, that actions that result in personal violence are responses to interpersonal situations rather than the result of a career in criminally defined activity.

[34] See David J. Pittman and William Handy, "Patterns in Criminal Aggravated Assault," *Journal of Criminal Law, Criminology and Police Science,* 55 (December, 1964), pp. 462–470; Richard A. Peterson, David J. Pittman, and Patricia O'Neal, "Stabilities in Deviance: A Study of Assaultive and Non-Assaultive Offenders," *Journal of Criminal Law, Criminology and Police Science,* 53 (March, 1962), pp. 44–49; Marvin E. Wolfgang, *Patterns in Criminal Homicide* (Philadelphia: University of Pennsylvania Press, 1958); John L. Gillin, *The Wisconsin Prisoner* (Madison: University of Wisconsin Press, 1946); Menachem Amir, "Patterns of Forcible Rape," in Clinard and Quinney, *Criminal Behavior Systems,* pp. 60–75.
[35] F. H. McClintock, *Crimes of Violence* (New York: St. Martins Press, 1963), p. 57.

Most murders and aggravated assaults represent a response, growing out of social interaction between one or more parties, in which a situation comes to be defined as requiring the use of violence. Generally in order for such an act to take place, all parties must come to perceive the situation as one requiring violence. If only one responds in a dispute, it is not likely to become violent; likewise, if only one of the disputants is accustomed to the use of violence, and the other is not, the dispute is likely to end only in a verbal argument. On the other hand, when a cultural norm is defined as calling for violence by a person in social interplay with another who harbors the same response, serious altercations, fist fights, physical assaults with weapons, and violent domestic quarrels, all of which may end in murder, may result. In the process of an argument, A and B both define the initial situation as a serious threat, B then threatens A physically, A threatens B, and B then threatens A. By circular reaction, the situation can then rapidly build up to a climax in which one takes serious overt action, partly because of fear. Consequently, the victim, by being a contributor to the circular reaction of an argument increasing in its physical intensity, may precipitate his own injury or death.[36]

Because of the presence of interaction between persons in a situation of violence, the *victim* is a crucial agent in the action that is taken. Victims, in other words, tend to precipitate their own victimization. A study of homicide found that one in four criminal homicides were instigated in this way, in that the victim first showed or used a deadly weapon or struck a physical blow.[37] Not included in this figure were homicides that involved the victim's use of vile names, his infidelity, or his failure to live up to expectations, such as failure to pay a debt. Similarly, the victim's role was found to be important in aggravated assault.[38] The researchers reported that nearly three-quarters of the cases of assault studied had been preceded by verbal arguments, including family arguments and disputes that arose in a public place. The victim of rape, as well, has much to do with the fact that she is raped. A large proportion of

---

[36] Clinard and Quinney, *Criminal Behavior Systems,* p. 27.
[37] Wolfgang, *Patterns in Criminal Homicide,* p. 252.
[38] Pittman and Handy, "Patterns in Aggravated Assault," p. 467.

rape victims either behave submissively or agree to sexual relations before defining the consequences as rape.[39]

The existence of previous interpersonal relationships between murderers and their victims has been documented in a number of studies. In a study of New Jersey murders, classified according to victim-offender relationships and the situations in which the murders took place, it was found that about two-thirds of the murders grew out of some altercation with acquaintances, sex rivals, relatives, or mistresses.[40] Likewise, a Philadelphia study found that approximately two-thirds of the criminal homicides took place between persons who had a previous interpersonal relationship.[41] In 28 per cent of the cases the victim was a close friend of the murderer, in 25 per cent a family relative, and in 14 per cent an acquaintance. A study of Wisconsin murders showed a similar proportion of victims who had a previous relationship with the offender.[42] In addition, studies in other countries have also revealed the importance of interpersonal relationships in criminal homicide: Nearly 80 per cent of the homicides in a London study were committed against relatives or a well known acquaintance; an Indian study indicated that most murders occur within the same caste and frequently involve a husband and wife; and a Danish study revealed that the murderer's victim was a relative or an acquaintance in nine out of ten cases and that strangers were seldom the victims.[43] Needless to say, most of the violent behaviors that end in a criminal definition occur within a specific, and personally meaningful, social context.

In a broader sense, beyond the immediate interpersonal context of personal offenses, persons vary in the extent to which they engage in violent behavior and in their perceptions of violence as an alternative to interpersonal problems. Evidence indicates that the

[39] Amir, "Patterns in Forcible Rape," pp. 67–69.

[40] E. Frankel, "One Thousand Murderers," *Journal of Criminal Law, Criminology and Police Science,* 29 (January, 1939), pp. 687–688.

[41] Wolfgang, *Patterns in Criminal Homicide,* p. 207.

[42] Gillin, *The Wisconsin Prisoner,* p. 60.

[43] McClintock, *Crimes of Violence,* p. 238; Edwin D. Drivers, "Interaction and Criminal Homicide in India," *Social Forces,* 40 (December, 1961), pp. 153–158; Kaare Svalastoga, "Homicide and Social Contact in Denmark," *American Journal of Sociology,* 62 (July, 1956), pp. 37–41.

use of violence varies socially and culturally in respect to a person's geographical residence, social class, occupation, race, sex, and age.[44] Hence, violence against another person appears to be differently institutionalized in the various segments of society. In the final analysis, the extent to which a person engages in violent personal actions that may be defined as criminal depends upon his location in society, and consequently, upon his exposure to particular social norms.

Occasional Property Offense Behavior. For those who only occasionally engage in an offense against property and who are seldom defined as criminal, there is little identification with crime and little attempt to integrate such activity into a way of life. Their law-violating actions are not sophisticated in technique or skill of commission. Most of these persons have little knowledge about the world of crime or the vocabulary of crime. Thus, because of the sporadic nature of their actions and the infrequency of contact with criminal definitions, such persons do not conceive of themselves as criminals and do not usually associate with those who engage more regularly in activity that may be criminally defined.

Occasional shoplifters, as contrasted with professionals, do not conceive of themselves as criminals or regard their activities as crimes.[45] Generally they are respectable employed persons or housewives, "pilfering" only occasionally for their own use. They rationalize their actions on the basis that the things they take are of modest price and belong to large department stores than can absorb the loss. Few of these persons have criminal records.

Likewise, the major portion of check forgeries are committed by persons who have no record of such activity.[46] In a study of "naive" check forgery, it was found that such persons do not usually come from an area of high delinquency or crime and that they do not associate with criminally defined persons. The naive check forger,

[44] See Ronald H. Beattie and John P. Kenney, "Aggressive Crimes," *Annals of the American Academy of Political and Social Science*, 365 (March, 1966), pp. 73–85. Also see Franco Ferracuti and Marvin E. Wolfgang, *The Subculture of Violence: Towards an Integrated Theory in Criminology* (London: Tavistock Publication, 1967).

[45] Mary Owen Cameron, *The Booster and the Snitch: Department Store Shoplifting* (New York: The Free Press of Glencoe, 1964).

[46] Edwin M. Lemert, "An Isolation and Closure Theory of Naive Check Forgery," *Journal of Criminal Law, Criminology and Police Science*, 44 (October, 1953), pp. 296–307.

rather, tends to be socially isolated. But, in a difficult situation, forgery is personally perceived as an available alternative.

A similar lack of commitment to crime as a part of one's life is reported in a study of young rural offenders who occasionally engage in property offenses.[47] It was found that (1) their law-violating behavior did not start early in life, (2) they exhibited little knowledge of criminal techniques, (3) such activity was not pursued as a means of livelihood, and (4) they did not conceive of themselves as criminals. Rather than identifying with crime, the offenders considered themselves as "reckless" and unattached to traditional ways. They were mobile, referred to their behavior as "fast," and engaged in law-violating activity as an adventure.

The occasional property offender has little long-term social or cultural support for his behavior. Although several persons may be collectively involved in acts of vandalism, the behavior that takes place is more the result of an immediate interactional situation than a product of any kind of subculture.[48] Vandalism tends to be a spontaneous outgrowth of concrete situations of group interaction. Each interactive response by a participant builds the intensity of actions of other participants until a focus develops and a group act of vandalism occurs. For the moment at least, each participant has a feeling of excitement and a sense of involvement in a group. One has to have something.

Occupational Offense Behavior. Persons who violate criminal laws in the course of their occupational activity do not conceive of themselves as criminals but as "respectable" citizens. The fact that the offender is a member of a legitimate occupation also makes it difficult for others to conceive of occupational offenders as being real criminals. Consequently, because of the lack of public disapproval of occupational offenders, persons who violate laws that regulate occupational activity are not likely to incorporate a criminally defined role into their life organizations.

The maintenance of a noncriminal self-concept is one of the principal elements in the occupational offender's development of action

[47] Marshall B. Clinard, "Rural Criminal Offenders," *American Journal of Sociology,* 50 (July, 1944), pp. 38–45.

[48] Andrew L. Wade, "Social Processes in the Act of Juvenile Vandalism," in Clinard and Quinney, *Criminal Behavior Systems,* pp. 94–109.

patterns. This process has been observed in a study of embezzlers, which concluded that persons engage in such behavior only when they are able to apply to their own conduct verbalizations which allow them to adjust their concepts of themselves as trusted persons with their concepts of themselves as users of entrusted funds or property.[49] The trust violators thus defined the situation by rationalizations which enabled them to regard their violations as essentially noncriminal. They rationalized that their behavior was merely "borrowing," that it was justified by the presence of a nonsharable problem which could be resolved by violating their position of trust.

The respectable backgrounds of occupational offenders have been shown in several studies. A study of prosecuted cases of price and rationing violations during World War II found that less than one violator in ten had a criminal record.[50] In studies of other occupational offenders, it has been shown that the overwhelming majority of the offenders reside in the most desirable areas of the city.[51] Similarly, the respectability of the defendants involved in the 1961 criminal antitrust case in the heavy electrical equipment industry was described by a reporter as "middle-class men in Ivy League suits — typical businessmen in appearance, men who would never be taken for lawbreakers."[52] One of the defendants, a General Electric vice-president who was eventually sentenced to prison, was earning $135,000 a year. His background has been summarized as follows:

> He had been born in Atlanta and was 46 years old at the time he was sentenced to jail. He had graduated with a degree in electrical engineering from Georgia Tech, and received an honorary doctorate degree from Sienna College in 1958, was

[49] Donald R. Cressey, *Other People's Money* (New York: The Free Press of Glencoe, 1953).

[50] Marshall B. Clinard, *The Black Market: A Study of White Collar Crime* (New York: Holt, Rinehart and Winston, 1952), p. 295.

[51] Frank E. Hartung, "A Study in Law and Social Differentiation, as Exemplified in Violations of the Emergency Price Control Act in the Detroit Wholesale Meat Industry," unpublished Ph.D. dissertation, University of Michigan, 1949, p. 221; and Richard Quinney, "Retail Pharmacy as a Marginal Occupation: A Study of Prescription Violation," unpublished Ph.D. dissertation, University of Wisconsin, 1962, p. 261.

[52] Quoted in Gilbert Geis, "White Collar Crime: the Heavy Electrical Equipment Antitrust Cases of 1961," in Clinard and Quinney, *Criminal Behavior Systems*, p. 140.

married, and the father of three children. He had served in the Navy during the Second World War, rising to the rank of lieutenant commander, was a director of the Schenectady Boys Club, on the board of trustees of Miss Hall's School, and not without some irony, was a member of Governor Rockefeller's Temporary State Committee on Economic Expansion.[53]

The importance of group association and group support in the violation of occupational laws was indicated in a study of the criminal decisions rendered against seventy large corporations.[54] Occupational violations appeared to be normative in some businesses, and some persons, if isolated from other norms, learned motives, techniques, and rationalizations favorable to violation of law. Several factors isolate businessmen from unfavorable definitions of illegal activity, including the lenient coverage of such violations in the mass media and the lack of severe criticism by government officials. Furthermore, businessmen associate chiefly with other businessmen, both at work and in their social activities. Similar conclusions of the association with certain behavior patterns and the isolation from others have been reached in a study of the violation of labor relations laws and trade practices laws in a number of manufacturing firms.[55]

A person's commitment to the norms favorable to violation within an occupation or business depends upon the roles he plays in his work. The significance of the role structure of an occupation and the orientation of the members to the roles has been shown in a study of prescription violation among retail pharmacists.[56] Because the occupation of a pharmacist is structured according to two divergent occupational roles — professional and business — pharmacists experience the problem of adapting to one of several "occupational role organizations." The types of role organizations, in turn, differ in the extent to which they produce tendencies toward violating pre-

[53] Geis, "White Collar Crime," p. 147.

[54] Edwin H. Sutherland, *White Collar Crime* (New York: Holt, Rinehart and Winston, 1949).

[55] Robert A. Lane, "Why Businessmen Violate the Law," *Journal of Criminal Law, Criminology and Police Science,* 44 (August, 1953), pp. 151–165. Also see Clinard, *The Black Market,* pp. 298–313.

[56] Richard Quinney, "Occupational Structure and Criminal Behavior: Prescription Violation by Retail Pharmacists," *Social Problems,* 11 (Fall, 1963), pp. 179–185.

scriptions. Pharmacists who are oriented to a professional role are bound by a system of occupational control which includes guides for compounding and dispensing prescriptions. The business oriented pharmacists, on the other hand, are interested in the general business goal of monetary gain, subscribing to the popular belief in business that self-employment carries with it independence and freedom from control. The professional norms, as incorporated in the prescription laws, exercise little control over the occupational behavior of the pharmacists who are oriented to the business role. Thus, it was found that violations occur most frequently among business pharmacists and least often among professional pharmacists, with pharmacists who are oriented to both roles and pharmacists who are not oriented to either role being intermediate in frequency of violations. It was therefore concluded that prescription violation is related to the structure of the occupation and the "differential orientation" of retail pharmacists to the roles within the occupation.

Political Offense Behavior. An increasing amount of criminally defined behavior consists of action patterns that are pursued in the attempt to protest, express beliefs about, or alter in some way the social structure. Such political activities are variously named by the authorities of the state: treason, sedition, espionage, sabotage, war collaboration, military draft evasion, and civil disobedience. The actions — whether they violate laws created for the suppression of such behavior or laws created for other purposes (such as loitering and parading without a permit) — are regarded by political authorities as detrimental to the state and its institutions. Certain behaviors, therefore, become defined as criminal because the political actions of some persons are regarded by the authorities as politically threatening to the structure of the state.

The political behaviors that may result in criminality are many and varied. Nevertheless, characteristics are shared by those who are defined as political offenders. Most do not engage in criminally defined activity as a full-time career. Persons who commit political crimes do not usually conceive of themselves as criminals and do not identify with crime. They violate the law only when such action seems to be the most appropriate means for achieving certain ends. The ends, to the actor, are not strictly personal but are deemed desirable for the larger society. The behavior is regarded by the offender as symbolic of a higher purpose. Such persons carry on their criminally defined activities in pursuit of an ideal.

Thus, political offenders are usually committed to a larger social order.

> The social order they have in mind, however, may differ from the existing order. It is because of their commitment to something beyond themselves and conventional society that they are willing to engage in criminal behavior. Persons who occasionally engage in political crime are interested in their society, but at times find it lacking in important ways. They may then sever their commitment to the society in place of a social order which could exist. The social order to which they are committed may be a modification of the one that exists or may possibly be an entirely new order. Nevertheless, the existing society always serves as a reference point for political offenders.[57]

During political socialization and experience, persons develop a conception about the relative legitimacy of political institutions. In general, a political system is viewed as legitimate when the authority and objectives of those in control are respected and when the available procedures in the political process are believed to be adequate. Furthermore, persons regard a political system as legitimate or illegitimate according to the way in which the values of the system correspond to their own. Groups that do not share these values are more likely to question the legitimacy of the system at times. Such groups are likely to engage in political behaviors ("extremist politics") which may be defined as criminal. Their political actions may be of a variety either to the "right" or to the "left" of what is regarded as politically traditional in a society.[58]

[57] Clinard and Quinney, *Criminal Behavior Systems*, p. 180.

[58] For some of the research and writing on political offense behavior, see Ralph S. Brown, *Loyalty and Security* (New Haven: Yale University Press, 1958); Karl O. Christiansen, "Collaborators with the Germans in Denmark During World War II," in Clinard and Quinney, *Criminal Behavior Systems*, pp. 231–246; Arnold Foster, "Violence on the Fanatical Left and Right," *Annals of the American Academy of Political and Social Science*, 364 (March, 1966), pp. 141–148; Joseph C. Mouledoux, "Political Crime and the Negro Revolution," in Clinard and Quinney, *Criminal Behavior Systems*, pp. 217–231; Robert K. Murray, *Red Scare: A Study in National Hysteria, 1919–1920* (Minneapolis: University of Minnesota Press, 1965); Herbert L. Packer, "Offenses Against the State," *Annals of the American Academy of Political and Social Science*, 339

The pursuit of illegal activities during political action is not regarded as an important consideration by most political offenders. For such persons the violation of a particular criminal law actually represents an appeal to a higher norm, possibly even an appeal to the federal law. The person who is viewed by the authorities and the public as disloyal to his country is nevertheless being true to higher loyalties.⁵⁹ Such persons are conscientiously following norms and values which differ from those of the political majority.

The intensity of group support received by political offenders varies, of course, from one kind of political activity to another. But the fact that such activity has group support is evident in almost all forms of criminally defined political activity. Nearly all those prosecuted for conscientious objection during World War II were members of groups and organizations committed to peace and opposition to war.⁶⁰ Such religious groups as the Society of Friends, Jehovah's Witnesses, Mennonites, and Church of the Brethren provided support for those who opposed military service on religious grounds. The philosophical objectors, those not basing their objections on religious grounds, also found group support for their actions. They were united by such organizations as the Pacifist Research Bureau, the War Resisters League, and the National Council Against Conscription. Some of these groups, and many new groups, continue to provide support and assistance for opposition and resistance to the draft and to military service.

The social nature of political offenses varies according to not only the extent and means of group support but also such social characteristics as the size of the supporting group or organization, the cohesiveness of the group, formality of organization, duration of the group, geographical dispersion of the members, and patterns of leadership.⁶¹ Also, the groups to which political offenders belong

(January, 1962), pp. 77–89. William Preston, Jr., *Alien Dissenters: Federal Suppression of Radicals, 1903–1933* (Cambridge, Mass.: Harvard University Press, 1963).

⁵⁹ See Robin M. Williams, *American Society* (New York: Alfred A. Knopf, 1960), pp. 379–380; Mabel A. Elliott, *Crime in Modern Society* (New York: Harper & Row, 1951), pp. 179–197; Morton Grodzins, *The Loyal and Disloyal: Social Boundaries of Patriotism and Treason* (Chicago: University of Chicago Press, 1956).

⁶⁰ Mulford Q. Sibley and Ada Wardlow, *Conscientious Objectors in Prison, 1940–1945* (Ithaca, N.Y.: Pacifist Research Bureau, 1945), chap. 1.

⁶¹ See Lemert, *Social Pathology,* pp. 175–235.

differ greatly in their aims and their ideologies. Finally, the forms of political criminality differ in the techniques and tactics used by the members: oratory, face-to-face persuasion, writing and propaganda, nonviolent action, passive resistance, demonstrations, sit-ins, marches, strikes, suicide, and guerrilla warfare. All these actions may become defined as criminal during the attempt to achieve political goals.

Public Order Offense Behavior. The largest proportion of crime consists of violations against public order. Included among these behaviors, which may be criminally defined in various ways, are prostitution, homosexual relations, and drug addiction. In most of the behaviors no real injury is suffered by another person. Rather, the behaviors violate the sense of order in the community. And as the community reacts to the behavior of public order offenders, these persons tend to become segregated from community life and may begin to play the criminal role.

Prostitutes are introduced to their activity by those who are closely associated with prostitution. But once a person becomes committed to prostitution as part of a life organization, a further period of apprenticeship is necessary in order to ensure some success in prostitution. For the call girl, in particular, a culture must be learned which includes a philosophy as well as techniques of operation.

> The structure of the apprenticeship period seems quite standard. The novice receives her training either from a pimp or from another more experienced call girl, more often the latter. She serves her initial two to eight months of work under the trainer's supervision and often serves this period in the trainer's apartment. The trainer assumes responsibility for arranging contacts and negotiating the type and place of the sexual encounter.
>
> The content of the training pertains both to a general philosophical stance and to some specifics (usually not sexual) of interpersonal behavior with customers and colleagues. The philosophy is one of exploiting the exploiters (customers) by whatever means necessary and defining the colleagues of the call girl as being intelligent, self-interested and, in certain important respects, basically honest individuals. The interpersonal techniques addressed during the learning period consist primarily of "pitches," telephone conversations, per-

sonal and occasionally sexual hygiene, prohibition against alcohol and dope while with a "john," how and when to obtain the
fee, and specifics concerning the sexual habits of particular
customers. Specific sexual techniques are very rarely taught.
The current sample included a considerable number of girls
who, although capable of articulating this value structure, were
not particularly inclined to adopt it.[62]

Because prostitutes encounter a duality of social values regarding
their behavior — values that stigmatize such activity and values
that support it — self-conceptions tend to be both ambivalent and
subject to change.[63] Yet, since prostitutes can rationalize their behavior by reference to the value of commercial success, an appropriate self-image can be maintained. In addition, a prostitute is able
to sustain her role by interaction with other prostitutes and with
those who associate with prostitutes. A specialized language, an
argot, also provides a sense of group solidarity for prostitutes.[64]
Furthermore, contact with the law through repeated arrests
strengthens the self-conceptions of prostitutes and reinforces the
rationalizations that they have for their actions.

Homosexuality, whether or not it is defined as criminal in some
way, involves learning a social role. The role is learned in association with others and includes the defining of oneself as a homosexual.
The self-conception as a homosexual is also derived from the negative reactions of others in the community. The homosexual may, in
turn, seek more and more associations within the world of homosexuality. Thus, social pressures tend to push persons along a progression of stages of homosexual behavior, although some individuals do not necessarily progress to the final stages and others may
still maintain contact with the rest of the community.

 1. The first stage usually occurs in the late teens or early
 twenties. As his friends start to go out with girls and eventually
 marry, the homosexual finds other interests and drifts away
 from their company. Sometimes he is scarcely aware of his

[62] James H. Bryan, "Apprenticeships in Prostitution," *Social Problems,* 12
(Winter, 1965), p. 294.

[63] Norman R. Jackman, Richard O'Toole, and Gilbert Geis, "The Self-Image
of the Prostitute," *Sociological Quarterly,* 4 (Spring, 1963), pp. 150–161.

[64] David W. Maurer, "Prostitutes and Criminal Argots," *American Journal of
Sociology,* 44 (January, 1939), pp. 546–550.

homosexual tendencies or has not come to terms with them, but gradually he becomes conscious of his isolation. Many young homosexuals have described their dismay when they have discovered that the sort of things which interest their friends hold no appeal for them.

2. Thus the young homosexual finds he is driven away from the company of ordinary men and women at just the time when he most needs their help. As he loses his friends he begins to regard himself as an outcast. He finds to his dismay that will-power and self-control are not the answer to his problem. The more extrovert homosexual will soon pass through this second stage and quickly make friends with other homosexuals. But others lead lonely lives, plagued by feelings of guilt and accepting the role of the social isolate.

3. At the third stage the young man meets other homosexuals and begins to go to their meeting places and joins a homosexual group. Some of them soon tire of this opportunity to mix in a group of like-minded individuals, but others accept the chance eagerly. Here a homosexual can feel at ease because he does not have to hide his true inclinations. Indeed, this is such a relief that much of the talk in these groups is about sex. It is here that the two worlds conflict. He must make sure that his friends from the other world do not meet his friends from the homosexual group. He has to explain his absences from the other world, think up convincing stories, and learn to lead two lives. Some homosexuals resolve this dilemma by moving on to the fourth stage.

4. At this last stage the homosexual way of life monopolizes his interests and absorbs all his time. He gives up his efforts to resolve the conflicts between the outside world and the homosexual way of life. He moves exclusively in a homosexual group and adopts a hostile attitude towards all those not in the group. He has, in fact, adopted all the characteristics of an introverted minority group.[65]

A large proportion of homosexuals have developed stable homosexual relationships and a style of life centering around the homosexual role. These are the confirmed homosexuals, most of whom never come to the attention of the police. These persons, as shown in one study, tend to start their homosexual relations with other

[65] Michael Schofield, *Sociological Aspects of Homosexuality: A Comparative Study of Three Types of Homosexuals* (Boston: Little, Brown, 1965), p. 181.

boys before the age of seventeen, eventually developing long-standing relations with men.[66] They establish special meeting places for their associations as they become segregated from the rest of the community. Consequently, a homosexual "subcommunity" is created. The homosexual community has its "own status symbols and mythology, and may provide the same kind of social and psychological support that a family group provides for other people."[67]

Persons who use drugs do not necessarily conceive of themselves as criminals. But in recent times, with the emphasis the Federal Bureau of Narcotics has placed on the sale and possession of drugs and with the subsequent legislation and administrative rulings, drug users have found that their action is criminally defined. The legal and public stigmatizing of the drug user has thus tended to force the user to define his own drug using actions as criminal, although the rest of his action patterns may not be so defined.

Most persons are initiated into the use of drugs by association with friends or acquaintances. They start experimenting with drugs out of curiosity as to their effects and, ultimately, to conform to the expectations of their group.[68] Some adolescents in slum areas take drugs for the "kick," as something to heighten and intensify the present moment of experience, and to differentiate their lives from the routine daily life of the "square."[69] For many of these, however, continual drug use requires a change in reference group orientation and association. As one researcher has stated, the person who progresses in drug use not only learns to appreciate the effects of drug use to the fullest, but shifts his group and ideological commitments:

> Moving along the career line toward confirmed use depends upon the user's having a positive physical response to heroin and learning how to enjoy the effects of "the high." Once the

[66] *Ibid.,* pp. 100–143.

[67] *Ibid.,* p. 183. Also see Maurice Leznoff and William A. Westley, "The Homosexual Community," *Social Problems,* 3 (April, 1956), pp. 257–263; Gordon Westwood, *A Minority: A Report on the Life of the Male Homosexual in Great Britain* (London: Longmans, Green, 1960), pp. 83–86.

[68] Julius Klein and Derek L. Phillips, "From Hard to Soft Drugs: Temporal and Substantive Changes in Drug Usage Among Gangs in a Working-Class Community," *Journal of Health and Social Behavior,* 9 (June, 1968), pp. 139–145.

[69] Harold Finestone, "Cats, Kicks, and Color," *Social Problems,* 5 (July, 1957), pp. 3–4.

user finds pleasure in drug use and prefers his dreamy state to the action world of non-using friends, he disengages himself from the usual routines of the stand-up cat ideology and learns to believe in a new ideology that is consistent with the pleasurable effects of heroin. The speed with which the new drug user disengages himself from his former reference group depends upon the way the members adhere to the ideology of the stand-up cat.[70]

Beyond the fact of drug use itself, the social context and the personal meaning of drug use vary considerably. The observations above apply primarily to drug use among lower class adolescents. However, with the rise of the "hippie" phenomenon other patterns have emerged. In a study of drug use among hippies in the Haight-Ashbury section of San Francisco, it was found that two patterns of drug use exist in the same area, a "head" pattern consisting of those who use LSD ("acid" users) and a "freak" pattern, those who inject Methedrine ("speed shooters").[71] Each recruits a different kind of person and is accompanied by a different style of life.

Yet another pattern of drug use is found among college students. A study of drug use (primarily marijuana) among college students found that the students who used drugs adhered to what might be characterized as a "hang-loose" ethic.[72] That is, drug use tends to occur among those students whose behavior, attitudes, and self-images represent an opposition to the traditional, established order. A sequence of events associated with drug use among college students has been suggested:

Adherence to the "hang-loose" ethic is more likely to occur among certain predisposed personality types (i.e., rebellious, cynical) and in certain social sub-groups (i.e., males, non-religious); such adherence is likely to lead to a favorable attitude toward smoking marijuana both for its "high" effects and its symbolism of rebellion against authority; this favorable attitude will be supported by other students who also

[70] Harvey W. Feldman, "Ideological Supports to Becoming and Remaining a Heroin Addict," *Journal of Health and Social Behavior*, 9 (June, 1968), p. 138.
[71] Fred Davis with Laura Munoz, "Heads and Freaks: Patterns and Meanings of Drug Use Among Hippies," *Journal of Health and Social Behavior*, 9 (June, 1968), pp. 156–164.
[72] Edward A. Suchman, "The Hang-loose Ethic and the Spirit of Drug Use," *Journal of Health and Social Behavior*, 9 (June, 1968), pp. 146–155.

embrace the "hang-loose" ethic and engage in similar overt and covert expressions of rejection of the established order. Finally, given this climate of opinion and behavior, the smoking of marijuana becomes almost a "natural" act for many students far removed from the public's current efforts to define it either as a legal or a health problem.[73]

With increasing dependence on drugs and association with other drug users, persons involved in some patterns of drug use tend to progress into the role of drug addict. Their addiction finds support in an elaborate set of group norms that center around what one writer has called a "survival system."[74] The system furnishes the addict with the justification and the ideology for dependence on drugs. Addicted persons then recruit new members in order to sell them drugs to support their own habit. There is also defensive communication, with its own argot for drugs, supplies, and drug users, which must be learned by the initiates. Through a "neighborhood warning system" addicts provide mutual protection against arrest by the police. Because of the illegality of drug sales, addicts depend upon a complex distribution network for securing their drugs. In order to secure drugs, addicts often have to violate laws in other ways.[75] Finally, then, imposing criminal definitions on drug users and drug addicts not only defines their possession of drugs as criminal but promotes other actions that may be criminally defined. As unintended as these consequences may be, the criminal law has its own capacity for producing personal action patterns.

Conventional Offense Behavior. Some persons who are defined as delinquent during adolescence continue into adulthood with action

---

[73] *Ibid.*, pp. 153–154. For research on other patterns of drug use, see John C. Ball, "Two Patterns of Narcotic Drug Addiction in the United States," *Journal of Criminal Law, Criminology and Police Science,* 56 (June, 1965), pp. 203–211; Alfred R. Lindesmith, *Opiate Addiction* (Bloomington: Indiana University Press, 1947); Charles Winick, "The Use of Drugs by Jazz Musicians," *Social Problems,* 7 (Winter, 1959–1960), pp. 240–254.

[74] Seymour Fiddle, "The Addict Culture and Movement into and out of Hospitals," in Senate Committee on the Judiciary, Subcommittee to Investigate Juvenile Delinquency, *Hearings,* Part 13 (Washington, D.C.: U.S. Government Printing Office, 1963), p. 3156.

[75] See Harold Finestone, "Narcotics and Criminality," *Law and Contemporary Problems,* 22 (Winter, 1957), pp. 69–85; John O'Donnell, "Narcotic Addiction and Crime," *Social Problems,* 13 (Spring, 1966), pp. 374–385; Schur, *Crime Without Victims,* pp. 120–168.

patterns that become criminally defined. Such a career usually involves early experience with a juvenile gang. The members learn social roles and achieve status by participating in gang activities. They continuously learn techniques and rationalizations for their behavior. Gradually such persons move from petty to more serious offenses — from truancy, destruction of property, and street fighting to auto theft, robbery, and burglary. By the time they are young adults they are likely to have an extensive record of contact with the law, including experiences with the police, juvenile authorities, courts, reformatories, and possibly prisons. These experiences add to the person's sophistication in criminally defined activities and to his conception of himself as a criminal.

The progression from early juvenile gang activity to adult conventional offense behavior has been observed in several studies. In a study of Negro armed robbers it was found that the offenders had a history of arrests:

> An early patterning of stealing from their parents, from school, and on the street; truancy, and suspension or expulsion from school; street fighting, association with older delinquents, and juvenile delinquent gang memberships, all were usually evident in their social backgrounds. When compared with the men in the other criminal categories, it was found that there was more destruction of property in their delinquent activities, and there were more frequent fights with schoolmates, male teachers, and delinquent companions. There was a higher incidence of "mugging" and purse snatching. They had more often been the leaders of delinquent gangs, and they claimed they were leaders because of their superior size and physical strength.[76]

A similar career in juvenile gang activity has been called the "semiprofessional property criminal." These offenders represent the usual outcome of patterns of gang delinquency, because "many juvenile gang offenders continue in criminality as semi-professionals."[77]

[76] Julian B. Roebuck and Mervyn L. Cadwallader, "The Negro Armed Robber as a Criminal Type: The Construction and Application of a Typology," *Pacific Sociological Review*, 4 (Spring, 1961), p. 24.
[77] Don C. Gibbons, *Changing the Lawbreaker* (Englewood Cliffs, N.J.: Prentice-Hall, 1965), p. 105. For further documentation of the progression from juvenile offenses to adult conventional offenses, see Harold S. Frum, "Adult Criminal Offense Trends Following Juvenile Delinquency," *Journal of Criminal*

Most of the behaviors included in conventional offenses, whether juvenile or adult, are related to property in one way or another. As a person progresses in conventional offenses, he engages in these actions to supplement or completely make a living. When offense behavior has thus become a part of one's life organization a whole complex of factors is involved, including personal commitment to crime, self-conception, social reactions, and further continuance in a life of crime.

> As juvenile offenders progress into conventional career crime, they become more committed to crime as a way of life and develop a criminal self-conception. Because of repeated offenses, and because of subsequent arrests and convictions, conventional offenders eventually identify with crime. For occasional property offenders who pursue criminal activity only sporadically, there is vacillation in self-conception. But for conventional criminals who regularly commit offenses and who are continually isolated from law-abiding segments of society, a criminal self-conception is virtually inescapable. In addition, because property offenders are dealt with rather severely before the law, through arrest and sentencing, such offenders readily come to regard themselves as criminals. The criminal record is a constant reminder that the person has been stigmatized by the society. The record may provide a vicious circle whereby the offender, once stigmatized, often cannot enter into law-abiding society and must continue in a life of crime.[78]

One of the occupational hazards of the conventional offender is the *risk* of being detected, arrested, and convicted. But because conventional offenders develop some skill and organization in their activities, they are able to minimize the chances of being criminally defined.[79] As indicated by criminal statistics, only about a quarter of property offenses (and only those *known* to the police) are cleared

---

Law, Criminology and Police Science, 49 (May–June, 1958), pp. 29–49; Clifford R. Shaw, Henry D. McKay, and James F. McDonald, *Brothers in Crime* (Chicago: University of Chicago Press, 1938).

[78] Clinard and Quinney, *Criminal Behavior Systems*, p. 321.

[79] Observations on risk-taking among offenders are found in Edwin M. Lemert, "Social Structure, Social Control, and Deviation," in Marshall B. Clinard (ed.), *Anomie and Deviant Behavior* (New York: The Free Press of Glencoe, 1964), pp. 73–75; Daniel S. Claster, "Comparison of Risk Perception Between Delinquents and Non-Delinquents," *Journal of Criminal Law, Criminology and Police Science*, 58 (March, 1967), pp. 80–86.

by arrest. For many career offenders, then, the often-quoted adage that "crime does not pay" is a myth maintained by and for law-abiding members of society.

When criminal offenses are pursued as a means of livelihood with some success, other ways of living are not readily observed, understood, or desired by the offender. Furthermore, the excitement and notoriety of a criminal career may be more rewarding than the prospects of hard work, responsibility, and monotony provided by a respectable, law-abiding career. Also, association and involvement with other offenders provides a group consciousness that makes movement to a law-abiding life less comprehensible and desirable.

Why some conventional offenders discontinue their criminally defined activities in their mid-twenties or early thirties is, therefore, the problem to be explained: "It is much easier to determine why offenders continue in criminal careers than it is to understand what makes them quit."[80] It may be that as a person grows older he tends to lose touch with his earlier associates because of marriage and family responsibilities. Such a change in life style is probably more important in breaking an offense pattern than are the many attempts at rehabilitation. Because of certain external factors, then, a person may find that a law-abiding career may hold greater personal possibilities than a career which has the potential of being periodically defined as criminal.

Organized Offense Behavior. Some persons violate criminal laws or become defined as criminal by participating in business enterprises that are organized for making economic gain illegally. The persons involved in such activity variously occupy positions within a hierarchical system of specifically defined relationships with mutual obligations and privileges. At the top of the hierarchy are the powerful leaders, the "lords" of the underworld, who make the important decisions and run the organization. A middle echelon of gangsters, henchmen, and lieutenants carry out the commands of the leaders. At the bottom are persons marginally associated with organized crime — narcotics peddlers, prostitutes, bookies, runners — who deal directly with the public.

The hierarchic structure of organized crime, with its diversity of

---

[80] Walter C. Reckless, *The Crime Problem*, 3rd ed. (New York: Appleton-Century-Crofts, 1961), p. 164.

personnel, makes generalization about the careers of its members difficult. Many persons in organized crime, especially those lower in the hierarchy, have careers similar to that of the conventional offender.[81] They tend to have a life history of association with juvenile gangs and a long series of delinquent and criminal offenses. Instead of ending their careers in their early twenties, however, they have continued their activities in association with persons in organized crime.

The juvenile gang of the slum produces the adult "gangster" who uses strong-arm methods and is employed for his talents by illegal organized groups. Such persons usually come from large cities, frequently have long criminal records of armed robberies, and conceive of themselves as "tough." Those who are successful in organized crime sometimes become its leaders. Organized crime may thus provide persons with the opportunity for a lifetime career in illegal activity.

Progression into organized crime increasingly isolates the offender from conventional society. Though there are variations according to the person's location within the hierarchy, most organized offenders are committed to the world of crime. Most of their activities are in continuous violation of the law. But by a process of justification, based in part on a contempt for the rest of society, they are able to maintain an appropriate self-image. Underworld leaders may, however, choose to live segmented lives, retiring to the seclusion of pseudo-respectability.[82] Their commitment, nevertheless, remains with the world of crime, where they receive their prestige, power, and are provided with a luxurious way of life.

Throughout their careers persons in organized crime associate regularly with other offenders. These associations and the support received from them are provided by the very nature of organized crime. That is, the crime syndicate which is organized to maintain a large-scale business enterprise for the coordination and control of products and services, ensures the association of persons involved in similar illegal activities. A description of this organization of

[81] See Reckless, *The Crime Problem,* p. 203; Solomon Kobrin, "The Conflict of Values in Delinquency Areas," *American Sociological Review,* pp. 653–661; Gus Tyler, "The Roots of Organized Crime," *Crime and Delinquency,* 8 (October, 1962), pp. 325–338.

[82] See Virgil W. Peterson, "The Career of a Syndicate Boss," *Crime and Delinquency,* 8 (October, 1962), pp. 339–354.

common illegal activity has recently been provided.[83] According to the report, the core of organized crime today consists of twenty-four groups (or "families"), which operate as criminal cartels in large cities across the country. In the internal structure of each of these groups, membership varies from as many as 700 men to as few as 20. Each family is structured according to a number of well defined positions. Outside the structure of the family is the "commission," which is a combination of legislature, supreme court, board of directors, and arbitration board for the coordination of the entire family system. The commission is composed of the bosses of the most powerful families and varies from nine to twelve men. The balance of power of this nationwide council currently rests with the leaders of the five families of New York, which is considered the headquarters of the entire operation of organized crime in the United States.

Finally, organized crime must be viewed in its relationship to the legal system. The existence of organized crime, in fact, depends on the way in which the criminal law is enforced and administered. In order to continue its operations, organized crime must maintain some amount of immunity from the law. This immunity is achieved in several ways.

> First, the leaders of organized crime are not usually arrested and prosecuted because they stay behind the scenes of operation. Gangland activity cannot be readily traced to its leaders. Second, persons lower in the hierarchy of organized crime, if arrested, are likely to be released by action from their superiors. Such release and avoidance of prosecution and punishment are assured through what is popularly known as the "fix." For various reasons, persons not directly involved in criminal activity contribute to the protection of organized criminals. Law enforcement officials, judges, doctors, businessmen, and others may at times provide needed services for the protection of organized criminals.

> A third way in which organized crime may acquire immunity is by gaining political power through contribution to polit-

[83] President's Commission on Law Enforcement and Administration of Justice, *The Challenge of Crime in a Free Society* (Washington, D.C.: U.S. Government Printing Office, 1967), pp. 191–196. Also see Robert T. Anderson, "From Mafia to Cosa Nostra," *American Journal of Sociology*, 71 (November, 1965), pp. 302–310.

ical organizations. Elected officials may owe their election to organized criminals. Furthermore, regular "payoffs" to officials provide protection for organized crime. Thus, on a permanent basis, organized crime may be immune to law enforcement through political graft and corruption. Fourth, because organized crime provides the public with illicit and desired services, such as prostitution, gambling and narcotics, a certain amount of immunity from arrest and prosecution results from public toleration of organized crime.

A fifth means of immunity is found in the functioning of the law itself. Existing laws and enforcement procedures have not been especially successful in coping with organized crime. The survival and continuance of organized crime is possible because legal action is kept at a minimum. Lack of effective legislation and weak law enforcement are, in turn, a reflection of public toleration of organized crime in the United States.

Finally, through the infiltration of legitimate business, organized crime is able to evade the law. Organized crime today often operates behind the facade of legitimate business, obscuring its operation and making its detection difficult. Also, in the case of racketeering, organized crime escapes the law because intimidated businessmen must contend with reprisal if a report is made. In addition, organized crime and legitimate business may mutually assist one another, as in the regulation of prices of given commodities or through the enforcement of labor contracts. . . . The interdependence of the underworld of crime and the upperworld of business assures the maintenance of both systems. Mutual assistance, accompanied by public espousal of the profit motive under almost any arrangement, provides considerable assurance of immunity for organized crime.[84]

Thus, organized crime is maintained, and the offenders within the organization are assured of their way of life, by the relationship of organized crime to the administration of criminal law.

Professional Offense Behavior. Some persons, remaining outside organized crime, spend the majority of their time in illegal activities. They engage in specialized offenses, all of which are directed toward economic gain. By means of skill and elaborate

[84] Clinard and Quinney, *Criminal Behavior Systems,* pp. 386–387.

techniques, they are able to acquire considerable sums of money by "professional" thievery or fraud. Their activities include pick-pocketing, shoplifting, sneak-thieving from stores, stealing from jewelry stores by substituting articles, stealing from hotel rooms, and miscellaneous rackets, such as passing illegal checks and extorting money from others engaged in illegal behavior. These activities are carried out for the most part without being detected by the offender. In the unusual cases when they are apprehended, professional offenders generally find ways to have the charge dropped.

Of all the types of offenders, professionals have the most highly developed careers in crime. In addition to being more skilled in their activity, they are able to operate without violence and strong-arm tactics. Regarding themselves as professionals, they tend to avoid other types of offenders and associate primarily with one another. Furthermore, professional offenders tend to come from better economic backgrounds than do the conventional and orga-nized offenders. Many start in legitimate employment as salesmen, hotel clerks, waiters, or bellboys.[85] They may continue to engage in legitimate employment until they have progressed so that their entire livelihood can be achieved through illegal means.

The professional offender is likely to begin his career in illegal activities at a relatively late age. Once he is engaged in professional offenses, however, he tends to continue in them for the rest of his life.

> The con man begins his special career at a much older age than other criminals, or perhaps it is better said that he continues his criminal career at a time when others may be relinquishing theirs. Unemployment occasioned by old age does not seem to be a problem of con men; age ripens their skills, insights, and wit, and it also increases the confidence they inspire in their victims. With age the con man may give up the position of the roper and shift to being an inside man, but even this may not be absolutely necessary. It is possible that cultural changes outmode the particular con games older men have been ac-customed to playing and thereby decrease their earnings some-

[85] See Edwin H. Sutherland, *The Professional Thief* (Chicago: University of Chicago Press, 1937), pp. 21–25.

what, but this seems unlikely. We know of one con man who is seventy years of age and has a bad heart, but he is still as effective as he ever was.[86]

The longevity of the professional offender results, of course, in part from the fact that very few are ever arrested, tried, convicted, or sentenced to prison.

Professional offenders develop a philosophy of life to justify their actions and to enhance their self-images. Basic to this philosophy is the belief that all men are actually dishonest. They also justify their behavior by the belief that all persons would violate the law if they had the skill and opportunity. As Joseph "Yellow Kid" Weil, a successful confidence man, said of himself:

> The men I fleeced were basically no more honest than I was. One of the motivating factors in my action was, of course, the desire to acquire money. The other motive was a lust for adventure. The men I swindled were also motivated by a desire to acquire money, and they didn't care at whose expense they got it. I was particular. I took money only from those who could afford it and were willing to go in with me in schemes they fancied would fleece others.[87]

The professional offender can thus justify his own behavior by the conduct of his victim, who, after all, has been willing to participate in an illegal act. Such rationalizations are shared and supported by professional offenders in their association with one another.

The importance of group associations among professional offenders is indicated in the way in which persons are recruited into that world. Recognition by other professional offenders is the essential quality.[88] Without such recognition, no amount of knowledge and experience can provide the offender with the qualifications for a successful career built around the social role of the professional offender.

Included in the procedure of acquiring recognition by established professional offenders are two necessary elements: selection and tutelage. Selection takes place as professional offenders come in

[86] Lemert, *Social Pathology*, pp. 323–324.
[87] Joseph R. Weil and W. T. Brannon, *"Yellow Kid" Weil* (Chicago: Ziff-Davis, 1948), p. 293.
[88] Sutherland, *The Professional Thief*, pp. 197–228.

contact with other offenders (amateur thieves, burglars), with persons on the fringes of crime (pimps, "fences"), or with persons engaged in legitimate occupations. The contracts are made in places where professional offenders are working, in jails, or in places of leisure-time activities. Selection, which must be by mutual agreement between established and prospective professionals, is followed by a probationary period in which the neophyte learns the skills, techniques, attitudes, and values of the professional offender. In addition, he assimilates standards of group morality, such as honesty among professionals and not to inform on others. Gradually he becomes acquainted with other professional offenders. He eventually acquires the special language or argot by which members communicate with one another.[89] On the basis of such knowledge and expertise, the person develops action patterns in a world he shares with fellow professional offenders.

There is some indication that professional offense behavior may be changing as other changes are taking place in society.

> At the end of the last century, persons and organizations that were the victims of professional crime, especially of forgery, established as a reaction to professional crime a number of schemes which subsequently brought about a change in the organization and operation of professional crime. The establishment of the bankers' associations, the creation of merchants' protective agencies, and improvements in police methods made the risks of organized professional forgery exceedingly great. Also important to the decline of professional forgery has been the increasingly widespread use of business and payroll checks as well as personal checks. Because of these reactions the systematic check forger no longer has to resort to criminal associates or to employ the more complex procedures used in past decades. Thus, it can be seen that professional crime, as is true of other types of crime, is related to the structure of society. As society and the reaction to crime change, so do the organization and operation of the types of crime.[90]

[89] David W. Maurer, *The Big Con* (New York: Signet Books, 1962); David W. Maurer, *Whiz Mob* (New Haven: College and University Press, 1964).

[90] Clinard and Quinney, *Criminal Behavior Systems*, p. 436. Regarding these changes, see Edwin M. Lemert, "The Behavior of the Systematic Check Forger," *Social Problems*, 6 (Fall, 1958), pp. 141–149. Other studies of professional offenders are found in Cameron, *The Booster and the Snitch;* Ted Polsky, "The Hustler," *Social Problems*, 12 (Summer, 1964), pp. 3–15; Julian B. Roebuck,

PERSONAL MEANING
OF ACTION

Each man seeks a meaningful existence. In abstraction the possible paths to man's existential salvation are many. But each person is bound by the social space he occupies in his own time in history. The alternatives that are at his command are limited. A man's horizons are set by his perceptions of the possibilities of being human and by the opportunities that are structured about him.

The action patterns that persons develop for themselves are solutions to the multiple problems of being socially human. Each person's actions, including a patterning of self-images and overt behaviors, are shaped by his relationships with others. It is within a socially structured environment, with the help of his friends (and others), that a person creates a meaningful life for himself.

The substance of a person's action is problematic. Though the content of the actions is shaped by the social and cultural location of the person in society, actions are ultimately the product of each individual. But the name that will be given the behavior is also an enterprise of others. And the names tend to be simplistic — like "good" or "bad," "virtuous" or "sinful," "law-abiding" or "criminal."

I have maintained throughout this chapter that personal actions are meaningful to the actors and that the actions are constructed in part through the reactions of other persons. The person may, consequently, develop a way of behaving — including a supporting style of life — that takes its reference from criminal definitions. Criminal definitions not only provide behavior with the quality of criminality, but also assist in living a life.

"The Negro Number Man as a Criminal Type: The Construction and Application of a Typology," *Journal of Criminal Law, Criminology and Police Science,* 54 (March, 1963), pp. 48–60; Julian B. Roebuck and Ronald C. Johnson, "The 'Short Con' Man," *Crime and Delinquency,* 10 (July, 1964), pp. 235–248; Edwin M. Schur, "Sociological Analysis of Confidence Swindling," *Journal of Criminal Law, Criminology and Police Science,* 48 (September–October, 1957), pp. 296–304.

5

Construction
of Criminal
Conceptions

CHAPTER NINE

Public
Conceptions
of Crime

Man constructs his own reality. And with the help of others, he creates a social world. The construction of this world is related to the knowledge man develops, the ideas to which he is exposed, and the manner in which he selects and interprets information to fit the world he is shaping. Man behaves, then, in reference to his conceptions of reality.

Included in man's social reality are conceptions about crime. Wherever the concept of crime exists, images are communicated in society about the meaning of crime, the nature of the criminal, and the relationship of crime to the social order. *Criminal conceptions* are thus constructed and diffused throughout society by various means of communication. For purposes of analysis, conceptions of crime can be discussed according to (1) social reaction to crime, (2) the diffusion of criminal conceptions, (3) social types in the world of crime, (4) public attitudes toward crime, and (5) public attitudes toward the control of crime. All these issues in the construction of criminal conceptions affect the development of criminal definitions and behavior patterns in a society.

SOCIAL REACTION TO CRIME

The reaction of the public to crime is both a product of the social reality of crime and a source in the construction of conceptions of crime. On the one hand, social reactions to crime are a consequence of the reality the public has constructed in regard to crime. Persons react in specific ways to the occurrence of criminally defined activity, to the enforcement and administration of the law, and to the treatment of the offender. Without a social reality of crime, there would be no reaction to crime. But, on the other hand, the reactions that are elicited in response to crime are at the same time shaping the social reality of crime. As persons react to crime, they develop patterns for the responses of the future.

In spite of the often spontaneous quality of personal responses to crime, reaction to crime takes place in a social and cultural context. That is to say, social reaction to crime is socially structured and is patterned according to a system of norms. All societies have a variety of *reactive norms* that prescribe the appropriate reactions for particular situations and specify how and by whom the reactions are to be administered.[1] For many areas of human activity both *legal* and *extralegal* reactions are prescribed. The violation of a particular criminal law, for example, is accompanied by a set of appropriate formal sanctions. The formal sanctions are, in turn, administered through procedures established by law. The same violation is likewise subject to extralegal sanctions, including such public reactions as stigmatization of the offender and denial of employment.[2] Moreover, social reactions are normatively patterned according to such contingencies as the type of offense, the personal and social characteristics of the offender, the social location of the offense, and the degree to which the offense violates other social norms. All these affect the manner and the regularity with which reactions (both legal and extralegal) will be practiced. Thus, social reactions, like all other forms of behavior, are to be understood according to their social patterning and cultural regulation.

The reactive norms within any society are not generalized for the entire society, but vary considerably from one segment to another. Extralegal prescriptions, in particular, vary throughout a population according to such social characteristics as the age, sex, ethnicity,

[1] See Alexander L. Clark and Jack P. Gibbs, "Social Control: A Reformulation," *Social Problems,* 12 (Spring, 1965), pp. 402–406; Jack P. Gibbs, "Sanctions," *Social Problems,* 14 (Fall, 1966), pp. 152–154.

[2] See Richard D. Schwartz and Jerome H. Skolnick, "Two Studies of Legal Stigma," *Social Problems,* 10 (Fall, 1962), pp. 133–142.

religion, and social class of the reactors.[3] Among the legal reactions are specific prescriptions in the criminal codes of the respective political units. But the legal codes provide alternative reactions for any offense. Because of the latitude of prescriptions, the patterns of legal reaction differ from one kind of criminal case to another, varying in such matters as the types of sanctions utilized and the consistency with which the reactions are imposed and administered. Hence, social reactions, whether legal or extralegal, are not socially monolithic in either their cultural prescription or their actual patterning. Variations in social reactions are to be sought and explained as reflecting the segmental organization of society.

From the perspective of the individual, responses to crime are influenced by *knowledge* about crime and *perceptions* about the meaning of crime. The attitudes of persons toward such matters as criminal behavior, law enforcement, and the handling of offenders are affected by the kinds and amounts of knowledge they have about these matters. Persons differ greatly in their knowledge about the existence and substance of laws in the society.[4] Reaction to all that is associated with crime initially rests upon knowledge about crime. Likewise, perception of the crime phenomenon underlies any social reaction to crime. How a person perceives crime provides a framework for his own understanding of and subsequent reaction to crime.

> Attitudes to crime and criminals then, vary, not so much in terms of the intrinsic nature of the criminal act, but in terms of the likelihood of the act being an established part of the observer's own social world. Crime is in the last analysis what the other person does. What I do, if it is against the law, is susceptible to redefinition through rationalization. Even if the observer is unlikely to commit the particular crime in question, his attitude to it will be conditioned by a degree of modification which may result in either a lenient tolerance or a

[3] In respect to variations in social reactions regarding homosexuals, see John I. Kitsuse, "Societal Reaction to Deviant Behavior: Problems of Theory and Method," *Social Problems*, 9 (Winter, 1962), p. 256.

[4] Torgny T. Segerstedt, "A Research into the General Sense of Justice," *Theoria*, 15 (1949), pp. 323–338. Also see Frederick Beutel, *Some Potentialities of Experimental Jurisprudence as a New Branch of Social Science* (Lincoln: University of Nebraska Press, 1957).

punitive rejection, depending upon how far the crime threatens the observer, or the group to which they all belong.[5]

Perception precedes a response of any kind.

Criminal conceptions are gradually constructed. The social reactions of today must be viewed within a cultural framework that has developed *historically*. With this in mind, it has been suggested that the early Puritan image of deviation continues to be reflected in many of our modern reactions to crime.[6] For the Puritans in Massachusetts Bay, crime was an act against the symmetry and orderliness of nature itself. The criminal, in keeping with the Puritans' theological doctrine, was relegated to a category of permanent misfits who were predestined to oppose the social order by engaging in unacceptable activities. As a result of these attitudes the Puritans developed a "deployment pattern" in regard to crime and deviance:

> To characterize the New England deployment pattern in a word, we may say (1) that the Puritans saw deviant behavior as the special property of a particular class of people who were more or less frozen into deviant attitudes; and (2) that they generally thought it best to handle the problem by locking these people into fairly permanent deviant roles. Puritan theories of human development began with the assumption that men do not change a great deal as they mature or are exposed to different life experiences, and in this sense the settlers of the Bay had little faith in the promise that men might "reform" or overcome any pronounced deviant leanings. A person's character, like his social estate, is fixed by the preordained pattern of human history, and if he should somehow indicate by his surly manners and delinquent ways that he is not a very promising candidate for conversion, the community was not apt to waste many of its energies trying to change him or mend his character. In a very real sense, he belonged to a deviant "class" and was not expected to improve upon that condition.[7]

The Puritan heritage is still very much a part of our public and legal reaction to crime. Our image of the criminal is predicated on a

[5] Terence Morris, "The Social Toleration of Crime," in Hugh J. Klare (ed.), *Changing Concepts of Crime and Its Treatment* (Oxford: Pergamon Press, 1966), pp. 33–34.

[6] Kai T. Erikson, *Wayward Puritans: A Study in the Sociology of Deviance* (New York: John Wiley, 1966).

[7] *Ibid.*, pp. 196–197.

belief in the irreversibility of human nature. Strengthened by positivistic assumptions in our criminology, we tend in our social reactions to place the criminal in a class by himself.

> Now, as then, we leave few return routes open to people who try to resume a normal social life after a period of time spent on the community's boundaries, because most of us feel that anyone who skids off into the more severe forms of aberrant expression is displaying a serious defect of character, a deep blemish which cannot easily be erased. We may learn to think of such people as "sick" rather than "reprobate," but a single logic governs both of these labels, for they imply that nothing less than an important change of heart, a spiritual conversion or a clinical cure, can eliminate that inner seed which leads one to behave in a deviant fashion.[8]

DIFFUSION OF CRIMINAL CONCEPTIONS

Once a society has a generalized criminal mythology, conceptions of crime are diffused throughout the population. The *diffusion* of criminal conceptions simultaneously involves the *construction* of conceptions of crime among individuals and groups. This mutual process is accomplished in a number of ways. All the means which facilitate construction of conceptions, however, are mediated by the social context of diffusion and by the interpersonal relations associated with the adoption of criminal conceptions.

Among the most important agents in the diffusion of criminal conceptions are the media of mass communication. Crime coverage in the newspapers, television, and movies affect a person's estimate of the frequency of crime as well as the interpretations that he attaches to crime. Research has shown that a special reality is presented in the newspapers in respect to crime. In one study, it was found that the amount of crime news in each of four Colorado newspapers varied independently of the amount of crime in the state as reflected by crime statistics.[9] Persons were then asked, in a public opinion poll, to estimate the amount of crime in the state. The results indicated

---

[8] *Ibid.*, pp. 204–205.

[9] F. J. Davis, "Crime News in Colorado Newspapers," *American Journal of Sociology*, 57 (January, 1952), pp. 325–330.

that public opinion about crime tended to reflect trends in the amount of crime news rather than the actual crime rates. Coverage of crime in the newspapers created a conceptual reality that was meaningful to the public in spite of any other social reality of crime.

Moreover, the mass media provide varying and often divergent portrayals of crime. Perusal of different newspapers in the same city on the same day is enough to illustrate that one's construction of a conception of crime depends upon which newspaper he happens to read. One of the most striking examples is a comparison of two newspapers in New York City that have considerably different orientations to news presentation: the New York *Daily News* and *The New York Times*. In a content analysis of the two newspapers, it was found that over three months the *Daily News* presented nearly twice as many items about juvenile delinquency as did the *Times*.[10] In front-page coverage, the *Daily News* carried four stories for each one displayed in the *Times*. Furthermore, there were differences between the two papers in the emotionality with which the news items were presented. Differences were seen, especially, in the terminology and phraseology of the headlines of the two papers. Typical of the *Daily News* headlines were: "Cops Nab Two In Cat-Mouse Roof Top Chase," "Stolen Kiss Traps Robber of Girl In Hall," "Hunt Two Boy Bullies Who Killed Lad," "Thugs Finger A Fingerman," and "Beer Gets Guv's Girl Canned From College." The headlines from the *Times,* in comparison, were mild and unemotional: "Museum Theft Laid To Delinquents," "Third Slain In Youth Violence," "Youth Crime Rise Is Held Magnified," and "Three Fires Set In Bronx School."

Thus public conceptions of crime and delinquency are constructed and diffused on the basis of "news" presentations. Specific conceptions are shaped by what is considered to be news about the subject of crime. Since the press is one of the chief dispensers of information about crime, conceptions of crime and delinquency are influenced by the newspaper coverage to which one is exposed. A recent portrayal of the crime problem in the *Daily News,* for instance, as shown in the cartoon (page 283) dramatically presents an image of crime for the Sunday viewer.

[10] Rita Bachmuth, S. M. Miller, and Linda Rosen, "Juvenile Delinquency in the Daily Press," *Alpha Kappa Delta,* 30 (Spring, 1960), pp. 47–51.

STREET WALKER

The style and content of much of the media represent a continual preoccupation with crime. For the many persons who find this sort of coverage to their liking, the real world is a selective one, a crime-centered one. Not only is attention focused on crime, but the more sensational and adventuresome aspects of crime are portrayed. The routine nature of the major portion of crime is also neglected. Coverage of crime in the mass media, therefore, is not only selective but is a distortion of the everyday world of crime. But such is the stuff from which reality worlds are constructed for much of the population.

The effect of the coverage of crime in the mass media has been a topic for considerable speculation and research.[11] Many educators, social observers, and parents have worried about the possible effects of the depiction of crime and violence in the media. It is not my purpose here, however, to survey and evaluate the many arguments and findings. I have no doubt of the selective nature of the coverage of crime in the mass media. Likewise, I am convinced that crime as presented in the media affects the recipient's attitudes and behavior. I am also certain that in some cases persons are "tried" by the press before their cases are decided in a court of law.[12] But, first, the relationship that I perceive between exposure to media and the attitudes and behaviors of persons is on a more general level. That is, public conceptions of crime are created in part by the images of crime in the mass media. And, second, the relationship must be viewed along with the mediating forces of social context and interpersonal relations.

Recent research on mass communications has confirmed that the possible effects of the mass media are mediated by interpersonal networks of communication and by such contextual matters as integration in social groups and membership in various kinds of groups.[13] Personal contacts in a social context influence one's interpretation of the content of the mass media. Moreover, mass communication, in

[11] Much of the research is reviewed in Joseph T. Klapper, *The Effects of Mass Communications* (New York: The Free Press of Glencoe, 1960), pp. 135–165.

[12] See Alfred Friendly and Ronald L. Goldfarb, *Crime and Publicity: The Impact of News on the Administration of Justice* (New York: Vintage Books, 1968).

[13] See Elihu Katz, "The Two-Step Flow of Communication: An Up-to-Date Report of an Hypothesis," *Public Opinion Quarterly*, 21 (Spring, 1957), pp. 61–78; John W. Riley, Jr. and Mathilda White Riley, "Mass Communications

working through mediators, reinforces existing conceptions. The social nature of exposure to mass media, therefore, influences the nature and impact of the portrayal of crime in mass communication.

The implication of the above idea is that exposure to such images affects individuals differently according to their past experiences and their present associations. In particular, it appears that persons who are involved in patterns of criminally defined activity are more likely to be influenced by crime portrayals than persons not so involved.[14] On an even more subtle level, however, the effect of exposure to crime in the mass media may not be significant until a personal problem or a particular social condition presents itself. Exposure in the past may thus furnish a future alternative for action.

Certainly we can convincingly argue that mass communications are socially mediated. Nevertheless, there would be nothing to mediate if a particular image did not exist in the mass media in the first place. Mass communications *do* make a difference. My argument, reinterpreting the thesis of the effects of mass media, is that a specific kind of crime coverage in the media provides the source for building criminal conceptions. A conception of crime is presented in the mass media. That conception, diffused throughout the society, becomes the basis for the public's view of reality. Not only is a symbolic environment created within the society, but personal actions take their reference from that environment. Indeed, the construction of a conceptual reality is also the creation of a social reality of actions and events.

SOCIAL TYPES IN THE
WORLD OF CRIME

All the nuances of crime cannot be vividly communicated. In communication, images must be simplified, sharpened, and reduced to their essentials. Thus, in order to facilitate the diffusion of conceptions of crime, *stereotypes* of crime and criminals are created. Of-

---

and the Social System," in Robert K. Merton, Leonard Broom, and Leonard S. Cottrell, Jr. (eds.), *Sociology Today* (New York: Basic Books, 1959), pp. 537–578; Everett M. Rogers, *Diffusion of Innovations* (New York: The Free Press of Glencoe, 1962), pp. 57–75, 208–253.

[14] Herbert Blumer and Philip Hauser, *Movies, Delinquency, and Crime* (New York: Macmillan, 1933).

fenders, accordingly, are grouped by the public into such categories as the thief, the burglar, the robber, the sex offender, and the murderer. Categories such as these furnish the boundaries for the public's view of crime.

On the basis of stereotypes, then, persons construct their conceptual realities of crime. The criminal becomes a *social type*.[15] As a social type, "the criminal" can be understood by the observer as one who possesses attributes that are believed to be characteristic of a class of people. The criminal, as socially typed, is a construct that incorporates a description of what such persons are like, why they act as they do, and how they should act in the future. All that is associated with crime has the possibility of being categorized by the public. Such is the basis of human understanding.

Some systematic evidence exists on the public stereotyping of criminals. In a series of pilot studies the extent and nature of stereotyped images of deviants were investigated.[16] The researcher found, first, public stereotypes for such deviant categories as homosexuals, drug addicts, prostitutes, murderers, and juvenile delinquents. It was then determined that persons also tend to consistently portray each type of deviant in a particular way. Homosexuals were likely to be described as being sexually abnormal, perverted, mentally ill, and maladjusted, whereas marijuana smokers were characterized as persons looking for kicks, escapists, insecure, lacking self-control, and frustrated. It was concluded that "discernible stereotypes of at least several kinds of deviants do exist in our society and that there is a fair amount of agreement on the content of these stereotypes."[17] Hence, imputed deviance, including deviance which may also be criminally defined, is publicly stereotyped. These stereotypes of human behavior are structured and patterned in society.

On a more general level, the category of "criminal" tends to incorporate its own stereotyped set of characteristics. According to public conception, the criminal is a social type. The principal model for the type is the *villain*, one who is feared, hated, and ridiculed. The criminal is generally the "bad guy" in popular conception. Crim-

---

[15] The concept of social type is from Orrin E. Klapp, *Heroes, Villains, and Fools* (Englewood Cliffs, N.J.: Prentice-Hall, 1962), pp. 1–24.

[16] J. L. Simmons, "Public Stereotypes of Deviants," *Social Problems,* 13 (Fall, 1965), pp. 223–232.

[17] *Ibid.,* p. 229.

inals are the enemies of law and order (desperadoes, rebels, flouters, rogues, troublemakers), villainous strangers (intruders, suspicious isolates, monsters), disloyal and underhanded types (renegades, traitors, deceivers, sneak-attackers, chiselers, shirkers, corrupters), or are among the miscellaneous social undesirables (vagrants, derelicts, convicts, outcasts).[18] Such villains are with us in popular conception, nominally as criminals. The public concept of crime is used to cover a multitude of sins.

But the criminal as a social type incorporates other than the image of villain. He may also be cast in the role of *hero*. Noted outlaws are an example:

> Billy the Kid did not make a good villain because he was blonde, blue-eyed, well built, and rather handsome; women fell for him. He was brave and a square shooter. Such discrepancies in the character of a bad man made him resemble others (Robin Hood, Don Juan, François Villon, Pancho Villa), who perhaps should have been villains but were not.[19]

Paradoxically (perhaps), the villainous criminal can also be a popular favorite of heroic proportions.

A major reason for the ambiguity between villainous and heroic criminal conceptions is that the roles of villain and hero support similar value themes. Both types depend upon aggressiveness, cleverness, and the ability to "outdo" others in some way.

> Not only in fiction but in real life confusion between good guys and bad guys occurs. Since Edwin H. Sutherland's epochal studies, Americans have gotten rather used to the idea that a whitecollar criminal looks very like an honest businessman. Expense account chiseling, kickbacks, payoffs, tax evasion, even a little fraud or larceny, may be all in a day's work. If the old distinction between honesty and dishonesty has become blurred, no less has the quaint notion that "crime does not pay" (if you want to get a laugh from an audience, just smile when you say this). When the Brinks Express robbers were caught a few years back, a housewife remarked, "I was kind of sad. It seemed a shame, when they had only a few days to go before the statute of limitations would have let them keep all that money." A

[18] Klapp, *Heroes, Villains, and Fools*, pp. 50–67.
[19] *Ibid.*, p. 50.

strange kind of casing is occurring today — good guys do not have to live up to codes, bad guys do not have to be caught and punished (especially if they look enough like good guys); it may be that the distinction is ceasing to be important.[20]

With a bit more humor, Mark Twain observed the same American tendency to respect what is also regarded as criminal:

And he grew up and married and raised a large family, and brained them all with an ax one night, and got wealthy by all manner of cheating and rascality; and now he is the infernalest wickedest scoundrel in his native village, and is universally respected, and belongs to the legislature.[21]

The ambiguous reaction to crime can be traced in part to the tradition of the *romantic outlaw*. Tales of the maverick who defied the law are legend.

Even today annual celebrations are devoted to Jesse James at Northfield, Minnesota (because he happened to ride through and rob a bank there), and to Wild Bill Hickock at Deadwood, South Dakota. Were a proposal made to abolish the outlaw tradition, there would probably be a storm of protest from movie-makers, writers, and the public. Crooks like John Dillinger, the "Yellow Kid" Weil, and Al Capone, get wrapped in glamor, even outlaws from other countries, such as Pancho Villa, who, in spite of train robberies and murders, became as much of a celebrity in America as Buffalo Bill; reporters stayed with his staff to tell of the women he kidnapped or how he ordered a thousand-dollar bathtub from a firm in Chicago.[22]

Certainly the romantic outlaw is more than villain. He is also something else — "too good to be a villain, too bad to be a hero, too serious to be a mere clown, too interesting to forget."[23]

Perhaps some criminals capture the modern imagination as *anti-heroes*. As anti-hero, the criminal represents the attempt to make it outside the system. Inevitable failure gives charisma to his noble attempt. And, along the way, such a criminal is likely to assist those

[20] *Ibid.*, pp. 145–146. Also see Nathan Hare, "The Ambivalent Public and Crime," *Crime and Delinquency*, 9 (April, 1963), pp. 145–151.
[21] "Story of the Bad Little Boy," in *The Complete Short Stories of Mark Twain*, ed. by Charles Neider (New York: Bantam Books, 1957), pp. 8–9.
[22] Klapp, *Heroes, Villains, and Fools*, p. 146.
[23] *Ibid.*, p. 147.

who are made to fail in other ways because of the system. Woody Guthrie had Pretty Boy Floyd singing in Shawnee, Oklahoma:

> You say that I'm an outlaw
> You say that I'm a thief
> Here's a Christmas dinner
> For the families on relief

Then adding:

> Now as through this world I ramble
> I see lots of funny men
> Some will rob you with a six gun
> And some with a fountain pen.
>> But as through your life you roam
>> You won't never see an outlaw
>> Drive a family from their home.[24]

Respect for some criminals, in addition, is a product of the American fascination with violence. Violence has become a hallowed tradition in American culture:

> If we could formulate a generalized image of America in the eyes of foreign peoples from the eighteenth century to the present, it would surely include, among other things, a phantasmagoria of violence, from the original Revolution and Indian wars to the sordid history of lynching; from the casual killings of the cowboy and bandit to the machine-gun murders of racketeers. If America has often been considered a country of innocence and promise in contrast to a corrupt and immoral Europe, this sparkling, smiling, domestic land of easygoing friendliness, where it is estimated that a new murder occurs every forty-five minutes, has also glorified personal whim and impulse and has ranked hardened killers with the greatest folk heroes. Founded and preserved by acts of aggression, characterized by a continuing tradition of self-righteous violence against suspected subversion and by a vigorous sense of personal freedom, usually involving the widespread possession of firearms, the United States has evidenced a unique tolerance of homicides.[25]

[24] "Pretty Boy Floyd," *American Folksong, Woody Guthrie,* edited by Moses Asch (New York: Oak Publications, 1961), p. 27.
[25] David Brion Davis, *Homicide in American Fiction, 1798–1860: A Study in Social Values* (Ithaca, N.Y.: Cornell University Press, 1957), pp. vii–viii.

Little wonder, then, that there is public confusion in the evaluation of acts that involve violence. Violence itself has its own legitimacy.

Criminals are not the only social types that fill the public world of crime. Also included are the social types that are associated with criminals. Policemen, lawyers, and detectives have become socially typed through the various forms of communication. The detective, in particular, has been the object of a great deal of characterizing in the mystery novel. Edgar Allan Poe, interested in unraveling puzzles by reasoning, wrote a number of stories in which the detective played the dominant role. In 1852 Charles Dickens introduced readers of *Bleak House* to a Scotland Yard detective, Inspector Bucket. But it was not until Arthur Conan Doyle introduced Sherlock Holmes to the public in "A Study of Scarlet" in the 1880's that the detective story became a public favorite. Sherlock Holmes represented to readers not only a "consulting detective," but a cultured gentleman who transcended the law with his own code of right and wrong. In the world of Holmes the business of upholding the right fell upon the shoulders of private men rather than public officials.[26] Holmes was always, morally and scientifically, beyond the reach of Lestrade of Scotland Yard.

The crime-fighting heroes of today display virtues for another age. These characters are more likely to be found in suspense and science fiction stories than in detective stories.[27] The "private eye," such as Dashiell Hammett's Sam Spade or Raymond Chandler's Philip Marlowe, is a tough guy, cynical, hard-boiled, and hard drinking, who is at war with criminals in his *own* way, often outside the law. Mickey Spillane's Mike Hammer killed numerous innocent people in his pursuits against crime. But perhaps James Bond of Ian Fleming's novels best presents the modern figure in a world of crime. As a secret agent, Bond is licensed to kill — and with great finesse. He is talented also as a lover, sportsman (who cheats), and a connoisseur of fashionable luxuries. Ian Fleming symbolizes something that appeals to every good man.

> What he offers his readers is the beguiling modern dream of life
> of total self-sufficiency and sophisticated self-indulgence. Soli-

[26] See Martin Maloney, "A Grammar of Assassination," *Etc.*, 11 (Winter, 1954), pp. 83–95.

[27] See Christopher Hibbert, *The Roots of Evil: A Social History of Crime and Punishment* (Harmondsworth, Eng.: Penguin Books, 1966), pp. 302–314.

tary, composed, self-assured, acting with ritualistic deliberation and meeting his trials single-handedly and resourcefully, Bond is an existential deep-sea diver. In his casual moments (enjoying a good meal or an evening with a lovely woman) he projects the satisfaction of feeling cool and superior; at critical times he demonstrates the capacity of the lone individual to pull through unaided. His only use for society is as a hospital, where he can recoup his strength for the next plunge into the void.[28]

Images such as these have been presented to a wide audience by television and the movies as well as by fictional literature. Detective heroes have been portrayed in leading roles as being "smarter than the cops, craftier than the crooks, too quick to be caught and domesticated by the classiest doll."[29] And we have been presented with the shadowy figure of Perry Mason, a lawyer who behaves like a private detective in preparing his cases. The list need not be extended. It is enough to say that the world of crime is readily before us for the taking.

I am not necessarily being critical of the ways in which the characters of the world of crime are presented. The portrayals by criminologists probably have not been any more convincing. I *do*, however, argue that the world of fiction is also the world of reality. Fiction is fact when it is believed and taken as the object of action. When criminals and their counterparts are characterized in a particular way, they are already becoming social types which find their fulfillment in society. Social reality begins in the imagination.

PUBLIC ATTITUDES
TOWARD CRIME

The nature and intensity of the public's concern about crime varies from time to time; it has periodically been acute throughout the twentieth century. Fluctuations in attention to crime are indicated by the perennial appointment of legislative and private committees to

[28] Albert Goldman, "Elegant Narcissist," *The New York Times Book Review,* December 11, 1966, p. 36. (A review of John Pearson, *The Life of Ian Fleming* [New York: McGraw-Hill, 1966].) Also see Lycurgus M. Starkey, Jr., *James Bond's World Values* (Nashville, Tenn.: Abingdon Press, 1966).

[29] Quoted in Hibbert, *The Roots of Evil,* p. 311 (originally from *Time,* October, 1959). Also see Melvin L. De Fleur, "Occupational Roles as Portrayed on Television," *Public Opinion Quarterly,* 28 (Spring, 1964), pp. 57–74.

investigate the crime problem. The public's perception of crime is
variable. The construction and diffusion of criminal conceptions are
part of a process that is continually changing in substance and intensity.

Public anxiety about crime is now especially critical — in response,
the President's Commission on Law Enforcement and Administration
of Justice was established in 1965.[30] One part of the Commission's
task was to investigate the anxiety itself. Attitudes toward crime
were assessed by analyzing national public opinion polls and surveys
conducted for the Commission.

The Commission, indeed, found that crime is perceived by the public as one of the most serious of all domestic problems.[31] In a national survey conducted for the Commission by the National Opinion
Research Center, citizens were asked to choose from a list of six
major domestic problems facing the nation the one to which they
had been paying the most attention recently. Crime was the second
most frequently selected problem. Only race relations was selected
by more people. Furthermore, most persons thought the crime situation in their own community was getting worse. A Gallup survey of
April, 1965, showed that this pessimistic perception of the crime
problem occurred among many segments of the population — men
and women, well educated and less educated, and all age, regional,
income, and residential groupings.

Personal *fear* of crime, the Commission found, is especially great
about personal safety and to some extent the fear that personal property will be taken. Most intense is the fear of being accosted by a
stranger on the street or that a stranger will break into the home
and attack them. Although these are the crimes that occur least frequently, fear about them significantly affects personal lives. The
Commission reported the following:

> Perhaps the most revealing findings on the impact of fear of
> crime on people's lives were the changes people reported in their

[30] For the summary report, see President's Commission on Law Enforcement
and Administration of Justice, *The Challenge of Crime in a Free Society*
(Washington, D.C.: U.S. Government Printing Office, 1967).

[31] See President's Commission on Law Enforcement and Administration of
Justice, "Public Attitudes Toward Crime and Law Enforcement," *Task Force
Report: Crime and Its Impact — An Assessment* (Washington, D.C.: U.S.
Government Printing Office, 1967), pp. 85–95. Or see Jennie McIntyre, "Public
Attitudes Toward Crime and Law Enforcement," *Annals of the American
Academy of Political and Social Science,* 374 (November, 1967), pp. 34–46.

regular habits of life. In the high-crime districts surveyed in Boston and Chicago, for example, five out of every eight respondents reported changes in their habits because of fear of crime, some as many as four or five major changes. Forty-three percent reported they stayed off the streets at night altogether. Another 21 percent said they always used cars or taxis at night. Thirty-five percent said they would not talk to strangers any more.[32]

The Commission also found that there are differences in the intensity of concern about crime according to personal characteristics of the population. In a national survey of anxiety about crime, supplemented by a survey in Washington, it was found that Negro women have the highest degree of anxiety, followed in order by Negro men, white women, and white men. Also, anxiety about crime is more pronounced among the lower income levels for both Negroes and whites.[33]

One of the first pieces of research on public attitudes toward crime investigated attitudes of persons to stealing from three kinds of organizations.[34] The main objective of the research was to determine how the size of the victim organization affects public attitudes toward stealing. In general, it was found that if obliged to choose, most persons disapprove less of stealing from large, impersonal business and governmental organizations than from small, personal organizations. The findings were, however, modified by the characteristics of the respondents. It was observed that regardless of organizational size, the lower the socioeconomic status of the respondent the greater the approval of stealing. Similarly, women were more inclined to approve of stealing than men, though they showed the greatest differences in attitudes when the size of the victim or-

[32] President's Commission on Law Enforcement and Administration of Justice, *Task Force Report: Crime and Its Impact — An Assessment,* p. 88.

[33] Phillip H. Ennis, *Criminalization in the United States: A Report of a National Survey,* President's Commission on Law Enforcement and Administration of Justice, Field Survey II (Washington, D.C.: U.S. Government Printing Office, 1967), pp. 72–79; Albert D. Biderman, Louise A. Johnson, Jennie McIntyre, and Adrianne W. Weis, *Report on a Pilot Study in the District of Columbia on Victimization and Attitudes Toward Law Enforcement,* President's Commission on Law Enforcement and Administration of Justice, Field Survey I (Washington, D.C.: U.S. Government Printing Office, 1967), pp. 119–134.

[34] Erwin O. Smigel, "Public Attitudes Toward Stealing as Related to Size of the Victim Organization," *American Sociological Review,* 21 (June, 1956), pp. 320–327.

ganization was considered. The conclusion was that while size of organization affects public attitudes toward stealing, the attitudes are also affected by the characteristics of the respondents.

Similar research was conducted in a study of public attitudes toward the violation of unemployment compensation laws.[35] Three major circumstances were considered: (1) knowledge of the laws, (2) social norms of the respondents, and (3) socioeconomic status. The evidence supported the hypothesis that knowledge of the law plays a part in determining attitudes toward violation of the law. Individuals who approved of the illegal behavior were likely to be ignorant of the law and unaware that violations were involved. It was found that when the social norms are in conflict with the goals of the law, there is a divergence in attitudes toward violation. Respondents who had poor jobs and low socioeconomic status were more inclined to approve of violation of unemployment compensation laws, whereas those who had good jobs and high status were more likely to disapprove of the violations. Finally, the opportunity to violate the law and personal experiences with unemployment increased the tendency to approve or at least be indifferent toward the violation of unemployment compensation laws.

Attitudes toward offenses in which the public itself is the victim may also be considered. Violations of the Federal Food, Drug and Cosmetic Act directly affect the consumer. With such pure food violations as misbranding and adulteration in mind, a sample of consumers was asked to judge selected cases of violation to show how they would react to the violations.[36] The responses of the consumers were then compared with actual decisions in the cases and with possible decisions provided in the federal law. The respondents reacted to the pure food violations without regard for their class position: "That is, even though they vary greatly by income, occupation, and educational level, by degree of awareness and familiarity with these violations, and by amount of organized consumer activity, their choices of penalties do not differ significantly from one such grouping to another."[37] Yet, according to their reactions, the re-

[35] Erwin O. Smigel, "Public Attitudes Toward 'Chiseling' with Reference to Unemployment Compensation," *American Sociological Review*, 18 (February, 1953), pp. 59–67.

[36] Donald J. Newman, "Public Attitudes Toward a Form of White Collar Crime," *Social Problems*, 4 (January, 1957), pp. 228–232.

[37] *Ibid.*, p. 231.

spondents tended to view food adulteration as more comparable to serious traffic violations than to burglary. The respondents, thus, tended to view such violators as "law breakers" rather than "criminals." But pure food offenses against the customer have only recently become a matter of public interest. Greater awareness of this form of violation in the future may be accompanied by a stronger public reaction toward the offenses.

Criminal conceptions also refer to offenses that are without victims. Public knowledge about and reaction to three forms of such offenses (abortion, homosexuality, and drug addiction) were investigated in one study.[38] Respondents in the San Francisco area were asked to indicate the degree to which they approve of changes in social policies toward abortion, homosexuality, and drug addiction. Other questions probed for misconceptions about the facts regarding these activities. The researchers found that the levels of social tolerance for these behaviors varied according to (1) the degree to which the behaviors are interpreted as being dangerous to the participants or to other members of society and (2) the accuracy of their knowledge about the behaviors. Also, it was found that tolerance for abortion, homosexuality, and drug addiction was related to variations in the social background of the respondents. Men were more tolerant than women, younger persons than older persons, educated persons than less educated persons, and Protestants and Jews than Catholics. Finally, regardless of these social correlates of attitudes, it was found that persons were most tolerant of abortion, less tolerant of proposed changes in laws and practices regarding homosexuals, and least accepting of changes in the handling of drug addicts.

Members of a community are likely to develop a pattern of reactions to crime peculiar to their own community. Public reaction to crime within a particular community setting has been studied in research conducted for the President's Commission on Law Enforcement and Administration of Justice in a middle-sized eastern industrial city, given the fictitious name of "Wincanton."[39] A survey of the city's residents indicated a general tolerance of gambling and

[38] Elizabeth A. Rooney and Don C. Gibbons, "Social Reactions to 'Crime Without Victims,'" *Social Problems*, 13 (Spring, 1966), pp. 400–410.

[39] John A. Gardiner, "Public Attitudes Toward Gambling and Corruption," *Annals of the American Academy of Political and Social Science*, 374 (November, 1967), pp. 123–134.

related activities, but hostility toward all forms of official corruption
The respondents displayed both a tolerance of illicit services and a
demand for honesty on the part of local officials. The residents apparently did not realize the paradox that in order for illicit services
to be supplied, dishonesty of local officials was necessary. A major
reason for the public ignorance of the connection between gambling
and corruption, the study suggests, is that the illegal activities of the
officials are hidden from public view, becoming known only during
a reform investigation. The following conclusions were offered about
the nature and significance of public attitudes toward gambling and
corruption:

> First, public attitudes are much more permissive toward gam-
> bling than the statutes which are common in the United States;
> gambling is either positively desired or else not regarded as
> particularly reprehensible by a substantial proportion of the
> population. Second, citizens value official honesty and impar-
> tial administration of the laws even if they do not expect that
> all officials will, in fact, live up to these standards. Third, while
> there was little awareness of the extent of corruption in the
> city, citizens reacted strongly whenever investigations revealed
> the relationship between organized crime and local officials.
> While local residents are inadequately aware of the costs of the
> support for the services offered by organized crime, they re-
> spond positively whenever choices are clearly and dramatically
> presented to them.[40]

The implication is that the conclusions apply as well to public attitudes toward crime in other communities.

PUBLIC ATTITUDES TOWARD
THE CONTROL OF CRIME

Associated with public attitudes toward crime are thoughts on controlling it. Public conceptions develop in regard to law and its enforcement, judicial administration of criminal law, and penal and
correctional administration. As with other attitudes, these become
patterned within the segments of society. Actions, in turn, find their
source in such conceptions.

Attitudes toward the control of crime tend to be moralistic. The

---

[40] *Ibid.,* p. 134.

surveys regarding beliefs about the causes of crime indicate a concern with the morals of the country and the moral training of youths.[41] A Gallup poll of 1965 showed that few persons blame social conditions or law enforcement for the increase in crime. Rather, most answers reflected poor parental guidance or inadequate home life and supervision of teenagers. In another survey, also asking similar questions about the causes of crime, it was found that 68 per cent of the persons interviewed believed that upbringing or bad environment were the main causes of crime. Few suggested poor or inadequate social conditions.

Although the public attributes an increase in crime to the lowering of moral standards, most would depend on the police and related agencies for controlling crime; connected with this reliance on law enforcement is the generally positive attitude the public has toward the police. According to opinion polls, most of the public has a high opinion of the work of the police. A poll in 1967 showed that 77 per cent of the public had a "great deal" of respect for the police, 17 per cent had "some" respect, and only 4 per cent had "hardly any" respect.[42] Similarly, the national survey in 1965 by the National Opinion Research Center (NORC) showed that 67 per cent of the persons interviewed thought that the police were doing a good to excellent job of enforcing the law.[43] The later finding, however, was qualified by the income, race, and sex of the respondents. It was found in the NORC study that upper income groups are consistently more favorable in their evaluation of the police, that Negroes at all income levels have fairly strong negative attitudes toward the police, and that Negro women are more critical than Negro men of the job the police are doing. Furthermore, although Negroes more than whites feel that the police are not "respectful" to them, persons of both races and sexes tend to feel that the police are not sufficiently respectful.

Nevertheless, in spite of some criticism, there is a general public reliance on the police for the control of crime. Associated with this

[41] See McIntyre, "Public Attitudes Toward Crime and Law Enforcement," pp. 41–44.

[42] George Gallup, "U.S. Public Gives Police Big Vote of Confidence," *The Gallup Report* (Princeton, N.J.: American Institute of Public Opinion, August 30, 1967).

[43] Ennis, *Criminalization in the United States*, pp. 52–72. Also see Phillip H. Ennis, "Crime, Victims, and the Police," *Trans-Action*, 4 (June, 1967), pp. 36–44.

acceptance (and mandate) is the public's willingness to permit the police considerable range in their efforts to control crime. A majority of those (73 per cent) interviewed in Washington, D.C., agreed that the police have the right to act tough when deemed necessary.[44] More than half (56 per cent) thought that there should be more use of police dogs. In the national survey, 52 per cent of the respondents believed that the police should have more power, and 42 per cent believed that police should risk arresting an innocent person rather than risk missing an offender.[45] Yet, the surveys found a concern among the public for protection of the civil rights of the individual in enforcement of the law. Some of this concern is related to a belief that there is discrimination against certain economic and racial groups.

The general positive acceptance of the police in America is a reflection of "the sacredness of the police as a social institution, especially among the less sophisticated lower-middle class — the people with 'Support your local police' bumper stickers who enliven their lives by reading about child molesters in the Sunday supplements."[46] It is not so much that we respect the law, but that we submit to popular sovereignty. Law *enforcement* represents something more and something other than the law. The police are allowed to operate a kind of order that limits any challenge to the social functions of the institution of law enforcement. It is assumed that law enforcement is good in itself. There may be occasional criticisms of incidents of police brutality, but to critically examine law enforcement as an institution is not an especially pressing interest of Americans.

Another indication that the public believes that repressive measures, rather than changes in social conditions, are the most effective means of controlling crime is found in attitudes about court actions. A Gallup survey in 1969 found that 75 per cent of adults believe that the courts do not deal harshly enough with criminals.[47] Only 2 per cent said that the courts in their area deal "too harshly" with criminals, while 13 per cent agreed that the treatment by the courts

[44] Biderman, Johnson, McIntyre, and Weis, *Report on a Pilot Study in the District of Columbia on Victimization and Attitudes Toward Law Enforcement*, pp. 144–149.

[45] Ennis, *Criminalization in the United States*, pp. 58–60.

[46] Edgar Z. Friedenberg, "Hooked on Law Enforcement," *The Nation* (October 16, 1967), pp. 360–361.

[47] *The New York Times*, February 16, 1969, p. 47.

is "about right." Further evidence of the public's desire to crack down on crime was indicated when 58 per cent of the respondents agreed that it was a good idea to give a double sentence to anyone who commits a crime with a gun. Similarly, 71 per cent of the respondents believed that it is a good idea to deny parole to a person convicted of crime a second time.

The public apparently believes that the courts are too lenient in their sentencing practices. Aside from this evaluative matter, the public has a fairly definite idea of the kinds of penalties that the courts should give for specific crimes. This was documented in a study conducted some years ago of the judgments of students in assigning punishments to thirteen selected felonies.[48] On the basis of a questionnaire, the students were asked to respond as if they were judges in criminal cases. A principal finding was a significant discrepancy between the penal law, the application of the law, and the judgments as to how the law should be applied in the assignment of sentences for the crimes. Severe child beating by a father was regarded as much more serious, in the penalty it deserves, than indicated in the law and actual sentences. There was, as well, a consistent and stable hierarchy of crimes and associated penalties in the minds of most of the students. Moreover, there were predictable relationships between an individual's personal characteristics (sex, socioeconomic status, and rural-urban backgrounds) and the punishments he assigned to the offenses. Women were inclined to assign longer prison sentences than men for such offenses as child beating and bigamy and shorter ones for assault with a deadly weapon; persons with an upper class background were inclined to assign longer prison sentences than those with a lower class background for such offenses as bribing a witness and child beating; and persons from rural areas were more inclined than those from urban areas to assign harsher punishments for such crimes as arson, attempted burglary, and grand larceny. To generalize from the findings, the public judgments were assigned according to the crime and its cultural meaning, in relation to the personal characteristics of the evaluators.

More recent research continues to show a pattern of public atti-

[48] Arnold M. Rose and Arthur E. Prell, "Does the Punishment Fit the Crime? A Study in Social Valuation," *American Journal of Sociology*, 61 (November, 1955), pp. 247–259.

tudes toward the punishment of specific offenses. In a national survey conducted in 1967, the public was asked the best way of dealing with an adult convicted of a specific crime.[49] The alternative sentences, from a list of seven crimes ranging from embezzlement to murder, were probation, a short prison sentence with parole, or a long prison sentence. The use of probation found little favor with the public. Considering each of the crimes, only about a quarter of the respondents felt that probation was an appropriate sentence. Only for prostitution, judged more harshly by women than men, did as much as 26 per cent of the public feel probation should be used. A further breakdown by education showed an increasingly severe attitude as the amount of education decreased. That is, those with less than a high school education were the most willing to have someone sent to prison.

Public attitudes toward the control of crime are not always logically consistent. Some ambivalence or even contradiction is to be expected in attitudes toward various means of crime control. Ultimately, opinions are based on valuation. One forced response on an issue may simultaneously call a number of divergent values into play. Consistency in attitudes toward crime and the control of crime is more often an accident than a logical association of underlying values.

Ambivalence in attitudes toward crime control can be found in the public opinion surveys and research studies. A study of adult attitudes toward the control of juvenile delinquency found that respondents in Wisconsin believed delinquents should be punished but, at the same time, that they should be treated.[50] Although differences followed social status, with persons of high social status showing less ambivalence between the espousal of a legalistic-punitive approach and a treatment approach, punishment of the delinquent was generally emphasized whereas at the same time treatment was favored.

A similar pattern of responses can be observed in the national survey which contained questions on prisons and corrections.[51] More than half the adults polled felt that the prison system was doing a

[49] Louis Harris and Associates, *The Public Looks at Crime and Corrections* (Washington, D.C.: Joint Commission on Correctional Manpower and Training, 1968), pp. 11–12.

[50] William P. Lentz, "Social Status and Attitudes Toward Delinquency Control," *Journal of Research in Crime and Delinquency*, 3 (July, 1966), pp. 147–154.

[51] Harris, *The Public Looks at Crime and Corrections*, pp. 7–9.

good job in helping to deal with the problem of crime. (The more education the participant had, the less likely he was to give the prison a positive rating.) But though the majority of the respondents believed in the worth of the prison as a form of punishment, an even larger proportion (72 per cent) felt that rehabilitation should be the main emphasis within the prison. In addition, there was little interest (only 20 per cent) among the respondents in the increased use of parole to release inmates from prison.

A final consideration in public attitudes toward the control of crime is that of attitudes toward the death penalty. Changes in attitudes toward capital punishment are among the most sensitive indicators of shifts in the public's orientation to crime control. There has been a gradual shift in the United States from a punitive reaction to one that is less oriented to punishment. Since 1953 Gallup has been polling the American public on capital punishment, asking: "Are you in favor of the death penalty for persons convicted of murder?"[52] In the 1953 survey, 68 per cent of the national sample favored the death penalty. By 1960 the proportion who favored capital punishment shifted to 51 per cent, and by 1965 the figure had decreased to 45 per cent. In 1966, 42 per cent of the public favored the death penalty.

Other surveys and studies support and amplify the extent to which the public is undergoing changes in attitudes toward capital punishment.[53] The amount of support for the death penalty varies from one segment of the population to another, and shifts in opinion are occurring at varying rates. A greater proportion of men than women favor the death penalty. However, the greatest amount of change in attitude toward capital punishment in the last few years has occurred among men. Also, whereas occupational groups such as law enforcement officers still tend to favor the death penalty, other occupational groups such as psychiatrists, penologists, and social workers are tending to oppose the death penalty.

Attitudinal changes such as these, occurring among the general public and within the segments associated with penal and correc-

---

[52] George Gallup, "Opposition to the Death Penalty Continues to Mount," *The Gallup Poll* (Princeton, N.J.: American Institute of Public Opinion, July 1, 1966).

[53] See Hugo Adam Bedau (ed.), *The Death Penalty in America* (Garden City, N.Y.: Anchor Books, 1964), pp. 231–236.

tional practices, are likely to affect the control policies of the future. Public attitudes are relevant because basically they are the sources of action. That which is regarded and handled as criminal begins in the minds of persons in some segments of society.

CONSEQUENCES OF CRIMINAL CONCEPTIONS

So it is that conceptions of crime are constructed and diffused throughout the segments of society. And the conceptions are important because of their consequences. But since they vary from one segment to another, they have different effects on the total society. That is, the conceptions most critical in creating a social reality of crime are those held by the power segments of the society. These are the segments that impose their views and actions on others in the name of the whole society. The social reality of crime is basically constructed from the criminal conceptions held by the most powerful segments of society.

Any conception of crime has its own set of consequences. Each conception provides a perspective as to what is regarded as crime, how crime should be controlled, how criminals should be punished and treated, and how the population is to conduct itself in an environment of crime and criminals. All these issues are resolved in actions. As thoughts become deeds, a social reality is constructed.

But the most significant consequence of a criminal conception is the creation of crime. Without the concept of crime, crime would not exist as a phenomenon. It follows that the more concern that surrounds the concept of crime, the greater is the probability that criminal definitions will be formulated and applied. The concept of crime must be reified in order to justify its existence.

CHAPTER TEN

The Politics
of Reality

The conceptions of crime within any society are many and varied. The reality of crime is a multifaceted world of an infinite number of realities. But in the social reality that is constructed to cope concretely with crime, some criminal conceptions are more important than others. Particular criminal conceptions, those of the powerful segments of society, ultimately determine the nature of the social reality of crime. These are the criminal conceptions that are responsible for creating crime.

Conceptions of crime — the subjective aspect of the social reality of crime — are constructed with intentions, not merely to satisfy the imagination. We end up with some realities rather than others for good reason — because someone has something to protect. That protection can be achieved by the perpetuation of a certain view of reality. Realities are, then, the most subtle and insidious of our forms of social control. No weapon is stronger than the control of one's world of reality. It is the control of one's mind.

By constructing a reality that we are all to believe in, those in positions of power *legitimize* their authority. That which is believed to be true, to be the "real" nature of things, is good in itself. It is right simply because it *is,* and is not to be questioned or refuted. Believing is accepting. Hence, the reality of crime that is constructed for all of us by those in a position of power is the reality we tend to accept as our own. By doing so, we grant those in power the authority to carry out the actions that best promote their interests.

This is the *politics of reality*. The social reality of crime in politically organized society is constructed as a political act. Both private and governmental groups have a vested interest in constructing particular criminal conceptions that instruct official policy. From beginning to end, then, the construction of the social reality of crime is a political matter.

PERIODIC INVESTIGATIONS
OF CRIME

At various times the public is made aware of the crime problem. Public alarm about crime fluctuates from one period to another.[1] And associated with each period is the belief in a new "crime wave." How and why are these waves manufactured? The answer can be found in part in the interests that have something to gain from constructing a reality that includes an aroused fear and anxiety about crime.

Concerted efforts to increase public concern about crime are often achieved by the appointment of committees to investigate what someone regards as the particular crime problem of the time. Crusades on crime have been organized for the explicit purpose of promoting a criminal conception. Realities of crime are shaped by such periodic investigations of crime.

Many of the crime commissions in the last fifty years have been organized in communities to investigate that which some leaders have regarded at the time as the local crime problem. In 1920 a number of civic groups in Cleveland (headed by the Cleveland Bar Association) commissioned a survey of crime. The final report concentrated on the machinery of criminal justice.[2] At about the same time the Chicago Crime Commission was established in response to a sensational case in which a gang of four men killed two armed guards carrying a factory payroll. The Chicago Crime Commission exists to this day, looking into various aspects of crime and criminal justice. Other cities, both in the past and in recent

[1] See Yale Kamisar, "When the Cops Were Not 'Handcuffed.'" *The New York Times Magazine,* November 7, 1965, p. 34.

[2] Roscoe Pound and Felix Frankfurter (eds.), *Criminal Justice in Cleveland* (Cleveland: The Cleveland Foundation, 1922).

times, have established commissions to investigate various aspects of the crime problem.[3]

New York, in particular, has been the setting for numerous criminal investigations. One of the earliest organizations was the Society for the Prevention of Crime, started in 1878. Eventually the Society developed a religious fervor under the leadership of the Reverend Charles Henry Parkhurst. In the 1920's, when a crime wave was the principal topic of conversation, the Society engaged the public by sponsoring an essay contest on how best to reduce crime. Professor Franklin H. Giddings and a panel of prominent citizens awarded the first prize of $2,500 to a former police captain and the second prize of $500 to a police detective. The proposals to curb crime included a criticism of the police commissioner, a recommendation that parole be eliminated, and the suggestion that the heads of prisoners be shaved and that they wear striped uniforms.

Following such efforts, a number of committees and citizen's groups concentrated on specific forms of crime and deviance in New York, especially on prostitution and organized crime. Criminal justice in the city received attention in the 1930's with the Appellate Court's appointment of the Seabury Commission. Considerable graft and corruption in the city government were exposed. Nevertheless, city officials, as could be expected, denounced and then ignored the investigation. Characteristically, Mayor Jimmy Walker responded by condemning those who called for further investigations as "slanderers of the fair name of the City we love."[4]

Crime commissions have been established to investigate the crime problem on the state as well as the local level. In 1925 the Missouri Bar Association called a meeting of civic and business leaders throughout the state to enlist their support for a statewide crime

[3] See Ralph G. Murdy, *Crime Commission Handbook* (Baltimore: Criminal Justice Commission, 1965), pp. 12–35. Also E. Connor, "Crime Commissions and Criminal Procedure in the United States since 1920," *Journal of Criminal Law, Criminology and Police Science*, 21 (May, 1930), pp. 129–144; Allen Eaton, *A Bibliography of Social Surveys* (New York: Russell Sage Foundation, 1930); A. F. Kuhlman (ed.), *A Guide to Material on Crime and Criminal Justice* (New York: H. W. Wilson, 1929); Virgil Peterson, *Crime Commissions in the United States* (Chicago: Chicago Crime Commission, 1945).

[4] William B. Northrop, *The Insolence of Office — the Story of the Seabury Investigations* (New York: G. P. Putnam's Sons, 1932), p. 54.

survey. Research by a staff covered a number of topics, including law enforcement, prosecution, penal sanctions, and corrections.[5] Although recommendations on the criminal justice system were made, few were implemented. The proposals, if they had been instituted, would have destroyed the political machines in the metropolitan areas of the state. Corrupt and inefficient criminal "justice" systems, as well as crime, are not such serious considerations when the interests of those who hold political power are at stake.

Similar commissions, with similar results, completed their tasks in other states during this same period.[6] The conclusion that can be drawn from all these efforts is that crime commissions have been appointed primarily for political reasons. Politicians would like to give the appearance to their constituents that something is being done about crime. But when the recommendations of the commissions go counter to the interests of the politicians, legislation is more likely to be restricted to controlling "the criminal" rather than to be directed toward reforming the criminal justice system. Yet, everyone can be happy with the results of a criminal investigation. Civic, business, and professional groups have been active; the researchers have carried out their study; politicians have fought crime without upsetting the political apparatus; and nothing has changed. All this has been accomplished by appointing a crime commission.

Until recent times, the major experiment with a crime commission on the national level has been the Wickersham Commission. The commission, formally titled the National Commission on Law Observance and Enforcement, and chaired by former United States Attorney General George W. Wickersham, was established by an act of Congress in 1929. From the beginning, the commission was the fulfillment of a campaign promise by Herbert Hoover to conduct a thorough inquiry into the enforcement of the prohibition laws.

Things had been going rather badly for the prohibition laws. Basically they seemed to be unenforceable. Furthermore, the lack of their

[5] Missouri Association for Criminal Justice, *The Missouri Crime Survey* (New York: Macmillan, 1926).

[6] Illinois Association for Criminal Justice, *The Illinois Crime Survey* (Chicago: Illinois Association for Criminal Justice, 1929); Wayne Morris and Ronald H. Beattie, *Survey of the Administration of Justice* (Eugene: University of Oregon Press, 1932).

enforcement was making a mockery of the American legal system. In response, the commission, with a large staff of researchers, assistants, and writers, completed an impressive report that ran to fifteen volumes.[7] Included in the volumes was material that extended beyond the enforcement of prohibition laws to such topics as the causes of crime, crime among the foreign born, child offenders, criminal statistics, the costs of crime, criminal courts, deportation, criminal procedure, and penal institutions.

The recommendations of the Wickersham Commission in regard to its primary focus, the enforcement of prohibition laws, were confusing and contradictory, indicating the desire of the commission to satisfy opposing interests. On the one hand, the federal government could rest with the satisfaction that there were no recommendations for a repeal of the prohibition laws. But on the other hand, the public was told that the laws were unenforceable. Prohibition ended shortly, nevertheless, out of its own exhaustion.

Today it is commonplace to condemn the Wickersham Commission as an ineffectual body and to bemoan the fact that no significant legislation and reform followed as a result of the commission's work. However, the immediate significance of the commission was considerable. For it provided a *forum* for the clash of diverse political, intellectual, and philosophical positions regarding crime and justice in America. That should be worth something, since such conflicts usually remain blurred and disguised from public view.

The lack of any long-term results from the crime commissions of the past is due to a number of factors which are now changing. The more recent crime commissions are closely tied to the power structure of the society. They are composed, moreover, of large technical staffs, representing the most respected institutions in the country. Furthermore, the commissions are organized along bureaucratic lines. Such organization assures some permanence and continuity, and also increases the possibility for the implementation of the proposals by the commissions. Finally, the activities of the commissions are made known today to most of the public. Through mass communication, we are all being presented with the image that crime is a national problem. The whole population is being alerted

[7] See especially National Commission on Law Observance and Enforcement, *Report on the Enforcement of the Prohibition Laws of the United States* (Washington, D.C.: U.S. Government Printing Office, 1931).

to a social reality of crime that is being constructed by government-appointed commissions.

THE PRESIDENT'S CRIME COMMISSION

On March 9, 1966, Lyndon Johnson told the nation:

> *The problems of crime bring us together. Even as we join in common action, we know there can be no instant victory. Ancient evils do not yield to easy conquest. We cannot limit our efforts to enemies we can see. We must, with equal resolve, seek out new knowledge, new techniques, and new understanding.*[8]

Johnson's resolve in a "war on crime" had been confirmed less than a year before (July 23, 1965) in the signing of an Executive Order that established the President's Commission on Law Enforcement and Administration of Justice.

The President's Crime Commission was composed of 19 commissioners, 63 staff members, 175 consultants, and hundreds of advisers. During the investigation, the commission called three national conferences, conducted five national surveys, held hundreds of meetings, and interviewed tens of thousands of persons. A number of publications resulted from the efforts of the commission and its staff. Several Task Force Reports were made on specific subjects and a series of Field Surveys reported the research findings. The investigation is summarized in the volume *The Challenge of Crime in a Free Society*.[9] The general report also contains the commission's recommendations — more than 200 specific proposals.

The appointment of the President's Crime Commission was basically an expedient political move.[10] During the presidential campaign of the previous year, Barry Goldwater had campaigned on the theme of "lawlessness." Although he lost the election, the

---

[8] President Lyndon B. Johnson, Message to the Congress, March 9, 1966.

[9] President's Commission on Law Enforcement and Administration of Justice, *The Challenge of Crime in a Free Society* (Washington, D.C.: U.S. Government Printing Office, 1967).

[10] See Isidor Silver, "Crime and Punishment," *Commentary*, 45 (March, 1968), pp. 68–73; Isidor Silver, "Introduction," *The Challenge of Crime in a Free Society* (New York: Avon, 1968), pp. 17–36.

theme became ingrained in the public's reality of crime. Johnson, recognizing the fears upon which the theme of "lawlessness" played, reacted by organizing something very American: a commission that would identify a broad evil, a thorough study of that problem, and proposals that would offend no one. Moreover, a "war on crime" would divert the public's attention from a nasty and unpopular war abroad to a common evil at home.

The commission was composed of "men and women of distinction," most of the members being ignorant of the problem they were supposed to analyze. All the commissioners, however, had a vested interest in the analysis of the crime problem. In typical Johnson consensus style, the commission's composition was a careful balance of recognized constituencies: members from the law enforcement establishment, lawyers, judges, the mayor of New York, a publisher, a university president, a couple of law professors, a civil rights leader, and two women. Although the group covered a range of opinion about crime, the report was noncontroversial and clearly within the bounds of the established political and legal order.

The recommendations of the commission reflect the "liberal" thinking of the Johnson consensus. The specific recommendations are related to the commission's conclusion that crime reduction is possible by the "vigorous" pursuit of the following objectives:

> First, society must seek to prevent crime before it happens by assuring all Americans a stake in the benefits and responsibilities of American life, by strengthening law enforcement, and by reducing criminal opportunities.
>
> Second, society's aim of reducing crime would be better served if the system of criminal justice developed a far broader range of techniques with which to deal with individual offenders.
>
> Third, the system of criminal justice must eliminate existing injustices if it is to achieve its ideals and win the respect and cooperation of all citizens.
>
> Fourth, the system of criminal justice must attract more people and better people — police, prosecutors, judges, defense attorneys, probation and parole officers, and corrections officials with more knowledge, expertise, initiative, and integrity.
>
> Fifth, there must be much more operational and basic re-

search into the problems of crime and criminal administration, by those within and without the system of criminal justice.

Sixth, the police, courts, and correctional agencies must be given substantially greater amounts of money if they are to improve their ability to control crime.

Seventh, individual citizens, civic and business organizations, religious institutions, and all levels of government must take responsibility for planning and implementing the changes that must be made in the criminal justice system if crime is to be reduced.[11]

With the expenditure of enough energy and money, the reasoning goes, crime can be abolished without any significant alteration of American institutions.

Certainly the President's Crime Commission did not suggest any major alteration in the American legal system. For the commission, the causes of crime were to be found in the nature of individuals ("criminals") and in social conditions. That criminal law is in itself the "cause" of crime was not considered. No assessment was offered of the use of the criminal law as a sanction for human behavior.[12] The criminal law as a force in defining and perpetuating crime was not conceived of as being part of the reality of the crime problem. For the commission, crime is not that which the law defines as criminal, but is an evil that exists in spite of the law. Such evil, according to the President's Commission, can be eradicated in an ultimate victory over crime.

The President's Crime Commission has thus provided us with a particular conception of the reality of crime. The war on crime has become a political weapon to accomplish the objectives of those in positions of power. Moreover, the criminal reality that is being constructed for us is resulting in a reality of events. Our state of mind is leading to a particular kind of social order.

THE LAW AND ORDER CHALLENGE

The war on crime at the end of the 1960's culminated in legislation that has consequences for the future reality of crime. The legisla-

[11] President's Commission on Law Enforcement and Administration of Justice, *The Challenge of Crime in a Free Society*, p. vi.
[12] Herbert L. Packer, "Copping Out," *New York Review of Books*, 9 (October 12, 1967), pp. 17–20.

tion gave those who use crime as a political weapon the criminal reality they desired. The war on crime was thus escalated to the lofty issue of "law and order" in society.

On June 19, 1968, Lyndon Johnson signed the Omnibus Crime Control and Safe Streets Act. As originally conceived, the bill was to assist state and local governments in reducing the incidence of crime by increasing the effectiveness of law enforcement and criminal administration.[13] By the time the bill was passed, however, several controversial amendments were added embodying the increasing concern with law and order. One amendment (Title II) was a deliberate attempt to overturn previous Supreme Court decisions that supposedly were responsible for "coddling criminals" and "handcuffing the police." In the bill that was enacted, all voluntary confessions and eyewitness identifications — regardless of whether a defendant has been informed of his rights of counsel — could be admitted in federal trials. In another provision (Title III) state and local law enforcement agencies were given broad license to tap telephones and engage in other forms of eavesdropping. Law enforcement officials were permitted to engage in these practices for brief periods without even a court order. A final provision of the bill provided that any persons convicted of "inciting a riot or civil disorder," "organizing, promoting, encouraging, or participating in a riot or civil disorder," or "aiding and abetting any person in committing" such offenses shall be disqualified for employment by the federal government for five years. In the background of the law was the attempt to control by means of the criminal law any behavior that would threaten the established social and political order.

In signing the Crime Bill, President Johnson sounded a cautious note.[14] Though stating that the bill contained "more good than bad," he said that Congress "has taken a potentially dangerous step by sanctioning eavesdropping and wiretapping by federal, state, and local officials in an almost unlimited variety of situations." If the nation is not careful, he observed, some provisions of the bill "could result in producing a nation of snoopers bending

[13] Richard Harris, "Annals of Legislation: The Turning Point," *The New Yorker* (December 14, 1968), pp. 68–179.

[14] "Transcript of Johnson's Statement on Signing Crime and Safety Bill," *The New York Times,* June 20, 1968, p. 23.

through the keyholes of the homes and offices in America, spying on our neighbors." Despite such shortcomings, however, the president concluded that the new law "will help lift the stain of crime and the shadow of fear from the streets of our communities."

The law and order issue continues to be a politically potent device. In the presidential campaign of 1968, each of the candidates developed his own version of law and order as a battle cry for the campaign. Richard Nixon, then the Republican candidate, touched it off in his acceptance speech at Miami, charging that "some of our courts in their decisions have gone too far in weakening the peace forces as against the criminal," and adding that "if we are to restore order and respect for law in this country, there's one place we're going to begin: we're going to have a new Attorney General of the United States of America."[15] In even greater detail, Nixon presented his position on law and order in a paper "Toward Freedom from Fear." His position was made clear:

> Just as justice dictates that innocent men go free, it also means that guilty men must pay the penalty for their crimes. It is this second part of justice to which the nation must begin to address itself in earnest. . . . By now Americans, I believe, have learned the hard way that a society that is lenient and permissive for criminals is a society that is neither safe nor secure for innocent men and women.[16]

Hubert Humphrey, the Democratic candidate, responded by promising to halt "rioting, burning, sniping, mugging, traffic in narcotics and disregard for law." But he added that "the answer lies in reasoned effective action by our authorities, not in attacks on our courts, our laws or our Attorney General."

The former governor of Alabama, George Wallace, running as an independent candidate, took the most extreme position on the law and order issue. His solution was simple: free the police of all restraint. Wallace repeated his position every place he went, usually bringing the house down with the passage: "If you walk out of this hotel tonight and someone knocks you on the head,

---

[15] Quoted in Fred J. Cook, "There's Always A Crime Wave — How Bad's This One?" *The New York Times Magazine*, October 6, 1968, p. 38. The quotations from the other presidential candidates are also in Cook's article.

[16] Quoted in Albert J. Reiss, "Crime, Law and Order as Election Issues," *Trans-Action*, 5 (October, 1968), p. 3.

he'll be out of jail before *you're* out of the hospital, and on Monday morning they'll try the policeman instead of the criminal. That's right, we're going to have a *police* state for folks who burn the cities down. They aren't going to burn any more cities." The law and order issue was also becoming a racist euphemism for suppressing the demands of blacks in the urban ghettoes.

The law and order issue became part of the public domain by the end of the campaign. Even the candidates for lesser offices assisted by jumping on the law and order bandwagon. Other political men, such as J. Edgar Hoover, whose job as director of the FBI was assured by Nixon's election, contributed as well. Hoover's statement perhaps best captures the implication of the demand for law and order. By the time of election, Hoover could proclaim with all seriousness: "Justice is incidental to law and order." A distinct conceptual reality of crime and justice had been established.

CRIME AND LEGITIMACY OF AUTHORITY IN A FREE SOCIETY

The drive for law and order brings into sharp focus questions about the nature of the state and the relation of the individual to the state. In particular, the conflict between two fundamental rights is made clear in the law and order issue. That conflict involves, on the one hand, the state's right to protect its citizens and property and, on the other, the citizen's right to individual freedom. Moreover, the question arises of the extent to which the state can claim and exercise authority over the citizenry.

According to the democratic principle, the state's power is legitimate only when it is so regarded by the citizens. Furthermore, the state's authority to govern is legitimate only as long as certain constitutional guarantees are not violated in the course of governing. When the state's use of power to control others does not rest on consent and legal guarantees, the authority of the state is illegitimate and need not be obeyed. In fact, obeying illegitimate authority would be an unprincipled act. A society can only be "a free society," to use the phraseology of the President's Crime Commission, when the authority of the state is legitimate.

In the fervor of the war on crime and in the issue of law and order, basic individual rights have been jeopardized. Parts of the

Omnibus Crime Control and Safe Streets Act are undoubtedly unconstitutional (making suspect the legitimacy of the government). By statute, Congress has violated several provisions of the Constitution and decisions of the Supreme Court that guarantee individual rights. The Bill of Rights is in danger of being tacitly repealed in the name of law and order. For the moment at least, the forces that would restrict individual freedom are dominating the forces that would protect the individual from the aggression of the state.

The civil liberties of the citizen are further being attacked by prominent legal authorities. By the end of 1968, such persons as Judge Henry J. Friendly of the United States Court of Appeals in New York were proposing constitutional amendments that would substantially limit the self-incrimination clause of the Fifth Amendment.[17] Former governor Thomas E. Dewey, in his endorsement of the Friendly proposal, even went beyond the proposal by suggesting that "we could get along just as well if we repealed the Fifth Amendment." Proposals such as these have the possibility of establishing a government tyranny through the cause of law and order. In trying to promote a free society, these forces could easily negate the very principle of a free society.

More recently President Nixon has affirmed the tendency toward the restriction of civil liberties. Soon after his election, Nixon advanced an anti-crime program for the District of Columbia that would deprive the citizen of a basic civil liberty.[18] Nixon asked for authority "whereby dangerous hard-core recidivists could be held in temporary pretrial detention when they have been charged with crimes and when their continued pretrial release presents a clear danger to the community." This "preventive detention" proposal is a breach of the legal doctrine that presumes innocence until guilt is proved in court. We have reached a point in the war on crime in which serious consideration can be given to the reversal of the presumption of a citizen's innocence in favor of the presumption of the citizen's guilt.

The state has attempted to obtain support for its anti-civil libertarian challenge by claiming that such actions must be taken

---

[17] See Sidney E. Zion, "How It Would Be Without the Fifth," *The New York Times,* December 8, 1968, p. E 9.

[18] Fred P. Graham, "When Bail Is a License for Crime," *The New York Times,* February 2, 1969, p. E 11.

in order to control "violence." Increased use of police power has been justified as necessary to combat civil disorder. But the paradox is that the violence that the police attempt to control is inspired in many instances by the police themselves. And more important, much of the violence in these situations is actually committed by the police.

The state, quite understandably, does not regard its own actions as violence, or if such actions are considered, they are defined at best as "legitimate violence." So it is that looting of property during race "riots" is defined as violence by the state, but killing of looters is legitimate.[19] And those who would peaceably demonstrate against injustices of various kinds are subject to similar displays of police rioting and violence.[20] Many people tend to be led to a belief in the justified use of force by the state.

> American society has always endorsed legitimate violence. In fact, most of us do not consider it violence at all. Respect for law has become one of the nastiest features of the American character. Anything we can get legitimated passes without question. We feel free to destroy Vietnam as long as we enjoy the complicity of its officially recognized government — even though we know that government to be a fictional piece of apparatus we ourselves helped to install. And any disruptive social group to which lawlessness can be imputed is a fair target for violent suppression.[21]

Law enforcement can in itself be a form of instant violence. Those who call for law and order are supporters of this "legitimate violence," since it is being used to defend the established social order.

Violence, then, is the most direct form of state power. And since law is a monopoly of the state, violence when carried out by the state is usually legal.[22] But when the citizens no longer grant

---

[19] See *Report of the National Advisory Commission on Civil Disorders* (New York: Bantam Books, 1968), pp. 299–336.

[20] *Rights in Conflict, A Report Submitted by Daniel Walker to the National Commission on the Causes and Prevention of Violence* (New York: Bantam Books, 1968).

[21] Edgar Z. Friedenberg, "Legitimate Violence," *The Nation* (June 24, 1968), p. 822. Also see Paul Goodman, "Reflections on Civil Disobedience," *Liberation* (July–August, 1968), pp. 11–15.

[22] H. L. Nieburg, "Violence, Law and the Social Process," *American Behavioral Scientist,* 11 (March–April, 1968), pp. 17–19.

the state the authority to conduct violence, such violence is no longer legitimate, no matter how legal it may be. The time may be coming when state power exercised through the threat or use of violence will no longer be regarded as legitimate. No government can rule — practically or morally — without legitimacy. Power is legitimate only when it is granted by the citizenry. The law and order challenge has brought into the open the conflict between those who grant legitimacy to state violence and those who do not. A conceptual reality of crime is being constructed which recognizes this conflict. The result is not yet clear. Only the future holds the resolution. Let us hope that the war on crime will not be won if it means the further legitimation of state violence and the denial of individual freedom.

CONCLUSION

Crime begins in the mind. In this sense a conceptual reality of crime is constructed. But the consequence of such construction is a world of actions and events; that is, a phenomenal reality. The whole developmental complex of conception and phenomenon, in reference to crime, is the construction of the social reality of crime.

As I have argued throughout this book, crime is a definition of human conduct that becomes part of the social world. Furthermore, the most important conceptions of crime are those held by the powerful segments of society. Criminal definitions in their official formulations, consequently, are the most powerful means of social control, used to control actions which conflict with the interest of those who create these criminal definitions. Such is the dynamic process of the construction of the social reality of crime.

In recent times the theme of law and order has shaped the official conception of crime. That conception of reality has already influenced the phenomenal reality of crime. The state has used its power through the law to define as criminal what it regards as a threat to the social and political order. Crime has become a political weapon that is used to the advantage of those who control the processes of government.

In many ways, the war on crime has become a substitute for the older war on internal communism. Crime today is similarly being billed as "a threat to the American way of life."[23] We are all being told to join the struggle. "What can the individual citizen do?" The campaign calls us:

> Officials have stated that the police, the courts and the correctional agencies, acting alone, cannot control the problem. Crime and delinquency *can* be reduced when each citizen recognizes that it is his problem, too, and when he becomes personally involved in the struggle. In fact, it is maintained that the *only* answer to reducing crime significantly is *vigorous citizen action.*[24]

There is no end. The conceptions, with their inflammatory rhetoric, and the consequential events go on. It can only be hoped that in constructing the social reality of crime the protection of individual rights will also be included. The social reality of crime is indeed very much a part of the modern world. In constructing this reality, some of the most important problems of modern times are being played out.

[23] *Crime Control Projects for Citizens and Their Organizations* (New York: National Council on Crime and Delinquency, 1968), p. 4.

[24] *Crime, Delinquency and You,* pamphlet printed by Kemper Insurance for the National Council on Crime and Delinquency, Chicago, 1967, p. 1. Various anti-crime groups for citizens are discussed in Murdy, *Crime Commission Handbook,* pp. 36–43.

Index to Names

Index to Subjects

Zero makes me hungry   Zero makes me hungry
Zero makes me hungry   Zero makes me hungry
Zero makes me hungry   Zero makes me hungry
Zero makes me hungry   Zero makes me hungry
Zero makes me hungry   Zero makes me hungry
Zero makes me hungry   Zero makes me hungry
Zero makes me hungry   Zero makes me hungry
Zero makes me hungry   Zero makes me hungry
Zero makes me hungry   Zero makes me hungry
Zero makes me hungry   Zero makes me hungry
Zero makes me hungry   Zero makes me hungry
Zero makes me hungry   Zero makes me hungry
Zero makes me hungry   Zero makes me hungry

Zero makes me hungry

a collection of poems for today

Compiled by **Edward Lueders** and **Primus St. John**

Scott, Foresman and Company • Glenview, Illinois

Dallas, Tex. • Oakland, N. J. • Palo Alto, Cal. • Tucker, Ga. • Brighton, England

ISBN: 0-673-3456-9   ISBN: 0-673-3457-7

12345678910-RRW-858483828180797877675

Acknowledgments

Title: "Zero makes me hungry" from the poem "Numbers." Reprinted with permission of Macmillan Publishing Co., Inc. from THE REAL TIN FLOWER by Aliki Barnstone. Copyright © 1968 by Aliki Barnstone.

"The Act." William Carlos Williams, COLLECTED LATER POEMS. Copyright 1948 by William Carlos Williams. Reprinted by permission of New Directions Publishing Corporation. "After Supper" by Hugh McNamar. Reprinted by permission of the author. "Alarm Clock." From FINDING A POEM by Eve Merriam. Copyright © 1970 by Eve Merriam. Used by permission of Atheneum Publishers and Eve Merriam c/o International Creative Management. "Ancestors" by Grey Cohoe. From THE WHISPERING WIND, Terry Allen, Editor. Copyright 1972. Doubleday and Company. Used by permission of the author. "And They Lived Happily Ever After for a While." from FAST AND SLOW by John Ciardi. Copyright © 1975 by John Ciardi. Reprinted by permission of Houghton Mifflin Company. "The Artist." William Carlos Williams, PICTURES FROM BRUEGHEL AND OTHER POEMS. Copyright 1954 by William Carlos Williams. Reprinted by permission of New Directions Publishing Corporation. "At Grandmother's" by John Haislip from NOT EVERY YEAR. Copyright © 1971 by the University of Washington Press. Reprinted by permission. "At quitting time . . ." from BUNCH GRASS, by Robert Sund. Copyright © 1969 by Robert Sund. Reprinted by permission of University of Washington Press.

"Back Yard, July Night." From A BOOK OF NATURE POEMS, edited by William Cole. Copyright © 1969 by William Cole. Reprinted by permission of The Viking Press, Inc. "Battle Won Is Lost" by Philip George from NATIVE AMERICAN ARTS #1, published by the Institute of American Indian Arts. Reprinted by permission of the author. "Breaklight." From AN ORDINARY WOMAN, by Lucille Clifton. Copyright © 1974 by Lucille Clifton. Reprinted by permission of Random House, Inc., and Curtis Brown, Ltd.

"The Cat." From SLEEK FOR THE LONG FLIGHT, by William Matthews. Copyright © 1971, 1972 by William Matthews. Reprinted by permission of Random House, Inc. "The Chinese Greengrocers" by Pat Lowther from THE FIDDLEHEAD, January-February 1970. Reprinted by permission of the author. "Constellations" by Primus St. John. Reprinted by permission of the author.

"The Day We Die" by anonymous (the Kalahari Bushmen), from THE REBIRTH OF THE OSTRICH by Arthur Markowitz. Copyright 1971 by Arthur Markowitz. Reprinted by permission of the publishers, Campbell Museum, Gaborone, Botswana. "Days" from THE WHITSUN WEDDINGS by Philip Larkin. Copyright © 1960, 1961, 1962, 1964, by Philip Larkin. Reprinted by permission of Faber and Faber Ltd. "Don Larsen's Perfect Game." Copyright © 1967 by Paul Goodman. Reprinted from COLLECTED POEMS, by Paul Goodman, edited by Taylor Stoehr, by permission of Random House, Inc. "Done With." From THE DESCENT by Ann Stanford. Copyright © 1970 by Ann Stanford. Reprinted by permission of The Viking Press, Inc. "Don't Tell Anybody." Reprinted from COMPLETE POETRY OF OSIP EMILEVICH MANDELSTAM, translated by Burton Raffel and Alla Burago, by permission of the State University of New York Press, Burton Raffel and Alla Burago. Copyright © 1973 by State University of New York Press. "Drawing by Ronnie C., Grade One" by Ruth Lechlitner, is reprinted from A CHANGING SEASON, by Ruth Lechlitner, copyright 1973, by Branden Press, Inc. Reprinted by permission of Branden Press, Inc. and Ruth Lechlitner. "The Driver" by Joel Lueders from THE SATOR-IAN, 1970. Reprinted by permission of the author. "The Duck" from VERSES FROM 1929 ON by Ogden Nash (British title: FAMILY REUNION). Copyright, 1931, 1933, 1935, 1936, 1937, 1938, 1939, 1940, 1945, by Ogden Nash. Reprinted by permission of Little, Brown and Co. and J.M. Dent & Sons Ltd.

Table of Contents

A Project for Freight Trains

Sitting at crossings and waiting for freights to pass, we have all noticed words—COTTON BELT / ERIE / BE SPECIFIC—SAY UNION PACIFIC / SOUTHERN SERVES THE SOUTH—going by. I propose to capitalize on this fact in the following way:

All freight cars that have high solid sides—boxcars, refrigerator cars, tank cars, hopper cars, cement cars —should be painted one of eight attractive colors, and have one large word printed on them:

1. Burnt orange freight cars with the word CLOUD in olive drab.
2. Peagreen freight cars with the word STAR in charcoal gray.
3. Rose-red freight cars with the word MEADOW in salmon pink.
4. Glossy black freight cars with the word STEAM in gold.
5. Peach-colored freight cars with the word AIR in royal blue.
6. Peach-colored freight cars with the word PORT in forest green.
7. Lavender freight cars with the word GRASS in vermillion or scarlet.
8. Swiss blue freight cars with the word RISING in chocolate brown.

When this has been accomplished, freight cars should continue to be used in the usual ways, so that the word and color combinations will be entirely random, and unpredictable poems will roll across the landscape.

Freight cars without words (i.e., without high or solid sides, such as flatcars, cattle cars, gondolas, automobile transporters, etc.) should all be painted white, to emphasize their function as spaces in the poems. Cabooses can be this color too, with a large black dot, the only punctuation.

Approximations of these random train poems can be arrived at by using the numbers above, plus 9 and 0 for spaces, and combining serial numbers from dollar bills, social security numbers, birthdates, and telephone numbers. The 5-6 combination, which makes AIRPORT, is to be considered a lucky omen. 2-6 may be even luckier.

This project would need to be carried out over the entire United States at once. Every five years a competition could be held among poets to see who can provide the best set of colors and words for the next time.

David Young

Progress

There are two ways now
To cross the mountain.

One is a foot-path;
My father walked it beside his *burro*,
The *burro* loaded with eggs in boxes
To trade for *chile* and plums and apples
    In Chimayó.

One is a highway;
Your automobile, I watch it climbing
In such a hurry, on easy curvings
That slide beneath you and wave behind you—
    Pronto! You pass!

The path takes longer;
A week in going, a week in coming;
A man can see more, hear more, and feel more,
Learn more of the wisdom in long, slow thinking
    Along the trail.

But, as *senōr* says,
We have the highway. All the old wisdom
Does not much matter. If I could buy me
An automobile, I would not trade it
    For any *burro!*

Edith Agnew

Pony Song

i do not ride a painted pony
i've never felt his strong lean stride
    i ride a car from detroit
        and i sit in class
where they teach me about the great
                        white
                        romans
and not of my dry brown mother
the painted ponies have all gone
        only my grandmother remembers
    i ride a car from detroit
and my dry brown earth-mother
      will not speak to me now.

Rudy Bantista

Learning About the Indians

He danced in feathers, with paint across his nose.
Thump, thump went the drum, and bumped our blood,
And sent a strange vibration through the mind.
White Eagle, he was called, or Mr. White,

And he strutted for money now, in schoolrooms built
On Ohio's plains, surrounded by the graves
Of all of our fathers, but more of his than ours.
Our teachers called it Extracurricular.

We called it fun. And as for Mr. White,
Changed back to a shabby salesman's suit, he called it
Nothing at all as he packed his drums, and drove,
Tires screeching, out of the schoolyard into the night.

Mary Oliver

NEEDS

I want something suited to my special needs
I want chrome hubcaps, pin-on attachments
and year round use year after year
I want a workhorse with smooth uniform cut,
dozer blade and snow blade & deluxe steering
wheel
I want something to mow, throw snow, tow, and sow with
I want precision reel blades
I want a console-styled dashboard
I want an easy spintype recoil starter
I want combination bevel and spur gears, 14
gauge stamped steel housing and
washable foam element air cleaner
I want a pivoting front axle and extrawide turf tires
I want an inch of foam rubber inside a vinyl
covering
and especially if it's not too much, if I
can deserve it, even if I can't pay for it
I want to mow while riding

A. R. Ammons

THROUGH
THE AUTOMATIC CARWASH

Through the automatic carwash,
windows closed, water zinging
on metal, the windshield fogging,
the moving tread gives us
the idea of moving through a summer
thundershower in Missouri
at ten miles an hour,
windshield fogging,
hailstones banging on the hood,
darkness settling on us—and
the giant rollerbrushes thundering
down make my son say
I don't like this, and I
switch on the overhead light.

Robert Vas Dias

The Owl on the Aerial

Just at dusk
As the full moon rose
And filled his canyon,
Out of his crevice
Floated the owl,
His down-edged wings
Silent as moonlight.

With three-foot wingspread,
Claws that could paralyze
Rabbit or squirrel,
He battened on beetles
Drawn to the manlight,
And just for a little
He lit on the aerial,
His curved claws clutching
The shining metal.

Softly the moonlight
Sheened on his feathers
While under his feet,
Unfelt by him,
The moon lay still
And men like those
In the house below
Floated upon it.

Clarice Short

THE TELEVISION

Unaccustomed
to movement
and real life
it crept
to the window
and,
delicately
lifting the blind
with a long
aluminum
tentacle,
sat
looking out
at the night.

Geoffrey Godbey

JETLINER

now he takes his mark
at the very farthest end of the runway
looking straight ahead, eager, intense
with his sharp eyes shining

he takes a deep, deep breath
with his powerful lungs
expanding his massive chest
his burning heart beating like thunders

then . . . after a few . . . tense moments . . . of pondering
he roars at his utmost
and slowly begins to jog
kicking the dark earth hard
and now he begins to run
kicking the dark earth harder
then he dashes, dashes like mad, like mad
howling, shouting, screaming, and roaring

then with a most violent kick
he shakes off the earth's pull
softly lifting himself into the air
soaring higher and higher and higher still
piercing the sea of clouds
up into the chandelier of stars

Naoshi Koriyama

BACK YARD, JULY NIGHT

Firefly, airplane, satellite, star—
How I wonder which you are.

William Cole

And They Lived
Happily Ever After for a While   John Ciardi

It was down by the Dirty River
  As the Smog was beginning to thin
Because we had been so busy
  Breathing the worst of it in,

That the worst remained inside us
  And whatever we breathed back
Was only—sort of—grayish,
  Or at least not entirely black.

It was down by the Dirty River
  That flows to the Sticky Sea
I gave my heart to my Bonnie,
  And she gave hers to me.

I coughed: "I love you, Bonnie
  And do you love me true?"
The tears of joy flowed from my eyes
  When she sneezed back: "Yes—Achoo!"

It was high in the Garbage Mountains,
  In Saint Snivens by the Scent,
I married my darling Bonnie
  And we built our Oxygen Tent.

And here till the tanks are empty
  We sit and watch TV
And dream of the Dirty River
  On its way to the Sticky Sea.

Here till the needles quiver
  Shut on the zero mark
We sit hand in hand while the TV screen
  Shines like a moon in the dark.

I cough: "I love you, Bonnie.
  And do you love me true?"
And tears of joy flow from our eyes
  When she sneezes: "Yes—Achoo!"

MAN IN ORBIT

******

*While*freighting*f
rom*Earth*to*Venus*we
*passed*a*man*without*a
*spacesuit.*He*was*not*pleasant
*to*look*at,*orbiting*the*Sun.
*And*I*remembered*how*he*w
ould*repeat*a*modish*phrase*ba
ck*on*Earth,*endlessly—*Stop*
the*world,*I*want*to*get
*off.*And*it*appeared*t
hat**someone*had.*

******

D. O. Pitches

For Poets

Stay beautiful
but don't stay down underground too long
Don't turn into a mole
or a worm
or a root
or a stone

Come on out into the sunlight
Breathe in trees
Knock out mountains
Commune with snakes
& be the very hero of birds

Don't forget to poke your head up
& blink
Think
Walk all around
Swim upstream

Don't forget to fly

Al Young

Don't Tell Anybody

Don't tell anybody,
forget everything you saw—
a bird, an old woman, a jail,
anything. . .

Or else, the minute you unlock
your lips, when dawn comes
you'll start to shake
like a fine-firred pine tree.

And you'll remember a wasp at the summer cottage,
a children's pencil-case,
or forest blueberries
you never picked.

Osip Emilevich Mandelstam

Translated by Burton Raffel
and Alla Burago

THE SECRET

Two girls discover
the secret of life
in a sudden line of
poetry.

I who don't know the
secret wrote
the line. They
told me

(through a third person)
they had found it
but not what it was
not even

what line it was. No doubt
by now, more than a week
later, they have forgotten
the secret,

the line, the name of
the poem. I love them
for finding what
I can't find,

and for loving me
for the line I wrote,
and for forgetting it
so that

a thousand times, till death
finds them, they may
discover it again, in other
lines

in other
happenings. And for
wanting to know it,
for

assuming there is
such a secret, yes,
for that
most of all.

Denise Levertov

THE UNWRITTEN

Inside this pencil
crouch words that have never been written
never been spoken
never been thought

they're hiding

they're awake in there
dark in the dark
hearing us
but they won't come out
not for love not for time not for fire

even when the dark has worn away
they'll still be there
hiding in the air
multitudes in days to come may walk through them
breathe them
be none the wiser

what script can it be
that they won't unroll
in what language
would I recognize it
would I be able to follow it
to make out the real names
of everything

maybe there aren't
many
it could be that there's only one word
and it's all we need
it's here in this pencil

every pencil in the world
is like this

W. S. Merwin

Tartars, Uzbeks, Samoyeds

Tartars, Uzbeks, Samoyeds,
all the Ukrainians,
even the Volga Germans
are waiting for their translators.

And maybe this very minute
some Japanese is translating
me into Turkish
and has reached the depths of my soul.

Osip Emilevich Mandelstam

Translated by Burton Raffel
and Alla Burago

POEM:
A REMINDER

Capital letters prompting every line,
Lines printed down the center of each page,
Clear spaces between groups of these, combine
In a convention of respectable age
To mean: "Read carefully. Each word we chose
Has rhythm and sound and sense. This is not prose."

Robert Graves

Winter Poem

once a snowflake fell
on my brow and i loved
it so much and i kissed
it and it was happy and called its cousins
and brothers and a web
of snow engulfed me then
i reached to love them all
and i squeezed them and they became
a spring rain and i stood perfectly
still and was a flower

Nikki Giovanni

White Butterfly

What wisdom do you offer me,
Little white butterfly?
You open your wordless pages, and
Close again your wordless pages.

In your opened pages:
Solitude;
In your closed pages:
Solitude.

Tai Wang-Shu

Translated by Kai-yu Hsu

Drawing
by Ronnie C., Grade One

For the sky, blue. But the six-year-
old searching his crayon-box, finds
no blue to match that sky
framed by the window—a see-through shine
over treetops, housetops. The wax colors
hold only dead light, not this waterflash
thinning to silver
at morning's far edge.
Gray won't do, either:
gray is for rain that you make with
dark slanting lines down-paper.

Try orange!

—Draw a larger corner circle for sun, egg-yolk solid,
with yellow strokes leaping outward
like fire bloom—a brightness shouting
flower-shape wind shape joy shape!

The boy sighs, with leg-twisting bliss creating. . .

It is done. The stubby crayons
(all ten of them) are stuffed back
bumpily into their box.

Ruth Lechlitner

MAGIC WORDS

In the very earliest time,
when both people and animals lived on earth,
a person could become an animal if he wanted to
and an animal could become a human being.
Sometimes they were people
and sometimes animals
and there was no difference.
All spoke the same language.
That was the time when words were like magic.
The human mind had mysterious powers.
A word spoken by chance
might have strange consequences.
It would suddenly come alive
and what people wanted to happen could happen.
Nobody could explain this:
That's the way it was.

Netsilik origin (Eskimo)

Translated by Edward Field

38

DAYS

What are days for?
Days are where we live.
They come, they wake us
Time and time over.
They are to be happy in:
Where can we live but days?

Ah, solving that question
Brings the priest and the doctor
In their long coats
Running over the fields.

Philip Larkin

DON LARSEN'S PERFECT GAME

Everybody went to bat three times
except their pitcher (twice) and his pinch hitter,
but nobody got anything at all.
Don Larsen in the eighth and ninth looked pale
and afterwards he did not want to talk.
This is a fellow who will have bad dreams.
His catcher Berra jumped for joy and hugged him
like a bear, legs and arms, and all the Yankees
crowded around him thick to make him be
not lonely, and in fact in fact in fact
nothing went wrong. But that was yesterday.

Paul Goodman

The Act

There were the roses, in the rain.
Don't cut them, I pleaded.
    They won't last, she said
But they're so beautiful
    where they are.
Agh, we were all beautiful once, she
    said,
and cut them and gave them to me
    in my hand.

William Carlos Williams

SEVENTY-SIX

A man is born gentle and weak.
At his death he is hard and stiff.
Green plants are tender and filled with sap.
At their death they are withered and dry.

Therefore the stiff and unbending is the disciple of death.
The gentle and yielding is the disciple of life.

Thus an army without flexibility never wins a battle.
A tree that is unbending is easily broken.

The hard and strong will fall.
The soft and weak will overcome.

Lao Tsu

Translated by Gia-fu Feng
and Jane English

At Grandmother's

She lay in bed on the second floor,
Dying in quiet that whole season—
While I played catch behind the barn
Each afternoon,
And bounced the ball against the fence,
The wall, the chopping block, the trees.
But never against the empty metal drums,
The wooden well, the sill, the double doors,
Never against the chancy echoing dark.

John Haislip

Incident in a Rose Garden

Gardener: Sir, I encountered Death
                 Just now among our roses.
                 Thin as a scythe he stood there.

                 I knew him by his pictures.
                 He had his black coat on,
                 Black gloves, a broad black hat.

                 I think he would have spoken,
                 Seeing his mouth stood open.
                 Big it was, with white teeth.

                 As soon as he beckoned, I ran.
                 I ran until I found you.
                 Sir, I am quitting my job.

                 I want to see my sons
                 Once more before I die.
                 I want to see California.

Master: Sir, you must be that stranger
                 Who threatened my gardener.
                 This is my property, sir.

                 I welcome only friends here.
Death: Sir, I knew your father.
                 And we were friends at the end.

                 As for your gardener,
                 I did not threaten him.
                 Old men mistake my gestures.

                 I only meant to ask him
                 To show me to his master.
                 I take it you are he?

                 Donald Justice

The Day We Die

The day we die
the wind comes down
to take away
our footprints.

The wind makes dust
to cover up
the marks we left
while walking.

For otherwise
the thing would seem
as if we were
still living.

Therefore the wind
is he who comes
to blow away
our footprints.

Kalahari origin (Africa)

Translated by Arthur Markowitz

Today Is a Very Good Day to Die

Today is a very good day to die.
Every living thing is in harmony with me.
Every voice sings a chorus within me.
All beauty has come to rest in my eyes.
All bad thoughts have departed from me.
Today is a very good day to die.
My land is peaceful around me.
My fields have been turned for the last time.
My house is filled with laughter.
My children have come home.
Yes, today is a very good day to die.

Nancy Wood

And when we die at last,
we really know very little about what happens then.
But people who dream
have often seen the dead appear to them
just as they were in life.
Therefore we believe life does not end here on earth.

HEAVEN
AND
HELL

We have heard of three places where men go after death:
There is the Land of the Sky, a good place
where there is no sorrow and fear.
There have been angatoks who went there
and came back to tell us about it:
They saw people playing ball, happy people
who did nothing but laugh and amuse themselves.
What we see from down here in the form of stars
are the lighted windows of the villages of the dead
in the Land of the Sky.

Then there are two other worlds of the dead underground:
Way deep down is a place just like here on earth
except on earth you starve
and down there they live in plenty.
The caribou graze in great herds
and there are endless plains
with juicy berries that are nice to eat.
Down there too, everything
is happiness and fun for the dead.

But there is another place, the Land of the Miserable,
right under the surface of the earth we walk on.
There go all the lazy men who were poor hunters,
and all women who refused to be tattooed,
not caring to suffer a little to become beautiful.
They had no life in them when they lived
so now after death they must squat on their haunches
with hanging heads, bad-tempered and silent,
and live in hunger and idleness
because they wasted their lives.
Only when a butterfly comes flying by
do they lift their heads
(as young birds open pink mouths uselessly after a gnat)
and when they snap at it, a puff of dust
comes out of their dry throats.

Of course it may be
that all I have been telling you is wrong
for you cannot be certain about what you cannot see.
But these are the stories that our people tell.

Netsilik origin (Eskimo)　　　Translated by Edward Field

The Artist

Mr. T
        bareheaded
                in a soiled undershirt
his hair standing out
        on all sides
                stood on his toes
heels together
        arms gracefully
                for the moment
curled above his head!
        Then he whirled about
                bounded
into the air
        and with an entrechat
                perfectly achieved
completed the figure.
        My mother
                taken by surprise
where she sat
        in her invalid's chair
                was left speechless.
"Bravo!" she cried at last
        and clapped her hands.
                The man's wife
came from the kitchen:
        "What goes on here?" she said.
                But the show was over.

William Carlos Williams

jumped
off

jumped off
the garage once
& landed both
ways
on my feet
like a cat
& on my head
like any dumb animal

thought i was
superman or
rocketman maybe
& i guess
everybody wants
to fly sometime
even if your
wings take you
straight down

Don Gray

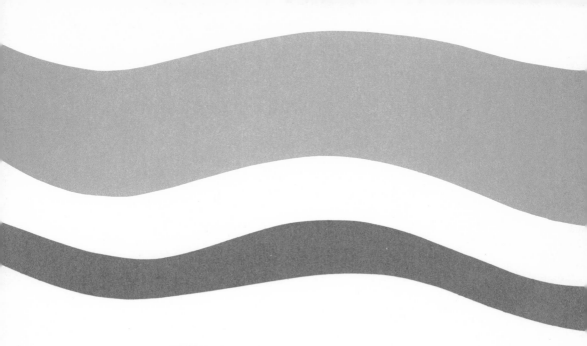

Plea

To my friend
who can no longer see
animals in the clouds

and takes it
as a sign of madness:

Hang on. Keep watch.

They must be gathering now
over the Pacific,

great, soft herds of elephants,
cirrous alligators
and horses being pulled apart

with no pain.

Judith Hemschemeyer

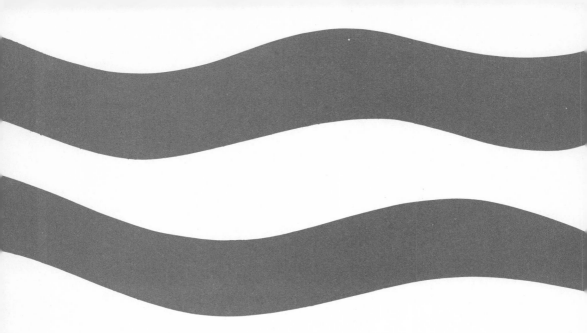

Piano Lessons

i used to sit at piano lessons
and cry
or hear my sisters crying
in the other room.
the old woman would snap
and say tight-lipped
"you are no good. what is wrong
with you."
but every year she would invite us
to her dogs' birthday party.
only the dogs got hats.
and in the summer
her funny smell would fill
the screen porch
where we waited our turns
to be defeated.
i would sit in the hammock
with the green terry cover,
and the candy in those
crystal dishes
(we never really knew if it
was there to eat)
it always tasted a million years old.

Candy Clayton

RIDING LESSON

I learned two things
from an early riding teacher.
He held a nervous filly
in one hand and gestured
with the other, saying, "Listen.
Keep one leg on one side,
the other leg on the other side,
and your mind in the middle."

He turned and mounted.
She took two steps, then left
the ground, I thought for good.
But she came down hard, humped
her back, swallowed her neck,
and threw her rider as you'd
throw a rock. He rose, brushed
his pants and caught his breath,
and said, "See, that's the way
to do it. When you see
they're gonna throw you, get off."

Henry Taylor

How to Paint
the Portrait of a Bird

First paint a cage
with an open door
then paint
something pretty
something simple
something fine
something useful
for the bird
next place the canvas against a tree
in a garden
in a wood
or in a forest
hide behind the tree
without speaking
without moving . . .
Sometimes the bird comes quickly
but it can also take many years
before making up its mind
Don't be discouraged
wait
wait if necessary for years
the quickness or the slowness of the coming
of the bird having no relation
to the success of the picture

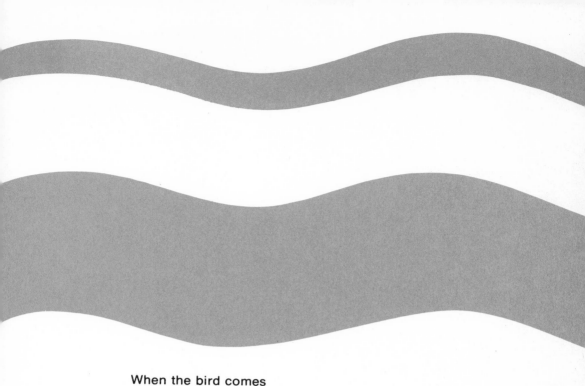

When the bird comes
if it comes
observe the deepest silence
wait for the bird to enter the cage
and when it has entered
gently close the door with the paint-brush
then
one by one paint out all the bars
taking care not to touch one feather of the bird
Next make a portrait of the tree
choosing the finest of its branches
for the bird
paint also the green leaves and the freshness of the wind
dust in the sun
and the sound of the insects in the summer grass
and wait for the bird to decide to sing
If the bird does not sing
it is a bad sign
a sign that the picture is bad
but if it sings it is a good sign
a sign that you are ready to sign
so then you pluck very gently
one of the quills of the bird
and you write your name in a corner of the picture.

Jacques Prévert   Translated by Paul Dehn

400-METER FREESTYLE

THE GUN full swing the swimmer catapults and cracks
  s
   i
    x
feet away onto that perfect glass he catches at
a
n
d
throws behind him scoop after scoop cunningly moving
   t
    h
     e
water back to move him forward. Thrift is his wonderful
  s
e
  c
ret; he has schooled out all extravagance. No muscle
   r
    i
     p
ples without compensation wrist cock to heel snap to
h
i
s
mobile mouth that siphons in the air that nurtures
   h
    i
     m
at half an inch above sea level so to speak.

```
    T
    h
    e
    astonishing   whites   of   the   soles   of   his   feet   rise
                                                                    a
                                                                      n
                                                                        d
    salute  us  on  the  turns.  He  flips,  converts,  and  is  gone
    a
    l
    l
    in  one.  We  watch  him  for  signs.  His  arms  are  steady  at
                                                                     t
                                                                      h
                                                                       e
    catch,  his  cadent  feet  tick  in  the  stretch,  they  know
    t
    h
    e
    lesson  well. Lungs  know,  too;  he  does  not  list  for
                                                              a
                                                                i
                                                                  r
    he  drives  along  on  little  sips  carefully  expended
    b
    u
    t
    that  plum  red  heart  pumps  hard  cries  hurt  how  soon
                                                                i
                                                                  t
                                                                    s
    near one more and makes its final surge        TIME: 4:25:9
```

Maxine Kumin

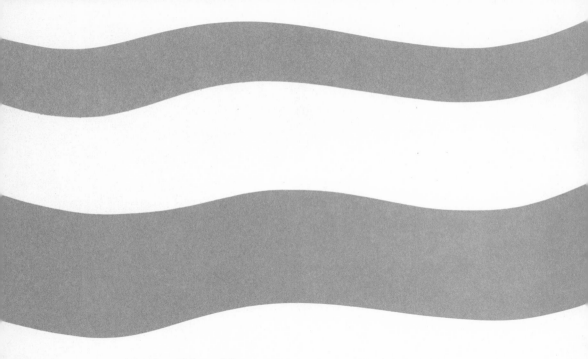

Pole Vault

He is running like a wasp,
Hanging on a long pole.
As a matter of course he floats in the sky,
Chasing the ascending horizon.
Now he has crossed the limit,
And pushed away his support.
For him there is nothing but a descent.
Oh, he falls helplessly.
Now on that runner, awkwardly fallen on the ground,
Once more
The horizon comes down,
Beating hard on his shoulders.

Shiro Murano

Translated by Satoru Sato
and Constance Urdang

Sky Diving

In the engine sound like many people together
beating and singing at incredible speed
to find a way out of the body into flight
and the spirit, I sit
strapped up and buckled, feeling my blood
beat hard in my fingers, temples
and lips. I have climbed my fear
to this place
to die a little and be born
a little in the air.

Twelve thousand feet, thinking more
now of my weight
than ever before, and it is hard to lift
my arms, though in a moment
I must. The others tell me
not to look out the window, so I do not move
from the corner
where the fuselage against my back easily becomes
a wall, and we are all sitting
in a small whistling room
not talking much
to each other.

Two and a half miles is a long
fall, but I have fallen
farther
with nearly as much
to lose.
I am almost ready. I am ready. I will
stand and walk out the door, surprised
to see what is really there and go
down without breathing, with a strange
good sensation
in my groin.

Rod Taylor

What My Uncle Tony Told My Sister, Angie, and Me

respect your mother and father
respect your brothers and sisters
respect your uncles and aunts
respect your land, the beginning
respect what is taught you
respect what you are named
respect the gods
respect yourself
everything that is around you
is part of you.

Simon J. Ortiz

SELF EXPRESSION

Mother has caught her head
in the bubble-gum machine
looking for her purple leotard.
Her black one she's saving
for funerals, she said.
Now if someone will answer her ad
and return her feather boa
constrictor, maybe she will stop
sharpening her fingers
and begin to cook again.

Ann Darr

You Had to Go to Funerals

You had to go to funerals
Even if you didn't know the
People
Your Mama always did
Usually your Pa.
In new patent leather shoes
It wasn't so bad
And if it rained
The graves dropped open
And if the sun was shining
You could take some of the
Flowers home
In your pocket
Book. At six and seven
The face in a gray box
Is always your daddy's
Old schoolmate
Mowed down before his
Time.
You don't even ask
After a while
What makes them lie so
Awfully straight
And still. If there's a picture of
Jesus underneath
The coffin lid
You might, during a boring sermon,
Without shouting or anything
Wonder who painted it

And how he would like
All eternity to stare
It down.
                                        Alice Walker

Have You Ever Hurt About Baskets?

Have you ever hurt about
  baskets?

I have, seeing my grandmother
  weaving for a long time.

Have you ever hurt about work?
I have because my father works
  too hard and he tells how
  he works.

Have you ever hurt about cattle?
I have because my grandfather
has been working on the cattle
  for a long time.

Have you ever hurt about school?

I have because I have learned
  lots of words from school,
and they are not my words.

Marylita Altaha

Lineage

My grandmothers were strong.
They followed plows and bent to toil.
They moved through fields sowing seed.
They touched earth and grain grew.
They were full of sturdiness and singing.
My grandmothers were strong.

My grandmothers are full of memories
Smelling of soap and onions and wet clay
With veins rolling roughly over quick hands
They have many clean words to say.
My grandmothers were strong.
Why am I not as they?

Margaret Walker

THE CHINESE GREENGROCERS

They live their days in a fragrance
of white and black grapes
and tomatoes and the fresh
water smell of lettuce.

They know with their hands
and noses the value
of all things grown.
They will make you a bargain price
on overripe cantaloupe.

They wash with clear water
their bunches of carrots
and radishes. They crank out
a canvas awning to shelter them.

Their babies suckle on unsold bananas.
By the age of six
they can all make change
and tell which fruits are ripe.

The grandmothers know only numbers
in English, and the names
of fruits and vegetables.

They open before the supermarkets open,
they are open all day,
they eat with an eye on the door.

They keep sharp eyes
for shoplifting children.
They know every customer's
brand of cigarettes.

After the neighbourhood movies are out
and the drugstores have all closed
they bring in their blueberries
and cabbages and potted flowers.

In the rooms behind the store
they speak in their own language.
Their speech flies around the rooms
like swooping, pecking birds.

Far into the night I believe
they weigh balsa baskets
of plums, count ears of corn
and green peppers.

No matter how they may wash
their fingers, their very pores
are perfumed with green,
and they sleep with parsley and peaches
oranges and onions
and grapes and running water.

Pat Lowther

Game After Supper

This is before electricity,
it is when there were porches.

On the sagging porch an old man
is rocking. The porch is wooden,

the house is wooden and grey;
in the living room which smells of
smoke and mildew, soon
the woman will light the kerosene lamp.

There is a barn but I am not in the barn;
there is an orchard too, gone bad,
its apples like soft cork
but I am not there either.

I am hiding in the long grass
with my two dead cousins,
the membrane grown already
across their throats.

We hear crickets and our own hearts
close to our ears;
though we giggle, we are afraid.

From the shadows around
the corner of the house
a tall man is coming to find us:

He will be an uncle,
if we are lucky.

Margaret Atwood

PROSPECTUS

I was raised on the Reservation
In an adobe house, with neither
A running water.
My bed was cradleboard
A sheepskin and the earth.
My food was my Mother's breast,
Goat's milk and cornmeal.
My play partners were puppies,
The lamb and the lizards.
I ate with my fingers,
I went barefoot at most time,
I washed my hair with yucca roots,
I carried water from the ditch.
My Mom ground corn for food.
Sometimes I went without eating.
I only spoke my language.
I prayed to the Great Spirit.
Someday I'll learn to speak English.

Joe Nieto

Kit, Six Years Old,
Standing by the Dashboard
Keeping Daddy Awake
on a Trip Home from the Beach

We'd have a old car, the kind that gets
flat tires, but inside would be wolfskin on
the seats and warm fur on the steering wheel,
and wolf fur on all the buttons. And we'd
live in a ranch house made out of logs with
a loft where you sleep, and you'd walk a
little ways and there'd be the farm with
the horses. We'd drive to town, and we'd
have flat tires, and be sort of old.

William Stafford

ANCESTORS

On the wind-beaten plains
    once lived my ancestors.

In the days of peaceful moods,
    they wandered and hunted.

In days of need or greed,
    they warred and loafed.

Beneath the lazy sun, kind winds above,
    they laughed and feasted.

Through the starlit night, under the moon,
    they dreamed and loved.

Now, from the wind-beaten plains,
    only their dust rises.

Grey Cohoe

The Giveaway

Saint Bridget was
A problem child.
Although a lass
Demure and mild,
And one who strove
To please her dad,
Saint Bridget drove
The family mad.
For here's the fault in Bridget lay:
She would *give everything away.*

To any soul
Whose luck was out
She'd give her bowl
Of stirabout;
She'd give her shawl,
Divide her purse
With one or all.
And what was worse,
When she ran out of things to give
She'd borrow from a relative.

Her father's gold,
Her grandsire's dinner,
She'd hand to cold
And hungry sinner;
Give wine, give meat,
No matter whose;
Take from her feet
The very shoes,
And when her shoes had gone to others,
Fetch forth her sister's and her mother's.

She could not quit.
She had to share;
Gave bit by bit
The silverware,
The barnyard geese,
The parlor rug,
Her little niece-
'S christening mug,
Even her bed to those in want,
And then the mattress of her aunt.

An easy touch
For poor and lowly,
She gave so much
And grew so holy
That when she died
Of years and fame,
The countryside
Put on her name,
And still the Isles of Erin fidget
With generous girls named Bride or Bridget.

Well, one must love her.
Nonetheless,
In thinking of her
Givingness,
There's no denial
She must have been
A sort of trial
To her kin.
The moral, too, seems rather quaint.
Who *had the patience of a saint,*
From evidence presented here?
Saint Bridget? Or her near and dear?

Phyllis McGinley

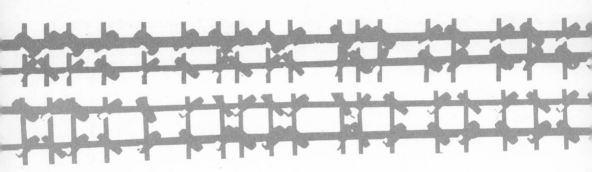

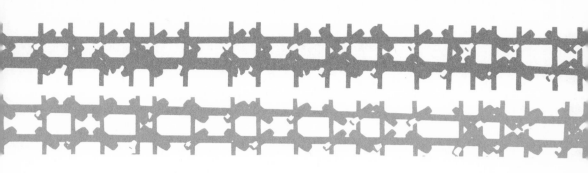

Love Song for a Jellyfish

How amazed I was, when I was a child,
To see your life on the sand.
To see you living in your jelly shape,
Round and slippery and dangerous.
You seemed to have fallen
Not from the rim of the sea,
But from the galaxies.
Stranger, you delighted me. Weird object of
The stinging world.

Sandra Hochman

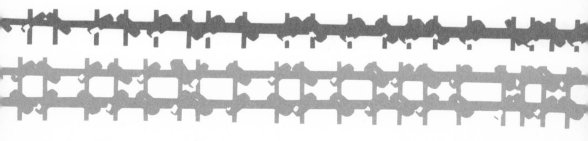

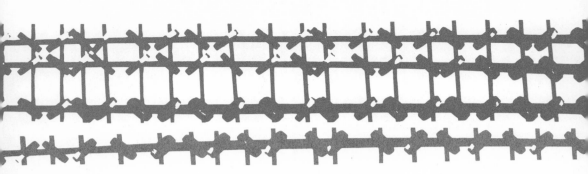

Flying Crooked

The butterfly, a cabbage-white,
(His honest idiocy of flight)
Will never now, it is too late,
Master the art of flying straight,
Yet has—who knows so well as I?—
A just sense of how not to fly:
He lurches here and here by guess
And God and hope and hopelessness.
Even the aerobatic swift
Has not his flying-crooked gift.

Robert Graves

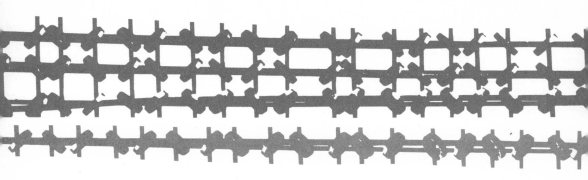

Pigeons

They paddle with staccato feet
in powder-pools of sunlight,
small blue busybodies
strutting like fat gentlemen
with hands clasped
under their swallowtail coats;
and as they stump about,
their heads like tiny hammers
tap at imaginary nails
in non-existent walls.

Elusive ghosts of sunshine
slither down the green gloss
of their necks an instant, and are gone.

Summer hangs drugged from sky to earth
in limpid fathoms of silence:
only warm dark dimples of sound
slide like slow bubbles
from the contented throats.

Raise a casual hand—
with one quick gust
they fountain into air.

Richard Kell

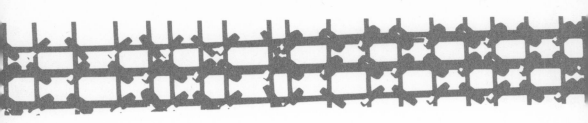

The
Cat

While you read
the sleepmoth begins
to circle your eyes
and then—
a hail of claws
lands the cat
in your lap.
The little motor
in his throat
is how a cat says
Me. He rasps the soft
file of his tongue
along the inside
of your wrist.
He licks himself.
He's building
a pebble of fur
in his stomach.
And now he pulls
his body in a circle
around the fire of sleep.

William Matthews

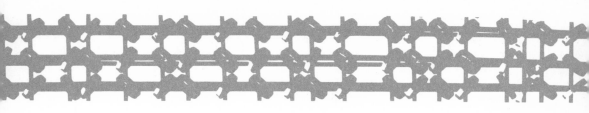

FELINE LESSON

We watched slant-eyes
come over the fence
and drop with a thump
on the barbered lawn.
Crouched under the gardenia,
he began the interrogation of
a prize-some tiny field
mouse hardly worth the
effort, it would seem,
to tease and pat and fawn
to excite his lust.

When we approached,
he took it almost all,
leaving just the sliver of
a tail outside his mouth.
He would not obey, of course,
and hunched and held,
wary-eyed against persuasion.

The mouse was not our pet,
and I knew well the cat.
What else could you expect of him?
But still my youngest son
cried half the night away.

Hugh McNamar

THE SHARK

My dear, let me tell you about the shark.
Though his eyes are bright, his thought is dark.
He's quiet—that speaks well of him.
So does the fact that he can swim.
But though he swims without a sound,
Wherever he swims he looks around
With those two bright eyes and that one dark thought.
He has only one but he thinks it a lot.
And the thought he thinks but can never complete
Is his long dark thought of something to eat.
Most anything does. And I have to add
That when he eats his manners are bad.
He's a gulper, a ripper, a snatcher, a grabber.
Yes, his manners are drab. But his thought is drabber.
That one dark thought he can never complete
Of something—anything—somehow to eat.

Be careful where you swim, my sweet.

John Ciardi

SARDINES

A baby Sardine
Saw her first submarine:
She was scared and watched through a peephole.

"Oh, come, come, come,"
Said the Sardine's mum,
"It's only a tin full of people."

Spike Milligan

The Duck

Behold the duck.
It does not cluck.
A cluck it lacks.
It quacks.
It is specially fond
Of a puddle or pond.
When it dines or sups,
It bottoms ups.

Ogden Nash

Point of View

The little bat hangs upside down,
And downside up the possum.
To show a smile they have to frown,
Say those who've run across'em.

David McCord

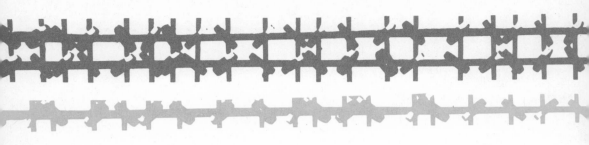

While
the Snake Sleeps

his dinner sits
in his stomach
bathing in acid

snake's tail is flat
his head is flat
his ribs in front and back
of his dinner are flat

his lidless eyes
turn in on themselves
his tongue rests
in his mouth

Judith Sampson

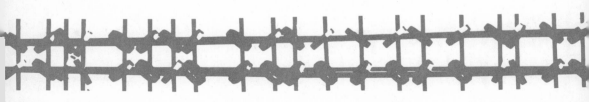

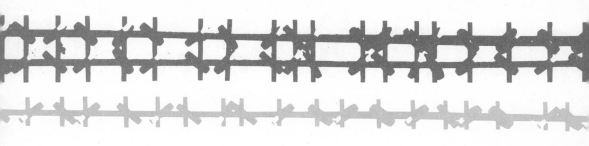

Snake Hunt

David Wagoner

On sloping, shattered granite, the snake man
From the zoo bent over the half-shaded crannies
Where rattlesnakes take turns out of the sun,
Stared hard, nodded at me, then lunged
With his thick gloves and yanked one up like a root.

And the whole hillside sprang to death with a hissing,
Metallic, chattering rattle; they came out writhing
In his fists, uncoiling from daydreams,
Pale bellies looping out of darker diamonds
In the shredded sunlight, dropping into his sack.

As I knelt on rocks, my blood went cold as theirs.
One snake coughed up a mouse. I saw what a mouse
Knows, as well as anyone. There, beside me,
In a cleft a foot away from my braced fingers,
Still in its coils, a rattler stirred from sleep.

It moved the wedge of its head back into shadow
And stared at me, harder than I could answer,
Till the gloves came down between us. In the sack,
Like the disembodied muscles of a torso,
It and the others searched among themselves

For the lost good place. I saw them later
Behind plate glass, wearing their last skins.
They held their venom behind wide-open eyes.

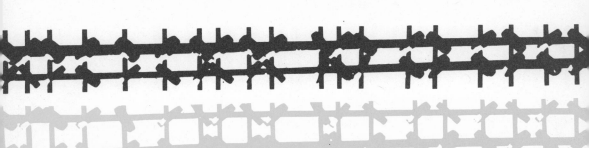

ZOO

Evolution dies out.
The cats fall as they are born
To sleep, without movement
To go after, movement to catch
Their deadly fascination.
Without wild heat
Rippling the distance, stripes
Rest easy on the zebra.
Gazelle are safe with nowhere
To run. There is only a flicker
Of something in the shudder of muscle
Fighting off the flies.

Michael Allin

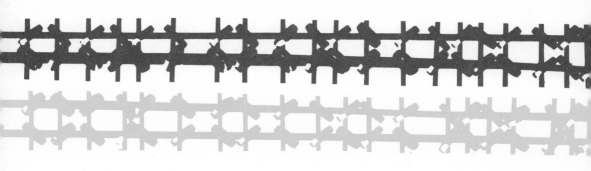

THE FALL

The European Bison fell from grace.
So did the white-tailed Gnu.
Likewise the Blesbok, as also the Mountain Zebra.
The Giant Tortoise must have sinned too.

Everyone knows about the Dodo;
The same goes for the Great Auk.
The inoffensive Okapi's crime
Was trying to be other beasts at the same time.
And there is the case of the Blue-Buck.

They all came to a halt and are dissolved in mystery.
Who remembers, now, Steller's cullionly Sea-Cow?
It, too, through its innocent fault
Failed the finals in history.

Muriel Spark

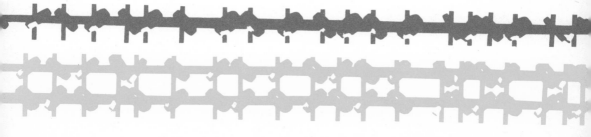

THROUGH THE WINDOW

Through the window
I see the soft rain.

Through the soft rain
I see the neighbor's fence.

And just above the fence
I see fully opened umbrellas
Softly flowing from left to right
On and on.

Hidden by the neighbor's fence
I can not see
Who goes there
Under each of the umbrellas.

But, I see each umbrella
Softly flowing from left to right
On and on,
Shading the someone under it
In the soft morning rain.

Naoshi Koriyama

The Driver

Someday I'm going to pick up
An east-bound hitchhiker and take him
Wherever he wants to go.
I'll ask him where he's headed
And he'll say "Boston"
And I'll say "Boston it is."

He'll probably think twice
About riding with me, then.
But after a while
He'll see that I'm normal
And we'll get to Boston
And I'll say "so long"
And he'll no longer exist
For me.

I'll pick up two girls
Who are headed for California,
And say "California it is."
They'll think twice because
They'll know that I'm normal.
But after a while they'll
See that I only intend to
Take them wherever they want to go
And I'll leave them in L.A.
Or San Francisco and say
"So long" and they'll cease
To exist for me.

So I'll spend my whole life
Giving rides to people
Who couldn't exist where
They found themselves living.
I'll go all directions
And never take money.
And I'll die when I
Pick up the killer.

Joel Lueders

Isleta Indian Girl

smooth dark eyes, wanting
touches me, looking at her,
so small, each gesture a
reaching

       little animals move
through forests the way
she folds her paper, sighs,
lips murmuring apologies
for her poor English she
follows surely out of
this room a trail older
than any university: most
languages would take note
of those simple graces.

Keith Wilson

After Supper

After supper I would trail
the scrape and thump of my brothers'
boots across the yard
to where it met the pasture;
both were really one
except one nearer,
the other more important.

Watching the cattle feed, my brothers
could talk an hour. Men governed by the seasons,
they could speak of hay to gather
before the rain—
but not too soon, a well marked Holstein,
those still with calves to suck.
As meadowlarks called from
somewhere along the fence-row,
the favorites were
watched with reverence as they fed.
There was communion while those
closest to the fence
allowed their foreheads to be stroked.

To me, though, listening
on those evenings,
they still stood just spotted brutes,
flinching beneath their flies.

Hugh McNamar

Looking North to Taos

I saw the pueblo beneath the blue
mountain, the older
buildings crumbling,
melting into mud. I watched
the old men, their heads
hidden beneath blankets,
and I wondered.

I have heard the round dance songs
from a thousand miles away,
have held the record cover in my
hands and seen the young boys
pictured on the back, their braids
long, their smiles not showing.
And I have wondered.

I sit still in the cool grass
toward evening,
legs crossed and tongue silent,
thinking as I look into the
dancing supper fires, "Am I
an Indian?" And I wonder.

Rudy Bantista

Religion

I'm a believer.
    I believe in kids
    Who ride their bikes
    Without holding on.

    I believe in the chances
    We take.
    To be complete
    For one moment
    With something we need.

    I believe in the crawling
    And struggling
    Of a baby
    Much more than I believe
    In his first step.

    I believe in trees,
    Especially willows,
    That do not try to fight the wind.

    And I believe in you,
    Whoever you are.
I believe.

Merrit Malloy

Breaklight

light keeps on breaking
i keep knowing
the language of other nations.
i keep hearing
tree talk
water words
and i keep knowing what they mean.
and light just keeps on breaking.
last night
the fears of my mother came
knocking and when i
opened the door
they tried to explain themselves
and i understood
everything they said.

Lucille Clifton

Weather

On sunny afternoons
baby carriages gather
outside launderettes
to plot their escape.

On cold mornings
large men at bus stops
stand like old smudge pots
waiting to be collected.

On hot nights
windows open
like sleepy eyes
and people hear
each other's music.

Robert Hershon

How to Tell a Tornado

Listen for noises.
If you do not live
near railroad tracks,
the freight train you hear
is not the Northern Pacific
lost in the storm:
that is a tornado
doing imitations of itself.
One of its favorite sounds
is no sound.
After the high wind, and
before the freight train,
there is a pocket of nothing:
this is when you think
everything has stopped:
do not be fooled.
Leave it all behind
except for a candle
and take to the cellar

Afterwards
if straws are imbedded
in trees without leave,
and your house—except
for the unbroken bathroom mirror—
has vanished
without a trace,
and you are naked
except for the right leg
of your pants,
you can safely assume
that a tornado
has gone through your life
without touching it.

Howard Mohr

Nothing at All

A cellar and an attic are friends
the cellar works hard for his keep
and has for his pains a furnace in his throat
and a bellyful of boiling water
the attic sits in the clouds from morning to night
with nothing at all in his head
but a rocking horse and a broken chair

from time to time the attic speaks of going away
sick of the bickering maples
sick of distance
sick of the gaping sky
he would get a place in the city
How can you bear me *he sighs*

the cellar shrugs No no
it's nothing at all
he wallows in the earth
like an ark of stone in a windless sea
nor will he take the attic seriously

one night a storm comes bellowing down from the hills
looking for trouble
its mane crackles with flame
rain drools from its jowls
it takes the house in its teeth and shakes it
from side
to side

a while the friends hold fast
but the attic
weak from want of exercise
lets go in the end
rising like a bat on great ungainly wings
he clatters away over the horrified maples

in time the storm grows bored and mutters off
the cellar crouches in the cooling mire
the fire in his throat is out
his belly gives him peace at last
but through the cracks he watches the sky
for the first time open
its clear blue idiot eye
and sees to the back of heaven
nothing at all
not a sheltering cloud
not a shadow
not a broken chair
the maples drop a few last tears and doze in the sun

Donald Finkel

Hello, Hello Henry

My neighbor in the country, Henry Manley,
with a washpot warming on his woodstove,
with a heifer and two goats and yearly chickens,
has outlasted Stalin, Roosevelt and Churchill
but something's stirring in him in his dotage.

Last fall he dug a hole and moved his privy
and a year ago in April reamed his well out.
When the county sent a truck and poles and cable,
his *Daddy* ran the linemen off with birdshot
and swore he'd die by oil lamp, and did.

Now you tell me that all yesterday in Boston
you set your city phone at mine, and had it ringing
inside a dead apartment for three hours
room after empty room, to keep yours busy.
I hear it in my head, that ranting summons.

That must have been about the time that Henry
walked up two miles, shy as a girl come calling
to tell me he has a phone now, 264, ring two.
It rang one time last week—wrong number.
He'd be pleased if one day I would think to call him.

Hello, hello Henry? Is that you?

Maxine Kumin

Poem

I loved my friend.
He went away from me.
There's nothing more to say.
The poem ends,
Soft as it began—
I loved my friend.

Langston Hughes

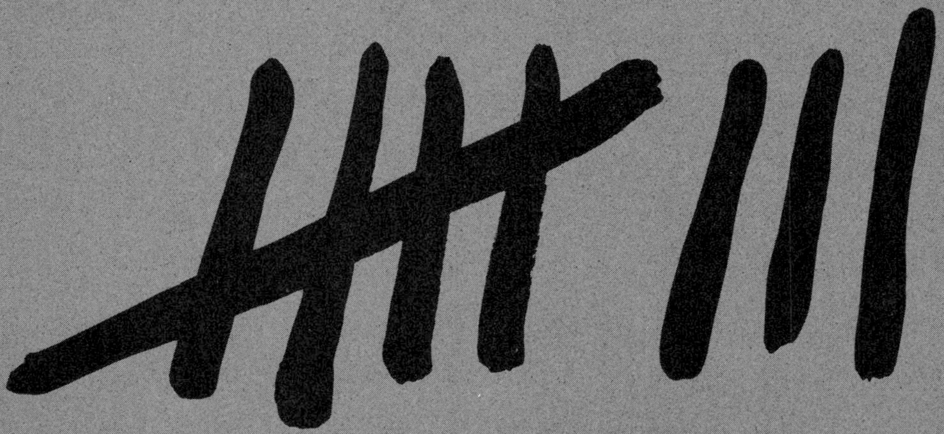

Worms and the Wind

Worms would rather be worms.
Ask a worm and he says, "Who knows what a worm knows?"
Worms go down and up and over and under.
Worms like tunnels.
When worms talk they talk about the worm world.
Worms like it in the dark.
Neither the sun nor the moon interests a worm.
Zigzag worms hate circle worms.
Curve worms never trust square worms.
Worms know what worms want.
Slide worms are suspicious of crawl worms.
One worm asks another, "How does your belly drag today?"
The shape of a crooked worm satisfies a crooked worm.
A straight worm says, "Why not be straight?"
Worms tired of crawling begin to slither.
Long worms slither farther than short worms.
Middle-sized worms say, "It is nice to be neither long nor short."
Old worms teach young worms to say, "Don't be sorry for me unless you
    have been a worm and lived in worm places and read worm books."
When worms go to war they dig in, come out and fight, dig in again,
    come out and fight again, dig in again, and so on.
Worms underground never hear the wind overground and sometimes they
    ask, "What is this wind we hear of?"

Carl Sandburg

Race Prejudice

Little mouse:
Are you
some rat's little child?
I won't love you if you are.

Alfred Kreymborg

MIGRATION

She stood hanging wash before sun
and occasionally watched the kids
gather acorns from the trees,
and when her husband came,
complaining about the tobacco spit on him
they decided to run North
for a free evening.
She stood hanging wash in the basement
and saw the kids sneak puffs from cigarettes,
fix steel traps with cheese
and when her husband came,
complaining of the mill's drudgery,
        she burst—
said he had no hunter's heart
beat him with a broom,
became blinded by the orange sun
racing into steel mill flames
and afterwards,
sat singing spirituals to sons.

Carole Gregory Clemmons

Done With

My house is torn down—
Plaster sifting, the pillars broken,
Beams jagged, the wall crushed by the bulldozer.
The whole roof has fallen
On the hall and the kitchen
The bedrooms, the parlor.

They are trampling the garden—
My mother's lilac, my father's grapevine,
The freesias, the jonquils, the grasses.
Hot asphalt goes down
Over the torn stems, and hardens.

What will they do in springtime
Those bulbs and stems groping upward
That drown in earth under the paving,
Thick with sap, pale in the dark
As they try the unrolling of green.

May they double themselves
Pushing together up to the sunlight,
May they break through the seal stretched above them
Open and flower and cry we are living.

Ann Stanford

Roaches

Last night when I got up
to let the dog out I spied
a cockroach in the bathroom
crouched flat on the cool
                porcelain,
                        delicate
antennae probing the toothpaste cap
        and feasting himself on a gob
                of it in the bowl:
I killed him with one unprofessional
                        blow,
scattering arms and legs
        and half his body in the sink . . .

I would have no truck with roaches,
crouched like lions in the ledges of sewers
their black eyes in the darkness
                        alert for tasty slime,
breeding quickly and without design,
laboring up drainpipes through filth
                        to the light;
I read once they are among
        the most antediluvian of creatures,
        surviving everything,
        and in more primitive times
thrived to the size of your hand . . .

yet when sinking asleep
        or craning at the stars,
I can feel their light feet
                probing in my veins,
their whiskers nibbling
                the insides of my toes;
and neck arched,
        feel their patient scrambling
up the dark tubes of my throat.   Peter Wild

105

Battle Won Is Lost

They said, "You are no longer a lad."
    I nodded.
They said, "Enter the council lodge."
    I sat.
They said, "Our lands are at stake."
    I scowled.
They said, "We are at war."
    I hated.
They said, "Prepare red war symbols."
    I painted.
They said, "Count coups."
    I scalped.
They said, "You'll see friends die."
    I cringed.
They said, "Desperate warriors fight best."
    I charged.
They said, "Some will be wounded."
    I bled.
They said, "To die is glorious."
    They lied.

Phil George

The Locust Swarm

Locusts laid their eggs in the corpse
Of a soldier. When the worms were
Mature, they took wing. Their drone
Was ominous, their shells hard.
Anyone could tell they had hatched
From an unsatisfied anger.
They flew swiftly towards the North.
They hid the sky like a curtain.
When the wife of the soldier
Saw them, she turned pale, her breath
Failed her. She knew he was dead
In battle, his corpse lost in
The desert. That night she dreamed
She rode a white horse, so swift
It left no footprints, and came
To where he lay in the sand.
She looked at his face, eaten
By the locusts, and tears of
Blood filled her eyes. Ever after
She would not let her children
Injure any insect which
Might have fed on the dead. She
Would lift her face to the sky
And say, "O locusts, if you
Are seeking a place to winter,
You can find shelter in my heart."

Hsu Chao

The Wolves

Last night knives flashed. LeChien cried
And chewed blood in his bed.
Vanni's whittling blade
Had found flesh easier than wood.

Vanni and I left camp on foot. In a glade
We came on a brown blossom
Great and shining on a thorned stem.
"That's the sensitive brier," I said.

"It shrinks at the touch," I added.
Soon we found buffalo. Picking
A bull grazing by itself, I began
The approach: while the shaggy head

Was turned I sprinted across the sod,
And when he swung around his gaze
I bellyflopped in the grass
And lay on my heartbeat and waited.

When he looked away again I made
Enough yardage before he wheeled
His head: I kneeled, leveled
My rifle, and we calmly waited.

It occurred to me as we waited
That in those last moments he was,
In fact, daydreaming about something else.
"He is too stupid to live," I said.

His legs shifted and the heart showed.
I fired. He looked, trotted off,
He simply looked and trotted off,
Stumbled, sat himself down, and became dead.

I looked for Vanni. Amid the cows he stood,
Only his arms moving as he fired,
Loaded, and fired, the dumb herd
Milling about him sniffing at their dead.

I called and he retreated.
We cut two choice tongues for ourselves
And left the surplus. All day wolves
Would splash blood from those great sides.

Again we saw the flower, brown-red
On a thorn-spiked stem. When Vanni
Extended his fingers, it was funny,
It shrank away as if it had just died.

They told us in camp that LeChien was dead.
None of us cared. Nobody much.
Had liked him. His tobacco pouch,
I observed, was already missing from beside his bed.

Galway Kinnell

Plaint of the Summer Vampires

DEERFLY   Winged sizzling pellet am I
and mottled flat triangle. Shrieking
blood-lust animates me as Soul
Body her pupa. My meal is the thin pain
where your hair divides in oil, my life a headlong
hurtling upon crowns of heads—your own
succulent head, the huge hard
unswishable heads of horses. You are wrong
to hate me; if I torment you
that is my doom.

MOSQUITO   I am all thin: subtlety on a thin
whine, six cocked legs hair-fine;
your skin where they touch down
is thicker. I am all
pin-striped, pin-slender, head
a perfect pinhead, mouth whose tiny puncture
can slip between nerveends more needle-
sharp than any pin. Sweat
is my Siren scent, my greed is boundless
witless and impersonal, my nature
none of my choosing.

TOGETHER   O to turn aphid! O
for unresistant leaf-juices and no
murderous mammoth hands whacking! Never to be
tangled again in hair or spotted on your wrist
sipping, and no chance for a getaway.
—Though you knock ME senseless a dozen times—
—Or flail *me* away—what can we do
but sort our wings and legs and try again
again and yet again? Starve or be slapped to death
is what it comes to. Pity us.
The thirst for blood is a curse.   Judith Moffett

Waking

I said to myself one morning:
   "Annie, the world is fair;
You'd better be up and combing
   The tangles out of your hair."

Quickly myself made answer:
   "The world is horrid and queer,
And if you don't go to sleep again
   You're going to be sorry, dear."

Annie Higgins

Alarm Clock

in the deep sleep forest
there were ferns
there were feathers
there was fur
and a soft ripe peach
on a branch within my

      r-r-r-r-r-r-r-r-r-r-r-r-r-r-r-r-r-r-r-r-r-r-r-r-r-r-r-r-r-r

Eve Merriam

FORMULA

To dream,
you don't have to ask permission,
nor cry out,
nor humble yourself,
nor put on lipstick;
it's enough to close your eyes halfway
and feel distant.
Perhaps the night dreams
that it is no longer night;
the fish, that they are boats;
the boats, fish;
the water, crystal.
To dream. . .
is a simple thing;
it doesn't cost a cent,
you need only to turn your back
on the hours that pass
and cover over pain,
your ears,
your eyes
and stay so,
stay. . .
until we are awakened
by a blow upon the soul

Ana María Iza

Translated by Ron Connally

Two Ways to Wake a Sleepwalker

I

Not too abruptly, now;
any shock may start up
something none of us can
finish. Maybe a little
tug on his pajama sleeve
will serve. No sudden noises
please. I read somewhere
it's bad to bring them
out of it too suddenly.

He doesn't know what's
going on or where he's
headed. Give him some
direction or he'll simply
drift in mystery from
room to room. He doesn't
really see what lies
ahead of him. Best to
guide him back to bed.

When morning comes, he
won't remember anything.
We can joke about it
then. Best without a doubt
to keep him half asleep
and let him dream it out.

Edward Lueders

II

Kick him. Nothing like
a sudden jolt to bring him
out of that unearthly
lethargy. Can't stand
to see a human being
anything but wide awake—
much less this dumb body
going through such empty
mindless motions.

           Slap
his stupid face until
he realizes who and
where he is. I bet he'll
thank us when he learns we
wouldn't stand for stupor.
Whole damn world is watching
every move we make, so
do it quick. There's
got to be some pain.

Kick him hard so he'll
remember who it was
that brought him howling
out of it and taught him
what it really means
to really be awake.

Preoccupation

Chaff is in my eye,
A crocodile has me by the leg,
A goat is in the garden,
A porcupine is cooking in the pot,
Meal is drying on the pounding rock,
The King has summoned me to court,
And I must go to the funeral of my mother-in-law:
In short, I am busy.

Mbundu origin (Africa)

Translated by Merlin Ennis

WHERE?

There's a place the man always say
Come in here, child
No cause you should weep
Wolf never catch the rabbit
Golden hair never turn white with grief
Come in here, child
No cause you should moan
Brother never hurt his brother
Nobody here ever wander without a home
There must be some such place somewhere
But I never heard of it.

Kenneth Patchen

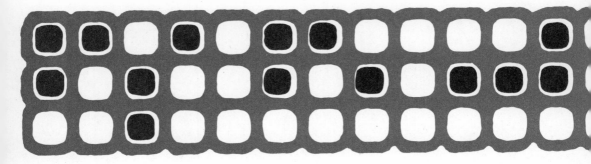

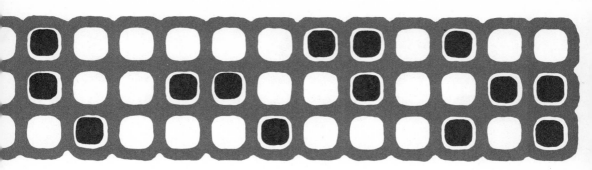

Explanations of Love

There is a place where love begins and a place
where love ends.

There is a touch of two hands that foils all
dictionaries.

There is a look of eyes fierce as a big Bethlehem open hearth
furnace or a little green-fire acetylene torch.

There are single careless bywords portentous as a
big bend in the Mississippi River.

Hands, eyes, bywords—out of these love makes
battlegrounds and workshops.

There is a pair of shoes love wears and the coming
is a mystery.

There is a warning love sends and the cost of it
is never written till long afterward.

There are explanations of love in all languages
and not one found wiser than this:

There is a place where love begins and a place
where love ends—and love asks nothing.

Carl Sandburg

With the Door Open

Something I want to communicate to you,
I keep my door open between us.
I am unable to say it,
I am happy only
with the door open between us.

David Ignatow

Simile

What did we say to each other
that now we are as the deer
who walk in single file
with heads high
with ears forward
with eyes watchful
with hooves always placed on firm ground
in whose limbs there is latent flight

N. Scott Momaday

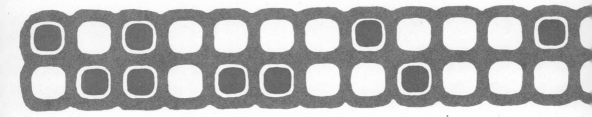

Water Color

The painter puts two thin lines
On one side of the page,
And one line on the other side.
Suddenly grass grows there!

Between them, a wavering line.
Water is moving!

Your two eyes look at me.
You lift one hand.

Suddenly my heart is growing toward you.
Suddenly I am moving toward you!

Paul Engle

Simple-song

When *we* are going toward someone we say
you are just like me
your thoughts are my brothers
word matches word
how easy to be together.

When we are leaving someone we say
how strange you are
we cannot communicate
we can never agree
how hard, hard and weary to be together.

We are not different nor alike
but each strange in his leather body
sealed in skin and reaching out clumsy hands
and loving is an act
that cannot outlive
the open hand
the open eye
the door in the chest standing open.

Marge Piercy

Mi Maestro

i wish
    you were
        a sponge—
that i could
    wring
       squeeze tightly
above my head;
With all
    the desire
       that i have
to learn
    from you
      about
        me.

Ana Castillo

Separation

Your absence has gone through me
Like thread through a needle.
Everything I do is stitched with its color.

W. S. Merwin

Intimates

Don't you care for my love? she said bitterly.

I handed her the mirror, and said:
Please address these questions to the proper person!
Please make all requests to head-quarters!
In all matters of emotional importance
please approach the supreme authority direct!—
So I handed her the mirror.

And she would have broken it over my head,
but she caught sight of her own reflection
and that held her spellbound for two seconds
while I fled.

D. H. Lawrence

In Golden Gate Park That Day

In Golden Gate Park that day
a man and his wife were coming along
thru the enormous meadow
which was the meadow of the world
He was wearing green suspenders
and carrying an old beat-up flute
in one hand
while his wife had a bunch of grapes
which she kept handing out
individually
to various squirrels
as if each
were a little joke

And then the two of them came on
thru the enormous meadow
which was the meadow of the world
and then
at a very still spot where the trees dreamed
and seemed to have been waiting thru all time
for them
they sat down together on the grass
without looking at each other
and ate oranges
without looking at each other
and put the peels
in a basket which they seemed
to have brought for that purpose
without looking at each other

And then
         he took his shirt and undershirt off
but kept his hat on
                    sideways
                         and without saying anything
         fell asleep under it
                  And his wife just sat there looking
at the birds which flew about
         calling to each other
                    in the stilly air
         as if they were questioning existence
         or trying to recall something forgotten

But then finally
         she too lay down flat
                         and just lay there looking up
                                   at nothing
         yet fingering the old flute
                            which nobody played
         and finally looking over
                         at him
without any particular expression
                    except a certain awful look
         of terrible depression

Lawrence Ferlinghetti

Haiku

there are things sadder
than you and I. some people
do not even touch.

Sonia Sanchez

My Rules

If you want to marry me, here's what you'll have to do
You must learn how to make a perfect chicken dumpling stew
And you must sew my holey socks and you must soothe my troubled mind
And develop the knack for scratching my back
And keep my shoes spotlessly shined
And while I rest you must rake up the leaves
And when it is hailing and snowing
You must shovel the walk, and be still when I talk
And—hey, where are you going??

Shel Silverstein

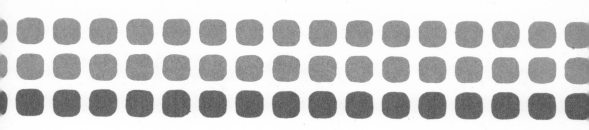

I Love You in Caves and Meadows

I love you in caves and meadows.
Flying, I love you.
In parks and streets and alleys I love you.
By the bones of my mother,
by the clenched fist of my father,
by sunlight and by starlight
by moonlight and by lamplight
by phosphorus match
and by fire lit of dated newspapers,
by fire of dried twigs, in dark woods alone
I love you
and by the nest of the mother bird
nervous and angry at the sight of me
I love you
I don't remember anything without love of you
I cannot remember living without drawing breath.

David Ignatow

128

Yei-ie's Child

I am the child of the Yei-ie.
Turquoise for my body, silver for my soul,
I was united with beauty all around me.
As turquoise and silver, I'm the jewel
    of my brother tribes and worn with pride.
The wilds of the animals are also my brother.
The bears, the deer, and the birds are a part
    of me and I am a part of them.
As brothers, the clouds are our long, sleek hair.
The winds are our pure breath.
As brothers, the rivers are our blood.
The mountains are our own selves.
As brothers, the universe is our home and
    in it we walk.
With beauty in our minds,
With beauty in our hearts, and
With beauty in our steps.
    In beauty we were born.
    In beauty we are living.
    In beauty we will die.
    In beauty we will be finished.

Charles C. Long

Two Girls Singing

It neither was the words nor yet the tune.
Any tune would have done and any words.
Any listener or no listener at all.

As nightingales in rocks or a child crooning
in its own world of strange awakening
or larks for no reason but themselves.

So on the bus through late November running
by yellow lights tormented, darkness falling,
the two girls sang for miles and miles together

and it wasn't the words or tune. It was the singing.
It was the human sweetness in that yellow,
the unpredicted voices of our kind.

Iain Crichton Smith

The Little Trumpet

All that is left
of the magic of the fair
is this little trumpet
of blue and green tin,
blown by a girl
as she walks, barefoot, through the fields.
But within its forced note
are all the clowns, white ones and red ones,
the band all dressed in gaudy gold,
the merry-go-round, the calliope, the lights.
Just as in the dripping of the gutter
is all the fearfulness of the storm
the beauty of lightning and the rainbow;
and in the damp flickers of a firefly
whose light dissolves on a heather branch
is all the wondrousness of spring.

Corrado Govoni

Translated by Carlo L. Golino

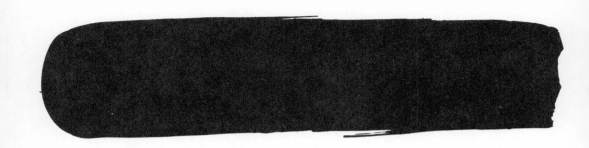

At Quitting Time

At quitting time
a combine clatters unseen behind a hill,
then emerges over the crest,
flowering orange against the sky.
The driver shuts off his engine.
Sweat and dust burn
in his swollen, red-rimmed eyes.
When he climbs off the seat and jumps down,
the field sways beneath him.
He is buried by silence,
lost in it.
Coming down the hill
to where he parked his car in the morning,
he is slowly becoming someone else,
entering another country.
Where he walks,
puffs of dust behind him
turn golden
in slanted sunlight.

Robert Sund

Laying the Dust

What a sweet smell rises
    when you lay the dust—
bucket after bucket of water thrown
on the yellow grass.
                The water
flashes
each time you
make it leap—
        arching its glittering back.
The sound of
          more water
pouring into the pail
almost quenches my thirst.
Surely when flowers
grow here, they'll not
smell sweeter than this
          wet ground, suddenly black.

Denise Levertov

Evening

The sun horse panting and snorting
Reaches the shores of evening
Kicking his hoofs and flicking red dust
His vermilion mane wet with perspiration
He throws red foam from his mouth

The mellow-colored Evening comes
And places her hand between his pricked ears
Her long fingers
Feel the hot breath from his nostrils
And take off the bridle from his mouth

The restive animal
Tamed and quietened
Walks behind the Evening slowly
And goes into the stable of darkness

Mohan Singh

Translated by Balwant Gargi

VESPER

Now sleep the mountain-summits, sleep the glens,
The peaks, the torrent-beds; all things that creep
On the dark earth lie resting in their dens;
Quiet are the mountain-creatures, quiet the bees,
The monsters hidden in the purple seas;
And birds, the swift of wing,
Sit slumbering.

Alcman of Sparta

Translated by F.L. Lucas

Swan and Shadow

```
                    Dusk
                Above the
            water hang the
                    loud
                    flies
                    Here
                    O so
                    gray
                    then
                    What        A pale signal will appear
                    When       Soon before its shadow fades
                    Where       Here in this pool of opened eye
                    In us       No Upon us As at the very edges
                of where we take shape in the dark air
                 this object bares its image awakening
                    ripples of recognition that will
                        brush darkness up into light
  even after this bird this hour both drift by atop the perfect sad instant now
                      already passing out of sight
                    toward yet-untroubled reflection
                  this image bears its object darkening
                 into memorial shades Scattered bits of
                light       No of water Or something across
                water       Breaking up No Being regathered
                 soon        Yet by then a swan will have
                 gone           Yes out of mind into what
                 vast
                 pale
                 hush
                 of a
                 place
                 past
        sudden dark as
            if a swan
              sang                        John Hollander
```

135

The Sky

The sky at night is like a big city
where beasts and men abound,
but never once has anyone
killed a fowl or a goat,
and no bear has ever killed a prey.
There are no accidents; there are no losses.
Everything knows its way.

Ewe origin (Africa)

Translated by Kafu Hoh

Constellations

Night time.
'fore I go to bed,
Grandma say,
Put the water to your head. . .
Shoo
Grandma ole
She say what she want to
And folks say it all true.
What is true. . .
Face all wet
'fore I sleep.
But,
Later on
In my bed
By the window,
I tug the quilt
Tight as the lights out. . .
Shoo
I look 'cross all the roofs I know
Feeling brave,
But the roofs ain't brave.
Farther out I see the bear—
Bear don't scare me—
Dip down
Deep in the blue water
O' grandma's God.
I hear grandma snore, loud
But the bear he don't move.
He stopped there
With the water on his face.
His child near by,
By a million years too. . .
Shoo
What going on that they do
What grandma say.
Everybody know
Grandma ole.

Primus St. John

NIGHT RAIN

I wake with the rain.
It has surprised me.
First, delight,
Then I think of outdoors:
The shovels and rakes I left in the garden
Rusting now in the mist,
The splintering of handles.
I think of car windows open
Tricycles
Canvas cots, trash cans
The hay uncovered
Mildew.

Well, they are out.
And the animals—
The cat, he is gone
The dog is the neighbor's
The horses have a tin roof
If they will stay under it.
And the wild things are there—
Birds, wet in the trees,
Deer in the brush, rabbits in hiding.
The leaves will all be washed
The wild lilacs, the walnuts.

I am sleepy and warm
I dream of the great hornéd owl
Snatching birds like plums out of trees.

Ann Stanford

138

NUMBERS

I hate and like math.
The letter O
and the number zero sound like
poems about O snowflake. Zero
makes me hungry. It is the emptiest
number in the universe
which is—and is not—round.
The wonder of zero, O snowflake
and the universe
will never be solved.
I want my lunch.

Aliki Barnstone

Author-Title Index

Pronunciation Glossary

angatok (ang'gə tok)
burro (bür'ō)
chile (chē'lā)
Chimayo (chē mī'ô)
entrechat (än trə shä′)
Gia-fu Feng (zhä fü fung)
Hsu Chao (shü shou)
Jacques Prévert (zhäk prä ver′)
Kafu Hoh (kä fü hō)
Kai-yu Hsu (kī yü shü)
Kalahari (kä′′lä hä′rē)
Lao Tsu (lou tsə)
Le Chien (lə shy ən′)
Mbundu (mə bün'dü)
Mi Maestro (mē mä es'trô)
Netsilik (nech'ə lik)
Osip Emilevich Mandelstam (ô'sēp ā mēl'ye vich man'dəl shtam)
Samoyed (sam′′ə yed′)
Satoru Sato (sä tô rü sä tô)
señor (se nyôr′)
Shiro Murano (shē rô mù rä nô)
Simon Ortiz (sē môn′ ôr'tēs)
Tai Wang-Shu (tī wäng shü)
Uzbek (üz'bek)
Yei-ie (yə̄ ē̄ə)

PRONUNCIATION KEY

a hat	i it	oi oil	ch child	ə =	a in about
ā age	ī ice	ou out	ng long		e in taken
ä far	o hot	u cup	sh she		i in pencil
e let	ō open	u̇ put	th thin		o in lemon
ē equal	ô order	ü rule	₮H then		u in circus
ėr term			zh measure		

Interpretation

A PROJECT FOR FREIGHT TRAINS (page 14)

In the first two stanzas, what words or phrases suggest how the speaker feels about freight trains? (The **speaker** is the person who is describing the events in a poem.)

What word does the combination 5–6 make? Why might it be considered lucky? Why might 2–6 be "even luckier"?

Do you agree with this statement: *A poem is a freight train of colorful words?* Why or why not? If you agree, what other "freight" besides colorful words does a poem carry?

PROGRESS (page 17)

Three persons are mentioned in this poem—the speaker ("I"), the speaker's father, and "you" (also addressed more respectfully as *señor*). How did the father cross the mountain? How does *señor* cross the mountain? How does the speaker cross the mountain?

How do the speaker and *señor* feel about the two ways of crossing? Which lines suggest how the father might feel about the two ways?

Does the title "Progress" reflect the attitude of the father? Of *señor*? Of the speaker? Of the person who wrote the poem? Explain.

PONY SONG (page 18)

Do you think "Car Song" would be an equally good title? Why or why not?

To what do the words "great/white/romans" refer? To what do the words "dry brown mother" refer? (Is the speaker talking about his father's wife?)

What tone of voice do you think the speaker is using?

LEARNING ABOUT THE INDIANS (page 19)

In what way is the man in the poem both White Eagle and Mr. White?

What was the students' attitude toward the performance? Mr. White's attitude?

What is meant by the statement that the plains are "surrounded by the graves/ of all our fathers, but more of his than ours"?

What do you think the students learned about Indians?

NEEDS (page 20)

What machine is the speaker describing? Where do you suppose the speaker picked up the particular language he uses to describe the machine?

What does the speaker "want"? What does the speaker "need"? Explain.

THROUGH THE AUTOMATIC CARWASH (page 21)

Have you ever driven through an automatic carwash? If so, what did it remind you of? What kinds of feelings did you experience?

Do you think the comparison of the carwash to a sudden thundershower is appropriate? Why or why not?

Why do you think the speaker's son becomes frightened? Can you think of any experiences you have had that caused you to react similarly? Explain.

THE OWL ON THE AERIAL (page 22)

What brings the owl out of its crevice?

What is going on above the owl, on the moon? What is going on below it, in the house?

What connection between the owl's activities and human activities does the poem suggest?

THE TELEVISION (page 23)

If you did not know the title, what image in the poem would help you to identify the "it"? (An **image** is a mental picture that words create in our imaginations.)

In what way is a television "unaccustomed to movement and real life"?

JETLINER (page 24)

The poetic device of giving human qualities to a nonhuman thing is called **personification**. Personification also occurs when we give living qualities to a nonliving thing.

What words or phrases in the poem accurately describe both a jetliner and a person? Both a jetliner and an animal?

BACK YARD, JULY NIGHT (page 25)

A **parody** is a humorous imitation of a more serious writing. This poem is a parody of an old, well-known song. The first two lines of the song are:

> Twinkle twinkle little star
> How I wonder what you are

In what ways is the poem similar to the song? In what ways is it different?

Would the second line of the poem have the same meaning for you if you did not know the song? Explain.

AND THEY LIVED HAPPILY EVER AFTER FOR A WHILE (page 26)

This poem is written in the style of a **ballad.** Many old songs that we now call folksongs came from traditional ballads. Find more information about the ballad form and read several of them in a literature anthology. In what ways is this poem similar to a traditional ballad? How does it differ? Do you think this poem is a parody of a traditional ballad? Why or why not?

MAN IN ORBIT (page 27)

Poetry in which the shape of the printed form is related to its subject matter is called **concrete poetry**. How is the shape of this poem related to the subject matter?

What do you think the man in the poem meant when he said "Stop the world, I want to get off"? In view of what happens to the man, what might the poem be suggesting about contemporary life?

FOR POETS (page 29)

What do you think the word "beautiful" means in the lines "Stay beautiful/ but don't stay down underground too long"?

A **symbol** is something that stands for or represents something else. Find words or phrases in this poem that are used as symbols. What does each symbolize?

DON'T TELL ANYBODY (page 30)

According to the speaker, what is the danger of talking about the things you observe?

How would the meaning of the poem be affected if the last line were omitted?

In what way does the advice given in this poem differ from the advice given in "For Poets"?

THE SECRET (page 31)

What is a secret? How is it possible that the girls could discover "the secret of life" in a line of poetry, and the speaker, who wrote the line, could not?

Explain how it is possible that the girls may discover the same secret a thousand times again in other lines.

Do you assume, as the speaker and the girls do, that poetry contains "the secret of life"? If so, is it the same as the secret of life that a scientist discovers? Explain.

THE UNWRITTEN (page 32)

Who is the speaker in this poem? What is the speaker doing?

Since the words cannot literally be living inside the pencil, where *are* they "living"?

What do you think the speaker has in mind by suggesting that we may need only one word? What word would you choose?

TARTARS, UZBEKS, SAMOYEDS (page 33)

The Tartars, Uzbeks, Samoyeds, Ukrainians, and Volga Germans are separate groups of people within the U.S.S.R. Each has its own distinct culture and language. The author, Osip Mandelstam, is also Russian.

What, besides its literal meaning, might the line "are waiting for their translators" imply? Explain how this idea is reinforced in the second stanza.

POEM: A REMINDER (page 34)

In this poem, the word "convention" means a rule based on common consent. According to the speaker, how old are the conventions of poetry? What conventions of poetry are present in this poem?

What is the significance of the title "Poem: A Reminder"?

WINTER POEM (page 34)

This poem, unlike "Poem: A Reminder," does not have capital letters prompting every line. Also, it does not rhyme. Is it less of a poem than "Poem: A Reminder"? Does it have rhythm and sound and sense? Explain.

WHITE BUTTERFLY (page 35)

To what object is the white butterfly indirectly compared in the first stanza? What are the "wordless pages"?

DRAWING BY RONNIE C., GRADE ONE (page 36)

Is this poem about *a* drawing or about *doing* a drawing?

What helps to create a mood of urgency and excitement in this poem? In what way does the mood change in the last stanza?

MAGIC WORDS (page 37)

Do you think the speaker in this poem really believes that at one time a person could change into an animal and an animal into a person? If not, what do you think the speaker is suggesting in this statement?

What ways can you think of in which words might still be magical today?

DAYS (page 39)

The speaker asks two questions. What is the answer to the first one? What must a person do in order to "solve" the second question?

Explain the significance of "the priest and the doctor."

DON LARSEN'S PERFECT GAME (page 40)

This poem is based on an actual game that was played during the 1956 World Series between the New York Yankees and the Brooklyn Dodgers. Don Larsen, a Yankee, pitched the first perfect game in the history of the World Series. (A perfect game is one in which no opposing player has been able to reach first base by any means—hit, walk, or error.) Yogi Berra's dash to the mound and the bearhug he gave Larsen are nearly as famous as Larsen's game.

Why will Don Larsen have bad dreams? What do you imagine those dreams will be about?

If, as the poem states, nothing went wrong, why is Don Larsen lonely? Can his teammates make him not lonely? Explain.

How does the last line affect the meaning of the poem? Would the meaning change if the last line were omitted? Why or why not?

THE ACT (page 41)

Why does the speaker want to leave the roses where they are? Why does the other person want to cut them?

How do you think each person feels about the roses after they have been cut?

SEVENTY-SIX (page 42)

In what ways can a person be like an unbending tree? Like a flexible tree?

In what sense do the first two lines of the poem specifically illustrate what the last two lines state generally?

AT GRANDMOTHER'S (page 43)

Which lines indirectly suggest that the speaker might be lonely?

Why does the speaker avoid bouncing the ball against certain objects? What is the echoing dark? In what way is the phrase "on the second floor" significant?

INCIDENT IN A ROSE GARDEN (page 44)

This poem is divided into three sections. Who is speaking to whom in each section?

Irony occurs when someone says something which is opposite of what is meant, or when something happens which is contrary to what would normally be expected. The former is *verbal irony;* the latter is *irony of situation.* What kind of irony occurs in this poem?

THE DAY WE DIE (page 45)

Do you think the speaker literally means that the wind comes down and blows away our footprints? What might the wind symbolize? The footprints?

TODAY IS A VERY GOOD DAY TO DIE (page 46)

What is the tone of this poem? (The **tone** of a poem is the speaker's attitude toward what he or she is describing. It is the speaker's tone of voice.)

If you were in the same position as the speaker, would you agree that "today is a very good day to die"? Why or why not?

HEAVEN AND HELL (page 47)

(*Angatoks* are people who have the power to control certain spirits.)

In what way is the picture of heaven and hell in this poem similar to or different from your own?

THE ARTIST (page 49)

(An *entrechat* is a ballet leap. Hands on hips, the dancer springs straight up and, with legs straight, crosses ankles several times before coming down in the same position from which the leap was started.)

Which lines tell you that Mr. T has probably taken ballet lessons? Do you think that Mr. T is a professional dancer? Why or why not?

What kind of picture of Mr. T do the first five lines evoke? How does the last line of the poem indirectly answer Mrs. T's question?

Do you think "The Audience" would be an equally good title? "The Performance"? Explain.

JUMPED OFF (page 50)

How do the two ways of landing differ from each other?

What, besides jumping off a garage, might this poem be about? What kind of "wings" is the speaker talking about in the second stanza?

PLEA (page 51)

To whom does the speaker address the plea? In which line is the plea stated?

In what sense are the herds of elephants "soft"? Why do the horses feel "no pain"? Explain the importance of the last line to the whole poem.

What, besides seeing animals in the clouds, might this poem be about?

PIANO LESSONS (page 52)

What facts about the piano teacher does the speaker give you? What more can you guess based on the facts given?

What is the speaker's attitude toward the lessons? Which lines tell you?

RIDING LESSON (page 53)

What were the two things that the speaker learned from the riding teacher?

How would you rephrase the teacher's advice at the end of the poem to make it apply to other learning experiences?

HOW TO PAINT THE PORTRAIT OF A BIRD (page 54)

In answering the following questions, keep in mind that the speaker's instructions have a symbolic meaning as well as a literal one.

Why is it important first to paint a cage with an open door?

What is important about the location where the canvas is placed?

Once the bird has been captured, why erase the cage?

Why is it a bad sign if the bird does not sing?

400-METER FREESTYLE (page 56)

How is the printed form of this poem related to the subject matter? In what sense has the author cheated in arranging the lines this way? Why do you suppose the first two words and the last word are in capital letters?

What does the line "he has schooled out all extravagance" mean? Do you think the description in this poem is effective? Why or why not?

POLE VAULT (page 58)

A **simile** is a figure of speech which compares two unlike things by use of the words *like* or *as* (for example, the blades of dry grass were *like* needles under my bare feet). Do you think the simile in this poem is appropriate? Why or why not?

Do you think the pole vaulter succeeds or fails? Find evidence in the poem to support your conclusion.

SKY DIVING (page 59)

What feelings does the speaker have while waiting? Why aren't the other people talking much to each other?

In what way does the poem imply that the anticipation of sky diving is different from the actual experience?

WHAT MY UNCLE TONY TOLD MY SISTER, ANGIE, AND ME (page 61)

What is the difference between respecting "what you are named" and respecting "yourself"?

Do you agree that "everything that is around you/ is part of you"? Explain.

SELF EXPRESSION (page 62)

How old do you think the speaker in this poem is?

In the first three lines what is the mother doing? What kind of machine is "the bubblegum machine"?

What responsibilities that the mother might be neglecting does the poem indirectly suggest? What would you guess is keeping her from fulfilling these responsibilities?

YOU HAD TO GO TO FUNERALS (page 63)

Compare the speaker in this poem with the speaker in "Self Expression."

In what ways are their observations typical of a young child's point of view?

HAVE YOU EVER HURT ABOUT BASKETS? (page 64)

What does the expression "Have you ever hurt about . . ." mean each time it is used?

What would you guess is the difference between the words the speaker has learned in school and the words she refers to as "my words"?

LINEAGE (page 65)

What is the significance of the change from the past tense in the first stanza to the present tense in the second?

What does the line "They have many clean words to say" mean?

THE CHINESE GREENGROCERS (page 66)

Where does the poem shift from a factual description of the Chinese green-grocers to an imaginary description of them?

What images in this poem do you think are especially effective?

GAME AFTER SUPPER (page 68)

Is the speaker talking about something that is happening in the present or that has happened in the past?

What kind of game are the speaker and two cousins playing? How do they feel?

In what way does the time of day add to the excitement of the game?

PROSPECTUS (page 69)

What is a *prospectus?* What does the title "Prospectus" contribute to the meaning of the poem?

KIT, SIX YEARS OLD, STANDING BY THE DASHBOARD KEEPING DADDY AWAKE ON A TRIP HOME FROM THE BEACH (page 70)

Who is the speaker in this poem? What is the speaker doing?

In what way is the language the speaker uses appropriate to the situation?

ANCESTORS (page 71)

What is the difference between grandparents and ancestors? Who do you suppose the speaker's ancestors are? Why do you think so? Could this poem be about your ancestors as well as the speaker's? Explain.

THE GIVEAWAY (page 72)

(*Stirabout* is an oatmeal or cornmeal porridge that is stirred as it boils until it thickens.)

What is the tone of this poem? What elements create the tone?

State the moral of the poem in your own words.

LOVE SONG FOR A JELLYFISH (page 75)

What is a jellyfish? What is dangerous about a jellyfish?

Why do you suppose the speaker was amazed and delighted?

In what sense is this poem a "love song"?

FLYING CROOKED (page 76)

The adjective *aerobatic* usually refers to airplane stunts such as loops, rolls, and dives. A *swift* is a fast-flying bird that appears to do graceful aerobatic stunts as it catches insects in flight. How does the butterfly's flight differ from that of the "aerobatic swift"?

Read this poem aloud. How is the sound particularly appropriate to the subject?

PIGEONS (page 77)

What images in this poem are especially effective in describing pigeons?

What mood is created in the second stanza? In what way does the third stanza affect that mood?

THE CAT (page 78)

This poem is written from a person's point of view. How would you reconstruct the poem from the cat's point of view?

FELINE LESSON (page 79)

What is the speaker's attitude toward the event described in the poem? Why do you suppose the speaker's son "cried half the night away"?

What is the lesson to which the title refers?

THE SHARK (page 80)

What is the speaker's attitude toward the shark? What words express this attitude?

What is the double meaning of the word "sweet" in the last line?

SARDINES (page 80)

To what or whom does the title refer?

THE DUCK (page 81)

Read this poem aloud. What do the sounds of the words contribute?

Explain the double meaning in the last line.

POINT OF VIEW (page 81)

What is the difference between "upside down" and "downside up"?

What is the significance of the title?

WHILE THE SNAKE SLEEPS (page 82)

In what ways is the description in this poem different from the usual descriptions of a snake?

SNAKE HUNT (page 83)

What are the speaker and the snake man doing in the first stanza?

Do you think the expression "sprang to death" describes the situation better than "sprang to life" would? Explain.

What line in the fourth stanza describes the terror of the speaker?

In the last stanza, what is the good place the snakes have lost? What phrase gives a clue as to what is going to happen to the snakes?

ZOO (page 84)

What kind of cats is the speaker referring to? What is the "movement" they lack? How are their lives different without it? In what sense do they fall asleep in the zoo?

In what sense does evolution die out in the zoo?

THE FALL (page 85)

What test ("finals") in history did all of these animals fail?

Find a picture of an okapi. How would *you* describe this animal?

THROUGH THE WINDOW (page 87)

What effect is created by having the events take place during a "soft rain" rather than during a downpour?

Do you think this is a poem about people? Why or why not?

THE DRIVER (page 88)

Why does the speaker expect the hitchhikers to think twice about riding with him? Would you think twice? Why or why not?

Which lines tell you the speaker's attitude toward the lives of others? Toward his own life?

ISLETA INDIAN GIRL (page 89)

In what "room" does this poem take place? What is the relationship of the speaker to the girl?

What does the speaker admire about the girl?

In what sense is the trail the girl follows "older than any university"?

AFTER SUPPER (page 90)

According to the first stanza, which was more important, the yard or the pasture?

What do the brothers do after dinner? What do they talk about?

How is the speaker different from his brothers?

LOOKING NORTH TO TAOS (page 91)

(*Taos* is a village in northern New Mexico. A *pueblo* is an Indian community.)

What is the speaker wondering about in each stanza? How would you answer the speaker's question in the last stanza?

RELIGION (page 92)

Is the speaker talking to a specific individual in the last stanza? What line tells you?

What do the first, second, third, and fifth stanzas have in common that the fourth stanza does not?

BREAKLIGHT (page 93)

The word "light" often symbolizes truth, knowledge, understanding, hope, or peace. Which of these meanings is intended in this poem?

The speaker in the poem calls upon the imagination of the reader. Do you feel this makes the poem more enjoyable than it would be if the speaker had been specific?

What do you imagine the fears of the mother could have been?

WEATHER (page 94)

Try writing two more stanzas to this poem in the same fashion as the three existing ones. Begin one "On rainy days . . ." and the other "On windy days. . . ."

HOW TO TELL A TORNADO (page 95)

What word in line three of the second stanza has a double meaning?

Which lines suggest the poem has a symbolic meaning? What might the tornado represent? What might be the significance of the "unbroken bathroom mirror"? The "candle"?

NOTHING AT ALL (page 96)

Explain the double meaning in the last line of stanza two.

Why is the attic bored? Why do you suppose the cellar refuses to take the attic seriously?

What feeling are you left with after reading this poem?

HELLO, HELLO HENRY (page 98)

Describe Henry and his way of life. What had been his father's attitude toward telephones?

Who might be the "you" addressed in the third stanza? What possible reason could this person have for wanting to keep the phone busy for three hours? Compare this person's attitude toward telephones to Henry's attitude.

POEM (page 99)

Does the line "I loved my friend" mean or feel the same to you at the end of the poem as at the beginning? Explain.

WORMS AND THE WIND (page 101)

In what ways are the attitudes of the worms in the poem similar to those of people?

RACE PREJUDICE (page 102)

Toward what is the speaker's prejudice directed? What quality does this prejudice share with all other prejudice?

MIGRATION (page 103)

Where is the family living at the beginning of the poem? Where do they move to?

In what ways does the family's life change after the move? What has not changed?

DONE WITH (page 104)

Who do you think "they" are in the second stanza? Who are "they" in the third and fourth stanzas?

What does the poem suggest is the reason for the house's being torn down?

In what way is the speaker "done with" the house? In what way is the speaker not "done with" the house?

ROACHES (page 105)

What is the speaker's attitude toward cockroaches? What is your attitude?

Readers of this poem have tended to like it very much or dislike it very much. What might be the reason for the differing reactions?

BATTLE WON IS LOST (page 106)

(A *coup* was a courageous or skillful blow executed by a warrior upon an enemy. Often, warriors would keep records of their achievements [*count coups*] by removing the scalps of their enemies.)

Who are "they" in the poem? What is the speaker's response to "them" throughout the poem? At what point does the reader realize that the speaker is dead?

What is the speaker's final attitude toward everything that "they" have said to him?

THE LOCUST SWARM (page 107)

What explanation is given for the undesirable features of the locusts?

What emotion in the woman prompts her to offer the locusts shelter in her heart?

THE WOLVES (page 108)

What takes place in stanza one?

In the last line of the seventh stanza, what impression do we get from "became dead" that we would not get from just "died"?

To what and whom does the title refer?

PLAINT OF THE SUMMER VAMPIRES (page 110)

What argument does each insect use in defense of itself?

What advantages do the deerfly and mosquito think the aphid has over them?

In the last stanza, what suggests that the deerfly is speaking? The mosquito?

WAKING (page 111)

In the first stanza, what does the speaker tell herself? In the second stanza, what second thoughts does she have? What might have prompted these second thoughts?

What do you think the speaker finally decides to do?

ALARM CLOCK (page 111)

Describe the feeling created by the speaker's account of the dream. In what way are the images appropriate to a "deep sleep"?

At what point in the dream is the speaker's account interrupted? What word would you choose to complete the speaker's account? Why?

FORMULA (page 112)

What is a *formula*? What is the formula in this poem?

Is the speaker talking about the kind of dream we have while we are sleeping or is she using the word dream to mean "imagine"? Explain.

What is meant by the "blow upon the soul"?

TWO WAYS TO WAKE A SLEEPWALKER (page 113)

What method of waking a sleepwalker does the first speaker recommend? What is his attitude toward the sleepwalker? What tone of voice does he use?

What method does the second speaker recommend? What is his attitude toward the sleepwalker? His tone of voice?

Which method do you recommend? If neither, what other method do you recommend?

Do you think the poem is more about being asleep or more about being awake? Explain.

PREOCCUPATION (page 114)

What is the tone of this poem? Which line contributes most to this tone?

WHERE? (page 115)

Who might "the man" in the first line be?

Is the speaker a realist or an idealist? Explain.

EXPLANATIONS OF LOVE (page 117)

What is the difference between what happens on a battleground and what happens in a workshop?

How can love make "battlegrounds and workshops" out of "hands, eyes, bywords"?

What is the warning love sends? Why is "the cost of it/ never written till long afterward"?

WITH THE DOOR OPEN (page 118)

What do you think the speaker wants to communicate? Why do you think the speaker is "unable to say it"? How does the speaker succeed in communicating that "something"?

SIMILE (page 119)

What are the "we" in the poem wary of? What do you suppose they said to each other to cause this wariness? Would the poem make better sense if we were to know what they said? Why or why not?

WATER COLOR (page 120)

What comparison is the speaker making in this poem?

SIMPLE-SONG (page 121)

According to the speaker, when we go toward or when we leave someone, what and whom are we really thinking of?

What is "the door in the chest" that stands open?

MI MAESTRO (page 122)

(*Mi Maestro* means "my teacher" in Spanish.)

What are the speaker's feelings for the person she is addressing?

What do you think the speaker wants to learn about herself?

SEPARATION (page 123)

Rephrase this poem in your own words.

How is the absent person still present in the speaker's life?

INTIMATES (page 123)

In stanza two, who is "the proper person" and "the supreme authority"?

What lines suggest who "she" really loves?

IN GOLDEN GATE PARK THAT DAY (page 124)

What is the mood in the first stanza? In what lines does the mood begin to change? What is the mood at the end of the poem?

What do you learn about the couple from the poem?

HAIKU (page 126)

What can you guess about the personal situation between the "you and I" in this poem?

MY RULES (page 126)

Which do you suppose the speaker in this poem is, a man or a woman? Defend your answer.

I LOVE YOU IN CAVES AND MEADOWS (page 127)

What feelings do you associate with caves? With meadows? Are there "caves and meadows" in Ferlinghetti's "In Golden Gate Park That Day"? Explain.

Restate the last two lines in your own words.

YEI-IE'S CHILD (page 129)

This poem is by a Navaho. In Navaho belief, the Yei-ie are holy, supernatural beings whose existence creates harmony and beauty in the world. The Navaho are known as fine craftsmen of turquoise and silver jewelry.

What does the jewelry that he makes and wears mean to the speaker? How does his attitude toward jewelry compare with those of people you know?

What do you think the speaker intends the last word of the poem to mean?

TWO GIRLS SINGING (page 130)

In the first two stanzas, what does the speaker suggest is the reason for the two girls singing?

In the last stanza, what does the speaker suggest is the effect of the singing on a possible listener?

What does the speaker mean by "the unpredicted voices of our kind"?

THE LITTLE TRUMPET (page 131)

How can the magic of a fair be contained in a little trumpet, the fearfulness of a storm in the dripping of a gutter, and the wondrousness of spring in the flicker of a firefly?

AT QUITTING TIME (page 132)

As the driver of the combine (a machine that harvests grain in the fields) leaves the field to go to his car, he is "becoming someone else." Who has he been and what kind of person might he be "becoming"? What "country" is he leaving and into what country might he be going?

LAYING THE DUST (page 133)

Out of the many appeals to the senses in this poem which one seems most important to the speaker? Which lines tell you?

Why do you suppose the speaker is thirsty when water is readily available?

EVENING (page 134)

In the first stanza, the speaker refers to the sun as a horse. What happens to the "sun horse" in the second stanza?

What has happened to the sun at the end of the poem?

Which of the two images, the "sun horse" or "evening" do you think is more appealing? Which one does the title suggest is more important?

VESPER (page 134)

A *vesper* is an evening song. This poem was written in Greece in the seventh century B.C. Do you think it is still appropriate to our time? Why or why not?

SWAN AND SHADOW (page 135)

How do you know where a new sentence in this poem begins? Why do you think the poet left out the punctuation marks?

Describe in your own words the event that takes place in the poem. What is the "pale signal"? In what way is the pool like an opened eye? Notice that the third line above the middle and the third line below are similar yet different. What does each describe?

A swan makes no sound that could be considered a song. In legend, however, a dying swan was thought to break into melodious song. Thus, the phrase "swan song" has come to mean any final statement or performance. Can this idea be applied to the final lines of this poem? Explain.

THE SKY (page 136)

What are the beasts and men to which the speaker refers in the second line?

Explain how you think the speaker feels about events in the night sky as compared to events on the earth.

CONSTELLATIONS (page 137)

What is the "bear" the speaker sees "farther out"? What is "his child near by"?

What do you think is the significance of "Put the water to your head . . ." and "Deep in the blue water / O' grandma's God"?

What do you think is the purpose of the refrain *"Shoo"*?

Describe the speaker of this poem with as many details as you can gather from the poem.

NIGHT RAIN (page 138)

In the first stanza, what kinds of things does the night rain make the speaker think about? What kinds of things does the speaker think about in the second stanza? What happens in the last stanza? What kinds of things would seem to be most important to the speaker?

NUMBERS (page 139)

What does "math" have to do with what follows in the poem? What do you think the speaker likes about math? Hates about math?

What do "zero," "O Snowflake," and "the universe" have in common for the speaker?

How does the speaker resolve the problem?

PARKINSON'S LAW

PARKINSON'S LAW

AND OTHER STUDIES IN ADMINISTRATION

BY

C. Northcote Parkinson

ILLUSTRATED BY

Robert C. Osborn

Sentry Edition

HOUGHTON MIFFLIN COMPANY BOSTON

The Riverside Press Cambridge

for Ann

PREFACE

To the very young, to schoolteachers, as also to those who compile textbooks about constitutional history, politics, and current affairs, the world is a more or less rational place. They visualize the election of representatives, freely chosen from among those the people trust. They picture the process by which the wisest and best of these become ministers of state. They imagine how captains of industry, freely elected by shareholders, choose for managerial responsibility those who have proved their ability in a humbler role. Books exist in which assumptions such as these are boldly stated or tacitly implied. To those, on the other hand, with any experience of affairs, these assumptions are merely ludicrous. Solemn conclaves of the wise and good are mere figments of the teacher's mind. It is salutary, therefore, if an occasional warning is uttered on this subject. Heaven forbid that students should cease to read books on the science of public or business administration — provided only that these works are classified as fiction. Placed between the novels of Rider Haggard and H. G. Wells, intermingled with volumes about ape men and space ships, these textbooks could harm no one. Placed elsewhere, among works of reference, they can do more damage than might at first sight seem possible.

Dismayed to realize what other people suppose to be the truth about civil servants or building plans, I have occasionally tried to provide, for those interested, a glimpse of reality. The reader of discrimination will guess that these glimpses of the truth are based on no ordinary experience. In the expectation, moreover, that some readers will have less discrimination than others, I have been careful to hint, occasionally, casually, at the vast amount of research upon which my theories are founded. Let the reader picture to himself the wall charts, card index cabinets, calculating machines, slide rules, and reference works that may be thought the indispensable background to a study such as this. Let him then be assured that the reality dwarfs all his imagining, and that the truths here revealed are the work not merely of an admittedly gifted individual but of a vast and costly research establishment. An occasional reader may feel that more detailed description should have been given of the experiments and calculations upon which these theories rest. Let him reflect, however, that a volume so elaborate would take longer to read and cost more to buy.

While it is undeniable that each one of these essays embodies the results from years of patient investigation, it must not be supposed that all has yet been told. The recent discovery in a certain field of warfare that the number of the enemy killed varies inversely with the number of generals on one's own side has opened a whole new field of research. A new significance has been quite recently attributed to the illegibility of signatures, the attempt being made to fix the point in a successful executive career at which the handwriting becomes meaningless even to the executive himself. New developments occur almost daily, making it virtually certain that later editions of this work will quickly supersede the first.

I wish to thank the editors who have given permission to reprint certain of these essays. Pride of place must go to the editor of *The Economist*, the journal in which Parkinson's law was first revealed to mankind. To the same editor I am indebted for permission to reprint the essay on "Directors and Councils," as also that on "Pension Point." Certain of the other articles have also appeared previously in *Harper's Magazine* and *The Reporter*.

To the artist, Robert C. Osborn, I am deeply grateful for adding a touch of frivolity to a work that might otherwise have seemed too technical for the general reader. To the publishers I am indebted for their encouragement, without which I should have attempted little and achieved still less. Last of all, I place on record the gratitude I feel toward the higher mathematician with whose science the reader is occasionally blinded and to whom (but for other reasons) this book is dedicated.

C. NORTHCOTE PARKINSON

Singapore
1957

CONTENTS

xi

PARKINSON'S LAW

1

PARKINSON'S LAW
OR THE RISING PYRAMID

WORK EXPANDS so as to fill the time available for its completion. General recognition of this fact is shown in the proverbial phrase "It is the busiest man who has time to spare." Thus, an elderly lady of leisure can spend the entire day in writing and dispatching a postcard to her niece at Bognor Regis. An hour will be spent in finding the postcard, another in hunting for spectacles, half an hour in a search for the address, an hour and a quarter in composition, and twenty minutes in deciding whether or not to take an umbrella when going to the mailbox in the next street. The total effort that would occupy a busy man for three minutes all told may in this fashion leave another person prostrate after a day of doubt, anxiety, and toil.

Granted that work (and especially paperwork) is thus elastic in its demands on time, it is manifest that there need be little or no relationship between the work to be done and the size of the staff to which it may be assigned. A lack of real activity does not, of necessity, result in leisure. A lack of occupation is not necessarily revealed by a manifest idleness. The thing to be done swells in importance and complexity in a direct ratio with the time to be spent. This fact is widely recognized, but less attention has been paid to its wider implications, more especially in the field of public administration. Politicians and taxpayers have assumed (with occasional phases of doubt) that a rising total in the number of civil servants must reflect a growing volume of work to be done. Cynics, in questioning this belief, have

imagined that the multiplication of officials must have left some of them idle or all of them able to work for shorter hours. But this is a matter in which faith and doubt seem equally misplaced. The fact is that the number of the officials and the quantity of the work are not related to each other at all. The rise in the total of those employed is governed by Parkinson's Law and would be much the same whether the volume of the work were to increase, diminish, or even disappear. The importance of Parkinson's Law lies in the fact that it is a law of growth based upon an analysis of the factors by which that growth is controlled.

The validity of this recently discovered law must rest mainly on statistical proofs, which will follow. Of more interest to the general reader is the explanation of the factors underlying the general tendency to which this law gives definition. Omitting technicalities (which are numerous) we may distinguish at the outset two motive forces. They can be represented for the present purpose by two almost axiomatic statements, thus: (1) "An official wants to multiply subordinates, not rivals" and (2) "Officials make work for each other."

To comprehend Factor 1, we must picture a civil servant, called A, who finds himself overworked. Whether this overwork is real or imaginary is immaterial, but we should observe, in passing, that A's sensation (or illusion) might easily result from his own decreasing energy: a normal symptom of middle age. For this real or imagined overwork there are, broadly speaking, three possible remedies. He may resign; he may ask to halve the work with a colleague called B; he may demand the assistance of two subordinates, to be called C and D. There is probably no instance in history, however, of A choosing any but the third alternative. By resignation he would lose his pension rights. By having B appointed, on his own level in the hierarchy, he would merely bring in a rival for promotion to W's vacancy when W (at long last) retires. So A would rather have C and D, junior men, below him. They will add to his consequence and, by dividing the work into two categories, as between C and D, he will have the merit of being the only man who comprehends them both. It is essential to realize at this point that C and D are, as it were, inseparable. To appoint C alone would have been impossible. Why? Because C, if by himself, would divide the work with A and so assume almost the equal status that has been refused in the first instance to B; a status the more emphasized if C is A's only possible successor. Subordinates must thus number two or more, each being thus kept in order by fear of the other's promotion. When C complains in turn of being overworked (as he certainly will) A will, with the concurrence of C, advise the appointment of two assistants to help C. But he can then avert internal friction only by advising the appointment of two more assistants to help D, whose position is much the same. With this recruitment of E, F, G, and H the promotion of A is now practically certain.

Seven officials are now doing what one did before. This is where Factor 2 comes into operation. For these seven make so much work for each other that all are fully occupied and A is actually working harder than ever. An incoming document may well come before each of them in turn. Official E decides that it falls within the province of F, who places a draft reply before C, who amends it drastically before consulting D, who asks G to deal with it. But G goes on leave at this point, handing the file over to H, who drafts a minute that is signed by D and returned to C, who revises his draft accordingly and lays the new version before A.

What does A do? He would have every excuse for signing the thing unread, for he has many other matters on his mind. Knowing now that he is to succeed W next year, he has to decide whether C or D should succeed to his own office. He had to agree to G's going on leave even if not yet strictly entitled to it. He is worried whether H should not have gone instead, for reasons of health. He has looked pale recently — partly but not solely because of his domestic troubles. Then there is the business of F's special increment of salary for the period of the conference and E's application for transfer to the Ministry of Pensions. A has heard that D is in love with a married typist and that G and F are no longer on speaking terms — no one seems to know why. So A might be tempted to sign C's draft and have done with it. But A is a conscientious man. Beset as he is with problems created by his colleagues for themselves and for him — created by the mere fact of these officials' existence — he is not the man to shirk his duty. He reads through the draft with care, deletes the fussy paragraphs added by C and H, and restores the thing back to the form preferred in the first instance by the able (if quarrelsome) F. He corrects the English — none of these young men can write grammatically — and finally produces the same reply he would have written if officials C to H had never been born. Far more people have taken far longer to produce the same result. No one has been idle. All have done their best. And it is late in the evening before A finally quits his office and begins the return journey to Ealing. The last of

6

the office lights are being turned off in the gathering dusk that marks the end of another day's administrative toil. Among the last to leave, A reflects with bowed shoulders and a wry smile that late hours, like gray hairs, are among the penalties of success.

From this description of the factors at work the student of political science will recognize that administrators are more or less bound to multiply. Nothing has yet been said, however, about the period of time likely to elapse between the date of A's appointment and the date from which we can calculate the pensionable service of H. Vast masses of statistical evidence have been collected and it is from a study of this data that Parkinson's Law has been deduced. Space will not allow of detailed analysis but the reader will be interested to know that research began in the British Navy Estimates. These were chosen because the Admiralty's responsibilities are more easily measurable than those of, say, the Board of Trade. The question is merely one of numbers and tonnage. Here are some typical figures. The strength of the Navy in 1914 could be shown as 146,000 officers and men, 3249 dockyard officials and clerks, and 57,000 dockyard workmen. By 1928 there were only 100,000 officers and men and only 62,439 workmen, but the dockyard officials and clerks by then numbered 4558. As for warships, the strength in 1928 was a mere fraction of what it had been in 1914 — fewer than 20 capital ships in commission as compared with 62. Over the same period the Admiralty officials had increased in number from 2000 to 3569, providing (as was remarked) "a magnificent navy on land." These figures are more clearly set forth in tabular form.

ADMIRALTY STATISTICS

Year	Capital ships in commission	Officers and men in R.N.	Dockyard workers	Dockyard officials and clerks	Admiralty officials
1914	62	146,000	57,000	3249	2000
1928	20	100,000	62,439	4558	3569
Increase or Decrease	−67.74%	−31.5%	+9.54%	+40.28%	+78.45%

The criticism voiced at the time centered on the ratio between the numbers of those available for fighting and those available only for administration. But that comparison is not to the present purpose. What we have to note is that the 2000 officials of 1914 had become the 3569 of 1928; and that this growth was unrelated to any possible increase in their work. The Navy during that period had diminished, in point of fact, by a third in men and two-thirds in ships. Nor, from 1922 onward, was its strength even expected to increase; for its total of ships (unlike its total of officials) was limited by the Washington Naval Agreement of that year. Here we have then a 78 per cent increase over a period of fourteen years; an average of 5.6 per cent increase a year on the earlier total. In fact, as we shall see, the rate of increase was not as regular as that. All we have to consider, at this stage, is the percentage rise over a given period.

Can this rise in the total number of civil servants be accounted for except on the assumption that such a total must always rise by a law governing its growth? It might be urged at this point that the period under discussion

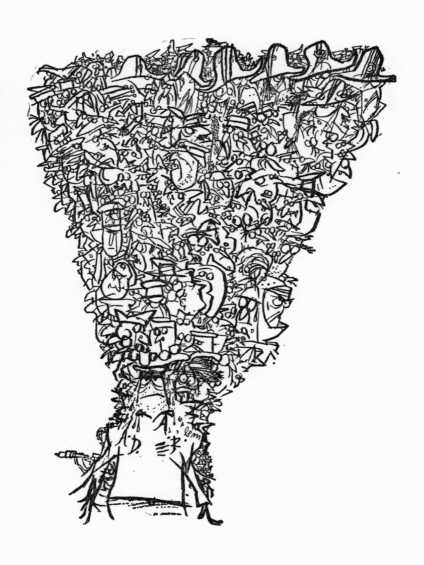

was one of rapid development in naval technique. The use of the flying machine was no longer confined to the eccentric. Electrical devices were being multiplied and elaborated. Submarines were tolerated if not approved. Engineer officers were beginning to be regarded as almost human. In so revolutionary an age we might expect that storekeepers would have more elaborate inventories to compile. We might not wonder to see more draughtsmen on the payroll, more designers, more technicians and scientists. But these, the dockyard officials, increased only by 40 per cent in number when the men of Whitehall increased their total by nearly 80 per cent. For every new foreman or electrical engineer at Portsmouth there had to be two more clerks at Charing Cross. From this we might be tempted to conclude, provisionally, that the rate of increase in administrative staff is likely to be double that of the technical staff at a time when the actually useful strength (in this case, of seamen) is being reduced by 31.5 per cent. It has been proved statistically, however, that this last percentage is irrelevant. The officials would have multiplied at the same rate had there been no actual seamen at all.

It would be interesting to follow the further progress by which the 8118 Admiralty staff of 1935 came to number 33,788 by 1954. But the staff of the Colonial Office affords a better field of study during a period of imperial decline. Admiralty statistics are complicated by factors (like the Fleet Air Arm) that make comparison difficult as between one year and the next. The Colonial Office growth is more significant in that it is more purely administrative. Here the relevant statistics are as follows:

1935	1939	1943	1947	1954
372	450	817	1139	1661

Before showing what the rate of increase is, we must observe that the extent of this department's responsibilities
was far from constant during these twenty years. The
colonial territories were not much altered in area or population between 1935 and 1939. They were considerably diminished by 1943, certain areas being in enemy hands.
They were increased again in 1947, but have since then
shrunk steadily from year to year as successive colonies
achieve self-government. It would be rational to suppose
that these changes in the scope of Empire would be reflected in the size of its central administration. But a glance
at the figures is enough to convince us that the staff totals
represent nothing but so many stages in an inevitable increase. And this increase, although related to that observed
in other departments, has nothing to do with the size — or
even the existence — of the Empire. What are the percent-
ages of increase? We must ignore, for this purpose, the
rapid increase in staff which accompanied the diminution of
responsibility during World War II. We should note
rather, the peacetime rates of increase: over 5.24 per cent
between 1935 and 1939, and 6.55 per cent between 1947
and 1954. This gives an average increase of 5.89 per cent
each year, a percentage markedly similar to that already
found in the Admiralty staff increase between 1914 and
1928.

Further and detailed statistical analysis of departmental
staffs would be inappropriate in such a work as this. It

is hoped, however, to reach a tentative conclusion regarding the time likely to elapse between a given official's first appointment and the later appointment of his two or more assistants.

Dealing with the problem of pure staff accumulation, all our researches so far completed point to an average increase of 5.75 per cent per year. This fact established, it now becomes possible to state Parkinson's Law in mathematical form: In any public administrative department not actually at war, the staff increase may be expected to follow this formula —

$$x = \frac{2k^m + l}{n}$$

k is the number of staff seeking promotion through the appointment of subordinates; l represents the difference between the ages of appointment and retirement; m is the number of man-hours devoted to answering minutes within the department; and n is the number of effective units being administered. x will be the number of new staff required each year. Mathematicians will realize, of course, that to find the percentage increase they must multiply x by 100 and divide by the total of the previous year, thus:

$$\frac{100 \ (2k^m + l)}{yn} \ \%$$

where y represents the total original staff. This figure will invariably prove to be between 5.17 per cent and 6.56 per cent, irrespective of any variation in the amount of work (if any) to be done.

The discovery of this formula and of the general principles upon which it is based has, of course, no political value. No attempt has been made to inquire whether departments *ought* to grow in size. Those who hold that this growth is essential to gain full employment are fully entitled to their opinion. Those who doubt the stability of an economy based upon reading each other's minutes are equally entitled to theirs. It would probably be premature to attempt at this stage any inquiry into the quantitative ratio that should exist between the administrators and the administered. Granted, however, that a maximum ratio exists, it should soon be possible to ascertain by formula how many years will elapse before that ratio, in any given community, will be reached. The forecasting of such a result will again have no political value. Nor can it be sufficiently emphasized that Parkinson's Law is a purely scientific discovery, inapplicable except in theory to the politics of the day. It is not the business of the botanist to eradicate the weeds. Enough for him if he can tell us just how fast they grow.

2

THE WILL OF THE PEOPLE
OR ANNUAL GENERAL MEETING

WE ARE ALL familiar with the basic difference between
English and French parliamentary institutions; copied respectively by such other assemblies as derive from each.
We all realize that this main difference has nothing to do
with national temperament, but stems from their seating
plans. The British, being brought up on team games, enter
their House of Commons in the spirit of those who would
rather be doing something else. If they cannot be playing
golf or tennis, they can at least pretend that politics is a
game with very similar rules. But for this device, Parliament would arouse even less interest than it does. So the
British instinct is to form two opposing teams, with referee
and linesmen, and let them debate until they exhaust themselves. The House of Commons is so arranged that the
individual Member is practically compelled to take one
side or the other before he knows what the arguments are,
or even (in some cases) before he knows the subject of
the dispute. His training from birth has been to play for
his side, and this saves him from any undue mental effort.
Sliding into a seat toward the end of a speech, he knows
exactly how to take up the argument from the point it has

reached. If the speaker is on his own side of the House, he will say "Hear, hear!" If he is on the opposite side, he can safely say "Shame!" or merely "Oh!" At some later stage he may have time to ask his neighbor what the debate is supposed to be about. Strictly speaking, however, there is no need for him to do this. He knows enough in any case not to kick into his own goal. The men who sit opposite

are entirely wrong and all their arguments are so much drivel. The men on his own side are statesmanlike, by contrast, and their speeches a singular blend of wisdom, eloquence, and moderation. Nor does it make the slightest difference whether he learned his politics at Harrow or in following the fortunes of Aston Villa. In either school he will have learned when to cheer and when to groan. But the British system depends entirely on its seating plan. If the benches did not face each other, no one could tell truth from falsehood — wisdom from folly — unless in-

15

deed by listening to it all. But to listen to it all would be ridiculous, for half the speeches must of necessity be nonsense.

In France the initial mistake was made of seating the representatives in a semicircle, all facing the chair. The resulting confusion could be imagined if it were not notorious. No real opposing teams could be formed and no one could tell (without listening) which argument was the more cogent. There was the further handicap of all the proceedings being in French — an example the United States wisely refused to follow. But the French system is bad enough even when the linguistic difficulty does not arise. Instead of having two sides, one in the right and the other in the wrong — so that the issue is clear from the outset — the French form a multitude of teams facing in all directions. With the field in such confusion, the game cannot even begin. Basically their representatives are of the Right or of the Left, according to where they sit. This is a perfectly sound scheme. The French have not gone to the extreme of seating people in alphabetical order. But the semicircular chamber allows of subtle distinctions between the various degrees of rightness and leftness. There is none of the clear-cut British distinction between rightness and wrongness. One deputy is described, politically, as to the left of Monsieur Untel but well to the right of Monsieur Quelquechose. What is anyone to make of that? What should we make of it even in English? What do they make of it themselves? The answer is, "Nothing."

All this is generally known. What is less generally recognized is that the paramount importance of the seating

plan applies to other assemblies and meetings, interna·
tional, national, and local. It applies, moreover, to meetings round a table such as occur at a Round Table Conference. A moment's thought will convince us that a
Square Table Conference would be something totally
different and a Long Table Conference would be different
again. These differences do not merely affect the length
and acrimony of the discussion; they also affect what (if
anything) is decided. Rarely, as we know, will the voting
relate to the merits of the case. The final decision is influenced by a variety of factors, few of which need concern us at the moment. We should note, however, that the
issue is actually *decided*, in the end, by the votes of the
center bloc. This would not be true in the House of Commons, where no such bloc is allowed to develop. But at
other conferences the center bloc is all important. This
bloc essentially comprises the following elements:

a. Those who have failed to master any one of the
memoranda written in advance and showered weeks beforehand on all those who are expected to be present.

b. Those who are too stupid to follow the proceedings
at all. These are readily distinguishable by their tendency
to mutter to each other: "What is the fellow talking
about?"

c. Those who are deaf. They sit with their hands cup-
ping their ears, growling "I wish people would speak up."

d. Those who were dead drunk in the small hours and
have turned up (heaven knows why) with a splitting head-
ache and a conviction that nothing matters either way.

e. The senile, whose chief pride is in being as fit as
ever — fitter indeed than a lot of these younger men. "I

walked here," they whisper. "Pretty good for a man of eighty-two, what?"

f. The feeble, who have weakly promised to support both sides and don't know what to do about it. They are of two minds as to whether they should abstain from voting or pretend to be sick.

Toward capturing the votes of the center bloc the first step is to identify and count the members. That done, everything else depends on where they are to sit. The best technique is to detail off known and stalwart supporters to enter into conversation with named middle-bloc types before the meeting actually begins. In this preliminary chat the stalwarts will carefully avoid mentioning the main subject of debate. They will be trained to use the opening gambits listed below, corresponding to the categories a to f, into which the middle bloc naturally falls:

a. "Waste of time, I call it, producing all these documents. I have thrown most of mine away."

b. "I expect we shall be dazzled by eloquence before long. I often wish people would talk less and come to the point. They are too clever by half, if you ask me."

c. "The acoustics of this hall are simply terrible. You would have thought these scientific chaps could do something about it. For half the time I CAN'T HEAR WHAT IS BEING SAID. CAN YOU?"

d. "What a rotten place to meet! I think there is something the matter with the ventilation. It makes me feel almost unwell. What about you?"

e. "My goodness, I don't know how you do it! Tell me the secret. Is it what you have for breakfast?"

f. "There's so much to be said on both sides of the

question that I really don't know which side to support.
What do you feel about it?"

If these gambits are correctly played, each stalwart will
start a lively conversation, in the midst of which he will
steer his middle-blocsman toward the forum. As he does
this, another stalwart will place himself just *ahead* of the
pair and moving in the same direction. The drill is best
illustrated by a concrete example. We will suppose that
stalwart X (Mr. Sturdy) is steering middle-blocsman Y
(Mr. Waverley, type f) toward a seat *near the front.* Ahead
goes stalwart Z (Mr. Staunch), who presently takes a seat
without appearing to notice the two men following him.
Staunch turns in the opposite direction and waves to
someone in the distance. Then he leans over to make a few
remarks to the man in front of him. Only when Waverley
has sat down will Staunch presently turn toward him and
say, "My dear fellow — how nice to see you!" Only some
minutes later again will he catch sight of Sturdy and start
visibly with surprise. "Hallo, Sturdy — I didn't think you
would be here!" "I've recovered now," replies Sturdy. "It
was only a chill." The seating order is thus made to appear completely accidental, casual, and friendly. That
completes Phase I of the operation, and it would be much
the same whatever the exact category in which the middle-
blocsman is believed to fall.

Phase II has to be adjusted according to the character
of the man to be influenced. In the case of Waverley
(Type f) the object in Phase II is to avoid any discussion
of the matter at issue but to produce the impression that
the thing is already decided. Seated near the front, Waverley will be unable to see much of the other members and

can be given the impression that they practically all think
alike.

"Really," says Sturdy, "I don't know why I bothered to
come. I gather that Item Four is pretty well agreed. All
the fellows I meet seem to have made up their minds to
vote for it." (Or against it, as the case may be.)

"Curious," says Staunch. "I was just going to say the
same thing. The issue hardly seems to be in doubt."

"I had not really made up my own mind," says Sturdy.

"There was much to be said on either side. But opposition would really be a waste of time. What do you think, Waverley?"

"Well," says Waverley, "I must admit that I find the question rather baffling. On the one hand, there is good reason to agree to the motion ... As against that ... Do you think it will pass?"

"My dear Waverley, I would trust your judgment in this. You were saying just now that it is already agreed."

"Oh, was I? Well, there does seem to be a majority.
... Or perhaps I should say ... "

"Thank you, Waverley," says Staunch, "for your opinion. I think just the same but am particularly interested
to find you agree with me. There is no one whose opinion
I value more."

Sturdy, meanwhile, is leaning over to talk to someone
in the row behind. What he actually says, in a low voice,
is this, "How is your wife now? Is she out of hospital?"
When he turns back again, however, it is to announce that
the people behind all think the same. The motion is as
good as passed. And so it is if the drill goes according to
plan.

While the other side has been busy preparing speeches
and phrasing amendments, the side with the superior technique will have concentrated on pinning each middle-
blocsman between two reliable supporters. When the
crucial moment comes, the raising of a hand on either
side will practically compel the waverer to follow suit.
Should he be actually asleep, as often happens with middle-
blocsman in categories d and e, his hand will be raised for
him by the member on his right. This rule is merely to
obviate both his hands being raised, a gesture that has
been known to attract unfavorable comment. With the
middle bloc thus secured, the motion will be carried with
a comfortable margin; or else rejected, if that is thought
preferable. In nearly every matter of controversy to be
decided by the will of the people, we can assume that the
people who will decide are members of the middle bloc.
Delivery of speeches is therefore a waste of time. The
one party will never agree and the other party has agreed

already. Remains the middle bloc, the members of which divide into those who cannot hear what is being said and those who would not understand it even if they did. To secure their votes what is needed is primarily the example of others voting on either side of them. Their votes can thus be swayed by accident. How much better, by contrast, to sway them by design!

HIGH FINANCE
OR THE POINT OF VANISHING INTEREST

PEOPLE WHO understand high finance are of two kinds: those who have vast fortunes of their own and those who have nothing at all. To the actual millionaire a million dollars is something real and comprehensible. To the applied mathematician and the lecturer in economics (assuming both to be practically starving) a million dollars is at least as real as a thousand, they having never possessed either sum. But the world is full of people who fall between these two categories, knowing nothing of millions but well accustomed to think in thousands, and it is of these that finance committees are mostly comprised. The result is a phenomenon that has often been observed but never yet investigated. It might be termed the Law of Triviality. Briefly stated, it means that the time spent on any item of the agenda will be in inverse proportion to the sum involved.

On second thoughts, the statement that this law has never been investigated is not entirely accurate. Some work has actually been done in this field, but the investigators pursued a line of inquiry that led them nowhere. They assumed that the greatest significance should attach to the order in which items of the agenda are taken. They assumed, further, that most of the available time will be spent on items one to seven and that the later items will be allowed automatically to pass. The result is well known. The derision with which Dr. Guggenheim's lecture was received at the Muttworth Conference may have been thought excessive at the time, but all further discussions on this topic have tended to show that his critics were right. Years had been wasted in a research of which the basic assumptions were wrong. We realize now that position on the agenda is a minor consideration, so far, at least, as this problem is concerned. We consider also that Dr. Guggenheim was lucky to escape as he did, in his underwear. Had he dared to put his lame conclusions before the later conference in September, he would have faced something more than derision. The view would have been taken that he was deliberately wasting time.

If we are to make further progress in this investigation we must ignore all that has so far been done. We must start at the beginning and understand fully the way in which a finance committee actually works. For the sake of the general reader this can be put in dramatic form thus:

Chairman   We come now to Item Nine. Our Treasurer, Mr. McPhail, will report.

Mr. McPhail   The estimate for the Atomic Reactor is before you, sir, set forth in Appendix H of the subcommittee's report. You will see that the general design and layout has been approved by Professor McFission. The total cost will amount to $10,000,000. The contractors, Messrs. Mc-Nab and McHash, consider that the work should be complete by April, 1959. Mr. McFee, the consulting engineer, warns us that we should not count on completion before October, at the earliest. In this view he is supported by Dr. McHeap, the well-known geophysicist, who refers to the probable need for piling at the lower end of the site. The plan of the main building is before you — see Appendix IX — and the blueprint is laid on the table. I shall be glad to give any further information that members of this committee may require.

Chairman   Thank you, Mr. McPhail, for your very lucid explanation of the plan as proposed. I will now invite the members present to give us their views.

It is necessary to pause at this point and consider what views the members are likely to have. Let us suppose that they number eleven, including the Chairman but excluding the Secretary. Of these eleven members, four — including the chairman — do not know what a reactor is. Of the remainder, three do not know what it is for. Of those who know its purpose, only two have the least idea of what it should cost. One of these is Mr. Isaacson, the other is Mr. Brickworth. Either is in a position to say something. We may suppose that Mr. Isaacson is the first to speak.

Mr. Isaacson   Well, Mr. Chairman. I could wish that I felt more confidence in our contractors and consultant. Had we gone to Professor Levi in the first instance, and had the contract been given to Messrs. David and Goliath, I should have been happier about the whole scheme. Mr. Lyon-Daniels would not have wasted our time with wild guesses about the possible delay in completion, and Dr.

Moses Bullrush would have told us definitely whether piling would be wanted or not.

Chairman   I am sure we all appreciate Mr. Isaacson's anxiety to complete this work in the best possible way. I feel, however, that it is rather late in the day to call in new technical advisers. I admit that the main contract has still to be signed, but we have already spent very large sums. If we reject the advice for which we have paid, we shall have to pay as much again.
(Other members murmur agreement.)

Mr. Isaacson   I should like my observation to be minuted.

Chairman   Certainly. Perhaps Mr. Brickworth also has something to say on this matter?

Now Mr. Brickworth is almost the only man there who knows what he is talking about. There is a great deal he could say. He distrusts that round figure of $10,000,000. Why should it come out to exactly that? Why need they demolish the old building to make room for the new approach? Why is so large a sum set aside for "contingencies"? And who is McHeap, anyway? Is he the man who was sued last year by the Trickle and Driedup Oil Corporation? But Brickworth does not know where to begin. The other members could not read the blueprint if he referred to it. He would have to begin by explaining what a reactor is and no one there would admit that he did not already know. Better to say nothing.

Mr. Brickworth   I have no comment to make.

Chairman   Does any other member wish to speak? Very
well. I may take it then that the plans and estimates are
approved? Thank you. May I now sign the main contract
on your behalf? *(Murmur of agreement)* Thank you. We
can now move on to Item Ten.

Allowing a few seconds for rustling papers and unrolling
diagrams, the time spent on Item Nine will have been just
two minutes and a half. The meeting is going well. But

some members feel uneasy about Item Nine. They wonder inwardly whether they have really been pulling their weight. It is too late to query that reactor scheme, but they would like to demonstrate, before the meeting ends, that they are alive to all that is going on.

Chairman   Item Ten. Bicycle shed for the use of the clerical staff. An estimate has been received from Messrs. Bodger and Woodworm, who undertake to complete the work for the sum of $2350. Plans and specification are before you, gentlemen.

Mr. Softleigh   Surely, Mr. Chairman, this sum is excessive. I note that the roof is to be of aluminum. Would not asbestos be cheaper?

Mr. Holdfast   I agree with Mr. Softleigh about the cost, but the roof should, in my opinion, be of galvanized iron. I incline to think that the shed could be built for $2000, or even less.

Mr. Daring   I would go further, Mr. Chairman. I question whether this shed is really necessary. We do too much for our staff as it is. They are never satisfied, that is the trouble. They will be wanting garages next.

Mr. Holdfast   No, I can't support Mr. Daring on this occasion. I think that the shed is needed. It is a question of material and cost . . .

The debate is fairly launched. A sum of $2350 is well within everybody's comprehension. Everyone can visualize a bicycle shed. Discussion goes on, therefore, for forty-five minutes, with the possible result of saving some $300. Members at length sit back with a feeling of achievement.

Chairman   Item Eleven. Refreshments supplied at meetings of the Joint Welfare Committee. Monthly, $4.75.

Mr. Softleigh   What type of refreshment is supplied on these occasions?

Chairman   Coffee, I understand.

Mr. Holdfast   And this means an annual charge of — let me see — $57?

Chairman   That is so.

Mr. Daring   Well, really, Mr. Chairman. I question whether this is justified. How long do these meetings last?

Now begins an even more acrimonious debate. There may be members of the committee who might fail to distinguish between asbestos and galvanized iron, but every man there knows about coffee — what it is, how it should be made, where it should be bought — and whether indeed it should be bought at all. This item on the agenda will occupy the members for an hour and a quarter, and they will end by asking the Secretary to procure further information, leaving the matter to be decided at the next meeting.

It would be natural to ask at this point whether a still smaller sum — $20, perhaps, or $10 — would occupy the Finance Committee for a proportionately longer time. On this point, it must be admitted, we are still ignorant. Our tentative conclusion must be that there is a point at which the whole tendency is reversed, the committee members

concluding that the sum is beneath their notice. Research has still to establish the point at which this reversal occurs. The transition from the $50 debate (an hour and a quarter) to the $20 debate (two and a half minutes) is indeed an abrupt one. It would be the more interesting to establish the exact point at which it occurs. More than that, it would be of practical value. Supposing, for example, that the point of vanishing interest is represented by the sum of $35, the Treasurer with an item of $62.80 on the agenda might well decide to present it as two items, one of $30.00 and the other of $32.80, with an evident saving in time and effort.

Conclusions at this juncture can be merely tentative, but there is some reason to suppose that the point of vanishing interest represents the sum the individual committee member is willing to lose on a bet or subscribe to a charity. An inquiry on these lines conducted on racecourses and in Methodist chapels, might go far toward solving the problem. Far greater difficulty may be encountered in attempting to discover the exact point at which the sum involved becomes too large to discuss at all. One thing apparent, however, is that the time spent on $10,000,000 and on $10 may well prove to be the same. The present estimated time of two and a half minutes is by no means exact, but there is clearly a space of time — something between two and four and a half minutes — which suffices equally for the largest and the smallest sums.

Much further investigation remains to be done, but the final results, when published, cannot fail to be of absorbing interest and of immediate value to mankind.

4

DIRECTORS AND COUNCILS
OR COEFFICIENT OF INEFFICIENCY

THE LIFE CYCLE of the committee is so basic to our knowledge of current affairs that it is surprising more attention has not been paid to the science of comitology. The first and most elementary principle of this science is that a committee is organic rather than mechanical in its nature: it is not a structure but a plant. It takes root and grows, it flowers, wilts, and dies, scattering the seed from which other committees will bloom in their turn. Only those who bear this principle in mind can make real headway in understanding the structure and history of modern government.

Committees, it is nowadays accepted, fall broadly into two categories, those (a) from which the individual member has something to gain; and those (b) to which the individual member merely has something to contribute. Examples of the B group, however, are relatively unimportant for our purpose; indeed some people doubt whether they are committees at all. It is from the more robust A group that we can learn most readily the principles which are common (with modifications) to all. Of the A group the most deeply rooted and luxuriant committees are those which confer the most power and prestige upon their mem-

33

bers. In most parts of the world these committees are called "cabinets." This chapter is based on an extensive study of national cabinets, over space and time.

When first examined under the microscope, the cabinet council usually appears — to comitologists, historians, and even to the people who appoint cabinets — to consist ideally of five. With that number the plant is viable, allowing for two members to be absent or sick at any one time. Five members are easy to collect and, when collected, can act

with competence, secrecy, and speed. Of these original members four may well be versed, respectively, in finance, foreign policy, defense, and law. The fifth, who has failed to master any of these subjects, usually becomes the chairman or prime minister.

Whatever the apparent convenience might be of restricting the membership to five, however, we discover by observation that the total number soon rises to seven or nine. The usual excuse given for this increase, which is almost invariable (exceptions being found, however, in Luxembourg and Honduras), is the need for special knowledge on more than four topics. In fact, however, there is another and more potent reason for adding to the team. For in a cabinet of nine it will be found that policy is made by three, information supplied by two, and financial warning uttered by one. With the neutral chairman, that accounts for seven, the other two appearing at first glance to be merely ornamental. This allocation of duties was first noted in Britain in about 1639, but there can be no doubt that the folly of including more than three able and talkative men in one committee had been discovered long before then. We know little as yet about the function of the two silent members but we have good reason to believe that a cabinet, in this second stage of development, might be unworkable without them.

There are cabinets in the world (those of Costa Rica, Ecuador, Northern Ireland, Liberia, the Philippines, Uruguay, and Panama will at once be called to mind) which have remained in this second stage — that is, have restricted their membership to nine. These remain, however, a small minority. Elsewhere and in larger territories cabinets have generally been subject to a law of growth. Other members come to be admitted, some with a claim to special knowledge but more because of their nuisance value when excluded. Their opposition can be silenced only by implicating them in every decision that is made. As they are brought in (and placated) one after another, the total membership rises from ten toward twenty. In this third stage of cabinets, there are already considerable drawbacks.

The most immediately obvious of these disadvantages is the difficulty of assembling people at the same place, date, and time. One member is going away on the 18th, whereas another does not return until the 21st. A third is never free on Tuesdays, and a fourth never available before 5 P.M. But that is only the beginning of the trouble, for, once most of them are collected, there is a far greater chance of members proving to be elderly, tiresome, inaudible, and deaf. Relatively few were chosen from any idea that they are or could be or have ever been useful. A majority perhaps were brought in merely to conciliate some outside group. Their tendency is therefore to report what happens to the group they represent. All secrecy is lost and, worst of all, members begin to prepare their speeches. They address the meeting and tell their friends afterwards about what they imagine they have said. But the more these merely representative members assert themselves, the more loudly do other outside groups clamor for representation. Internal parties form and seek to gain strength by further recruitment. The total of twenty is reached and passed. And thereby, quite suddenly, the cabinet enters the fourth and final stage of its history.

For at this point of cabinet development (between 20 and 22 members) the whole committee suffers an abrupt organic or chemical change. The nature of this change is easy to trace and comprehend. In the first place, the five members who matter will have taken to meeting beforehand. With decisions already reached, little remains for

37

the nominal executive to do. And, as a consequence of this, all resistance to the committee's expansion comes to an end. More members will not waste more time; for the whole meeting is, in any case, a waste of time. So the pressure of outside groups is temporarily satisfied by the admission of their representatives, and decades may elapse before they realize how illusory their gain has been. With the doors wide open, membership rises from 20 to 30, from 30 to 40. There may soon be an instance of such a membership reaching the thousand mark. But this does not matter. For the cabinet has already ceased to be a real cabinet, and has been succeeded in its old functions by some other body.

Five times in English history the plant has moved through its life cycle. It would admittedly be difficult to prove that the first incarnation of the cabinet — the English Council of the Crown, now called the House of Lords — ever had a membership as small as five. When we first hear of it, indeed, its more intimate character had already been lost, with a hereditary membership varying from 29 to 50. Its subsequent expansion, however, kept pace with its loss of power. In round figures, it had 60 members in 1601, 140 in 1661, 220 in 1760, 400 in 1850, 650 in 1911, and 850 in 1952.

At what point in this progression did the inner committee appear in the womb of the peerage? It appeared in about 1257, its members being called the Lords of the King's Council and numbering less than 10. They numbered no more than 11 in 1378, and as few still in 1410. Then, from the reign of Henry V, they began to multiply. The 20 of 1433 had become the 41 of 1504, the total reaching 172 before the council finally ceased to meet.

Within the King's Council there developed the cabinet's third incarnation — the Privy Council — with an original membership of nine. It rose to 20 in 1540, to 29 in 1547, and to 44 in 1558. The Privy Council as it ceased to be effective increased proportionately in size. It had 47 members in 1679, 67 in 1723, 200 in 1902, and 300 in 1951.

Within the Privy Council there developed the junto or Cabinet Council, which effectively superseded the former in about 1615. Numbering 8 when we first hear of it, its members had come to number 12 by about 1700, and 20 by 1725. The Cabinet Council was then superseded in about 1740 by an inner group, since called simply the Cabinet. Its development is best studied in tabular form. This is shown in Table I.

TABLE I – GROWTH OF THE ENGLISH CABINET

1740	5	1885	16	1945	16
1784	7	1900	20	1945	20
1801	12	1915	22	1949	17
1841	14	1935	22	1954	18
		1939	23		

From 1939, it will be apparent, there has been a struggle to save this institution; a struggle similar to the attempts made to save the Privy Council during the reign of Queen Elizabeth I. The Cabinet appeared to be in its decline in 1940, with an inner cabinet (of 5, 7, or 9 members) ready to take its place. The issue, however, remains in doubt. It is just possible that the British cabinet is still an important body.

Compared with the cabinet of Britain, the cabinet of the

United States has shown an extraordinary resistance to political inflation. It had the appropriate number of 5 members in 1789, still only 7 by 1840, 9 by 1901, 10 by 1913, 11 by 1945, and then — against tradition — had come down to 10 again by 1953. Whether this attempt, begun in 1947, to restrict the membership will succeed for long is doubtful. All experience would suggest the inevitability of the previous trend. In the meanwhile, the United States enjoys (with Guatemala and El Salvador) a reputation for cabinet-exclusiveness, having actually fewer cabinet ministers than Nicaragua or Paraguay.

How do other countries compare in this respect? The majority of non-totalitarian countries have cabinets that number between 12 and 20 members. Taking the average

TABLE II – SIZE OF CABINETS

No. of Members		No. of Members	
6	Honduras, Luxembourg	16	Iraq, Netherlands, Turkey
7	Haiti, Iceland, Switzer-land	17	Eire, Israel, Spain
		18	Egypt, Gt. Britain, Mexico
9	Costa Rica, Ecuador, N. Ireland, Liberia, Panama, Philippines, Uruguay	19	W. Germany, Greece, Indonesia, Italy
		20	Australia, Formosa, Japan
10	Guatemala, El Salvador, United States	21	Argentina, Burma, Canada, France
11	Brazil, Nicaragua, Pakistan, Paraguay	22	China
		24	E. Germany
12	Bolivia, Chile, Peru	26	Bulgaria
13	Colombia, Dominican R., Norway, Thailand	27	Cuba
		29	Rumania
14	Denmark, India, S. Africa, Sweden	32	Czechoslovakia
		35	Yugoslavia
15	Austria, Belgium, Finland, Iran, New Zealand, Portugal, Venezuela	38	USSR

of over 60 countries, we find that it comes to over 16; the most popular numbers are 15 (seven instances) and 9 (seven again). Easily the queerest cabinet is that of New Zealand, one member of which has to be announced as "Minister of Lands, Minister of Forests, Minister of Maori Affairs, Minister in charge of Maori Trust Office and of Scenery Preservation." The toastmaster at a New Zealand banquet must be equally ready to crave silence for "The Minister of Health, Minister Assistant to the Prime Minister, Minister in Charge of State Advances Corporation, Census, and Statistics Department, Public Trust Office and Publicity and Information." In other lands this oriental profusion is fortunately rare.

A study of the British example would suggest that the point of ineffectiveness in a cabinet is reached when the total membership exceeds 20 or perhaps 21. The Council of the Crown, the King's Council, the Privy Council had each passed the 20 mark when their decline began. The present British cabinet is just short of that number now, having recoiled from the abyss. We might be tempted to conclude from this that cabinets — or other committees — with a membership in excess of 21 are losing the reality of power and that those with a larger membership have already lost it. No such theory can be tenable, however, without statistical proof. Table II on the preceding page attempts to furnish part of it.

Should we be justified in drawing a line in that table under the name of France (21 cabinet members) with an explanatory note to say that the cabinet is not the real power in countries shown below that line? Some comitologists would accept that conclusion without further research. Others emphasize the need for careful investigation, more especially around the borderline of 21. But that the coefficient of inefficiency must lie between 19 and 22 is now very generally agreed.

What tentative explanation can we offer for this hypothesis? Here we must distinguish sharply between fact and theory, between the symptom and the disease. About the most obvious symptom there is little disagreement. It is known that with over 20 members present a meeting begins to change character. Conversations develop separately at either end of the table. To make himself heard, the member has therefore to rise. Once on his feet, he cannot help making a speech, if only from force of habit. "Mr. Chairman," he will begin, "I think I may assert without fear of contradiction — and I am speaking now from twenty-five (I might almost say twenty-seven) years of experience — that we must view this matter in the gravest light. A heavy responsibility rests upon us, sir, and I for one . . ." Amid all this drivel the useful men present, if there are any, exchange little notes that read, "Lunch with me tomorrow — we'll fix it then."

What else can they do? The voice drones on interminably. The orator might just as well be talking in his sleep. The committee of which he is the most useless member has ceased to matter. It is finished. It is hopeless. It is dead.

So much is certain. But the root cause of the trouble goes deeper and has still, in part, to be explored. Too many vital factors are unknown. What is the shape and size of the table? What is the average age of those present? At what hour does the committee meet? In a book for the non-specialist it would be absurd to repeat the calculations by which the first and tentative coefficient of inefficiency has been reached. It should be enough to state that prolonged research at the Institute of Comitology has given rise to a formula which is now widely (although not universally) accepted by the experts in this field. It should perhaps be explained that the investigators assumed a temperate climate, leather-padded chairs and a high level of sobriety. On this basis, the formula is as follows:

$$x = \frac{m^{\circ}(a - d)}{y + p\sqrt{b}}$$

Where m = the average number of members actually present; ° = the number of members influenced by outside pressure groups; a = the average age of the members; d = the distance in centimeters between the two members who are seated farthest from each other; y = the number of years since the cabinet or committee was first formed; p = the patience of the chairman, as measured on the Peabody scale; b = the average blood pressure of the three oldest members, taken shortly before the time of meeting. Then x = the number of members effectively present at the moment when the efficient working of the cabinet or other committee has become manifestly impossible. This is the coefficient of inefficiency and it is found to lie between 19.9 and 22.4. (The decimals represent partial attendance; those absent for a part of the meeting.)

It would be unsound to conclude, from a cursory inspection of this equation that the science of comitology is in an advanced state of development. Comitologists and subcomitologists would make no such claim, if only from

43

fear of unemployment. They emphasize, rather, that their studies have barely begun and that they are on the brink of astounding progress. Making every allowance for self-interest — which means discounting 90 per cent of what they say — we can safely assume that much work remains to do.

We should eventually be able, for example, to learn the formula by which the optimum number of committee members may be determined. Somewhere between the number of 3 (when a quorum is impossible to collect) and approximately 21 (when the whole organism begins to perish), there lies the golden number. The interesting theory has been propounded that this number must be 8. Why? Because it is the only number which all existing states (See Table II above) have agreed to avoid. Attractive as this theory may seem at first sight, it is open to one serious objection. Eight was the number preferred by King Charles I for his Committee of State. And look what happened to him!

THE SHORT LIST
OR PRINCIPLES OF SELECTION

A PROBLEM constantly before the modern administration, whether in government or business, is that of personnel selection. The inexorable working of Parkinson's Law ensures that appointments have constantly to be made and the question is always how to choose the right candidate from all who present themselves. In ascertaining the principles upon which the choice should be made, we may properly consider, under separate heads, the methods used in the past and the methods used at the present day.

Past methods, not entirely disused, fall into two main categories, the British and the Chinese. Both deserve careful consideration, if only for the reason that they were obviously more successful than any method now considered fashionable. The British method (old pattern) depended upon an interview in which the candidate had to establish his identity. He would be confronted by elderly gentlemen seated round a mahogany table who would presently ask him his name. Let us suppose that the candidate replied, "John Seymour." One of the gentlemen would then say, "Any relation of the Duke of Somerset?" To this the candidate would say, quite possibly, "No, sir." Then another gentleman would say, "Perhaps you are related, in that case, to the Bishop of Watminster?" If he said "No, sir" again, a third would ask in despair, "To whom then are you related?" In the event of the candidate's saying, "Well, my father is a fishmonger in Cheapside," the interview was virtually over. The members of the Board would exchange significant glances, one would press a bell and another tell the footman, "Throw this person out." One name could be crossed off the list without further discussion. Supposing the next candidate was Henry Molyneux and a nephew of the Earl of Sefton, his chances remained fair up to the moment when George Howard arrived and proved to be a grandson of the Duke of Norfolk. The Board encountered no serious difficulty until they had to compare the claims of the third son of a baronet with the second but illegitimate son of a viscount. Even then they could refer to a Book of Precedence. So their choice was made and often with the best results.

The Admiralty version of this British method (old pattern) was different only in its more restricted scope. The Board of Admirals were unimpressed by titled relatives as such. What they sought to establish was a service connection. The ideal candidate would reply to the second question, "Yes, Admiral Parker is my uncle. My father is Captain Foley, my grandfather Commodore Foley. My mother's father was Admiral Hardy. Commander Hardy is my uncle. My eldest brother is a Lieutenant in the Royal Marines, my next brother is a cadet at Dartmouth and my younger brother wears a sailor suit." "Ah!" the senior Admiral would say. "And what made you think of joining the Navy?" The answer to this question, however, would

scarcely matter, the clerk present having already noted the candidate as acceptable. Given a choice between two candidates, both equally acceptable by birth, a member of the Board would ask suddenly, "What was the number of the taxi you came in?" The candidate who said "I came by bus" was then thrown out. The candidate who said, truthfully, "I don't know," was rejected, and the candidate who said "Number 2351" (lying) was promptly admitted to the service as a boy with initiative. This method often produced excellent results.

The British method (new pattern) was evolved in the late nineteenth century as something more suitable for a democratic country. The Selection Committee would ask briskly, "What school were you at?" and would be told Harrow, Haileybury, or, Rugby, as the case might be. "What games do you play?" would be the next and invariable question. A promising candidate would reply, "I have played tennis for England, cricket for Yorkshire, rugby for the Harlequins, and fives for Winchester." The next question would then be "Do you play polo?" — just to prevent the candidate's thinking too highly of himself. Even without playing polo, however, he was evidently worth serious consideration. Little time, by contrast, was wasted on the man who admitted to having been educated at Wiggleworth. "Where?" the chairman would ask in astonishment, and "Where's that?" after the name had been repeated. "Oh, in *Lancashire!*" he would say at last. Just for a matter of form, some member might ask, "What games do you play?" But the reply "Table tennis for Wigan, cycling for Blackpool, and snooker for Wiggleworth" would finally delete his name from the list. There might even be some muttered comment upon people who deliberately wasted the committee's time. Here again was a method which produced good results.

The Chinese method (old pattern) was at one time so extensively copied by other nations that few people realize its Chinese origin. This is the method of Competitive Written Examination. In China under the Ming Dynasty the more promising students used to sit for the provincial examination, held every third year. It lasted three sessions of three days each. During the first session the candidate wrote three essays and composed a poem of eight couplets. During the second session he wrote five essays on a classical theme. During the third, he wrote five essays on the art of government. The successful candidates (perhaps two per cent) then sat for their final examination at the imperial capital. It lasted only one session, the candidate writing one essay on a current political problem. Of those who were successful the majority were admitted to the civil service, the man with the highest marks being destined for the highest office. The system worked fairly well.

The Chinese system was studied by Europeans between 1815 and 1830 and adopted by the English East India Company in 1832. The effectiveness of this method was investigated by a committee in 1854, with Macaulay as chairman. The result was that the system of competitive examination was introduced into the British Civil Service in 1855. An essential feature of the Chinese examinations had been their literary character. The test was in a knowledge of the classics, in an ability to write elegantly (both prose and verse) and in the stamina necessary to complete the course. All these features were faithfully incorporated in the Trevelyan-Northcote Report, and thereafter in the system it did so much to create. It was assumed that classical learning and literary ability would fit any candidate for any administrative post. It was assumed (no doubt rightly) that a scientific education would fit a candidate for nothing — except, possibly, science. It was known, finally, that it is virtually impossible to find an order of merit among people who have been examined in different subjects. Since it is impracticable to decide whether one man is better in geology than another man in physics, it is at least convenient to be able to rule them both out as useless. When all candidates alike have to write Greek or Latin verse, it is relatively easy to decide which verse is the best. Men thus selected on their classical performance were then sent forth to govern India. Those with lower marks were retained to govern England. Those with still lower marks were rejected altogether or sent to the colonies. While it would be totally wrong to describe this system as a failure, no one could claim for it the success that had attended the systems hitherto in use. There was no guarantee, to begin with, that the man with the highest marks might not turn out to be off his head; as was sometimes found to be the case. Then again the writing of Greek verse might prove to be the sole accomplishment that some candidates had or would ever have. On occasion, a successful applicant may even have been impersonated at the examination by someone else, subsequently proving unable to write Greek verse when the occasion arose. Selection by competitive examination was never therefore more than a moderate success.

Whatever the faults, however, of the competitive written examination, it certainly produced better results than any method that has been attempted since. Modern methods center upon the intelligence test and the psychological interview. The defect in the intelligence test is that high marks are gained by those who subsequently prove to be practically illiterate. So much time has been spent in studying the art of being tested that the candidate has rarely had time for anything else. The psychological interview has developed today into what is known as ordeal by house party. The candidates spend a pleasant weekend under expert observation. As one of them trips over the doormat and says "Bother!" examiners lurking in the background whip out their notebooks and jot down, "Poor physical coordination" and "Lacks self-control." There is no need to describe this method in detail, but its results are all about us and are obviously deplorable. The persons who satisfy this type of examiner are usually of a cautious and suspicious temperament, pedantic and smug, saying little and doing nothing. It is quite common, when appointments are made by this method, for one man to be chosen from five hundred applicants, only to be sacked a few weeks later as useless even beyond the standards of his department. Of the various methods of selection so far tried, the latest is unquestionably the worst.

What method should be used in the future? A clue to a possible line of investigation is to be found in one little-publicized aspect of contemporary selective technique. So rarely does the occasion arise for appointing a Chinese translator to the Foreign Office or State Department that the method used is little known. The post is advertised and the applications go, let us suppose, to a committee of five. Three are civil servants and two are Chinese scholars of great eminence. Heaped on the table before this committee are 483 forms of application, with testimonials attached. All the applicants are Chinese and all without exception have a first degree from Peking or Amoy and a Doctorate of Philosophy from Cornell or Johns Hopkins. The majority of the candidates have at one time held ministerial office in Formosa. Some have attached their photographs. Others have (perhaps wisely) refrained from doing so. The chairman turns to the leading Chinese expert and says, "Perhaps Dr. Wu can tell us which of these candidates should be put on the short list." Dr. Wu smiles enigmatically and points to the heap. "None of them any good," he says briefly. "But how — I mean, why not?" asks the chairman, surprised. "Because no good scholar would ever apply. He would fear to lose face if he were not chosen." "So what do we do now?" asks the chairman. "I think," says Dr. Wu, "we might persuade Dr. Lim to take this post. What do you think, Dr. Lee?" "Yes, I think he might," says Lee, "but we couldn't approach him ourselves of course. We could ask Dr. Tan whether he thinks Dr. Lim would be interested." "I don't know Dr. Tan," says Wu, "but I know his friend Dr. Wong." By then the chairman is too muddled to know who is to be approached by whom. But the great thing is that all the applications are thrown into the waste-paper basket, only one candidate being considered, and he a man who did not apply.

We do not advise the universal adoption of the modern Chinese method but we draw from it the useful conclusion that the failure of other methods is mainly due to there being too many candidates. There are, admittedly, some initial steps by which the total may be reduced. The formula "Reject everyone over 50 or under 20 plus every-one called Murphy" is now universally used, and its application will somewhat reduce the list. The names remaining will still, however, be too numerous. To choose between three hundred people, all well qualified and highly recommended, is not really possible. We are driven therefore to conclude that the mistake lies in the original advertisement. It has attracted too many applications. The disadvantage of this is so little realized that people devise advertisements in terms which will inevitably attract thousands. A post of responsibility is announced as vacant, the previous occupant being now in the Senate or the House of Lords. The salary is large, the pension generous, the duties nominal, the privileges immense, the perquisites valuable, free residence provided with official car and unlimited facilities for travel. Candidates should apply, promptly but carefully, enclosing copies (not originals) of not more than three recent testimonials. What is the result? A deluge of applications, many from lunatics and as many again from retired army majors with a gift (as they always claim) for handling men. There is nothing to do except burn the lot and start thinking all over again. It would have saved time and trouble to do some thinking in the first place.

Only a little thought is needed to convince us that the perfect advertisement would attract only one reply and that from the right man. Let us begin with an extreme example.

Wanted — Acrobat capable of crossing a slack wire 200 feet above raging furnace. Twice nightly, three times on Saturday.

Salary offered £25 (or $70 U.S.) per week. No pension and no compensation in the event of injury. Apply in person at Wildcat Circus between the hours of 9 A.M. and 10 A.M.

The wording of this may not be perfect but the aim should be so to balance the inducement in salary against the possible risks involved that only a single applicant will appear. It is needless to ask for details of qualifications and experience. No one unskilled on the slack wire would find the offer attractive. It is needless to insist that candidates should be physically fit, sober, and free from fits of dizziness. They know that. It is just as needless to stipulate that those nervous of heights need not apply. They won't. The skill of the advertiser consists in adjusting the salary to the danger. An offer of £1000 (or $3000 U.S.) per week might produce a dozen applicants. An offer of £15 (or $35 U.S.) might produce none. Somewhere between those two figures lies the exact sum to specify, the minimum figure to attract anyone actually capable of doing the job. If there is more than one applicant, the figure has been placed a trifle too high.

Let us now take, for comparison, a less extreme example.

Wanted — An archaeologist with high academic qualifications willing to spend fifteen years in excavating the Inca tombs at Helsdump on the Alligator River. Knighthood or equivalent honor guaranteed. Pension payable but never yet claimed. Salary of £2000 (or $6000 U.S.) per year. Apply in triplicate to the Director of the Grubbenburrow Institute, Sickdale, Ill., U.S.A.

Here the advantages and drawbacks are neatly balanced. There is no need to insist that candidates must be patient, tough, intrepid, and single. The terms of the advertisement have eliminated all who are not. It is unnecessary to require that candidates must be mad on excavating tombs. Mad is just what they will certainly be. Having thus reduced the possible applicants to a maximum of about three, the terms of the advertisement place the salary just too low to attract two of them and the promised honor *just* high enough to interest the third. We may suppose that, in this case, the offer of a K.C.M.G. would have produced two applications, the offer of an O.B.E., none. The result is a single candidate. He is off his head but that does not matter. He is the man we want.

It may be thought that the world offers comparatively few opportunities to appoint slack-wire acrobats and tomb excavators, and that the problem is more often to find candidates for less exotic appointments. This is true, but the same principles can be applied. Their application demands, however — as is evident — a greater degree of skill. Let us suppose that the post to be filled is that of Prime Minister. The modern tendency is to trust in various methods of election, with results that are almost invariably disastrous. Were we to turn, instead, to the fairy stories we learned in childhood, we should realize that at the period to which these stories relate far more satisfactory methods were in use. When the king had to choose a man to marry his eldest or only daughter and so inherit the kingdom, he normally planned some obstacle course from which only the right candidate would emerge with credit; and from which indeed (in many instances) only the right candidate would emerge at all. For imposing such a test the kings of that rather vaguely defined period were well provided with both personnel and equipment. Their establishment included magicians, demons, fairies, vampires, werewolves, giants, and dwarfs. Their territories were supplied with magic mountains, rivers of fire, hidden treasures, and enchanted forests. It might be urged that modern governments are in this respect less fortunate. This, however, is by no means certain. An administrator able to command the services of psychologists, psychiatrists, alienists, statisticians, and efficiency experts is not perhaps in a worse (or better) position than one relying upon hideous crones and fairy godmothers. An administration equipped with movie cameras, television apparatus, radio networks, and X-ray machines would not appear to be in a worse (or better) position than one employing magic wands, crystal balls, wishing wells, and cloaks of invisibility. Their means of assessment would seem, at any rate, to be strictly comparable. All that is required is to translate the technique of the fairy story into a form applicable to the modern world. In this, as we shall see, there is no essential difficulty.

The first step in the process is to decide on the qualities a Prime Minister ought to have. These need not be the same in all circumstances, but they need to be listed and agreed upon. Let us suppose that the qualities deemed essential are (1) Energy, (2) Courage, (3) Patriotism, (4) Experience, (5) Popularity, and (6) Eloquence. Now, it will be observed that all these are general qualities which all possible applicants would believe themselves to possess. The field could readily, of course, be narrowed by stipulating (4) Experience *of lion-taming*, or (6) Eloquence *in Mandarin*. But that is not the way in which we want to narrow the field. We do not want to stipulate a quality in a special form; rather, each quality in an exceptional degree. In other words, the successful candidate must be the most energetic, courageous, patriotic, experienced, popular, and eloquent man in the country. Only one man can answer to that description and his is the only application we want. The terms of the appointment must thus be phrased so as to exclude everyone else. We should therefore word the advertisement in some such way as follows:

Wanted — Prime Minister of Ruritania. Hours of work: 4 A.M. to 11.59 P.M. Candidates must be prepared to fight three rounds with the current heavyweight champion (regulation gloves to be worn). Candidates will die for their country, by painless means, on reaching the age of retirement (65). They will have to pass an examination in parliamentary procedure and will be liquidated should they fail to obtain 95% marks. They will also be liquidated if they fail to gain 75% votes in a popularity poll held under the Gallup Rules. They will finally be invited to try their eloquence on a Baptist Congress, the object being to induce those present to rock and roll. Those who fail will be liquidated. All candidates should present themselves at the Sporting Club (side entrance) at 11.15 A.M. on the morning of September 19. Gloves will be provided, but they should bring their own rubber-soled shoes, singlet, and shorts.

Observe that this advertisement saves all trouble about application forms, testimonials, photographs, references, and short lists. If the advertisement has been correctly worded, there will be only one applicant, and he can take office immediately — well, almost immediately. But what if there is no applicant? That is proof that the advertisement needs rewording. We have evidently asked for something more than exists. So the same advertisement (which is, after all, quite economical in space) can be inserted again with some slight adjustment. The pass mark in the examination can be reduced to 85 per cent with 65 per cent of the votes required in the popularity poll, and only two rounds against the heavyweight. Conditions can be successively relaxed, indeed, until an applicant appears.

Suppose, however, that two or even three candidates present themselves. We shall know that we have been insufficiently scientific. It may be that the pass mark in the examination has been too abruply lowered — it should have been 87 per cent, perhaps, with 66 per cent in the popularity poll. Whatever the cause, the damage has been done. Two, or possibly three, candidates are in the waiting room. We have a choice to make and cannot waste all the morning on it. One policy would be to start the ordeal and eliminate the candidates who emerge with least credit. There is, nevertheless, a quicker way. Let us assume that all three candidates have all the qualities already defined as essential. The only thing we need do is add one further quality and apply the simplest test of all. To do this, we ask the nearest young lady (receptionist or stenographer, as the case may be), "Which would you prefer?" She will promptly point out one of the candidates and so finish the matter. It has been objected that this procedure is the same thing as tossing a coin or otherwise letting chance decide. There is, in fact, no element of chance. It is merely the last-minute insistence on one other quality, one not so far taken into account: the quality of sex appeal.

6

PLANS AND PLANTS

OR THE ADMINISTRATION BLOCK

EVERY STUDENT of human institutions is familiar with the standard test by which the importance of the individual may be assessed. The number of doors to be passed, the number of his personal assistants, the number of his telephone receivers — these three figures, taken with the depth of his carpet in centimeters, have given us a simple formula that is reliable for most parts of the world. It is less widely known that the same sort of measurement is applicable, but in reverse, to the institution itself.

Take, for example, a publishing organization. Publishers have a strong tendency, as we know, to live in a state of chaotic squalor. The visitor who applies at the obvious entrance is led outside and around the block, down an alley and up three flights of stairs. A research establishment is similarly housed, as a rule, on the ground floor of what was once a private house, a crazy wooden corridor leading thence to a corrugated iron hut in what was once the garden. Are we not all familiar, moreover, with the layout of an international airport? As we emerge from the aircraft, we see (over to our right or left) a lofty structure wrapped in scaffolding. Then the air hostess leads us into

59

a hut with an asbestos roof. Nor do we suppose for a moment that it will ever be otherwise. By the time the permanent building is complete the airfield will have been moved to another site.

The institutions already mentioned — lively and productive as they may be — flourish in such shabby and makeshift surroundings that we might turn with relief to an institution clothed from the outset with convenience and dignity. The outer door, in bronze and glass, is placed centrally in a symmetrical façade. Polished shoes glide quietly over shining rubber to the glittering and silent elevator. The overpoweringly cultured receptionist will murmer with carmine lips into an ice-blue receiver. She will wave you into a chromium armchair, consoling you with a dazzling smile for any slight but inevitable delay. Looking up from a glossy magazine, you will observe how the wide corridors radiate toward departments A, B, and C. From behind closed doors will come the subdued noise of an ordered activity. A minute later and you are ankle deep in the director's carpet, plodding sturdily toward his distant, tidy desk. Hypnotized by the chief's unwavering stare, cowed by the Matisse hung upon his wall, you will feel that you have found real efficiency at last.

In point of fact you will have discovered nothing of the kind. It is now known that a perfection of planned layout is achieved only by institutions on the point of collapse. This apparently paradoxical conclusion is based upon a wealth of archaeological and historical research, with the more esoteric details of which we need not concern ourselves. In general principle, however, the method pursued has been to select and date the buildings which appear to have been perfectly designed for their purpose. A study and comparison of these has tended to prove that perfection of planning is a sympton of decay. During a period of exciting discovery or progress there is no time to plan the perfect headquarters. The time for that comes later, when all the important work has been done. Perfection, we know, is finality; and finality is death.

Thus, to the casual tourist, awestruck in front of St. Peter's, Rome, the Basilica and the Vatican must seem the ideal setting for the Papal Monarchy at the very height of its prestige and power. Here, he reflects, must Innocent III have thundered his anathema. Here must Gregory VII have laid down the law. But a glance at the guidebook will convince the traveler that the really powerful Popes reigned long before the present dome was raised, and reigned not infrequently somewhere else. More than that, the later Popes lost half their authority while the work was still in progress. Julius II, whose decision it was to build, and Leo X, who approved Raphael's design, were dead long before the buildings assumed their present shape. Bramante's palace was still building until 1565, the great church not consecrated until 1626, nor the piazza colonnades finished until 1667. The great days of the Papacy were over before the perfect setting was even planned. They were almost forgotten by the date of its completion.

That this sequence of events is in no way exceptional can be proved with ease. Just such a sequence can be found in the history of the League of Nations. Great hopes centered on the League from its inception in 1920 until about 1930. By 1933, at the latest, the experiment was seen to have failed. Its physical embodiment, however, the Palace

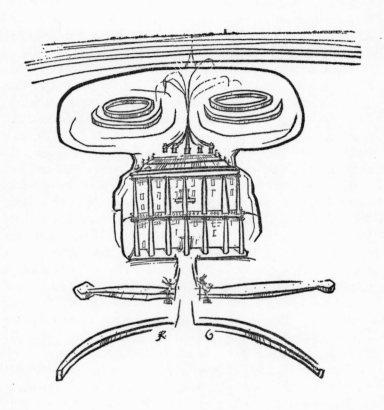

of the Nations, was not opened until 1937. It was a structure no doubt justly admired. Deep thought had gone into
the design of secretariat and council chambers, committee
rooms and cafeteria. Everything was there which ingenuity
could devise — except, indeed, the League itself. By the
year when its Palace was formally opened the League had
practically ceased to exist.

It might be urged that the Palace of Versailles is an instance of something quite opposite; the architectural embodiment of Louis XIV's monarchy at its height. But here
again the facts refuse to fit the theory. For granted that
Versailles may typify the triumphant spirit of the age, it
was mostly completed very late in the reign, and some of
it indeed during the reign that followed. The building of
Versailles mainly took place between 1669 and 1685. The
king did not move there until 1682, and even then the work
was still in progress. The famous royal bedroom was not
occupied until 1701, nor the chapel finished until nine
years later. Considered as a seat of government, as apart
from a royal residence, Versailles dates in part from as late
as 1756. As against that, Louis XIV's real triumphs were
mostly before 1679, the apex of his career reached in 1682
itself and his power declining from about 1685. According
to one historian, Louis, in coming to Versailles "was already sealing the doom of his line and race." Another says
of Versailles that "The whole thing . . . was completed
just when the decline of Louis's power had begun." A third
tacitly supports this theory by describing the period
1685–1713 as "The Years of Decline." In other words,
the visitor who thinks Versailles the place from which
Turenne rode forth to victory is essentially mistaken. It

would be historically more correct to picture the embarrassment, in that setting, of those who came with the news of defeat at Blenheim. In a palace resplendent with emblems of victory they can hardly have known which way to look.

Mention of Blenheim must naturally call to mind the palace of that name built for the victorious Duke of Marlborough. Here again we have a building ideally planned, this time as the place of retirement for a national hero. Its heroic proportions are more dramatic perhaps than convenient, but the general effect is just what the architects intended. No scene could more fittingly enshrine a legend. No setting could have been more appropriate for the meeting of old comrades on the anniversary of a battle. Our pleasure, however, in picturing the scene is spoiled by our realization that it cannot have taken place. The Duke never lived there and never even saw it finished. His actual residence was at Holywell, near St. Alban's, and (when in town) at Marlborough House. He died at Windsor Lodge and his old comrades, when they held a reunion, are known to have dined in a tent. Blenheim took long in building, not because of the elaboration of the design — which was admittedly quite elaborate enough — but because the Duke was in disgrace and even, for two years, in exile during the period which might otherwise have witnessed its completion.

What of the monarchy which the Duke of Marlborough served? Just as tourists now wander, guidebook in hand, through the Orangerie or the Galerie des Glaces, so the future archaeologist may peer around what once was London. And he may well incline to see in the ruins of Buckingham Palace a true expression of British monarchy. He will trace the great avenue from Admiralty Arch to the palace gate. He will reconstruct the forecourt and the central balcony, thinking all the time how suitable it must have been for a powerful ruler whose sway extended to the remote parts of the world. Even a present-day American might be tempted to shake his head over the arrogance of a George III, enthroned in such impressive state as this. But again we find that the really powerful monarchs all lived somewhere else, in buildings long since vanished — at Greenwich or Nonesuch, Kenilworth or Whitehall. The builder of Buckingham Palace was George IV, whose court architect, John Nash, was responsible for what was described at the time as its "general feebleness and triviality of taste." But George IV himself, who lived at Carlton House or Brighton, never saw the finished work; nor did William IV, who ordered its completion. It was Queen Victoria who first took up residence there in 1837, being married from the new palace in 1840. But her first enthusiasm for Buckingham Palace was relatively short-lived. Her husband infinitely preferred Windsor and her own later preference' was for Balmoral or Osborne. The splendors of Buckingham Palace are therefore to be associated, if we are to be accurate, with a later and strictly constitutional monarchy. It dates from a period when power was vested in Parliament.

It is natural, therefore, to ask at this point whether the Palace of Westminster, where the House of Commons meets, is itself a true expression of parliamentary rule. It represents beyond question a magnificent piece of planning, aptly designed for debate and yet provided with ample space for everything else — for committee meetings, for quiet study, for refreshment, and (on its terrace) for tea. It has everything a legislator could possibly desire, all incorporated in a building of immense dignity and comfort. It should date — but this we now hardly dare assume — from a period when parliamentary rule was at its height. But once again the dates refuse to fit into this pattern. The original House, where Pitt and Fox were matched in oratory, was accidentally destroyed by fire in 1834. It would appear to have been as famed for its inconvenience as for its lofty standard of debate. The present structure was begun in 1840, partly occupied in 1852, but incomplete when its architect died in 1860. It finally assumed its present appearance in about 1868. Now, by what we can no longer regard as coincidence, the decline of Parliament can be traced, without much dispute, to the Reform Act of 1867. It was in the following year that all initiative in legislation passed from Parliament to be vested in the Cabinet. The prestige attached to the letters "M.P." began sharply to decline and thenceforward the most that could be said is that "a role, though a humble one, was left for private members." The great days were over.

The same could not be said of the various Ministries, which were to gain importance in proportion to Parliament's decline. Investigation may yet serve to reveal that the India Office reached its peak of efficiency when accommodated in the Westminster Palace Hotel. What is more significant, however, is the recent development of the Colonial Office. For while the British Empire was mostly acquired at a period when the Colonial Office (in so far as there was one) occupied haphazard premises in Downing Street, a new phase of colonial policy began when the department moved into buildings actually designed for the purpose. This was in 1875 and the structure was well designed as a background for the disasters of the Boer War. But the Colonial Office gained a new lease of life during World War II. With its move to temporary and highly inconvenient premises in Great Smith Street — premises leased from the Church of England and intended for an entirely different purpose — British colonial policy entered that phase of enlightened activity which will end no doubt with the completion of the new building planned on the site of the old Westminster Hospital. It is reassuring to know that work on this site has not even begun.

But no other British example can now match in significance the story of New Delhi. Nowhere else have British architects been given the task of planning so great a capital city as the seat of government for so vast a population. The intention to found New Delhi was announced at the Imperial Durbar of 1911, King George V being at that time the Mogul's successor on what had been the Peacock Throne. Sir Edwin Lutyens then proceeded to draw up plans for a British Versailles, splendid in conception, comprehensive in detail, masterly in design, and overpowering in scale. But the stages of its progress toward completion correspond with so many steps in political collapse. The Government of India Act of 1909 had been the prelude to all that followed — the attempt on the Viceroy's life in 1912, the Declaration of 1917, the Montagu-Chelmsford Report of 1918 and its implementation in 1920. Lord Irwin actually moved into his new palace in 1929, the year in which the Indian Congress demanded independence, the year in which the Round Table Conference opened, the year before the Civil Disobedience campaign began. It would be possible, though tedious, to trace the whole story down to the day when the British finally withdrew, showing how each phase of the retreat was exactly paralleled with the completion of another triumph in civic design. What was finally achieved was no more and no less than a mausoleum.

The decline of British imperialism actually began with the general election of 1906 and the victory on that occasion of liberal and semi-socialist ideas. It need surprise no one, therefore, to observe that 1906 is the date of completion carved in imperishable granite over the British War Office doors. The campaign of Waterloo might have been directed from poky offices around the Horse Guards Parade. It was, by contrast, in surroundings of dignity that were approved the plans for attacking the Dardanelles.

The elaborate layout of the Pentagon at Arlington, Virginia, provides another significant lesson for planners. It was not completed until the later stages of World War II and, of course, the architecture of the great victory was not constructed here, but in the crowded and untidy Munitions Building on Constitution Avenue.

Even today, as the least observant visitor to Washington can see, the most monumental edifices are found to house such derelict organizations as the Departments of Commerce and Labor, while the more active agencies occupy half-completed quarters. Indeed, much of the more urgent business of government goes forward in "temporary" structures erected during World War I, and shrewdly preserved for their stimulating effect on administration. Hard by the Capitol, the visitor will also observe the imposing marble-

and-glass headquarters of the Teamsters' Union, completed not a moment too soon before the heavy hand of Congressional investigation descended on its occupants.

It is by no means certain that an influential reader of this chapter could prolong the life of a dying institution merely by depriving it of its streamlined headquarters. What he can do, however, with more confidence, is to prevent any organization strangling itself at birth. Examples abound of new institutions coming into existence with a full establishment of deputy directors, consultants and executives; all these coming together in a building specially designed for their purpose. And experience proves that such an institution will die. It is choked by its own perfection. It cannot take root for lack of soil. It cannot grow naturally for it is already grown. Fruitless by its very nature, it cannot even flower. When we see an example of such planning — when we are confronted for example by the building designed for the United Nations — the experts among us shake their heads sadly, draw a sheet over the corpse, and tiptoe quietly into the open air.

7

PERSONALITY SCREEN
OR THE COCKTAIL FORMULA

ESSENTIAL TO the technique of modern life is the Cocktail Party. Upon this institution hinges the international, the learned, and the industrial congress. Without at least one cocktail party these gatherings are known to be impossible. So far there has been too little scientific study of their function and possible use. The time has come to give this subject some careful thought. In planning a cocktail party what, exactly, do we hope to achieve?

This question can be answered in various ways, and it soon becomes evident that the same party can serve a variety of purposes. Let us take one possible object at random and see how it could be attained more completely and quickly by the application of scientific method. Take, for example, the problem of discovering the relative importance of the people there. We may assume that their official status and seniority is already known. But what of their actual importance in relation to the work being done? It often happens that the key men and women are not those of highest official standing. That these others are influential will be apparent by the end of the conference. How much more useful if we could have assessed their importance at the beginning! It is in this assessment that a cocktail party, held on the second day of the congress, may give invaluable aid.

For the purposes of the investigation it will be assumed that the space in which the party is to be held is all on one level and that there is only one formal entrance. It will be assumed, further, that the whole affair is to last two hours according to the invitation cards but two hours and twenty minutes in actual fact. It will be assumed, finally, that the drinks circulate freely throughout the area with which we have to deal; for a bar in visible operation would alter the nature of the problem. Given these assumptions, how are we to assess the real as opposed to the theoretical importance of the guests present?

The first known fact upon which we can base our theory is the direction of the human current. We know that the guests on arrival will drift automatically toward the left side of the reception floor. This leftward set of the tide has an interesting and partly biological explanation. The heart is (or to be exact, appears to be) on the left side of the body. In the more primitive form of warfare some form of shield is therefore used to protect the left side, leaving the offensive weapon to be held in the right hand. The normal offensive weapon was the sword, worn in a scabbard or sheath. If the sword was to be wielded in the right hand, the scabbard would have to be worn on the left side. With a scabbard worn on the left, it became physically impossible to mount a horse on the off side unless intending to face the tail — which was not the normal practice. But if you mount on the near side, you will want to have your horse on the left of the road, so that you are clear of the traffic while mounting. It therefore becomes natural and proper to keep to the left, the contrary practice (as adopted in some backward countries) being totally opposed to all the deepest historical instincts. Free of arbitrary traffic rules the normal human being swings to the left.

The second known fact is that people prefer the side of the room to the middle. This is obvious from the way a restaurant fills up. The tables along the left wall are occupied first, then those at the far end, then those along the right wall, and finally (and with reluctance) those in the middle. Such is the human revulsion to the central space that managements often despair of filling it and so create what is termed a dance floor. It will be realized that this behavior pattern could be upset by some extraneous factor, like a view of the waterfall from the end windows. If we exclude cathedrals and glaciers, the restaurant will fill up on the lines indicated, from left to right. Reluctance to occupy the central space derives from prehistoric instincts. The caveman who entered someone else's cave was doubtful of his reception and wanted to be able to have his back to the wall and yet with some room to maneuver. In the center of the cave he felt too vulnerable. He therefore sidled round the walls of the cave, grunting and fingering his club. Modern man is seen to do much the same thing, muttering to himself and fingering his club tie. The basic trend of movement at a cocktail party is the same as in a restaurant. The tendency is toward the sides of the space, but not actually reaching the wall.

If we combine these two known facts, the leftward drift and the tendency to avoid the center, we have the biological explanation of the phenomenon we have all observed in practice: that is the clockwise flow of the human movement. There may be local eddies and swirls — women will swerve to avoid people they detest, or rush crying "Darling!" toward people they detest even more — but the general set of the tide runs inexorably round the room. People who matter, people who are literally "in the swim," keep to the channel where the tide runs strongly. They move with the general movement and at very much the average speed. Those who appear to be glued to the walls, usually deep in conversation with people they meet every week, are nobodies. Those who jam themselves in the corners of the room are the timid and feeble. Those who drift into the center are the eccentric and merely silly.

What we have next to study is the time at which people arrive. Now we can safely assume that the people who matter will arrive at the time they consider favorable. They will not be among those who have overestimated the length of their journey and so arrive ten minutes before the party is due to begin. They will not be among those whose watches have stopped and who rush in, panting, when the party is nearly over. No, the people we want to identify will choose their moment. What moment will it be? It will clearly be a time fixed by two major considerations. They will not want to make an entrance before there are sufficient people there to observe their arrival. But neither will they want to arrive after other important people have gone on (as they always do) to another party. Their arrival will therefore be at least half an hour after the party begins and at least an hour before it is due to end. That gives us a bracket, suggesting the formula that the optimum arrival time will be exactly three-quarters of an hour after the time given on

73

the invitation card: 7.15, for example, if the party is supposed to start at 6.30. The temptation at this point is to conclude that the discovery of the optimum arrival time is the solution to the whole problem. Some students might say, "Never mind what happens afterwards. Observe the door with a stop watch and you have the answer." The more experienced investigator will treat that suggestion with gentle derision. For who is to know that the person arriving at 7.15 precisely was aiming to do just that? Some may arrive at that time because they meant to be there at 6.30 but could not find the place. Others may arrive at that hour thinking that the time is later than it is. A few might turn up then without even being invited — guests expected somewhere else and on another day. So, although safely concluding that the people who matter should arrive between 7.10 and 7.20, we would be entirely wrong to regard as important all who appear at about that time.

It is at this stage in the research project that we need to test and complete our theory by experimental means. Fully to understand the social current, we should resort to the technique used in a hydraulic laboratory. In such an establishment the scientist who wants to ascertain how water will flow round a bridge pier of a certain shape will add cochineal to the water which he sets flowing over a sheet of glass. On the glass he places his model pier. Then from above he photographs the pattern made by the color streaks in the water. What we should like to do would be to mark the people of known importance at a cocktail party — stain them, as it were, with cochineal — and photograph their progress from a gallery. It may be supposed that there are difficulties about pursuing an investigation on these lines.

Luckily, however, information came to hand about a certain British Colony where the "staining" of some specimens had already been done.

What had happened was that a former Governor, perhaps a century ago, tried to persuade the respectable male population to wear black evening dress instead of white. His persuasion and example failed completely so far as the merchants, bankers and lawyers were concerned but he was necessarily obeyed by the civil servants, who had no option in the matter. The result was that a tradition grew up and has been observed to this day. High government officers wear black and everyone else wears white. Now, as the officials are still important in this particular society, it was easy for investigators to follow their movement from a gallery. It was possible, moreover, to photograph their movement pattern on different occasions, confirming the theories so far described and leading us to the final discovery which we are now in a position to disclose. Careful observations proved, beyond a shadow of doubt, that the black coats arrived at some time between 7.10 and 7.20; that they circled left and so proceeded around the floor; that they avoided the corners and the walls; and that they shunned the middle. So far their behavior closely conformed to our theory. But we now noted a further and unexpected phenomenon. Having reached a point near the far right corner of the room — which they did in half an hour — they lingered in the same area for ten minutes or more. They then tended to leave rather abruptly. It was only after long and careful study of the films taken that we realized what this behavior meant. The pause, we finally concluded, was to allow the other important people to catch up, those who had arrived at 7.10 waiting for those who had arrived at 7.20. The actual foregathering of the important people did not take long. They each merely wanted to be seen by the others, as proof that they were there. This done, the withdrawal began and was, in every instance, complete by 8.15.

What we learned by observation in this one society is now believed to be applicable to any other; and the formula is easy to apply. To find the people who really matter, divide the whole floor area (mentally) into squares. Letter these from left to right, as you enter, as A, B, C, D, E, and F. Number the squares from the entrance to the far end as 1 to 8. The hour at which the party begins should be termed H. The moment when the last guest leaves will be approximately two hours and twenty minutes after the first people arrive. We shall call this $H + 140$. To find the people who really matter is now perfectly simple. They are the people grouped in square $E/7$ between $H + 75$ and $H + 90$. The most important person of all will be in the very center of the group.

Students will realize that the validity of this rule must depend upon its not being generally known. The contents of this chapter should therefore be treated as confidential and kept strictly under lock and key. Students of social science must keep this information to themselves and members of the general public are not on any account to read it.

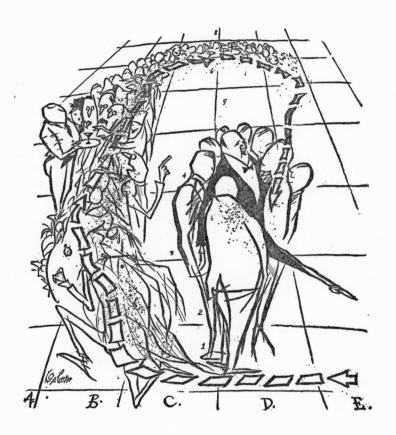

8

INJELITITIS
OR PALSIED PARALYSIS

WE FIND everywhere a type of organization (administrative, commercial, or academic) in which the higher officials are plodding and dull, those less senior are active only in intrigue against each other, and the junior men are frustrated or frivolous. Little is being attempted. Nothing is being achieved. And in contemplating this sorry picture, we conclude that those in control have done their best, struggled against adversity, and have finally admitted defeat. It now appears from the results of recent investigation, that no such failure need be assumed. In a high percentage of the moribund institutions so far examined the final state of coma is something gained of set purpose and after prolonged effort. It is the result, admittedly, of a disease, but of a disease that is largely self-induced. From the first signs of the condition, the progress of the disease has been encouraged, the causes aggravated, and the symptoms welcomed. It is the disease of induced inferiority, called Injelititis. It is a commoner ailment than is often supposed, and the diagnosis is far easier than the cure.

Our study of this organizational paralysis begins, logically, with a description of the course of the disease from the first signs to the final coma. The second stage of our inquiry concerns symptoms and diagnosis. The third stage should properly include some reference to treatment, but little is known about this. Nor is much likely to be discovered in the immediate future, for the tradition of British medical research is entirely opposed to any emphasis on this part of the subject. British medical specialists are usually quite content to trace the symptoms and define the cause. It is the French, by contrast, who begin by describing the treatment and discuss the diagnosis later, if at all. We feel bound to adhere in this to the British method, which may not help the patient but which is unquestionably more scientific. To travel hopefully is better than to arrive.

The first sign of danger is represented by the appearance in the organization's hierarchy of an individual who combines in himself a high concentration of incompetence and jealousy. Neither quality is significant in itself and most people have a certain proportion of each. But when these two qualities reach a certain concentration — represented at present by the formula I^3J^5 — there is a chemical reaction. The two elements fuse, producing a new substance that we have termed "injelitance." The presence of this substance can be safely inferred from the actions of any individual who, having failed to make anything of his own department, tries constantly to interfere with other departments and gain control of the central administration. The specialist who observes this particular mixture of failure and ambition will at once shake his head and murmur, "Primary or idiopathic injelitance." The symptoms, as we shall see, are quite unmistakable.

The next or secondary stage in the progress of the disease is reached when the infected individual gains complete or partial control of the central organization. In many instances this stage is reached without any period of primary infection, the individual having actually entered the organization at that level. The injelitant individual is easily recognizable at this stage from the persistence with which he struggles to eject all those abler than himself, as also from his resistance to the appointment or promotion of

anyone who might prove abler in course of time. He dare not say, "Mr. Asterisk is too able," so he says, "Asterisk? Clever perhaps — but is he *sound?* I incline to prefer Mr. Cypher." He dare not say, "Mr. Asterisk makes me feel small," so he says, "Mr. Cypher appears to me to have the better judgment." Judgment is an interesting word that signifies in this context the opposite of intelligence; it means, in fact, doing what was done last time. So Mr. Cypher is promoted and Mr. Asterisk goes elsewhere. The central administration gradually fills up with people stupider than the chairman, director, or manager. If the head of the organization is second-rate, he will see to it that his immediate staff are all third-rate; and they will, in turn, see to it that their subordinates are fourth-rate. There will soon be an actual competition in stupidity, people pretending to be even more brainless than they are.

The next or tertiary stage in the onset of this disease is reached when there is no spark of intelligence left in the whole organization from top to bottom. This is the state of coma we described in our first paragraph. When that stage has been reached the institution is, for all practical purposes, dead. It may remain in a coma for twenty years. It may quietly disintegrate. It may even, finally, recover. Cases of recovery are rare. It may be thought odd that recovery without treatment should be possible. The process is quite natural, nevertheless, and closely resembles the process by which various living organisms develop a resistance to poisons that are at first encounter fatal. It is as if the whole institution had been sprayed with a DDT solution guaranteed to eliminate all ability found in its way. For a period of years this practice achieves the desired result. Eventually, however, individuals develop an immunity. They conceal their ability under a mask of imbecile good humor. The result is that the operatives assigned to the task of ability-elimination fail (through stupidity) to recognize ability when they see it. An individual of merit penetrates the outer defenses and begins to make his way toward the top. He wanders on, babbling about golf and giggling feebly, losing documents and forgetting names, and looking just like everyone else. Only when he has reached high rank does he suddenly throw off the mask and appear like the demon king among a crowd of pantomime fairies. With shrill screams of dismay the high executives find ability right there in the midst of them. It is too late by then to do anything about it. The damage has been done, the disease is in retreat, and full recovery is possible over the next ten years. But these instances of natural cure are extremely rare. In the more usual course of events, the disease passes through the recognized stages and becomes, as it would seem, incurable.

We have seen what the disease is. It now remains to show by what symptoms its presence can be detected. It is one thing to detail the spread of the infection in an imaginary case, classified from the start. It is quite a different thing to enter a factory, barracks, office, or college and recognize the symptoms at a glance. We all know how an estate agent will wander round a vacant house when acting for the purchaser. It is only a question of time before he throws open a cupboard or kicks a baseboard and exclaims, "Dry rot!" (acting for the vendor, he would lose the key of the cupboard while drawing attention to the view from the window). In the same way a political scientist can recognize the symptoms of Injelititis even in its primary stage. He will pause, sniff, and nod wisely, and it should be obvious at once that he *knows*. But how does he know? How can he tell that injelitance has set in? If the original source of the infection were present, the diagnosis would be easier, but it is still quite possible when the germ of the disease is on holiday. His influence can be detected in the atmosphere. It can be detected, above all, in certain remarks that will be made by others, as thus: "It would be a mistake for us to attempt too much. We cannot compete with Toprank. Here in Lowgrade we do useful work, meeting the needs of the country. Let us be content with that." Or again, "We do not pretend to be in the first flight. It is absurd the way these people at Much-Striving talk of their work, just as if they were in the Toprank class." Or finally, "Some of our younger men have transferred to Toprank — one or two even to Much-Striving. It is probably their wisest plan. We are quite happy to let them succeed in that way. An exchange of ideas and personnel is a good thing — although, to be sure, the few men we have had from Toprank have been rather disappointing. We can only expect the people they have thrown out. Ah well, we must not grumble. We always avoid friction when we can. And, in our humble way we can claim to be doing a good job."

What do these remarks suggest? They suggest — or, rather, they clearly indicate — that the standard of achievement has been set too low. Only a low standard is desired and one still lower is acceptable. The directives issuing from a second-rate chief and addressed to his third-rate executives speak only of minimum aims and ineffectual means. A higher standard of competence is not desired, for an efficient organization would be beyond the chief's power to control. The motto, "Ever third-rate" has been inscribed over the main entrance in letters of gold. Third-rateness has become a principle of policy. It will be observed, however, that the existence of higher standards is still recognized. There remains at this primary stage a hint of apology, a feeling of uneasiness when Toprank is mentioned. Neither this apology nor unease lasts for long. The second stage of the disease comes on quickly and it is this we must now describe.

The secondary stage is recognized by its chief symptom, which is Smugness. The aims have been set low and have therefore been largely achieved. The target has been set up within ten yards of the firing point and the scoring has therefore been high. The directors have done what they set out to do. This soon fills them with self-satisfaction. They set out to do something and they have done it. They soon forget that it was a small effort to gain a small result. They observe only that they have succeeded — unlike those people at Much-Striving. They become increasingly smug and their smugness reveals itself in remarks such as this: "The chief is a sound man and very clever when you get to know him. He never says much — that is not his way — but he seldom makes a mistake." (These last words can be said with justice of someone who never does anything at all.) Or this: "We rather distrust brilliance here. These clever people can be a dreadful nuisance, upsetting established routine and proposing all sorts of schemes that we have never seen tried. We obtain splendid results by simple common sense and teamwork." And finally this: "Our canteen is something we are really rather proud of. We don't know how the caterer can produce so good a lunch at the price. We are lucky to have him!" This last remark is made as we sit at a table covered with dirty oilcloth, facing an uneatable, nameless mess on a plate and shuddering at the sight and smell of what passes for coffee. In point of fact, the canteen reveals more than the office. Just as for a quick verdict we judge a private house by inspection of the WC (to find whether there is a spare toilet roll), just as we judge a hotel by the state of the cruet, so we judge a larger institution by the appearance of the canteen. If the decoration is in dark brown and pale green; if the curtains are purple(or absent); if there are no flowers in sight; if there is barley in the soup (with or without a dead fly); if the menu is one of hash and mold; and if the executives are still delighted with everything — why, then the institution is in a pretty bad way. For self-satisfaction, in such a case, has reached the point at which those responsible cannot tell the difference between food and filth. This is smugness made absolute.

The tertiary and last stage of the disease is one in which apathy has taken the place of smugness. The executives no longer boast of their efficiency as compared with some other institution. They have forgotten that any other institution exists. They have ceased to eat in the canteen, preferring now to bring sandwiches and scatter their desks with the crumbs. The bulletin boards carry notices about the concert that took place four years ago, Mr. Brown's office has a nameplate saying, "Mr. Smith." Mr. Smith's door is marked, "Mr. Robinson," in faded ink on an adhesive luggage label. The broken windows have been repaired with odd bits of cardboard. The electric light switches give a slight but painful shock when touched. The whitewash is flaking off the ceiling and the paint is blotchy on the walls. The elevator is out of order and the cloakroom tap cannot be turned off. Water from the broken skylight drips wide of the bucket placed to catch it, and from somewhere in the basement comes the wail of a hungry cat. The last stage of the disease has brought the whole organization to the point of collapse. The symptoms of the disease in this acute form are so numerous and evident that a trained investigator can often detect them over the telephone without visiting the place at all. When a weary voice answers "Ullo!" (that most unhelpful of replies), the expert has often heard enough. He shakes his head sadly as he replaces the receiver. "Well on in the tertiary phase," he will mutter to himself, "and almost certainly inoperable." It is too late to attempt any sort of treatment. The institution is practically dead.

We have now described this disease as seen from within and then again from outside. We know now the origin, the progress, and the outcome of the infection, as also the symptoms by which its presence is detected. British medical skill seldom goes beyond that point in its research. Once a disease has been identified, named, described, and accounted for, the British are usually quite satisfied and ready to investigate the next problem that presents itself. If asked about treatment they look surprised and suggest the use of penicillin preceded or followed by the extraction of all the patient's teeth. It becomes clear at once that this is not an aspect of the subject that interests them. Should our attitude be the same? Or should we as political scientists consider what, if anything, can be done about it? It would be premature, no doubt, to discuss any possible treatment in detail, but it might be useful to indicate very generally the lines along which a solution might be attempted. Certain principles, at least, might be laid down. Of such principles, the first would have to be this: a diseased institution cannot reform itself. There are instances, we know, of a disease vanishing without treatment, just as it appeared without warning; but these cases are rare and regarded by the specialist as irregular and undesirable. The cure, whatever its nature, must come from outside. For a patient to remove his own appendix under a local anaesthetic may be physically possible, but the practice is regarded with disfavor and is open to many objections. Other operations lend themselves still less to the patient's own dexterity. The first principle we can safely enunciate is that the patient and the surgeon should not be the same person. When an institution is in an advanced state of disease, the services of a specialist are required and even, in some instances, the services of the greatest living authority: Parkinson himself. The fees payable may be very heavy indeed, but in a case of this sort, expense is clearly no object. It is a matter, after all, of life and death.

The second principle we might lay down is this, that the primary stage of the disease can be treated by a simple injection, that the secondary stage can be cured in some instances by surgery, and that the tertiary stage must be regarded at present as incurable. There was a time when physicians used to babble about bottles and pills, but this is mainly out of date. There was another period when they talked more vaguely about psychology; but that too is out of date, most of the psychoanalysts having since been certi-

fied as insane. The present age is one of injections and in-
cisions and it behooves the political scientists to keep in
step with the Faculty. Confronted by a case of primary infection, we prepare a syringe automatically and only hesi-
tate as to what, besides water, it should contain. In principle, the injection should contain some active substance
— but from which group should it be selected? A kill-
or-cure injection would contain a high proportion of Intolerance, but this drug is difficult to procure and sometimes too powerful to use. Intolerance is obtainable from
the bloodstream of regimental sergeant majors and is found
to comprise two chemical elements, namely: (a) the best
is scarcely good enough (GG^{nth}) and (b) there is no excuse for anything (NE^{nth}). Injected into a diseased institution, the intolerant individual has a tonic effect and may
cause the organism to turn against the original source of
infection. While this treatment may well do good, it is by
no means certain that the cure will be permanent. It is
doubtful, that is to say, whether the infected substance will
be actually expelled from the system. Such information as
we have rather leads us to suppose that this treatment is
merely palliative in the first instance, the disease remaining
latent though inactive. Some authorities believe that repeated injections would result in a complete cure, but
others fear that repetition of the treatment would set up
a fresh irritation, only slightly less dangerous than the original disease. Intolerance is a drug to be used, therefore,
with caution.

There exists a rather milder drug called Ridicule, but its
operation is uncertain, its character unstable, and its effects
too little known. There is little reason to fear that any

damage could result from an injection of ridicule, but neither is it evident that a cure would result. It is generally agreed that the injelitant individual will have developed a thick protective skin, insensitive to ridicule. It may well be that ridicule may tend to isolate the infection, but that is as much as could be expected and more indeed than has been claimed.

We may note, finally, that Castigation, which is easily obtainable, has been tried in cases of this sort and not wholly without effect. Here again, however, there are difficulties. This drug is an immediate stimulus but can produce a result the exact opposite of what the specialist intends. After a momentary spasm of activity, the injelitant individual will often prove more supine than before and just as harmful as a source of infection. If any use can be made of castigation it will almost certainly be as one element in a preparation composed otherwise of intolerance and ridicule, with perhaps other drugs as yet untried. It only remains to point out that this preparation does not as yet exist.

The secondary stage of the disease we believe to be operable. Professional readers will all have heard of the Nuciform Sack and of the work generally associated with the name of Cutler Walpole. The operation first performed by that great surgeon involves, simply, the removal of the infected parts and the simultaneous introduction of new blood drawn from a similar organism. This operation has sometimes succeeded. It is only fair to add that it has also sometimes failed. The shock to the system can be too great. The new blood may be unobtainable and may fail, even when procured, to mingle with the blood previously in circulation. On the other hand, this drastic method offers, beyond question, the best chance of a complete cure.

The tertiary stage presents us with no opportunity to do anything. The institution is for all practical purposes dead. It can be founded afresh but only with a change of name, a change of site, and an entirely different staff. The temptation, for the economically minded, is to transfer some portion of the original staff to the new institution — in the name, for example, of continuity. Such a transfusion would certainly be fatal, and continuity is the very thing to avoid. No portion of the old and diseased foundation can be regarded as free from infection. No staff, no equipment, no tradition must be removed from the original site. Strict quarantine should be followed by complete disinfection. Infected personnel should be dispatched with a warm testimonial to such rival institutions as are regarded with particular hostility. All equipment and files should be destroyed without hesitation. As for the buildings, the best plan is to insure them heavily and then set them alight. Only when the site is a blackened ruin can we feel certain that the germs of the disease are dead.

9

PALM THATCH TO PACKARD
OR A FORMULA FOR, SUCCESS

READERS WHO are all too familiar with popular works on anthropology may be interested to learn that some recent investigations have involved a completely novel approach. The ordinary anthropologist is one who spends six weeks or six months (or even sometimes six years) among, say, the Boreyu tribe at their settlement on the Upper Teedyas River, Darndreeryland. He then returns to civilization with his photographs, tape recorders, and notebooks, eager to write his book about sex life and superstition. For tribes such as the Boreyu, life is made intolerable by all this peering and prying. They often become converts to Presbyterianism in the belief that they will thereupon cease to be of interest to anthropologists; nor in fact has this device been known to fail. But enough primitive people remain for the purposes of science. Books continue to multiply, and when the last tribe has resorted to the singing of hymns in self-defense, there are still the poor of the backstreets. These are perpetually pursued by questionnaire, camera, and phonograph; and the written results are familiar to us all. What is new about the approach now being attempted is not the technique of investigation but the choice of a society in which to work. Anthropologists of this latest school ignore the primitive and have no time for the poor. They prefer to do their fieldwork among the rich.

The team whose work we shall now describe, and to which the present author is attached, made certain preliminary studies among Greek Shipping Magnates and went on to deal in greater detail with the Arab Chieftains of the Pipeline. When this line of investigation had to be abandoned, for political and other reasons, the team went on to study the Chinese Millionaires of Singapore. It is there we encountered the Flunky Puzzle. It is there we first heard of the Chinese Hound Barrier. During the early stages of our inquiry we did not know the meaning of either term. We did not even know whether they were different names for the same thing. What we can claim now is that we at least followed up the first clue to present itself.

This clue we obtained in the course of a visit to the Singapore palace of Mr. Hu Got Dow. Turning to the equerry who had shown him round the millionaire's collection of jade, Dr. Meddleton exclaimed, "Gee, and they say he began life as a coolie!" To this the inscrutable Chinese replied, "Only coolie can become millionaire. Only coolie can look like coolie. Only *velly* lich man can afford to look lich." Upon these few and enigmatic words (of which no further explanation was offered) we based our whole scheme of research. The detailed results are comprised in the Meddleton-Snooperage Report (1956) but there is no reason why they should not be presented in a simplified form for the general reader. What follows is just such an outline, with technicalities mostly omitted.

Up to a point, as we recognized, the problem of the

coolie-millionaire offers no real difficulty. The Chinese coolie lives in a palm-thatched hovel on a bowl of rice. When he has risen to a higher occupation — hawking peanuts, for example, from a barrow — he still lives on rice and still lives in a hovel. When he has risen farther — to the selling, say, of possibly stolen bicycle parts, he keeps to his hovel and his rice. The result is that he has money to invest. Of ten coolies in this situation, nine will lose their money by unwise speculation. The tenth will be clever or lucky. He will live, nevertheless, in his hovel. He will eat, as before, his rice. As a success technique this is well worthy of study.

In the American log cabin story the point is soon reached at which the future millionaire must wear a tie. He explains that he cannot otherwise inspire confidence. He must also acquire a better address, purely (he says) to gain prestige. In point of fact, the tie is to please his wife and the address to satisfy his daughter. The Chinese have their womenfolk under better control. So the prosperous coolie sticks to his hovel and his rice. This is a known fact and admits of two explanations. In the first place his home (whatever its other disadvantages) has undeniably brought him luck. In the second place, a better house would unquestionably attract the notice of the tax collector. So he wisely stays where he is. He will often keep the original hovel — at any rate as an office — for the rest of his life. He quits it so reluctantly that his decision to move marks a major crisis in his career.

When he moves it is primarily to evade the exactions of secret societies, blackmailers, and gangs. To conceal his growing wealth from the tax collector is a relatively easy matter; but to conceal it from his business associates is practically impossible. Once the word goes round that he is prospering, accurate guesses will be made as to the sum for which he can be "touched." All this is admittedly well known, but previous investigators have jumped too readily to the conclusion that there is only one sum involved. In point of fact there are three: the sum the victim would pay if kidnaped and held to ransom; the sum he would pay to keep a defamatory article out of a Chinese newspaper; the sum he would subscribe to charity rather than lose face.

Our task was to ascertain the figure the first sum will have reached (on an average) at the moment when migration takes place from the original hovel to a well-fenced house guarded by an Alsatian hound. It is this move that has been termed "Breaking the Hound Barrier." Social scientists believe that it will tend to occur as soon as the ransom to be exacted comes to exceed the overhead costs of the "snatch."

At about the time a prosperous Chinese changes house he has also to acquire a Chevrolet or Packard. Such a purchase often, however, antedates the change of address. So the spectacle of the expensive car outside the dingy office is too familiar to arouse much comment. No complete explanation has so far been offered. Conceding, as we may, the need for a car, we should rather expect it to share the squalor of its surroundings. For reasons not yet apparent, however, Chinese prosperity is first and fairly measured in terms of chromium, upholstery, make, and year. And the Packard will involve, very soon, a wire fence, barred windows, padlocked garage, and hound. A revolutionary change has occurred. If the Alsatian-owner does not go so far as to pay his taxes, he must at least know how to explain why no taxable income has so far come his way. And supposing he can avoid paying $100,000 to gangsters, he can hardly avoid payment of blackmail in some form. He must expect to receive obsequious journalists who claim credit for refusing to publish hostile articles about him in dubious journals. He must expect to see the same journalists a week later, this time collecting funds for some vaguely described orphanage. He must accustom himself to the visits of trade union officials offering for a consideration to discourage the industrial unrest that will otherwise affect his interests. He must resign himself, in fact, to the loss of a percentage.

One of our objects was to compile some detailed information about the Alsatian-owning phase of a Chinese businessman's career. This was, in some ways, the most difficult part of the whole investigation. There are types of knowledge only to be gained at the price of torn trousers and bandaged ankles. We are proud to think, in retrospect, that where risks were inevitable they were taken unflinchingly. No fieldwork was needed, however, to discover what actual amounts are paid in ransom. These figures are in fact generally known and often quoted in the local press with some pretense at accuracy. What is significant about these figures is the range between the smallest and the largest figures quoted. Sums appear to vary from $5000 to $200,000 — never as little as $2000 nor as much as $500,000. Nor can there be any doubt that the majority of extortions fall within a narrower range than that. Further research will, no doubt, establish what the average amount can be taken to be.

If we suppose that the minimum extortion represents a figure just high enough to yield a marginal profit, we shall as readily conclude that the maximum extortion represents all that can be extracted from the richest men that are ever kidnaped. It is manifest, however, that the very wealthiest men are never kidnaped at all. There would seem to be a point beyond which the Chinese gains immunity from blackmail. In this last phase, moreover, the millionaire

seeks to emphasize rather than conceal his wealth, demonstrating publicly that the point of immunity has been reached. So far, no social scientist of our team has been able to discover how this final immunity is achieved. Several have been thrown out of the Millionaires' Club when trying to collect evidence on this point. Concluding that it has something to do with the number of equerries, aides-de-camp, personal assistants, secretaries, and valets (all much in evidence at this stage) they have termed the problem "The Flunky Puzzle" and left it at that.

It is not to be supposed however that this problem will baffle us for long. Indeed, we know already that our choice lies, broadly speaking, between two alternative explanations, with the proviso that we may possibly end by accepting both. One guess has been that the flunkies are really gunmen forming an impenetrable bodyguard. The other guess is that the millionaire has bought up an entire secret society and one against which no other gang dare act. To test the former theory — by a carefully staged holdup — would be relatively simple. At the cost of a life or two the fact could be established beyond all reasonable doubt. To test the latter theory would need more brains and possibly more courage. With several casualties already among the brave dog-bitten members of our team, we did not feel justified in pursuing this line of research. We concluded that we had neither the men nor the funds to complete the investigation. Having since received timely aid from the Miss Plaste Trust (Far East branch) we hope to know the answer fairly soon.

A problem that remains, even after the publication of our interim report, is the enigma of Chinese tax evasion.

All that we could discover about this was that Western methods are not widely used. As is well known, the Western technique depends on discovering the standard delay (or S.D., as we call it among ourselves) in the department with which we have to deal. That is, of course, the normal lapse of time between the receipt of a letter and its being dealt with. It is, to be more exact, the time it takes for a file to rise from the bottom of the in-tray to the top of the pile. Supposing this to be twenty-seven days, the Western tax evader begins his campaign by writing to ask why he has received no notice of assessment. It does not matter, actually, what he says in the letter. All he wants is to ensure that his file, with its new enclosure, will be at the bottom of the heap. *Twenty-five days later* he will write again, asking why his first letter has not been answered. This sends his file back to the bottom again just when it was almost reaching the top. Twenty-five days later he writes again. . . . So his file is never dealt with at all and never in fact comes into view. This being the method known to us all, and known to be successful, we naturally concluded that it was known also to the Chinese. We found, however, that these is no S.D. in the East. Owing to variations in climate and sobriety, the government departments lack that ordered rhythm which would make them predictable. Whatever method the Chinese use, it cannot depend upon a known S.D.

To this problem we have, it should be emphasized, no final solution. All we have is a theory upon the validity of which it would be premature to comment. It was put forward by one of our most brilliant investigators and can be described as no more than an inspired guess. According to this supposition the Chinese millionaire does not wait for his assessment, but prefers to send the tax collector a check in advance for, say, $329.83. A covering note refers briefly to earlier correspondence and a previous sum paid in cash. The effect of this maneuver is to throw the whole tax-collecting machine out of gear. Disorganization turns to chaos when a further letter arrives, apologizing for the error and asking for twenty-three cents back. Officials are so perturbed and mystified that they produce no response of any kind for about eighteen months — and another check reaches them before that period has elapsed, this time for $167.42. In this way, the theory goes, the millionaire pays virtually nothing and the inspector of taxes ends in a padded cell. Unproved as this theory may be, it seems worthy of careful investigation. We might at least give it a trial.

10

PENSION POINT

OR THE AGE OF RETIREMENT

OF THE MANY problems discussed and solved in this work, it is proper that the question of retirement should be left to the last. It has been the subject of many commissions of inquiry but the evidence heard has always been hopelessly conflicting and the final recommendations muddled, inconclusive, and vague. Ages of compulsory retirement are fixed at points varying from 55 to 75, all being equally arbitrary and unscientific. Whatever age has been decreed by accident and custom can be defended by the same argument. Where the retirement age is fixed at 65 the defenders of this system will always have found, by experience, that the mental powers and energy show signs of flagging at the age of 62. This would be a most useful conclusion to have reached had not a different phenomenon been observed in organizations where the age of retirement has been fixed at 60. There, we are told, people are found to lose their grip, in some degree, at the age of 57. As against that, men whose retiring age is 55 are known to be past their best at 52. It would seem, in short, that efficiency declines at the age of R minus 3, irrespective of the age at which R has been fixed. This is an interesting fact in itself but not directly helpful when it comes to deciding what the R age is to be.

But while the R — 3 age is not directly useful to us, it may serve to suggest that the investigations hitherto pursued have been on the wrong lines. The observation often made that men vary, some being old at 50, others still energetic at 80 or 90, may well be true, but here again the fact leads us nowhere. The truth is that the age of retirement should not be related in any way to the man whose retirement we are considering. It is his successor we have to watch: the man (Y) destined to replace the other man (X) when the latter retires. He will pass, as is well known, the following stages in his successful career:

1. Age of Qualification   = Q
2. Age of Discretion   = $D \ (Q + 3)$
3. Age of Promotion   = $P \ (D + 7)$
4. Age of Responsibility   = $R \ (P + 5)$
5. Age of Authority   = $A \ (R + 3)$
6. Age of Achievement   = $AA \ (A + 7)$
7. Age of Distinction   = $DD \ (AA + 9)$
8. Age of Dignity   = $DDD \ (DD + 6)$
9. Age of Wisdom   = $W \ (DDD + 3)$
10. Age of Obstruction   = $OO \ (W + 7)$

The above scale is governed by the numerical value of Q. Now, Q is to be understood as a technical term. It does not mean that a man at Q knows anything of the business he will have to transact. Architects, for example, pass some form of examination but are seldom found to know anything useful at that point (or indeed any other point) in their career. The term Q means the age at which a professional or business career begins, usually after an elaborate training that has proved profitable only to those paid for organizing it. It will be seen that if Q = 22, X will not reach OO (the Age of Obstruction) until he is 72. So far as his own efficiency is concerned, there is no valid reason for replacing him until he is 71. But our problem centers not on him but on Y, his destined successor. How are the ages of X and Y likely to compare? To be more exact, how old will X have been when Y first entered the department or firm?

This problem has been the subject of prolonged investigation. Our inquiries have tended to prove that the age gap between X and Y is exactly fifteen years. (It is not, we find, the normal practice for the son to succeed the father directly.) Taking this average of fifteen years, and assuming that Q = 22, we find that Y will have reached AA (the Age of Achievement) at 47, when X is only 62. And that, clearly, is where the crisis occurs. For Y, if thwarted in his ambition through X's still retaining control, enters, it has been proved, a different series of stages in his career. These stages are as follows:

6. Age of Frustration (F) = A + 7
7. Age of Jealousy   (J)   = F + 9
8. Age of Resignation (R) = J + 4
9. Age of Oblivion   (O) = R + 5

When X, therefore, is 72, Y is 57, just entering on the Age of Resignation. Should X at last retire at that age, Y is quite unfit to take his place, being now resigned (after

a decade of frustration and jealousy) to a career of medi-
ocrity. For Y, opportunity will have come just ten years
too late.

The age of Frustration will not always be the same in
years, depending as it does on the factor Q, but its symptoms are easy to recognize. The man who is denied the
opportunity of taking decisions of importance begins to

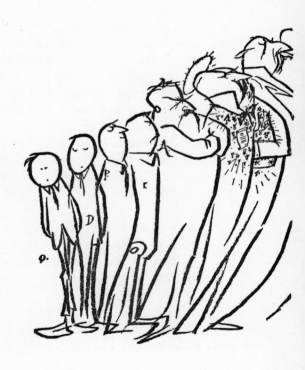

regard as important the decisions he is allowed to take. He becomes fussy about filing, keen on seeing that pencils are sharpened, eager to ensure that the windows are open (or shut), and apt to use two or three different-colored inks. The Age of Jealousy reveals itself in an emphasis upon seniority. "After all, I am still somebody." "I was never consulted." "Z has very little experience." But that period

drain

gives place to the Age of Resignation. "I am not one of these ambitious types." "Z is welcome to a seat on the Board — more trouble than it is worth, I should say." "Promotion would only have interfered with my golf." The theory has been advanced that the Age of Frustration is also marked by an interest in local politics. It is now known, however, that men enter local politics solely as a result of being unhappily married. It will be apparent, however, from the other symptoms described, that the man still in a subordinate position at 47 (or equivalent) will never be fit for anything else.

The problem, it is now clear, is to make X retire at the age of 60, while still able to do the work better than anyone else. The immediate change may be for the worse but the alternative is to have no possible successor at hand when X finally goes. And the more outstanding X has proved to be, and the longer his period of office, the more hopeless is the task of replacing him. Those nearest him in the seniority are already too old and have been subordinate for too long. All they can do is to block the way for anyone junior to them; a task in which they will certainly not fail. No competent successor will appear for years, nor at all until some crisis has brought a new leader to the fore. So the hard decision has to be taken. Unless X goes in good time, the whole organization will eventually suffer. But how is X to be moved?

In this, as in so many other matters, modern science is not at a loss. The crude methods of the past have been superseded. In days gone by it was usual, no doubt, for the other directors to talk inaudibly at board meetings, one merely opening and shutting his mouth and another nodding in apparent comprehension, thus convincing the chairman that he was actually going deaf. But there is a modern technique that is far more effective and certain. The method depends essentially on air travel and the filling in of forms. Research has shown that complete exhaustion in modern life results from a combination of these two activities. The high official who is given enough of each will very soon begin to talk of retirement. It used to be the custom in primitive African tribes to liquidate the king or chief at a certain point in his career, either after a period of years or at the moment when his vital powers appeared to have gone. Nowadays the technique is to lay before the great man the program of a conference at Helsinki in June, a congress at Adelaide in July, and a convention at Ottawa in August, each lasting about three weeks. He is assured that the prestige of the department or firm will depend on his presence and that the delegation of this duty to anyone else would be regarded as an insult by all others taking part. The program of travel will allow of his return to the office for about three or four days between one conference and the next. He will find his in-tray piled high on each occasion with forms to fill in, some relating to his travels, some to do with applications for permits or quota allocations, and the rest headed "Income Tax." On his completion of the forms awaiting his signature after the Ottawa convention, he will be given the program for a new series of conferences; one at Manila in September, the second at Mexico City in October, and the third at Quebec in November. By December he will admit that he is feeling his age. In January he will announce his intention to retire.

The essence of this technique is so to arrange matters

that the conferences are held at places the maximum distance apart and in climates offering the sharpest contrast in heat and cold. There should be no possibility whatever of a restful sea voyage in any part of the schedule. It must be air travel all the way. No particular care need be taken in the choice between one route and another. All are alike in being planned for the convenience of the mails rather than the passengers. It can safely be assumed, almost without inquiry, that most flights will involve takeoff at 2.50 A.M., reporting at the airfield at 1.30 and weighing baggage at the terminal at 12.45. Arrival will be scheduled for 3.10 A.M. on the next day but one. The aircraft will invariably, however, be somewhat overdue, touching down in fact at 3.57 A.M., so that passengers will be clear of customs and immigration by about 4.35. Going one way around the world, it is possible and indeed customary to have breakfast about three times. In the opposite direction the passengers will have nothing to eat for hours at a stretch, being finally offered a glass of sherry when on the point of collapse from malnutrition. Most of the flight time will of course be spent in filling in various declarations about currency and health. How much have you in dollars (U.S.), pounds (sterling), francs, marks, guilders, yen, lire, and pounds (Australian); how much in letters of credit, travelers checks, postage stamps, and postal orders? Where did you sleep last night and the night before that? (This last is an easy question, for the air traveler is usually able to declare, in good faith, that he has not slept at all for the past week.) When were you born and what was your grandmother's maiden name? How many children have you and why? What will be the length of your stay and where? What is the object of your visit, if any?. (As if by now you could even remember.) Have you had chicken pox and why not? Have you a visa for Patagonia and a re-entry permit for Hongkong? The penalty for making a false declaration is life imprisonment. Fasten your seat belts, please. We are about to land at Rangoon. Local time is 2.47 A.M. Outside temperature is 110° F. We shall stop here for approximately one hour. Breakfast will be served on the aircraft five hours after takeoff. Thank you. (For what, in heaven's name?) No smoking, please.

It will be observed that air travel, considered as a retirement-accelerator, has the advantage of including a fair amount of form-filling. But form-filling proper is a separate ordeal, not necessarily connected with travel. The art of devising forms to be filled in depends on three elements: obscurity, lack of space, and the heaviest penalties for failure. In a form-compiling department, obscurity is ensured by various branches dealing respectively with ambiguity, irrelevance, and jargon. But some of the simpler devices have now become automatic. Thus, a favorite opening gambit is a section, usually in the top right-hand corner, worded thus:

Return rendered in respect of the month of	

As you have been sent the form on February 16, you have no idea whether it relates to last month, this month or next. Only the sender knows that, but he is asking you. At this point the ambiguity expert takes over, collaborating closely with a space consultant, and this is the result:

109

Cross *out* the word which does not *apply*	Full name	Address	Domicile	When naturalized and why	Status
Mr. Mrs. Miss					

Such a form as this is especially designed, of course, for a Colonel, Lord, Professor, or Doctor called Alexander Winthrop Percival Blenkinsop-Fotheringay of Battleaxe Towers, Layer-de-la-Haye, near Newcastle-under-Lyme, Lincolnshire-parts-of-Kesteven (whatever that may mean). Follows the word "Domicile," which is practically meaningless except to an international lawyer, and after that a mysterious reference to naturalization. Lastly, we have the word "Status," which leaves the filler-in wondering whether to put "Admiral (Ret'd)" "Married," "American Citizen" or "Managing Director."

Now the ambiguity expert hands over the task to a specialist in irrelevance, who calls in a new space allocator to advise on layout:

Number of your identity card or passport	Your grandfather's full name	Your grandmother's maiden name	Have you been vaccinated, inoculated; when & why	Give full details

Note: The penalty for furnishing incorrect information may be a fine of £5000 or a year's penal servitude, or quite possibly both.

Then the half-completed work of art is sent to the jargon specialist, who produces something on these lines:

> What special circumstances[253] are alleged to justify the adjusted allocation for which request is made in respect of the quota period to which the former application[143] relates, whether or not the former level had been revised and in what sense and for what purpose and whether this or any previous application made by any other party or parties has been rejected by any other planning authority under subsection VII[35] or for any other reason, and whether this or the latter decision was made the subject of an appeal and with what result and why.

Finally, the form goes to the technician, who adds the space-for-signature section, the finish that crowns the whole.

> I/we [block capitals] . . . . declare under penalty that all the information I/we have furnished above is true to the best of my/our knowledge, as witness my/our signature signed this . . . . day of . . . . 19 . . . .,
>
> (*Signature*) . . . .
>
> WITNESS:
>
> | | | |
> |---|---|---|
> | *Name* . . . . | Photograph Passport Size | *Seal* . . . . |
> | *Address* . . . . | | *Thumb print* |
> | *Occupation* . . . . | | |

This is quite straightforward except for the final touch of confusion as to whose photograph or thumb print is wanted, the I/we person or the witness. It probably does not matter, anyway.

Experiment has shown that an elderly man in a responsible position will soon be forced to retire if given sufficient air travel and sufficient forms. Instances are frequent, moreover, of such elderly men deciding to retire before the treatment has even begun. At the first mention of a conference at Stockholm or Vancouver, they often realize that their time has arrived. Very rarely nowadays is it necessary to adopt methods of a severe character. The last recorded resort to these was in a period soon after the conclusion of World War II. The high official concerned was particularly tough and the only remedy found was to send him on a tour of tin mines and rubber estates in Malaya. This method is best tried in January, and with jet aircraft to make the climatic transition more abrupt. On landing at 5.52 P.M. (Malayan time) this official was rushed off at once to a cocktail party, from that to another cocktail party (held at a house fifteen miles from the hotel where the first took place), and from that to a dinner party (eleven miles in the opposite direction). He was in bed by about 2.30 A.M. and on board an aircraft at seven the next morning. Landing at Ipoh in time for a belated breakfast, he was then taken to visit two rubber estates, a tin mine, an oil-palm plantation, and a factory for canning pineapples. After lunch, given by the Rotary Club, he was taken to a school, a clinic, and a community center. There followed two cocktail parties and a Chinese banquet of twenty courses, the numerous toasts being drunk in neat brandy served in tumblers. The formal discussion on policy began next morning and lasted for three days, the meetings interspersed with formal receptions and nightly banquets in Sumatran or Indian style. That the treatment was too severe was fairly apparent by the fifth day, during the afternoon of which the distinguished visitor could walk only when supported by a secretary on one side, a personal assistant on the other. On the sixth day he died, thus confirming the general impression that he must have been tired or unwell. Such methods as these are now discountenanced, and have since indeed proved needless. People are learning to retire in time.

But a serious problem remains. What are we ourselves to do when nearing the retirement age we have fixed for others? It will be obvious at once that our own case is entirely different from any other case we have so far considered. We do not claim to be outstanding in any way, but it just so happens that there is no possible successor in sight. It is with genuine reluctance that we agree to postpone our retirement for a few years, purely in the public interest. And when a senior member of staff approaches us with details of a conference at Teheran or Hobart, we promptly wave it aside, announcing that all conferences are a waste of time. "Besides," we continue blandly, "my arrangements are already made. I shall be salmon fishing for the next two months and will return to this office at the end of October, by which date I shall expect all the forms to have been filled in. Goodbye until then." We knew how to make our predecessors retire. When it comes to forcing our own retirement, our successors must find some method of their own.